T0313992

FROM CONSENT TO COERCION

FOURTH EDITION

FROM **CONSENT**
TO **COERCION**

THE CONTINUING ASSAULT ON LABOUR

BRYAN EVANS
CARLO FANELLI
LEO PANITCH
DONALD SWARTZ

Foreword by Sam Gindin

UNIVERSITY OF TORONTO PRESS
Toronto Buffalo London

ISBN 978-1-4875-0646-9 (cloth)   ISBN 978-1-4875-3421-9 (EPUB)
ISBN 978-1-4875-2436-4 (paper)   ISBN 978-1-4875-3420-2 (PDF)

Library and Archives Canada Cataloguing in Publication

Title: From consent to coercion : the continuing assault on labour / Bryan Evans, Carlo Fanelli, Leo Panitch, Donald Swartz ; foreword by Sam Gindin.
Names: Panitch, Leo, author. | Evans, Bryan M., 1960–, author. | Fanelli, Carlo, 1984–, author. | Swartz, Donald, 1945–, author. | Gindin, Sam, writer of foreword.
Description: Fourth edition. | Revision of: Panitch, Leo. From consent to coercion. | Includes bibliographical references and index.
Identifiers: Canadiana (print) 20220470863 | Canadiana (ebook) 20220470901 | ISBN 9781487524364 (paper) | ISBN 9781487506469 (cloth) | ISBN 9781487534219 (EPUB) | ISBN 9781487534202 (PDF)
Subjects: LCSH: Labor unions – Canada – History. | LCSH: Labor unions – Law and legislation – Canada – History. | LCSH: Collective bargaining – Canada – History.
Classification: LCC HD6524 .P35 2023 | DDC 331.890971 – dc23

We welcome comments and suggestions regarding any aspect of our publications – please feel free to contact us at news@utorontopress.com or visit us at utorontopress.com.

Every effort has been made to contact copyright holders; in the event of an error or omission, please notify the publisher.

We wish to acknowledge the land on which the University of Toronto Press operates. This land is the traditional territory of the Wendat, the Anishnaabeg, the Haudenosaunee, the Métis, and the Mississaugas of the Credit First Nation.

University of Toronto Press acknowledges the financial support of the Government of Canada and the Ontario Arts Council, an agency of the Government of Ontario, for its publishing activities.

ONTARIO ARTS COUNCIL
CONSEIL DES ARTS DE L'ONTARIO
an Ontario government agency
un organisme du gouvernement de l'Ontario

Funded by the   Financé par le
Government   gouvernement
of Canada   du Canada

Contents

Illustrations

Graphs

Tables

Preface to the Third Edition

This new edition of *The Assault on Trade Union Freedoms* could not have been produced without the contributions of Dan Crow, Larry Savage, and Chuck Smith, who provided us with their outstanding research skills, helped in drafting various sections of the new Chapter 9, and, with the assistance of Travis Fast, updated all the tables. Greg Albo, Chris Boyle, and Byron Sheldrick provided us with equally indispensable assistance in the preparation of the earlier editions of this book. Few authors could have been as fortunate in having such capable and inspired researchers; they not only shared our sense of the importance of the project but contributed so much to the development of our ideas.

The origins of this book go back to 1982, when controversy still swirled around the Trudeau government's introduction of its "6 and 5" public-sector wage controls program. This program initiated a process whereby almost one-third of Canada's organized workers lost their right to strike for between two and three years. In October of that year, we argued in a conference paper (subsequently published in Swimmer and Thompson's edited volume, *Conflict or Compromise*, and in revised form in the journal *Labour/ Le Travail*) that this measure heralded the closing of an era of free collective bargaining and the shift towards a more coercive, less consensual system of state-labour relations. The paper was widely noted, with various versions of the argument also published inside the labour movement. In 1984, Garamond Press asked us to update the paper and extend our discussion of trends in the provinces. This update appeared as the monograph *From Consent to Coercion* in the spring of 1985.

In view of that monograph's relatively wide use among students and trade unionists, and continuing developments that seemed to confirm our argument, Garamond suggested in the summer of 1987 that we prepare a revised and updated edition. Before we finished documenting and analyzing the relevant material, including assessing the Charter of Rights and Freedoms' impact on trade union rights, it became clear to us that we were in the process of producing virtually a new book. This became the first edition of *The Assault on Trade Union Freedoms: From Consent to Coercion Revisited*, published in the summer of 1988.

This book became rather influential as well as controversial, and we were urged to update it further in light of developments after the mid-1980s. This proved to be no simple task, in view of the sheer amount of relevant events, legislation, and court judgments that needed to be researched and analyzed up to the early 1990s. The same has proved to be true in the preparation of this third edition, covering the events of the last ten years. We have thus added two new chapters: Chapter 9 covers all the relevant developments at the federal, provincial, and judicial levels; and Chapter 10 is an extensive reflection on the limits of the old labour strategies and what an effective set of new strategies for labour entails for the twenty-first century.

We could not have managed without the benefit of discussions and criticisms, as well as considerable help and encouragement, from many other friends and colleagues in the universities, the government, and the labour movement. In this regard, we would like to mention Harry Arthurs, Morna Ballantyne, Amy Bartholemew, Peter Bellefeuille, Steve Benedict, Geoff Bickerton, Jules Bloch, Linda Briskin, John Calvert, Stephanie Copeland, Barry Fleming, Patsy Gallagher, Michel Gauvin, Sam Gindin, Ian Green, Steve Jelly, Larry Katz, Greg Kealey, John Laing, Mike Lebowitz, Carla Lipsig-Mumme, Gil Levine, Stan Marshall, Gregor Murray, Merrill O'Donnell, Joe Roberts, Errol Sharpe, Sid Shniad, Gene Swimmer, Sharon Yandle, Rosemary Warskett, Reg Whitaker, and Sharon Wood. We are especially grateful for Judith Fudge, Harry Glasbeek, and Rosemary Warskett for having read and provided very helpful comments on the new chapters for this edition.

We also owe thanks, for their generous financial support at all stages of the project, to Carleton and York Universities, and to the Social Science and Humanities Research Council of Canada. We would like to thank Peter Saunders of Garamond Press for his help and encouragement over the years; and for providing us in the past with the considerable editorial assistance of Carmen

Palumbo, Sharon Nelson, Melodie Mayson, Ted Richmond and, for this edition, Margaret Tessman. Finally, we want to again thank Melanie Panitch and Jane Swartz and our children, for their warmth, understanding, and unceasing support.

Leo Panitch
Donald Swartz
February 2003

Preface to the Fourth Edition

The first edition of *From Consent to Coercion* was published by Leo Panitch and Donald Swartz in 1985. It argued, controversially, that Canada was witnessing the end of the era of free collective bargaining, which began in the mid-1940s, and the emergence of a new era where coercion would play a significantly greater role in securing the subordination of workers to capital. Since then, they twice updated the book, first in 1993 and again in 2003, as the evidence supporting their arguments grew. When Carlo Fanelli and Bryan Evans proposed undertaking a fourth edition that would bring the historical record up to the present, both Leo and Donald provided enthusiastic encouragement. Sadly, as many reading this will know, Leo passed away suddenly on 19 December 2020. It is bittersweet for us that Leo is not present to share in the joy of seeing several years' work concluded and made available to students and researchers. It would be impossible to briefly summarize the immense intellectual contributions of Leo's writing. Since his passing, a range of special issues has commemorated his lifelong works. This includes: *Studies in Political Economy*; *Monthly Review*; Socialist Project; *Jacobin*; *Canadian Dimension*; *Capitalism, Nature, Socialism*; *Labour/Le Travail*; and, of course, the *Socialist Registrar*, where he served as editor since 1985.

This new edition brings the study up to date while expanding its scope to encompass the austerity measures that served to undermine the living standards of Canadian workers. It also documents the growing trend towards authoritarian neoliberalism and the consequent impacts this has had on unionized and non-unionized workers, public services, and democratic practice.

It has also been reorganized in a way that expands the analysis in chronological form and emphasizes the need to develop a politics of a new kind. As is always the case with scholarly ventures, it is the result of many hands. In this regard, we would like to acknowledge and thank our friends and colleagues Greg Albo, Heather Whiteside, and Mark P. Thomas for their support and for generously allowing us to draw on work we have published together in developing the arguments in this book. These works have appeared as follows: G. Albo and B. Evans, "Permanent Austerity: The Politics of the Canadian Exit Strategy from Fiscal Stimulus," *Alternate Routes: A Journal of Critical Social Research* 22 (2011): 7–28; C. Fanelli and H. Whiteside, "COVID-19, Capitalism and Contagion," *Alternate Routes: A Journal of Critical Social Research* 31 (2020): 6–27; C. Fanelli and H. Whiteside, "In the Fight of Our Lives," *Alternate Routes: A Journal of Critical Social Research* 32 (2021): 5–12; C. Fanelli and M.P. Thomas, "Austerity, Competitiveness and Neoliberalism Redux: Ontario Responds to the Great Recession," *Socialist Studies* 7 (2011), 141–70; G. Albo and C. Fanelli, "Austerity Against Democracy: An Authoritarian Phase of Neoliberalism?" *Teoria Politica: An International Journal of Theory and Politics* 4 (2014), 65–88.

Several skilled research assistants also contributed to the updating of this edition, including Laurence Hamel-Roy, Gerard Di Trolio, Brent Toy, Andy Zhu, Shakiel Mendez, Maria Foggia, and Tamar Becker. In addition, we wish to acknowledge the financial support we received from the Centre for Labour Management Relations at Toronto Metropolitan University. Last and certainly not least, we want to thank Donald, who provided extensive comments on earlier drafts. Any errors in the expanded material are of course our responsibility.

Bryan Evans
Carlo Fanelli
August 2022

Foreword: Beyond Fatalism – Renewing Working-Class Politics

Sam Gindin

"We need to ask ourselves," Leo Panitch and Donald Swartz stated in the third edition of *From Consent to Coercion*, "whether free pertains to those who do business or whether it pertains also to the majority of Canadians who do not *do* business." Their book, now a classic, focused on a critical expression of the tension between liberal democratic principles and capitalist realities: the substantive right of workers to strike. Canadian workers were officially granted the basic democratic right to form unions, but the substance of that right – the withdrawal by workers of their labour power – was regularly suspended when workers successfully used it. This was so especially, but not only, in the public sector.

From Consent to Coercion (1985) was updated in 1993 and 2003 and, after a long and significant 20 years, is now updated here once more and in its original spirit by Bryan Evans and Carlo Fanelli. What makes the original book and all its updates such a definitive work is its meticulous research and an analytical framework that merged history, political economy, class conflicts, and the role of the state, all without ignoring the specificity of Canada. Scholarly yet accessible, it is unashamedly partisan in its support for unions without exempting unions from its critical gaze. Through addressing the move from "consent to coercion" in labour relations, it also captures the broader shift that emerged in late 1970s capitalism and was popularly summarized as "neoliberalism."

Neoliberalism revolved around a restructuring of class forces and social priorities in favour of competitiveness and private profits. At its advent, a good many progressives confidently argued that this new era would quickly collapse from its economic contradictions – and if not, it would be discredited and defeated once its class biases, false promises, and authoritarian tendencies were exposed. Three decades later, with neoliberalism still standing, it became common to hear that the state's active response to the 2008–2009 financial crisis had finally ended neoliberalism, a hasty declaration that was repeated regarding the COVID-19 pandemic.

Yet neoliberalism persists. It has remained the dominant form of capitalism framing all the editions of *From Consent to Coercion*. It is now the capitalist norm not just in Canada but near universally. What now appears the aberration in capitalist history isn't neoliberalism but the standard it is compared to – the mythologized postwar "golden age" with its expectations of steady progress for working people. Like the parrot in the Monty Python sketch, that earlier era "is dead, is no more, is bereft of life."

No other capitalism is today on offer; neoliberalism has become synonymous with capitalism itself. The working-class frustrations that accompanied this social shift did erode the legitimacy of political parties and the state. And capitalism itself no longer carries its past popular esteem. But neoliberalism's ongoing *authority* in organizing our lives endures. The latest update of *From Consent to Coercion* emphasizes what is most significant about neoliberalism's dominance since the early 1980s: it has been lamented but largely "uncontested."

Its duration now exceeds four decades (a decade longer than the period from the start of World War I to the end of World War II). Why has this anti-social restructuring of society, with its gross and rising inequalities, permanent insecurity, and ever-narrowing substantive democracy been tolerated for so long, especially by the labour movement? This is the central question today for the labour movement and left in developed capitalist countries.

Adolph Reed has aptly characterized neoliberalism as "capitalism without a working-class opposition." Reed, as does *From Consent to Coercion*, sees this as a crisis in liberal democracy with dangerous implications. But though the book is a call to end the undemocratic attack on labour rights so as to retain vital space for furthering a deeper democracy, its authors know full well that this is contingent on a renewal of the trade union movement. To that end, the last chapter of the book provides a number of creative, concrete, and eminently *practical* proposals for regenerating unions so they have the capacity to challenge this resilient scourge. Yet some very few exceptions aside, those proposals have till now not been seriously discussed in unions, never mind strategically taken up. Again: why?

Neoliberalism does not bear the full responsibility for the weakness of the labour movement. Rather, it consolidated weaknesses that were already there. Countering neoliberalism's hegemonic hold on society demands appreciating that the common contrast between neoliberalism and the "golden age" also included *continuities* in both the nature of the state's agenda and the limited responses of labour. Elaborating on this necessitates a brief historical interlude. In the first half of the twentieth century, capitalism had presided over two catastrophic world wars, the Great Depression, and the rise of dangerous nationalisms. What came into question was not only the tendency to globalization that Marx predicted, but liberal capitalism itself. In the closing years of World War II, the American state emerged to lead in overcoming this threat. The challenge was to replace the fragmented capitalism of empires, colonies, and protectionism with a world of sovereign states whose economies would be internationally open and linked by private corporations acting through markets.

The flow of natural resources, goods, and capital would be determined not by military strength or administrative barriers but by free trade, free capital flows, and competitiveness (with US military power in reserve for dealing with countries wavering in their acceptance of this new order). Each state would have a responsibility to establish the conditions for private capital accumulation within its own territories and guarantee equal treatment for domestic and foreign capital. All this would be constitutionalized via international treaties that superseded national parliaments. Canada became an early model of the integration of sovereign states into a world superintended by the American state. In the immediate aftermath of the war in Europe and Japan, aspects of this vision, such as the removal of trade barriers and especially free capital flows, necessitated compromises to deal with the pressing concerns of economic reconstruction, legitimation, and the restoration of capitalist power. But the direction of development was evident.

The continuity here – from the postwar making of a global capitalism committed to corporate freedoms and property rights to neoliberalism – is clear enough. However, this itself does not do away with the distinctiveness of neoliberalism. A major difference between the two periods remains, and it lies in the two eras' responses to capitalism's "labour problem."

In the postwar years, several factors coalesced to emphasize gaining workers' acceptance to capitalism's new road. In some countries the capitalist class had lost legitimacy during the war. As well, the requisites of Cold War ideological conflict gave significant weight to generally demonstrating capitalism's compatibility with democratic worker rights and material advances. And with the postwar boom in full swing, states in the developed capitalist countries generally had the capacity to meet at least some significant working-class demands (often, as in Europe, with the aid of the United States). Above all, workers came out of the war strong, confident, and determined to make up for their deprivations during the Depression and the war.

Especially critical here was the *form* taken by the postwar accommodations to the working class. To undermine postwar sentiments calling for a radical redistribution of wealth and economic power, working-class militancy was consciously channelled into individual consumption and cross-class cooperation in supporting growth. Unions were accepted, but only alongside the marginalization of their most radical activists and constraints on solidarity actions across workplaces. (The marginalization of the radical left was especially pivotal in countries like France, Italy, and Greece, where the anti-fascist role of communists during the war led to considerable popular support at the war's end).

The "welfare state" provided a measure of security for workers, but in a way that *supplemented* consumerism rather than looked to replace it with decommodified collective goods. Unemployment insurance, for example, was structured not to remove the discipline of unemployment but to keep laid off workers in the workforce and curb opposition to economic restructuring and imports. Canada's universal health care system, undoubtedly a great boon to working-class families, never went so far as to include pharmacare, dental care, and eye care, never mind socializing the production of drugs and hospital supplies.

This kind of integration into the capitalist project allowed for a degree of autonomy and militancy that made it possible for workers to make significant gains *within* the capitalist paradigm. By the end of the 1960s, however, with the postwar boom fading, this became a problem for corporations and the state. And absent a larger vision and political program on the part of labour, the crisis for capitalism became a crisis as well for labour.

With capitalist structures of economic and political power remaining largely untouched, the welfare state was vulnerable to reversals as circumstances changed. And labour, limiting itself to economic militancy and generally fragmented struggles, paid little attention to converting its strength at the time into a broader, robust social force. What bridged the fate of the labour movement across the two periods was that the limited horizons of the labour movement in "the best of times" foreshadowed its defeats in the making and perpetuation of the neoliberal times to come.

The state staggered through a decade of experimenting with various fixes to the crisis of the 1970s and when they all proved inadequate, the stumbling led capitalist elites and the state to the conclusion that there was no longer a middle ground. Options had become polarized. The impasse could only be broken by either greater regulations on corporations or breaking the working class and pressing ahead with *more* capitalism. Even though they were uncertain how working people would react, the capitalist elites and the state responded radically and decisively to this choice. The labour movement and its political arm, social democracy, did not – they hoped that this aggressive turn was temporary or looked instead for a non-existent middle ground.

Labour's response emboldened unremitting attacks on workers' gains. The partial accommodation to workers' needs gave way to an uncompromising assertion that "there is no alternative." Fatalism replaced legitimation as the key to reproducing capitalism. And it is fatalism that is now the labour movement's greatest enemy.

It was not that working people stopped fighting as neoliberalism was imposed. Bouts of resistance did keep resurfacing, but they remained localized, sporadic, and politically narrow. Consumption was maintained and even increased for most families despite austerity and stagnant wages. But in the absence of structures that could give workers confidence in *collective* struggles, workers were left with survival tactics that came at great cost and unintentionally reproduced neoliberalism's individualist ethos.

Individuals worked longer hours or picked up extra jobs. Total family hours in the workforce increased even as the alleged liberatory forces of technology marched on. Speedup and weaker health and safety conditions were tolerated, personal debt increased. Young people stayed longer with parents to save for a mortgage. Lower taxes were viewed as a de facto wage increase they had missed out on, even as this *implied* greater pressure on the social programs desperately needed. While competition among corporations drove some out of business, this created further opportunities for the strong and consolidated capital *as a class*. For workers, however, competition is death; it undermines the key strength that gives power to the right/freedom to withdraw their labour: their solidarity.

Looking back over the near four decades covered by this book, neoliberalism seems to be less something new than a particular phase of capitalism's fundamental drive to subordinate literally *everything* – human labour, social relations, social institutions, nature – to the unrelenting discipline of competitiveness and thereby to capital accumulation. This is a tendency, not an inevitability, but if this anti-social "logic" is to be challenged, then that challenge will have to come from a transformed labour movement.

What we now need to confront with "sober senses" is that there may be no dynamic internal to unions that can lead to such a union renewal. After all this time, the rampant frustrations with neoliberalism have not done it. The inequities and gaps in our health care and social protections have been dramatically exposed by the pandemic, but unions are not coming out of the pandemic more organized and mobilized (some major labour leaders even cozied up closer to conservative politicians). And though the environmental crisis looms with no plan to deal with its scale, here too labour has not taken on the potential of hegemonic leadership.

Union leaderships have either settled into the comfort zone of lowered membership expectations *easing* pressure on the leaders or reluctantly succumbed to the fatalism that neoliberalism so powerfully radiates. Or they mean well but have so very little in the way of recent experiences to encourage thinking and acting more ambitiously. For their part, workers seem too fragmented, too dependent on their bosses (even when they despise them), too drawn into immediate survival mode, too exhausted by work and the weight of daily life, and too alienated from even their own structures to participate in challenging and changing them. And perhaps above all, there is no organization of committed socialists to act as a catalyst to bring out the best of working people, including their prime organization – their unions.

The necessity of a party not only favouring workers but for achieving socialism was implicit in all the editions of *From Consent to Coercion*, but this latest edition poses it explicitly in the concluding paragraph of the book. The accumulated defeats in the absence of an institution explicitly committed to class formation have made addressing this imperative. How else to explicitly address class formation, democratize knowledge, develop the individual and collective capacities of working people to imagine a world beyond capitalism, analyze and understand their circumstances, debate without rancour, strategize, lead struggles, and win others over to the creation of a world not yet on the horizon?

Such a party cannot of course just be conjured up by fiat. The long-standing dilemma is that a party needs a popular base, but without a party it is hard to imagine such a base emerging. The only answer to this conundrum is to go beyond waiting for the "objective" circumstances, appreciate that a socialist party is a voluntarist intervention that will always be a "premature" leap into the semi-darkness, yet also respect that *some* base is still necessary.

The immediate goal must therefore be to set in motion processes that engage workers and the infrastructures and relationships that might at some point – indeterminate today – contribute to the creation of an institution capable of freeing us from the debilitating muck of neoliberalism/capitalism to the end of realizing our fullest collective potentials.

From Consent to Coercion has been so indispensable to this project because of what it exposes about both liberal democracy and the limits of the union response yet understands that unions remain an indispensable democratic force in capitalist society. The challenge the authors pose is the critical necessity of union renewal – not the conversion of unions into socialist organizations, which is not their role in representing workers with different politics, but into working-class institutions open to the socialist ideas that are, from a *practical* perspective, essential to better addressing their members' needs. That is, providing internal spaces for broader working-class education and deeper participation; seeing local unions as centres of working-class life; extending union battles to the class as a whole; joining the fight against other oppressions that are not "identified" as class struggles but are, at their core, inseparable from them; always raising expectations; and appreciating capitalist limits as contingent barriers to overcome.

Acronyms and Initialisms

ADQ	Action Dèmocratique du Québec
AEPA	Agricultural Employees Protection Act
ALRA	Agricultural Labour Relations Act
ATA	Alberta Teachers' Association
AUPE	Alberta Union of Public Employees
BCGEU	British Columbia Government Employees' Union
BQ	Bloc Québécois
CAQ	Coalition for Quebec's Future
CAW	Canadian Auto Workers
CBC	Canadian Broadcasting Corporation
CCA	Canadian Construction Association
CCB	Canada Child Benefit
CCF	Co-operative Commonwealth Federation
CCPA	Canadian Centre for Policy Alternatives
CEQ	Quebec Teachers' Federation
CERB	Canada Emergency Response Benefit
CEWS	Canada Emergency Wage Subsidy
CFIB	Canadian Federation of Independent Businesses
CFOA	Committee on Freedom of Association
CHST	Canada Health and Social Transfer
CIO	Congress of Industrial Organizations
CIRB	Canada Industrial Relations Board
CLAC	Christian Labour Association of Canada

CLC	Canadian Labour Congress
CP	Canadian Pacific
CPI	Consumer Price Index
CRB	Canada Recovery Benefit
CRCB	Canada Recovery Caregiving Benefit
CRHP	Canada Recovery Hiring Program
CRSB	Canada Recovery Sickness Benefit
CSN	Confédération des syndicats nationaux (Confederation of National Trade Unions)
CSQ	Centrale des syndicats du Québec
CUPE	Canadian Union of Public Employees
CUPW	Canadian Union of Postal Workers
CWB	Canada workers benefit
EI	Employment Insurance
ESA	Employment Standards Act
EU	European Union
FIIQ	Fédération des infirmières et infirmiers du Québec
FOS	final offer selection
FTA	Free Trade Agreement
FTQ	Fédération des travailleurs et travailleuses du Québec (Quebec Federation of Labour)
GDP	gross domestic product
GM	General Motors
G7	Group of Seven
GST	Goods and Services Tax
G20	Group of Twenty
HEU	Hospital Employees' Union
IAM	International Association of Machinists
IDIA	Industrial Disputes Investigation Act
ILO	International Labour Organization
IMF	International Monetary Fund
IRC	Industrial Relations Council
IRDIA	Industrial Relations and Disputes Investigations Act
IWA	Industrial, Wood and Allied Workers
MAC	Mining Association of Canada
MERF	market enhancement recovery fund
MLA	member of the Legislative Assembly

MRI	magnetic resonance imaging
NAFTA	North American Free Trade Agreement
NAPE	Newfoundland and Labrador Association of Public and Private Employees
NDP	New Democratic Party
NSCAD	Nova Scotia College of Art and Design
NSGEU	Nova Scotia Government Employees Union
NSNU	Nova Scotia Nurses Union
NSTU	Nova Scotia Teachers' Union
OCC	Ontario Chamber of Commerce
OECD	Organisation for Economic Co-operation and Development
OFL	Ontario Federation of Labour
OLRA	Ontario Labour Relations Act
OLRB	Ontario Labour Relations Board
OOP	Open Ontario Plan
OPG	Ontario Power Generation
OPSEU	Ontario Public Service Employees Union
PQ	Parti Québécois
PSAC	Public Service Alliance of Canada
PSESA	Public Service Essential Services Act
PSSRA	Public Service Staff Relations Act
PSSRB	Public Service Staff Relations Board
PWU	Power Workers' Union
RCMP	Royal Canadian Mounted Police
REO	representative employers' organization
RWDSU	Retail, Wholesale and Department Store Union
SCC	Supreme Court of Canada
SEIU	Service Employees International Union
SFL	Saskatchewan Federation of Labour
SGEU	Saskatchewan Government Employees Union
UAW	United Auto Workers
UCP	United Conservative Party
UFCW	United Food and Commercial Workers
UMFA	University of Manitoba Faculty Association
UTU	United Transportation Union
WB	World Bank
WTO	World Trade Organization

CHAPTER ONE

From the Era of Consent to the Era of Coercion

Chapter Summary: This chapter provides a broad historical overview of the ascent of neoliberalism from the margins of political and economic thought to mainstream orthodoxy. It outlines our central contention in this book that the period of neoliberalism has been characterized by the passing of an era of free collective bargaining in Canada, one where the state and capital sought, at least in part, to obtain the consent of workers and unions to act as subordinates in Canada's capitalist democracy. The current era of neoliberalism marks a return to a more open reliance by capital and the state on coercion to secure the subordination of workers in a period increasingly characterized as "authoritarian." In this context, worker power diminished as class inequality rapidly escalated.

INTRODUCTION

An era of free collective bargaining began with the federal government's 1944 Order-in-Council PC 1003. This cabinet order established legal recognition of the rights of private-sector workers across Canada to organize, bargain collectively, and strike, and it backed these rights up with state sanctions against employers who refused to recognize and bargain with trade unions. In 1948, Order-in-Council 1003 was superseded by the Industrial Relations and Disputes Investigation Act, giving these rights a permanent legislative basis for private-sector workers under federal jurisdiction. Over the next two decades, similar legislation was generally adopted by the provinces for private-sector and municipal workers in their jurisdictions. As subsequent chapters will show, in some jurisdictions it was not until the 1990s where public-service workers would see similar legislation passed extending the right to bargain and, in some cases, even strike. These legally established rights have been seen – and not least by the Canadian trade union movement itself – as the point at which Canada extended democracy to include **free collective bargaining**: the right to negotiate and bargain over wages and working conditions without threats and interference from lawmakers and/or employers.

It was not until about a quarter-century later that Canadian governments finally signed on to the General Principles proclaimed in the 1919 constitution of the **International Labour Organization (ILO)**: "First: The guiding principle … that labour should not be regarded as a commodity or article of commerce; Second: The right of association for all lawful purposes by the employed as well as by the employers." Despite the continuation of exclusions and limitations on union rights in Canada, it was widely assumed – and expressed the reformist **ideology** that prevailed in labour relations in the postwar era – that there would be steady if slow progress towards the ever-fuller realization of workers' rights. These reforms were thought to be irreversible and cumulative, although such a worldview inevitably outlived the social realities that gave rise to it. The social realities of the last four decades may have finally put this to rest.

This book is about the coercive assault against trade union rights and freedoms in Canada by both federal and provincial governments of every political stripe. We need to ask ourselves whether free pertains only to the freedom of those who do business or whether it pertains also to the freedom of the majority of Canadians who do not do business but, rather, work for those who own businesses, or who work for governments, which increasingly act as if they were businesses themselves. While the struggles of unionized workers are centred, this book explores the successive diminution of what vestiges remain of the Keynesian **welfare state** and the impacts it has had on broader working-class rights and standards of living.

It is one of the great ironies of our time that as the Canadian state finally moved to formally constitutionalize liberal democratic freedoms, it simultaneously moved towards restricting those elements of democracy that specifically pertain to workers' freedoms, in particular that of **freedom of association**. It might have been thought that federal and provincial governments thereby implicitly recognized the **right to strike** and bargain collectively, which alone make workers' rights to freedom of association meaningful. However, within months of the proclamation of the constitution, those rights were abrogated for almost one-third of all organized workers in Canada through a series of federal and provincial legislative measures.

The most important of these measures, because it clearly symbolized both the significance of the Charter's silences on the right to strike and a turning point in state policy **vis-à-vis** labour-capital affairs, was the federal Public Sector Compensation Restraint Act, introduced in June 1982. This Act tended to be characterized as imposing a two-year period of statutory wage restraint on federal employees in conformity with the slogan of "6 and 5." But the Act did much more – it completely suppressed the right to bargain and strike for all those public employees covered by the legislation. Most provinces quickly followed suit and, in nearly all cases, while the form of free collective bargaining was preserved, its substance was dramatically curtailed.

These measures were often initially presented as emergency responses – that is, "temporary" suspensions to free collective bargaining to deal with unprecedented "fiscal" pressures. Yet this was a case where the old French saying "*c'est seulement le provisoire qui dure* [it's only the provisional that lasts]" had particular merit. For these temporary measures were part of a long-term trend, which included the jailing of prominent union leaders from across the country; the increased **designation** of public- and private-sector workers as "essential," thereby removing their right to strike; the growing use of **back-to-work legislation**, which removed workers' right to strike when they actually exercised it; and the ongoing adoption of budgetary measures that included privatization and "permanent austerity" across all key social expenditures, especially health care, education, and employment supports.

Many work and labour studies experts viewed the restrictions on workers' trade union rights introduced in the early 1980s as mainly temporary, reflecting nothing more than a passing historical moment.[1] This statement of faith in the permanence of reform was then, as now, astonishingly naive. More insightful was the view that with the growing movement towards **deregulation** of the private sector and continued fiscal pressures in the public sphere, it would be premature to predict that we have seen the end of legislated wage restraint.[2] Developments in the range of laws governing industrial relations in Canada since that time have continued the movement away from the principles characteristic of the postwar era of free collective bargaining, instead moving towards institutionalizing permanent exceptionalism with, over the last decade, "authoritarian" characteristics.

Precisely because Canadian workers have resorted to lengthy strikes to defend their historic achievements, federal and provincial governments began to broaden their powers to intervene in collective bargaining. These interventions involved new measures that allowed the state to limit or suspend strike actions by workers and provided numerous mechanisms to undermine union bargaining power through interference in internal union affairs. Such measures, combined with new restrictions on picketing and **secondary strike action** by unions, essentially weakened the ability of workers to "take wages out of competition" while enhancing employers' access to non-union labour. Without destroying the formal structure of collective bargaining, governments have made further and avowedly permanent encroachments on workers' collective freedoms within that structure. Any government reforms that ran against this current were limited and reflected a marked change in the character of the labour relations regime in Canada.

In this regard, what we have witnessed, then, is the passing of the era of free collective bargaining in Canada, one in which the state and capital relied, more than before World War II, on obtaining the consent of workers generally, and unions in particular, to act as subordinates in Canada's capitalist democracy. The current era marks a return, albeit under quite different conditions, to the more open reliance of the state and capital on **coercion** – on force and on fear – to secure that subordination. This is not to suggest that coercion was in any sense absent from the postwar era or that coercion is the only, or even always the dominant, factor in labour relations. But there is a changing conjuncture in the Canadian political economy, and it marks a change in the form in which coercion and consent are related to one another, a change significant enough to demarcate permanence in this new era. This new era is broadly called neoliberalism, and since it is subject to various interpretations, the following section sets out our understanding.

NEOLIBERALISM AND PERMANENT AUSTERITY

The theoretical origins of **neoliberalism** can be traced back to the 1930s and a tiny group of liberal intellectuals meeting in Paris to discuss the prospects for war and the threats posed, as they saw it, by "totalitarianism" and "collectivist planning."[3] From its very beginnings, the new doctrine was quite consciously set as an unyielding defender of the institutions of private property, with priority given to market freedoms and in opposition to socialism as an alternate economic and democratic order to capitalism. In its specific programmatic mandate, neoliberalism was an offspring of the Great Depression and set against Keynesian state intervention. But however much its protagonists set themselves up as outsiders, neoliberalism was never an alien political doctrine to economic and political elites of western Europe and North America: neoliberal ideas (privileging economic freedoms) had always been incorporated as a legitimate component of state policy discussions, particularly in Germany, the United States, and Britain.

The foremost expositors of neoliberalism had the aim of recreating a liberalism in defence of market forces. The link between neoliberalism and more authoritarian forms of government that its founders recognized has not been given the attention that it deserves, something this book aims to rectify. This is best exemplified, in both their economic theories and political tracts, in the writings of Ludwig von Mises, Friedrich von Hayek, and Milton Friedman. Von Mises was a central figure in Austrian economics' opposition to Marxism and crusaded against state intervention in markets (including approving of Italian fascism in its crushing of the left). His wartime move to the United States was central to anchoring neoliberal thinkers on both sides of the Atlantic. But it was Hayek and his 1944 *Road to Serfdom* that best exemplified their political objectives and the controversial contention that market freedoms are a necessary prerequisite for democratic freedoms, as "only capitalism makes democracy possible." For Hayek, democracy is understood foremost in procedural terms as a "constitutionally-limited liberal democracy" that can safeguard against the potential market-inhibiting "abuses of democracy." In this vein, Hayek famously followed von Mises in his oft-noted preference for a "liberal dictator" to a "democratic government lacking liberalism."

Following World War II, neoliberal thought became more institutionalized, notably with the establishment of the Mont Pelerin Society in 1947. Neoliberalism was further nurtured in the postwar period by well-funded think tanks like the Institute of Economic Affairs, the Heritage Foundation, and the Fraser Institute, among others. Across the postwar boom, neoliberals proved relentless in their critique of state – and especially social – expenditures as excessive and unaffordable. For neoliberals, market freedoms were understood as a necessary check on the centralized power of the state. These views became canonized in Milton Friedman's 1962 book, *Capitalism and Freedom*, where he argued, "History suggests only that capitalism is a necessary condition for political freedom." As with Hayek, for Friedman, freedom is necessarily dependent upon market freedoms and private property, with democracy understood almost exclusively in formal and procedural terms.

The historically specific character of capitalist social relations and **liberal democracy** is marginalized from the core focus by neoliberals in theory, and the universalizing tendencies of market exchange and private property are privileged as the real spaces of human freedom. This is why neoliberalism as a political practice should not be read as a juxtaposition of (less) state against (more) market. Rather, as a set of policy practices, neoliberalism has been about a particular kind of state suited to the logic of capital in a specific historical phase of capitalist development. As such, it has been directed at reducing public services and assets in order to open up the state sector to new profit-making opportunities; lowering wages, benefits, and working conditions for a more flexible and market-dependent workforce; and deploying the coercive capacities of the state to enforce these "market measures."

By the late 1960s, neoliberalism had surfaced as both a recognizable set of ideas and a political movement. The economic recession of the 1970s provided a political opening that was rooted in the relative weakening of capital vis-à-vis labour amidst declining profit margins, leading to both rising unemployment and inflation. As well, the collapse of the **Bretton Woods** system in 1971 ended the convertibility of gold to US dollars and the subsequent move to flexible rates that further encouraged international capital flows. These changes occurred in conjunction with the rebuilding of the productive capacities of Europe and Japan, the 1973 Arab oil embargo, capital flight to newly emerging industrial regions with cheaper pools of labour and lower environmental standards, as well as technological and organizational restructuring in the manufacturing heartlands of North America and Europe.

By the 1980s, with Keynesians unable to address the economic impasse, neoliberalism offered an alternate policy kit to tackle "stagflation" (a situation where there is both high inflation and high unemployment) and a political practice firmly set against democratic and anti-capitalist demands. Neoliberal policy experiments had earlier precedents, in particular the Chilean military junta of Pinochet (which Hayek praised as a necessary "transitional dictatorship"). But its political materialization as an alternative governance project was represented by the election of Margaret Thatcher in the UK and Ronald Reagan in the United States, as well as the governments of Pierre Trudeau and Brian Mulroney in Canada, which in many ways led the global turn to neoliberalism. The effect was to create pressures to get ahead of the curve as the Canadian state took measures to ensure that Canadian enterprises remained competitive in the United States and international markets.

Because of the United States' capacity to manipulate the dollar price (the global reserve currency) and to exploit Wall Street's international financial dominance, this structural/institutional power meant the US could delay (or avoid) having to do what other states had to in order to remain globally competitive. In Canada's case, this meant using the whip of state power to accelerate capitalist restructuring, including adjusting the domestic economy to ensure high levels of domestic savings and investments; ensuring balance of payments; maintaining public and private indebtedness; and ensuring a strong financial sector so as to spur development and sustain consumption. Although the motivation appears as predominantly a product of internal pressures, external conditions played a significant role if Canadian enterprises were going to compete internationally.

This, in part, explains why Canada led the charge against inflation and demanded concessions from workers, which resulted in a significant restructuring of the role of the state in providing social services. Unlike the United States, Canada could not run huge deficits, otherwise capital would flow out. The effect of **austerity** measures was not only to make enterprises more competitive in world markets but to do so at the expense of devaluing previously sustainable livelihoods and occupations. By the 1980s, full-employment policies had been officially abandoned in Canada as inflation-targeting and deficit reduction were prioritized. The resulting high levels of unemployment worked to discipline labour and undermine the growing militancy of organized labour. Assets held by the state were relinquished onto the market, where capital could invest and discipline workers. These new spaces of commodification alleviated the problem of overaccumulation and, once set in motion, created pressures to continuously find more spaces where privatization could be achieved.

Over the next two decades, neoliberalism became not merely dominant but uncontested as the guiding vision of a democratic "market economy." This social vision translates into the programmatic core of the neoliberal policy matrix: an economic policy focus on inflation control and supply-side incentives; privatization and commercialization of public-sector assets and services; liberalization of trade in goods and capital movements; restructuring of labour (and business) regulations to reduce so-called market impediments; and societal commodification of goods and services. Around this policy hub, an enormous number of state initiatives followed that steadily transformed the social form of the state into a set of institutions and policy mechanisms supporting market disciplines. In terms of economic policy, neoliberalism sought regressive tax reform, constraints on the growth of social services, an export-led growth strategy, the lifting of controls on foreign direct investment and trade liberalization, and to keep real wage increases below increases in productivity. In terms of welfare policy, an ethos of personal responsibility and individual culpability supplemented by private charity, philanthropy, and volunteerism were prioritized in place of state-administered social programs.

The transformation of the public sector was linked to the adoption of so-called "new public management." This theory asserted that government and, more broadly, the public sector should function more like the private sector, looking to the market for inspiration and, whenever possible, emulating it. Something like a policy manual materialized for public-sector management: the privatization of public goods and services; a greater reliance on outsourcing and contracting out; the commercialization of state services such as user-pay provisions and monetization of public assets; and competition between public agencies alongside use of short-term and contract labour. In the neoliberal "lean" state, the privatization and commercialization of public services has steadily usurped any counter mechanisms – ombudspersons, freedom of information, citizen participation and review panels, new forms of democracy, and so forth – for democratic accountability and social provision.

The liberalization of trade and capital flows established a new international governance framework across the world market. This was a project to discipline the "Global South" to break from nationalist projects that favoured developing domestic industries and reducing reliance on foreign imports, as well as to facilitate the transition of the former East Bloc, China, and others into capitalism. These policy objectives – the so-called "Washington Consensus" – were institutionalized through various international agencies such as the World Bank (WB), International Monetary Fund (IMF), and World Trade Organization (WTO). In effect, national parliaments and executives were "disciplined" to follow the neoliberal policy course. A plethora of bilateral and regional "free trade" agreements further promoted trade and investment liberalization and the protection of private property, especially in the form of foreign direct investment, through trade-related investment and intellectual property rights clauses. The international governance framework, in other words, with its intricate web of external administrators, legal structures, and treaty frameworks led by the core capitalist states, became another disciplinary mechanism on democratic decision-making in favour of the world market.

Across the 1990s, workplace arrangements were redesigned to expose workers more forcefully to market forces. These labour market measures were designed to weaken protective regulations, restrict collective institutions, and strengthen pro-individualistic regulations. So-called flexibility arrangements increased the use of shift work, short-term contracts, workplace speedups, evening and overnight work, part-time labour, weekend work, rotating and split shifts, variable schedules, as well as casual and seasonal employment. These disciplinary mechanisms escalated the pace of work, led to a growing precariousness of job tenure, and heightened work-life conflicts owing to long hours of work and lack of control over working time. The Canadian economy was also reoriented towards the export of raw materials – agriculture, forestry, minerals, and energy. Many trade-sensitive industries were also damaged through sharp currency appreciation, contributing to stagnant productivity and innovation gains, and undermining the development of a sustainable and diversified economy able to weather volatile global commodities markets.

The reworking of state regulatory frameworks had the intent of limiting the scope of national discretion in altering distributional bargains, property rights, and market outcomes via state intervention. This has often appeared as an assault on the national state by the world market – but this is a fundamental misreading. It has in fact been a recasting of state functions through the upward transference of regulatory responsibilities to international bodies – an "internationalization of the state," in terms of specific regulatory functions – to structure national market frameworks, alongside the simultaneous devolution of operational responsibilities, particularly of the welfare state, to subnational governments – a "localization of the state" for policing and building infrastructure to support firm-level competitiveness – without matching fiscal supports. The neoliberal restructuring of the state not only blocked progressive governments from using their national or subnational authority to pursue "market-disengaging" policies, it also established a competitive regulatory dynamic internal to neoliberalism within and between governments. In other words, interjurisdictional competition locked in further neoliberalization – thus leading to the conclusion that "there is no alternative."

The neoliberal period has also been associated with the processes of financialization. This refers to the overall role of finance in economic activity and the enhanced standing of central banks and monetary policy in the economic policy function of the state. The rise of central banks to policy pre-eminence in the early phases of neoliberalism was the foundation for the "shock therapy" used to fight inflation. But it also meant that the wealth and income of creditors (i.e., the financial sector) would grow relative to other sectors; bank deregulation would increase the problem of overleveraging and systemic risk from bank failures; the internationalization of capital would be driven, in good part, by finance; and state debt management would become more deeply intertwined with the bond markets.

Finance, therefore, has occupied a more pivotal role as the central agency allocating surplus capital and credit between potential uses and thus in the disciplining of industry. Finance has also maintained continual pressure on the state for its project of "total privatization" and commodification of the public sector. Financialization and the accompanying volatility and credit crises became, not unexpectedly, one of the distinguishing features of neoliberalism. But each financial crisis surprisingly reinforced rather than undermined the leading position of central banks, credit, and finance in the economy and finance capital in the state and power structures. This dynamic was brought to a head in 2008 with the explosion of a global financial crisis and, about a decade later, with the COVID-19 pandemic.

THE GREAT RECESSION

What began as an unprecedented housing meltdown centred in the US economy in the fall of 2007 quickly turned into a banking and financial market downturn, and then a global insolvency crisis through 2008. Due to the highly integrated nature of financial institutions and their exposure to toxic assets associated with the subprime housing market and high levels of bank debt, a series of forced bank mergers and quasi-nationalizations soon followed. These private-sector bailouts by the public sector resulted in troubled assets being shifted onto the state sector or central banks, which also exposed other underlying problems such as increasing corporate and personal debt loads, an overheating commercial and housing market, credit-reliant consumption, stagnant real wages, and unprecedented levels of income and wealth polarization. A worldwide credit crunch soon emerged as subprime mortgage-backed securities were discovered in the portfolios of banks and hedge funds around the world.

The governments of the G7 and G20 intervened with trillions to guarantee inter-bank lending and the purchasing of government and commercial paper. To address the shock to aggregate demand, a coordinated turn to emergency fiscal expansion was led by the US government and the G20 states, with governments adopting, in general, fiscal deficits in the order of 2–5 percent of GDP (although with the severe banking crises and recession, these levels were much larger in the US and Britain).[4] Canada did not experience the severity of the financial crisis of Ireland, the UK, and the US, nor the long-term competitiveness and financial problems of Greece or other countries in the European periphery. This was primarily due to Canada's monopolistic financial sector, which had been protected by its market structure, the underwriting of high-risk mortgages by the state, and the support given by the Bank of Canada to the financial sector to maintain profit margins. There has been, as will be shown in subsequent chapters, a long-term pattern of fiscal austerity by federal and provincial governments dating back to the 1980s.

This was not, as is frequently argued, a return to **Keynesianism** and the state acting against volatile and uncontrolled markets – rather, this was the "emergency monetarism" that many neoliberals had long formulated as part of their necessary policy arsenal in the case of severe demand shocks caused by instability in financial markets depleting the available means of exchange. Additional stimulative measures included temporary public works programs, particularly those related to infrastructure, as a means of supporting effective demand and bolstering consumption. To avert any possible misinterpretations of their intents and affirm continued political fidelity to neoliberalism, all G20 member governments agreed to further open their markets to capital, guarantee credit availability, and monetize public assets.

With the economic crisis no longer in danger of spiralling out of control, states steadily reconstructed – and then deepened – the neoliberal policy mix. Executive power was reinforced, often at the expense of parliaments, and special economic agencies were formed, frequently at a distance from line departments and parliamentary accountability. As the credit crisis mutated into a sovereign debt crisis, "fiscal consolidation" became the technical operational mandate for a further shifting of the tax burden, reducing welfare state provisions, seeking union concessions, and a massive monetization of public assets. Given the potentially long period of stagnation and public debt, the core capitalist countries entered into a new phase of "permanent austerity" – a theme repeated by the international agencies, which suggested a 10- to 20-year horizon for working out the impacts of the crisis on government debt levels.

Building on the first major wave of privatization initiatives under the neoliberal mandate of the mid-1980s to the end of the 1990s in Latin America and the transitional economies of the former Soviet Union (China took a somewhat different path towards market capitalism), the process picked up steam in the early 2000s as many European countries liquidated assets during the post-9/11 recovery phase before slowing again with the onset of the 2008 financial crisis, when buyers were few and far between. However, by 2012, governments had brought about the third highest volume of privatizations by value on record and, by 2015, had "monetized" a record $319.9 billion through privatization sales worldwide, easily exceeding the previous record of $265.2 billion (€184.3 billion) set in 2009. Public-sector management reform was another source of restructuring, including privatization, public-private partnerships (P3s), contracting out, and leasing opportunities, as well as new management norms and balanced-budget legislation.

In the time since, the incidence of workers earning low wages has increased, rising from 16.7 percent in 2006 to 17.2 percent in 2014 across the European Union (EU). Within the Eurozone itself, the rise has been greater – from 14.3 to 15.7 percent over the same period. Whereas low-waged work accounted for 13 percent of all employment in Canada in 1989, it rose to more than 20 percent by 2007 (an increase of 53 percent). Between 1997 and 2013, the proportion of minimum wage earners rose from 5 percent to 6.7 percent across Canada (an increase of 34 percent). Likewise, between 2008 and 2013, the number of part-time jobs grew at nearly twice the rate of full-time work, 5.9 percent versus 3.3 percent, and accounted for 40 percent of all job growth. An astonishing 72 percent of all net new jobs created between 2009 and 2014, the "recovery" phase following the crisis, fell into precarious or low-paid categories, while the underemployment rate of 14.2 percent stood at double the unemployment rate of 7.1 percent. Meanwhile, the percentage of working-age Canadians rose 1.1 percent, outstripping the growth of jobs in the economy, which grew at only 0.7 percent. By the end of 2014, the labour participation rate had fallen to 65.7 percent, its lowest since 2000.

Changes in union density have been an important driver of growing income polarization and social inequality in Canada, as in many other countries, too, having undergone a period of protracted "deindustrialization" as governments facilitated the offshoring of manufacturing capacity to low-wage, often authoritarian, jurisdictions. A 1990 study by the Economic Council of Canada found that the "standard employment" relationship – that is, full-time jobs with a degree of security – was giving way to precarious work, jobs that were part-time, temporary, and provided little or no opportunity for career mobility. Of course, when considered historically, secure, full-time employment has been the exception, not the norm, representing only a small period over two centuries of capitalist development. If there is such a thing as a "standard" capitalist employment relationship, it is much more closely associated to the "iron law" of labour degradation articulated by Marx in the mid-nineteenth century than its mid-twentieth-century Keynesian interlude. This caveat aside, union density has since declined from an average of 20 percent to 17 percent across the Organisation for Economic Co-operation and Development (OECD) as a whole.

Though uneven across the provinces, there have been major structural shifts to the composition of union membership over the last three decades across Canada. Whereas public-sector union density has stayed relatively consistent since the 1980s, hovering around 70 percent, total Canadian private-sector density fell from a high of 35 percent to around 16 percent. In addition to being predominantly public sector-led, more women (32 percent) are unionized today compared with men (29 percent), albeit unevenly across the public and private sectors. While public-sector unionization rates have remained fairly consistent over the past three decades – buoying total union density (around 30 percent) – private-sector unionization has been nearly halved. As a result, the bargaining power of unions versus capital and the state has declined as bargaining strategies have become increasingly defensive. Even the IMF, hardly an advocate for labour rights, acknowledged that declining union strength and growing workplace productivity have contributed to the explosive growth of social inequality. Thus, over the neoliberal period, the primary mechanism for increasing labour income has been severely constrained.

The erosion of union density has coincided with workers' descent into lower-paid and non-unionized jobs, including decreased compensation as a proportion of GDP (see Graph 1.1).

A study by the Canadian Imperial Bank of Commerce (2015) noted that, since the late 1980s, the number of part-time jobs created has been rising at a significantly higher rate than full-time jobs. According to the bank's employment quality index – a measure that includes the distribution between full-time and part-time work, self-employment and paid employment, and the sectoral composition of full-time work – Canada's labour market has been on a downward trajectory for the previous 25 years. The report notes that the decline in employment quality is structural, not cyclical, and that the fastest growing segment of the labour market is also the one with the weakest bargaining power.

A study by the Toronto Dominion Bank led to similar conclusions. Based on a new index of labour market indicators that includes hours worked,

Graph 1.1. Share of Labour Compensation in GDP at Current National Prices in Canada, 1970–2020

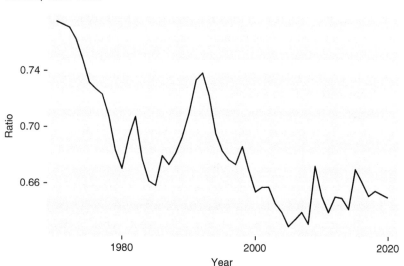

self-employment wage trends, and temporary work, the study demonstrated that the country's job market was "experiencing more weakness than is implied by looking at the headline unemployment rate alone." This weakness "is driven by elevated levels of labour underutilization, involuntary part-time employment, and long-term unemployment." These trends are amplified in the context of persistent gendered and racialized divisions of labour that exacerbate labour market exclusion. Across the labour market, racialized persons remain concentrated in low-income occupations, often falling below the average Canadian hourly wage and yearly salary. Consequently, racialized families are up to four times more likely to fall below low-income cut-off measures, with new immigrants more than twice as likely as those Canadian born to experience chronic low incomes, contributing to a broader racialization of poverty. Precarity of job tenure and lack of protection for immigrant workers is also widespread.

Despite labour productivity growing 1.12 percent per year between 1976 and 2014, median real hourly earnings grew by only 0.09 percent. This has contributed to both a general decline in labour's share of income and a deterioration of labour's purchasing power. In this context, wealth and income inequalities have rapidly risen. It is estimated that the wealthiest 10 percent of Canadians own more than 50 percent of the national wealth, while the richest

86 Canadian families alone own more than the bottom 11.4 million. In other words, the richest 0.002 percent of Canadians hold an amount of wealth equal to the bottom 34 percent of the population. In the decade of austerity following the **Great Recession**, Canada's 1 percent continued to pull away. Although corporate profits have historically tended to average less than 5 percent of sales, structural changes over the past decade have moved that average to over 6 percent, reaching a 27-year high in 2015, only to be surpassed in the context of the COVID-19 pandemic.

A CRISIS UNLIKE OTHERS: COVID-19

In March 2020, the World Health Organization declared COVID-19 to be a global pandemic. In previous crises, the most obvious being the Great Depression and 2008 global financial crisis, states intervened where markets had failed. COVID-19 was an entirely different order of problem. Here the goal was to suspend, through state directive, much of the social activity necessary for economic functioning. That response provided a glimpse to an alternative narrative.[5] Unlike the pre-pandemic period, once the threat posed by the virus was evident, governments "magically found a way to pay for all kinds of programs and supports written off as impossible before. The sky, it seems, is the limit."[6] The array of state interventions to replace lost income for both workers and employers brought to the fore fundamental questions regarding the prevailing social and economic order. Could not work and production be organized to meet basic human needs for food, shelter, decent employment, and health care?

As the COVID-19 crisis evolved, governments around the world intervened with trillions in broad tax relief, wage subsidies, grants, preferential loans, and other guarantees to prevent widespread economic collapse and support the recovery. Governments also took equity stakes in everything from energy, rail, automotive, and air transportation to support troubled firms. At the midway point of 2020, global economic stimulus amounted to $10 trillion, three times more than the collective responses to the Great Recession. By year's end, this had grown to over $20 trillion, with the value of COVID-19 fiscal stimulus packages as a percentage of GDP in some G20 countries surpassing more than 50 percent. A recent IMF report spoke of the "difficult trade-offs between implementing measures to support near-term growth and avoiding a further buildup of debt that will be hard to service down the road."

While it did recommend some modest tax and revenue measures to support the economy, it also cautioned of debt sustainability and reminded of the familiar trope to remove targeted support in the future.

Worldwide, unemployment levels spiked. In Canada, all job growth since the mid-1980s had been effectively wiped out as more than one-third of working-age Canadians (more than seven million people) sought basic income support through the new Canada Emergency Response Benefit (CERB), far surpassing the half million jobs lost in the first year of the 2008–2009 recession. South of the border, 15 percent of the American workforce (26 million people) applied for unemployment benefits, wiping out more than 22 million jobs created since 2010. While European job losses were less severe, due largely to more robust government wage-subsidy programs equal to 60–90 percent of wages and a broader social welfare net, it is estimated that upwards of 59 million jobs had been lost by mid-2020, on top of cuts in pay and hours worked, with the Eurozone experiencing the most significant economic contraction in its history. More than 1.5 billion workers across the Global South, equal to nearly half the global workforce, saw their income drop by more than 60 percent during the first year of the crisis.

Globally, poverty rates have risen sharply with close to 100 million joining the ranks of the extreme poor (earning less than US$1.90 per day) and an additional 80 million more people are undernourished than before the pandemic. Cumulative per capita income losses over 2020–2022, compared with pre-pandemic projections, are equivalent to 20 percent of GDP in emerging and developing countries (excluding China), while in advanced economies the losses are expected to be roughly half. COVID-19 has impacted the world of work and workers in unprecedented ways. An ILO report found that 255 million jobs have been lost, with global unemployment increasing by 33 million, while more than 80 million have left the ranks of the labour force altogether. Divergent recovery paths are reflected in accelerating inequality, within and across the Global North and South. Global labour income has declined by US$3.7 trillion (8.3 percent), or 4.4 percent of global GDP. Loss of income has disproportionately impacted youth, women, racialized and lower-educated workers, who have experienced the most dramatic declines in disposable income, which contrasts sharply with job growth in a number of higher-educated service sectors.

These differential impacts are likely to leave a generational scar on labour force participation, productivity growth, and global macroeconomic stability. The ILO's monitoring of the pandemic's impact on employment found that the equivalent of an additional 125 million full-time jobs would be lost by the end of 2021. Informal workers, who comprise some two billion people world-wide, often without labour rights and social protections, have had their earnings cut in half. For migrant workers, a sector dominated by long-standing employment and human rights violations and exemptions, work and living conditions have gone from bad to worse, with a growing preponderance of non- or underpayment for work performed. And for the first time in two decades, the number of child labourers has risen and now stands at more than 160 million worldwide – an increase of more than eight million, with estimates suggesting this number could rise by more than 46 million in the absence of extended social protections.

In the context of the crisis, the common definition of "essential workers" – expanded beyond the usual health professionals and first responders to embrace building cleaners, grocery clerks, food processing workers, food delivery workers, truck drivers, and restaurant kitchen workers, many of these occupations among the lowest paid – emerged as those who enabled capitalism to survive day to day. These workers moved from the ranks of the unacknowledged to being "heroes," albeit without the pay and recognition and for a staggeringly short period of time. Fractures also appeared within the elite neoliberal consensus, as reflected in a *Financial Times* editorial board opinion piece arguing that it was now necessary to reverse "the prevailing policy direction of the last four decades." The activist state, they wrote, was to be retrieved from the dustbin of history, with new investments in public services, more secure employment, and policies for redistribution central to this new **social contract**.[7] A transformation of this magnitude, however, requires political actors – that is, social agents with the organizational and ideological capacity to carry this program forward into the streets and the state.

As discussed more fully in Chapter 7, in April 2020, the federal government introduced the CERB to cope with the large gaps in Employment Insurance (EI) coverage, particularly for precarious, self-employed, and gig economy workers. Provincial governments also rolled out their own business support programs and prohibitions, such as the temporary moratorium on evictions introduced in Ontario. At the same time, provincial governments resisted calls to introduce paid sick days and equipped themselves with highly centralized and authoritarian powers to suspend the rights of workers to reject unsafe work, unilaterally deeming them as essential.[8]

Less than half of the Canadian workforce has access to employer-provided paid sick leave.[9] Although some paid sick leave was provided though the EI and CERB programs, eligibility requirements meant that many lower-income, precariously employed, and migrant workers were unable to access these benefits.[10] The inadequacy of existing income and social supports became evident when government directives ordered the shuttering of non-essential economic sectors with the resultant mass unemployment and, for the more fortunate, the turn to home-based work. The most common, and anaemic, response was that all provinces amended their respective employment standards legislation to provide job-protected leave during declared emergencies, including infectious disease outbreaks. Though varying across the provinces, employees were provided temporary unpaid leave benefits due to declared emergency powers or for reasons related to a designated infectious disease, but these benefits were largely inadequate in the context of the pandemic. The reluctance of governments to amend their employment standards legislation to include at least ten permanent paid sick days, as labour advocates have called for, is illustrative of the continued coercive assault.

And pointing to a more authoritarian expression of state power, several provinces empowered certain ministers to issue unilateral edicts that stood beyond the scrutiny of both cabinet and the legislature. In several provinces, the pandemic was the rationale for governments to suspend, or otherwise intervene, in collective bargaining or to override collective agreements. In Quebec, teachers' unions received notices stating that, in order to deal with the COVID-19 pandemic, their assignments, schedules, and workplaces could be modified at any time because their collective agreements were no longer considered binding. Emergency legislation in Ontario empowered employers to force shift changes, mandate extra hours, and deny vacation days in the health care sector. In Alberta, the emergency powers were particularly sweeping, where any minister was empowered to legislate through a ministerial order without legislative scrutiny. The Justice Centre for Constitutional Freedoms filed a constitutional challenge shortly after the Bill was introduced. The case was dismissed, however, when the Bill was repealed.[11]

Pandemic-induced insecurity has strengthened the grip of ruling classes worldwide. The speed and scale of billionaire growth has been unprecedented, with the world's 2,755 billionaires now worth $13.1 trillion, up more than 62 percent from $8 trillion in 2019. A report from Oxfam (2021) suggests that the world's ten richest men have seen their combined wealth increase by half a trillion dollars since the pandemic began.[12] Likewise, top financial institutions report record profits all while benefiting from a global tax system that conveys disproportionate advantages to the wealthy.[13] Billionaires may not have caused the pandemic, but the public policies enabling their wealth accumulation strategies have certainly exacerbated the "collateral damage," with foregone tax revenues and public investments, extreme inequality, poverty, and precarity of job tenure precipitating the pandemic and shaping the likely outcomes of current support measures. The COVID-19 era is thus a crisis of unprecedented proportions not only for its effects on production and reproduction, but through the coalescing of structural inequalities and cyclical instabilities equally characteristic of capitalism. State responses have been predictably handcuffed by governments' modes of production and status quo delimitation of future possibilities, making economic overhaul all the more urgent.

As a reminder of Marx's diagnosis of capitalist patterns of concentration and centralization, corporations are also looking to pick up assets pummelled by the virus, just as they did through the 2008 bankruptcies. COVID-19 began as a health emergency, but having emerged in the context of political-economic illness, it soon brought into sharp focus the significance of public services. Researchers at the Canadian Centre for Policy Alternatives estimated in 2009 that average Canadians received an amount equal to $17,000 from public services.[14] For some two-thirds of the Canadian population, the social wage – public services or benefits that supplement market income – made up more than half of household income. For Canadians in median-income households, this amounted to $41,000 worth of public services, like health care, education, and personal transfer payments. In 2019, Statistics Canada came to similar conclusions, estimating that average Canadians received over $6,000 in public services, $4,000 in education, and close to $9,000 in direct cash transfers (e.g., Employment Insurance, Old Age Security, Guaranteed Income Supplement), including another $2,500 in other public services like housing, recreation, culture, and environmental protection. In other words, on average, the social wage was valued at over $20,000, or about one-fifth of actual household consumption.[15]

Public services also reduce broader inequalities, particularly in times of economic difficulty or labour market uncertainty, and ensure that ordinary people can have a say in the quality and cost of those services. Even so, this has not stopped a cacophony of neoliberal hardliners from fanning the flames of deficit hysteria, calling for reductions and the outright elimination of the very public services and jobs that have buttressed the most severe effects of the crisis. Vampire-like ideology is, however, hard to kill, even if it means discarding an entire generation in the interests of balancing the books. Exposed as the vulgar charlatans that they are, proponents of neoliberalism and austerity are out of ideas; indeed, if they were really serious about the deficit, they need not look any further than the tens of trillions doled for corporate welfare and tax cuts for the wealthy.

From its origins in the liberal right's antagonism towards socialism, neo-liberalism has accepted that constraints on democracy may be necessary to defend capitalist markets. Thus, a "de-democratization" tendency has often been observed as a central feature of state practices over the neoliberal period. More overtly "authoritarian" measures can also be detected as reflected, for instance, in the resurgence of the far right and revival of neo-fascist and pop-ulist movements. We have also seen the further strengthening of executive power and insulation of economic policy from parliamentary accountability, as well as an incredible multiplication of legalized restrictions and policing modalities for the disciplining of dissent generally, and labour in particular, by the "austerity state." The new restrictions on free collective bargaining, trade unions, and social movements are consistent with the neoliberal view that a free society pivots around market freedoms and, occasionally, requires restraints on the "excesses of democracy."

In this regard, the authoritarian tendencies of neoliberalism as actual state practice have mutated into a "disciplinary democracy" that restricts trade un-ion and workers' rights more broadly. The substance of democracy as a pro-cess of struggle between social classes over alternative socio-economic orders and the development of citizenship capacities has been severely constrained. This is the case whether governance is exercised by hard right political re-gimes or social democratic parties of the centre-left accepting austerity for a turn at the seat of state power. What remains of democracy is the procedural legitimacy provided by elections offering a choice among teams of political elites who then defend the disciplines of the market and administer a pro-gressively more coercive state. In this regard, the impasse of labour – both as an organizational force and working-class movement – calls attention to the urgent task of rebuilding and renewing socialist politics – of getting people to think ambitiously again and of meeting new challenges through unique solutions left of social democracy, something we return to later in this book.

OUTLINE OF THE BOOK

This book provides a historical perspective in tracing out the shift from an era of regulated consent to an era characterized by an increasing normalization

of coercion by the state. In this respect, Chapter 2 begins with the early formation of trade unions in the late nineteenth century and the expansion of
working-class and trade union organization through the critical 1930s to 1945.
The postwar period is crucial in this history, as this is the so-called "golden
age" of capitalism, where trade unions representing workers' bargaining interests, as well as the legal and institutional frameworks for collective bargaining,
were established. This chapter examines the contradictions and limitations
embedded within the reforms of the 1940s. Moreover, it demonstrates that
the evolution of labour legislation in the subsequent decades did not corre-
spond to the gradualist assumptions of **reformist ideology**. What advances
were made, such as the extension of collective bargaining rights to federal and
provincial public servants, took place only under the specific economic and
political conditions of the 1960s. And even then, like the 1940s normalization,
this extension of "industrial citizenship" was restricted in important ways.

Chapter 3 covers the 1970s. It is in this pivotal decade that the postwar
paradigm begins to shift as the economic and political elements that sustained
the previous decades of growth began to transform. The central economic
characteristic of the 1970s was "stagflation." Here, high unemployment coincided with serious inflationary pressures, a combination that Keynesian
economic theory suggested was not possible. To defend its living standards,
the labour movement mobilized in ways not seen since the 1930s. For capital,
labour's growing bargaining power combined with a smaller share of profit
margins presented a threat. The Canadian state responded by introducing
wage controls to constrain pay increases for both public- and private-sector
workers. This moment established the era of coercion. Initially a temporary
measure, it has since been embedded otherwise permanently. And the New
Democratic Party (NDP), with several provincial governments endorsing the
controls regime, entered its own crisis of political legitimacy. In the 1970s, the
labour-capital compromises forged in the 1940s began to unravel, preparing
the ground for the neoliberal assault that was to come.

Chapter 4 examines the 1980s, wherein the assault against working-class
standards of living accelerated. In 1984, Brian Mulroney's Progressive Conservatives formed federal government, and they would remain in power until
1993. The Mulroney government's overall objective was to align the federal
state with the broader interests of business. The turn to free trade was central
to this agenda, but this included restricting the rights of federal **public-sector
workers**. Coercion took concrete form in the attenuation of the right to strike
via designation of workers as "essential," overseeing elaborate strikebreaking

schemes, including the use of scabs and introducing back-to-work legislation. In so doing, the Mulroney government provided a "how-to" manual for
ideologically like-minded provincial governments. Of course, the 1980s also
saw coercion mixed with elements of reform. The case of Ontario from 1985
to 1987 exemplifies this, where the Liberals brought the 42-year-long tenure
of the Progressive Conservatives in government to a conclusion. Given the
Liberals had four seats fewer than the Conservatives, leading government required a formal written "accord" with the NDP – which placed on the agenda
a number of worker-friendly legislative reforms covering employment standards, such as pay equity, labour relations, and occupational health and safety.
While most of North America was pursuing neoliberal restructuring, Ontario
appeared to have briefly opted to slow the process down and seek alternative
trajectories within capitalism.

While the turn to coercion accelerated through the 1980s as neoliberalism
became orthodoxy, it was consolidated in the 1990s. Chapter 5 delves into this
tumultuous history, which, while being a period of consolidation and setbacks
for workers and democratic institutions, was also a period of broad-based
resistance to an increasingly repressive neoliberalism. Throughout Canada,
every government provoked some manner of resistance as workers pushed
back against both austerity and efforts to curtail labour rights and protections.
Ontario is a particularly insightful case during this period as the NDP government moved from an initial reform agenda to one of austerity. This shattered
the party's electoral alliance with much of the labour movement, resulting in
the election of the Mike Harris-led Conservatives and the implementation
of the Common Sense Revolution platform, which set out to aggressively re-
write labour legislation and shrink the broader public sector. Trade unions
and a host of community organizations in turn launched the Days of Action
political strikes in an effort to put a halt to the government's agenda. In western Canada, NDP governments intervened to end strikes and usurp collective
bargaining. Quebec, similarly governed by the ostensibly social democratic
Parti Québécois, would turn to unilateral rewriting of collective agreements.
Previously, labour's enemies were well recognized, but through the 1990s,
even historical political allies had become unreliable. The Canadian fiscal
"miracle" of the 1990s was built upon the most significant program of austerity in the country's history. The Chrétien-Martin governments, together with
the provinces, consolidated this dismantling of the welfare state through a
program of labour coercion, which crushed the working-class militancy witnessed in earlier decades.

As Canada entered the twenty-first century, given the lessons of the 1990s, there would be no abatement from permanent austerity. The largely defeated resistance efforts of the 1990s now crafted a general sense of defeat as few signs suggested workers would employ the strike weapon to regain some losses or resist further ones. Chapter 6 turns to examining the years between 1999 and around 2013, a period where the federal and provincial strategy of punitive austerity resulted in budget surpluses. The 2006 federal election brought in the hard right Stephen Harper Conservative government that not only built on the fiscal austerity legacy of its Liberal predecessors but also made a sharp authoritarian turn in governance style and practice. This informed both the "rescue" and "exit" strategies to the 2008 global financial crisis. Irrespective of government party, each of the provinces embarked upon strategies ensuring workers – and, centrally, public-sector workers – would pay for the costs accumulated through the crisis, both directly, through wage and benefit concessions, and via the weakening of existing public services. All provinces restricted budget expenditures at or below 2 percent per year and looked to consolidate the assault on private-sector unionization by introducing new constraints on public-sector bargaining. By the second decade of the new millennium, governments had firmly placed coercion at the centre of the political and policy playbook.

The second decade of the twenty-first century was one of continuity and change: continuity in the sense of sustained austerity, and change in the sense that authoritarian politics accelerated. The federal structure of the Canadian state allows for uneven developments and paradoxical mixes of coercion and modestly reformist moments. Chapter 7 details these trajectories, including the defeat in 2015 of the Conservatives by the "progressive" Trudeau Liberals, which had campaigned in favour of deficit financing – a remarkable turn in itself. The Liberals, through the election, held out an olive branch to labour, promising more opportunities for input on the policy agenda. However, this was less than it appeared to be. And in the provinces, particularly those where right-wing parties governed, coercion, with a decidedly authoritarian bent, remained central. The provinces sought to institutionalize the austerity state through marketization, privatization, and labour policies that restructured the remnants of the postwar set of labour-capital compromises.

Chapter 8 explores how labour unions increasingly turned to the courts to defend and extend their right to free collective bargaining with reference to the Canadian Charter of Rights and Freedoms, in particular Sections 2(b) and 2(d), freedom of expression and freedom of association. It finds that the practical result of the first labour trilogy in the late 1980s was such that governments could essentially continue to ban or restrict strikes and to exclude specific groups of workers from collective bargaining with relative impunity. Over the next two decades, it seemed as though labour had reached an impasse with regard to using legal mechanisms to protect their rights – however, a series of decisions, most notably *BC Health Services*, brought a renewed sense of hope and optimism. And in 2015, with what has come to be known as the second labour trilogy, it seemed that proponents of a "legal road to labour rights" were proven right. In a series of decisions, the Supreme Court of Canada expanded the rights of workers to collectively bargain and, in some cases, to even strike. Subsequent decisions, however, poured cold water on the progressive potential of the courts. In the context of increasingly authoritarian governments, and the growing threat of using the notwithstanding clause (Section 33), the courts have done little to extend rights to non-unionized workers, let alone contribute to a reinvigorated and confident labour movement. In this regard, the double-edged sword involved in unions' four-decade-long reliance on labour law and the courts reaffirms that unions in Canada are in desperate need of a new strategy to broaden and deepen their connection with their members and working people more generally, along with building a renewed working-class politics.

Finally, we turn in Chapter 9 to the state of the labour movement today as well as that of its political and electoral strategies within the context of an increasingly authoritarian capitalism. **Antonio Gramsci**'s oft-cited remark that the "crisis consists precisely in the fact that the old is dying and the new cannot be born; in this interregnum a great variety of morbid symptoms appear" vividly captures the "moment" we are experiencing. As relates to this book, two bear emphasizing. If trade union renewal is to happen, it will be founded upon a vision and practice contributing to radical political and economic transformation. The work of trade unions will stretch beyond defensive bargaining and contribute to organizing a working-class offensive. Second, and connected to the preceding point, a politics of a new type necessarily requires new working-class organizations and party structures, which are organically interwoven. On both counts, it is about beginning again. **Democratic capitalism** has not simply reached its limits. It is dissolving. Only through a renewed socialist politics, rooted in working-class organization and speaking to the needs of the twenty-first century, will the turn to an **authoritarianism** in defence of plutocratic interests be challenged.

CHAPTER TWO

The Postwar Era of Free Collective Bargaining

Chapter Summary: This chapter addresses the historical roots of Canadian labour policy and politics from the late 1800s to the 1960s. It begins with an overview of the partial loosening of restrictions on trade union rights in the late nineteenth century in the context of the state's largely pro-business and anti-labour orientation. A key turning point was reached in the early to mid-1940s as the federal government was forced by widespread worker militancy to manage growing class conflict amid the need to maintain production during World War II. The political and legislative compromises over this period established the labour relations framework that largely predominated over the next three decades, a period known broadly as the postwar "golden age" of capitalism. As this chapter shows, however, the postwar class compromise – with its many exclusions and limitations – was a fleeting phenomenon from its inception, tied to the contextual specificity of capitalist social relations.

INTRODUCTION

The social relations under which capitalist production takes place embody a structural antagonism between employers and employees (i.e., class conflict).

Since the employment contract gives the employer, as the purchaser of labour time, the right to determine what work employees do, exercising this
right involves the use of power. In turn, workers have historically recognized
that collective organization and the threat of collective withdrawal of labour
are necessary to advance their interests vis-à-vis the employer. Both formally
free actors in the capitalist labour market, the employer and employee seek
to establish their interests – ideologically and legally – in terms of rights the
state recognizes: the rights of property and managerial prerogative, on the one
hand, and, on the other, the rights of association and to strike.

The evolution of liberal capitalist societies into liberal democratic societies
is conventionally understood in terms of voting rights. However, the distinction between a democratic or authoritarian capitalist regime is never only
one of voting rights. It is equally a distinction which rests on the absence or
presence of freedom of association. The long struggle of the working classes
for political representation within the state system was matched through the
nineteenth and twentieth centuries by an equally long struggle against the
legal prohibition of the right to free association for wage labour.

Liberal democracy not only brought the working class into the parliamentary representative system on the basis of individual, universalistic criteria; it
also involved the state's recognition of the collective, class-specific organization of labour – the trade unions – as legitimate representatives of workers.
Moreover, the independence of the trade unions from direct interference by
the state itself had to be established.

FROM COERCION TO CONSENT

Prior to 1872, trade unions in Canada were illegal, defined as "combinations"
(monopolies) in the "restraint of trade." The Masters and Servants Act (1847)
made the decision to leave one job for another a criminal and civil offence.
The act of "deserting employment" or "breach of contract" was punishable by
fines and jail time. However, if an employer did not pay wages for work completed, employers were only subject to civil fines and rarely prosecuted. The
Trade Unions Act of 1872 did not grant positive rights to unions (the right
to act), but only loosened some of the legal restrictions on unions, granting
their members a certain degree of immunity from criminal prosecution.[1] This
did not mean that the state did not act from this point forward to promote
union organization or collective bargaining. On the contrary, capital's right to

continue to resist unionization in the succeeding decades was the chief focus of industrial relations. For instance, shortly after the Trade Unions Act, the federal government passed the Criminal Law Amendment Act of 1872, which essentially made picketing illegal and reinforced this with penalties where violence or intimidation (on the part of workers, but not employers) was alleged to have occurred during organizing drives and strikes. Moreover, the legal status of union contracts was such that they were essentially unenforceable in a court of law.

The state's extensive use of force in defence of the unfettered rights of capital became a hallmark of Canadian labour history. As both the Royal Commission on Mills and Factories of 1882, and the Royal Commission on the Relations of Labour and Capital of 1889 graphically detailed, unemployment, low pay, long working hours, high living costs, unsafe work, and lack of housing were common working-class grievances through this period.[2] These concerns were compounded by employer blacklists, mass dismissals, and non-recognition of unions and collective bargaining, and they were legally institutionalized via the use of strikebreakers, police and military interventions by way of injunctions, and the use of the riot act and martial law.[3]

The establishment of the federal Department of Labour in 1900 and the passing of the Industrial Disputes Investigation Act (IDIA) of 1907 were illustrative of the state's attempts to moderate and contain class conflict. The IDIA prohibited strikes and lockouts pending the completion of an investigation and mandated attempts at conciliation by a board consisting of representatives of labour, employers, and the government. If the dispute remained unresolved, the law required 30 days' notice before a strike or lockout could be legally undertaken. The failure to comply with the provisions of the Act could be met with fines and jail time. As James Rinehart noted, "while the major [strike] weapon of workers was blunted, the IDIA contained no prohibition of employers' anti-union tactics, such as the use of scab labour, injunctions, victimization of unionists, or yellow-dog contracts. As a result of the act, striking workers found themselves confronted with a more or less united opposition of both employer and state."[4]

Even the most progressive manifestation of the ruling ideology vis-à-vis the "labour problem" in the first decades of the century rested on a blatantly political distinction between "legitimate" and "illegitimate" trade unionism. Mackenzie King, who had served as an industrial relations consultant to US business magnate J.D. Rockefeller, and as the first deputy minister of labour and later the first minister of labour on his way to becoming Liberal leader and prime minister, wrote of "the danger of this whole body being converted to socialism if employers fail to take them into a sort of partnership through agreements with recognized unions. The solution of the problem of strikes seems to me to lie along the business partnership arrived at by long-term agreements between responsible leaders of organized capital on the one side and organized labour on the other. The trade unions must be incorporated, and limits put on the right to strike without compliance and with safeguards in the constitution."[5] Even for unions regarded as fundamentally oriented towards class collaboration, and hence as "legitimate," the 1907 Act, and state practices under its rubric, were filled with coercive implications and restrictions on freedom of association, including the right to strike. In the characteristic fashion of the Canadian state until the 1940s, the Act was directed "towards the **ad hoc** suspension of hostilities," in the context of "a generalized defence of private property rights by the capitalist state."[6]

By the early decades of the 1900s, the trade union movement had reached an impasse, but things changed rapidly with Canada's entry into World War I. The massive growth of industry, rail, and harbour facilities, stimulated by the cheap availability of credit, set in motion vast technological, administrative, and organizational changes to the labour process. **Fordist** production methods and Taylorist managerial processes proliferated.[7] As the war waged, labour's bargaining power grew vis-à-vis the state and capital. While corporate profits soared, so too did the cost of living for workers. This served to fan the flames of workplace militancy, in Canada and abroad, and civil disobedience peaked, reaching its crescendo with the 1919 Winnipeg General Strike. The deployment of the Royal North West Mounted Police against the workers vividly symbolized the coercive role of the state at work.[8]

After more than three decades of unparalleled economic growth, the Great Depression radically halted the expansion of capitalism. By 1933, one in four workers was unemployed and half the working age population was on some form of work relief. Prime Minister Bennett tried to export the Depression's problems by turning to the usual scapegoats during times of crisis: immigrants and activists. From 1930 to 1935, Canada deported more than 28,000 alleged communist sympathizers, labour organizers, and those on some form of welfare relief. Canada became the first country with parliamentary institutions, apart from Japan, to outlaw communist organizations and to declare their property, belongings, and facilities subject to confiscation. Fearing urban unrest, Bennett segregated unemployed men in isolated northern work relief camps under slave labour conditions.[9]

In 1935, the "On-to-Ottawa Trek" reignited working-class organization and redefined the political possibilities of the time. A bout of sit-down strikes, plant occupations, and other militant outbursts erupted across the country in concert with the homeless, poor, immigrants, and communists who began agitating for a "New Deal." Illustrative of the renewed working-class militancy was the strike by the United Auto Workers (UAW) at Oshawa on 8 August 1937, when 4,000 workers struck against General Motors due to the company's unwillingness to recognize the union, wage rollbacks, unsafe work, and long hours. After two weeks on strike, workers won union recognition, an increase in pay and benefits, grievance mechanisms, and health and safety improvements, ushering a new era of industrial militancy.[10]

It was only with Canada's entry into World War II that the Great Depression would be overcome. "The War Measures Act converted Canada overnight from a confederation into a unitary state; the government overrode or supplanted most of the normal procedures of peace; it became the largest and much the most important employer of labour; it used its fiscal capacity and monetary powers to effect maximum war production; [it] borrow[ed] billions, raising billions by taxation, and then bringing into play a reserve power by borrowing many millions from the banking system to inflate the economy to full war capacity."[11] Increasing with intensity under national mobilization for war and the return of full employment, Canada witnessed an unprecedented tide of sustained and comprehensive working-class mobilization and politicization through the 1940s. As historian H.A. Logan has noted, "the trade union world seethed with discontent over the injustices resulting from the refusal of both private and government corporations to bargain collectively."[12] By 1943, one out of every three trade union members were engaged in strike action. Over the next five years, union membership nearly doubled from 17 to 30 percent of the non-agricultural workforce.[13]

It was at this point when the state turned away from ad hoc coercive mechanisms vis-à-vis workers' struggles for union recognition and began to recognize the principle of freedom of association for workers. As Hal Draper has argued, "It is the pattern in all countries that, as soon as the bourgeoisie reconciles itself to the fact that trade unionism is here to stay, it ceases to denounce the institution as a subversive evil that has to be rooted out with fire and sword in order to defend God, country, and motherhood, and turns instead to the next line of defence: domesticating the unions, housebreaking them, and fitting them into the national family as one of the tame cats."[14] With the passing of Privy Council Order 1003, the Wartime Labour Relations

Regulations Act, the rights of workers to organize and bargain collectively were for the first time enshrined in federal law. It developed certification procedures, mandated compulsory union recognition, defined unfair labour practices, and established an administrative framework to enforce these regulations. One of the first major conflicts to test the parameters of PC 1003 occurred on 12 September 1945, when more than 10,000 UAW workers went on strike at the Ford Windsor plant. The dispute lasted more than three months, resulting in a wave of cross-Canada sympathy strikes involving more than 8,000 workers at 25 plants, before both sides agreed to go to binding arbitration.[15] Six weeks later, Justice Ivan Rand issued his landmark ruling.

His decision provided for compulsory dues check-off for all employees in the bargaining unit whether they were members of the union or not, since all workers in the workplace benefited in some form from the union. The "**Rand formula**" prohibited all strikes during the term of a collective agreement and instituted a system of financial penalties, to be drawn from union dues, which would be levied against the union in the event of an illegal strike. It must be stressed that this new era in labour relations did not evolve suddenly from the minds of legislators, judges, and industrial relations experts. Nor had capitalists miraculously been transformed into far-sighted social philosophers (as Rand's ruling against the Ford Motor Company itself attests).[16] Rather, the labour legislation of the 1940s was the product of an unprecedented shift in the balance of class forces in Canadian society.

This industrial militancy was politically expressed by the dramatic rise of the Co-operative Commonwealth Federation (CCF) in the opinion polls, by Communist and CCF victories in the 1943 federal by-elections, and by the rather hasty conversion of the Liberal and Conservative parties to reforms along the lines of the Keynesian welfare state. While the threat of any direct political challenge to capitalism had largely evaporated by 1945 – as evidenced in the Ontario and federal elections of that year – industrial militancy did not pass away. The temporary industrial relations reform initiated by Privy Council Order 1003 became permanent legislation in 1948 with the passing of the Industrial Relations and Disputes Investigations Act (IRDIA). The IRDIA cemented the legislative rights first passed with PC 1003 and extended these to a limited number of public corporations and agencies – thus beginning the era of free collective bargaining.

The use of the word "free" has a crucial double meaning. It suggests that a balance of power exists between capital and labour, that they face each other as equals, otherwise any bargain struck could scarcely be viewed as one that was freely achieved. It also suggests that the state's role is akin to that of an umpire involved in applying, interpreting, and adjusting impartial rules. In the case of the first meaning, the structured inequality between capital and labour is obscured; in the second, the use of the state's coercive powers on behalf of capital is overlooked. Industrial relations orthodoxy in the postwar era of free collective bargaining was premised on an acceptance of both meanings of the word "free." We will not dwell here on the continued structural inequality between capital and labour.[17] It will suffice to mention the massive inequality in resources available to each party in the relationship. First, in sheer scale, flexibility, and durability, capital's material resources continue to overwhelm those of labour. Second, the organizational and ideological resources of labour remain scarcely measurable against the network of associations, organizations, advisory bodies, in-house publications, and mass media that are owned by, or financially beholden to, capital. Capital's greater access to the state throughout the postwar period has been well documented.[18] As Ellen Wood has noted, although capitalist class relations give the unique impression that the labourer is a "free vendor of his labour-power" market dependence is an instituted compulsion: capital has a choice, while wage labour does not.[19]

The supremacy of capital in this era of free collective bargaining, in both its ideological and coercive dimensions, was captured well by Harold Laski:

> The right to call on the service of the armed forces ... is normally and naturally regarded as a proper prerogative of the ownership of some physical property that is seen to be in danger.... But we should be overwhelmed if a great trade union in an industrial dispute, asked for, much less received, the aid of the police, or the militia or the federal troops to safeguard it in a claim to the **right to work** which it argued was as real as the physical right to visible and corporal property, like a factory.[20]

Laski recognized that in "a political democracy set within the categories of capitalist economies ... the area within which workers can maneuver for concessions is far wider than in a dictatorship." But he also understood the fact that even within capitalist democracy, the labour movement is confronted with "an upper limit to its efforts beyond which it is hardly likely to pass."[21] This reference to capital's privileged access to the coercive apparatus of the state returns us directly to the second meaning of "free." The very same legislation that supported the right to recognition and guaranteed the right to strike also constrained in a highly detailed manner the nature of bargaining and the exercise of union power.

The true thrust of the legislation in this respect was made apparent by Paul Weiler in defence of the conventional interpretation of free collective bargaining: "There are two parts of a labour code which are central to the balance of power between union and employer. One is the use of the law to facilitate the growth of union representation of organized workers. The other is the use of the law to limit the exercise of union economic weapons (the strike and the picket line) once a collective bargaining relationship has become established."[22] The other part of the labour legislation of the 1940s that Weiler referred to was precisely the extensive set of restrictions placed on collective action by unions, which established in Canada one of the most restrictive and highly juridified frameworks for collective bargaining in any capitalist democracy.

Modelled after the American Wagner Act, Canadian legislation went "beyond it," as Logan noted: "(1) in naming and proscribing unfair practices by unions ... (2) in assuming a responsibility by the state to assist the two negotiating parties ... [and] (3) in forbidding strikes and lockouts during negotiations for the term of the agreement."[23] Part and parcel of union recognition and the promoting of collective bargaining were a broad set of legal restrictions on eligibility for membership and the precise circumstances for legal strike action. Apart from restrictions on picketing and secondary boycotts, the most important restriction on the right to strike was the ban on strikes during the term of a collective agreement.

It is crucial to understand that the new mechanisms promoting the institutionalization of union recognition and free collective bargaining were, as Rand said, "devised to adjust, toward an increasing harmony, the interests of capital, labour and the public," in light of the shift in the balance of class forces that had taken place over the preceding decades. It was an adjustment devised not to undermine but to secure and maintain under new conditions capital's "long run ... dominant position."[24] The postwar settlement between capital and labour, which involved limited measures to reduce unemployment, the introduction of welfare state reforms, and the new labour legislation, certainly created real gains for working people. These reforms, however, did not create equality between the contending classes. While these measures gave the appearance that the scope of market penetration had been constrained, in practice these measures quietly consolidated capital's control over the labour process by legitimating the social subordination of labour via impartial social welfare inducements as a patch onto the flawed fabric of the capitalist system. In other words, "decommodification" had the paradoxical effect of actually deepening and extending market relations.[25]

Through formal mechanisms for negotiation and redistribution, consent came to play a visibly dominant role in inter-class relations, while coercion, still crucially present, was in the background. Coercion in capital-labour relations became less ad hoc and arbitrary: as the state's rationalization and institutionalization of workers' freedoms of association became more formal, so too did coercion. What before had taken the appearance of the charge of the Mounties now increasingly took the form of the rule of law by which unions policed themselves in most instances. Where they did not, as Chapter 8 shows, the courts were often quick to act with injunctions and additional restrictions on picketing that reflected a judicial perpetuation, alongside the new legal framework, of the tradition of ad hoc interventions, to the benefit of capital.

Finally, even in the context of the overarching theme of consensual industrial relations that marked the era, it was still necessary to distinguish between what the state regarded as "legitimate" and "illegitimate" trade unionism. On even more blatantly political grounds than at the beginning of the century, the state and the bulk of the reformist wing of the labour leadership cooperated in applying extensive coercion, overtly as well as covertly, against communists and other radicals in the union movement. Many of labour's most committed and able industrial organizers not only had their civil liberties abused but were also pushed out of or marginalized within the trade union. These actions were taken in the context of an international Cold War that often involved a clandestine war against political radicalism in the domestic labour movement.[26] This, too, was an element in the postwar settlement and an important measure of the state coercion – as well as of the unions' self-policing – was embedded in it.

THE MYTH OF GRADUALISM

The passage of the IRDIA, accompanied by similar provincial legislation, signified that legal protection of workers' freedom to organize and bargain would be a central element of the postwar settlement. The labour movement undoubtedly expected that the reforms were permanent gains that would be gradually extended to other workers. Moreover, given that the settlement also expanded the role of the state, it might also have been expected that the extension of bargaining rights would begin among public employees. However, little growth of bargaining rights occurred; on the contrary, the only changes involved imposing additional restrictions on existing collective rights.[27]

The end to this impasse came not gradually but suddenly in the mid-1960s. The decade of the sixties is frequently portrayed as one of student radicalism and militancy contrasted with working-class consumerism and acquiescence.[28] This contrast is much overdrawn, as the "revolt" of the sixties was in broad measure generational. More importantly, consumerism is not without its contradictions. As Ralph Miliband observed, taking issue with the omnipotence ascribed to corporate demand management through advertising by John Galbraith and others, "The point is rather that business is able freely to propagate an ethos in which private acquisitiveness is made to appear as the main if not the only avenue to fulfillment, in which 'happiness' or 'success' are therefore defined in terms of private acquisition."[29]

Happiness and success are, however, relative terms. By the 1960s, the character of the working class was being transformed as much by the postwar generation as were the universities. Young workers' frames of reference did not include the Depression or the Cold War, with many coming of age just as the myth of a classless, affluent society was reaching its apogee. The contrast between this image and the reality of working-class life did not tarnish the image so much as inspire them to make it part of their own reality. Increasingly, the only way to achieve incomes consistent with the image was through collective bargaining, an understanding that manifested in the wave of strikes that punctuated the 1960s, as workers challenged the authority of their bosses, and even the law, under conditions of high employment. This wave established a new record in terms of the number of strikes and workers involved. As Stuart Jamieson noted, these strikes differed sharply from those of the 1950s in that wage demands figured much more prominently. An uncommonly large number of strikes – one-third of the total in 1966 – were "wildcats," often conducted in defiance of union leaders and, at times, even against them.[30] The government, not surprisingly, saw workers' realization of their bargaining power and their determination to use it as a manifestation of an industrial relations crisis, and it was prompted to establish the Woods Task Force, the major postwar enquiry on labour relations.[31]

However, the state's response to this new climate cannot be understood except in relation to the particular, and even more profound, set of changes at work in Quebec.[32] The previous 25 years had seen a transformation of both the economic base and the working class in Quebec, including the growth of unionization. Despite this transformation, the Quebec government remained in the grip of conservative interests. The province's response to a succession of strikes, from the 1949 Asbestos strike through to the strike by copper miners and smelter workers at Murdochville in 1957, was hostile and repressive, fostering a relatively radical working class and intelligentsia. The 1961 election victory of the Lesage Liberals formally broke the hold of the old regime on the province and initiated rapid political change. This change necessitated a political settlement with labour as no less than that which had been necessary elsewhere in Canada in the 1940s.

The basis of this settlement was the extension of bargaining rights to Quebec's public-sector workers in 1965. The breakthrough in Quebec sent shockwaves reverberating through the Canadian state because the reforms went well beyond what had been achieved in English Canada. In Quebec, federal public-sector workers were politicized as part of the working class and were galvanized to intensify their efforts to win the same demands from their own employer. Pressure from Quebec was a powerful boost to the growing general insistence by federal workers for bargaining rights after the Diefenbaker government, faced with the 1958–1961 recession, broke precedent by rejecting the pay increase proposed by the bipartite National Joint Council that had advised the government on these matters since 1944.[33]

It was clear that significant political restructuring was inevitable, not only in Quebec but also at the federal level. The new Quebec Liberal Party, reflecting the initiatives of the radical intelligentsia, provided a beacon to the federal Liberals, who needed to find a new image after the St. Laurent-C.D. Howe government of the 1950s was routed by the populist Diefenbaker Conservatives in 1958. The apparent appeal of the recently formed NDP and the fading bloom of postwar settlement across English Canada intensified the Liberal Party's need for a new image, which they hoped would bring them a quick return to their accustomed position as the governing party.

At the federal level, the new reality was reflected in the rise of the "three wise men," Trudeau, Pelletier, and Marchand, to leadership roles within the Liberal Party. The second wave of the welfare state in Canada, undertaken by the minority Liberal governments of the mid-1960s, was in good part an outcome of these developments. A significant element of this policy shift, apart from medicare and pension reform, was the appointment of the 1963 Heeney Commission to examine the question of collective bargaining rights for federal workers.[34] It was a foregone conclusion that Heeney would recommend in favour of collective bargaining for federal workers; what was at issue was how free it would actually be.

The government's commitment to the rights of its workers was no deeper than that of capital. As employers, governments have a unique rationale for restricting their employees' freedom of association – the supremacy of parliament. As a result, while finally conceding federal employees' collective bargaining rights in 1967, the federal government insisted on restrictions beyond those imposed on private-sector workers. Vital issues, including pensions, job classifications, technological change, staffing, and the use of part-time or casual labour, were wholly or partly excluded from the scope of bargaining. Serious consideration was also given to denying federal workers the right to strike, but in the end the right to strike was granted, largely because postal employees, particularly in Quebec and British Columbia, waged a number of what were, in effect, recognition strikes in the mid-1960s. These strikes did much to persuade the government that making strikes illegal did not guarantee preventing them.[35]

The reverberations of the Quiet Revolution in Quebec were also felt in the other provinces, where collective bargaining became the order of the day for most public-sector workers. That these reforms were meaningful is beyond a doubt. Nonetheless, it is striking how limited a version of trade union freedoms was conceded. The challenge to the law that the 1960s wave of strikes often represented was met not by liberalizing but by broadening the inclusiveness of Canada's restrictive, legalized collective bargaining regime. In most provinces, and at the federal level, a number of crucial issues were decreed to be outside the scope of public-sector bargaining. In several cases – Alberta, Ontario, Prince Edward Island, and Nova Scotia – provincial employees, and others such as hospital workers, continued to be denied the right to strike and bargain collectively.

CONCLUSION: THE LIMITS OF REFORM

The much-touted breakthrough that extended union rights in Canada in the 1960s must therefore be seen in terms of their continually narrowing limits. It would be wrong to ascribe these limits just to the resistance of particular sections of capital or to the ideology of liberal politicians. An equally important and largely ignored factor was the remarkable conservatism of the English Canadian labour movement, which repeatedly proved itself incapable of taking the initiative in generating demands or mobilizing support for reforms that challenged the terms of the postwar settlement. Few Canadian union leaders, for example, questioned the principle of the ban on strikes during the life of a collective agreement, although they sometimes sought specific exemptions from its application (e.g., unsafe working conditions). They even went along with the requirement that they act as agents of the law by formally notifying their members of the legal obligation to abide by this ban. During the 1960s and early 1970s, union leaders occasionally joined their members in defying the law as it applied to a given dispute, but they very rarely questioned the general framework of legal regulation.

As already noted, this conservatism must be attributed in part to the effects of the Cold War on the labour movement. The anti-communist crusade after World War II was directed against socialist ideas and militant rank-and-file struggle, as much as at members of the Communist Party, who then symbolized, albeit imperfectly and not exclusively, that tradition. As a result, control of the labour movement was assumed by people who were characterized, as David Lewis delicately put it, "by the absence of a sense of idealism."[36] There is no little irony in Lewis providing this description, given that his own central role in trying to build a base for the CCF in the union movement involved him trying "to wrest control from the communists wherever possible."[37] In this struggle, the CCF allied themselves with the most conservative and opportunistic elements of the labour movement, who, upon winning this internecine struggle, placed their own indelible stamp on the movement.

But other factors were involved as well, not least because objective circumstances typically exert more influence over action than subjective intention. In this respect, the adverse effect of the 1940s legislation on the character of the Canadian labour movement must be considered. Bourgeois reforms, however much they are the product of class struggle, are not without their contradictions. Left unchallenged, they can undermine the very conditions that called them into existence and open the way for future defeats. In reflecting on the legislative approach to union recognition, H.A. Logan observed: "The powerful weapon of the strike as an aid to negotiation through militant organization was weakened in its usefulness where the approach to recognition had to be certification."[38] Logan's reference to the way the legislation devalued militant organization is crucial. Unlike the capitalist firm, with its naturally given singularity of purpose, unions aggregate discrete individuals with their own purposes. The power of unions lies in the willingness of their numbers to act collectively, and for that to happen, a common purpose must be developed. The development of collective purpose is a social process – an outcome of education and organization that involves sustained interaction between the leaders and the led – and one that requires particular skills. Moreover, the incessant centrifugal pressures of a liberal consumerist society make this development a never-ending process.

The certification approach to union recognition did more than just weaken the apparent importance of militant organization – it directed the efforts of union leaders away from mobilizing and organizing and instead towards the juridical arena of the labour boards. In this context, different skills were necessary. It was critical, above all, to know the law – including legal rights, procedures, and precedents. These juridical activities tended to foster a legalistic practice and consciousness in which union rights appeared as privileges bestowed by the state, rather than democratic freedoms won and to be defended by collective struggle.

The ban on strikes during collective agreements and the institution of compulsory arbitration to resolve disputes while agreements were in force had a similar effect. Under these circumstances, it was unnecessary to maintain and develop collective organization between negotiations. Indeed, union leaders had a powerful incentive to do the reverse: to suppress any sign of spontaneous militancy. Industrial relations legislation inevitably treats unions as legal entities that are distinct from their members. This distinction was evidenced by the much greater penalties imposed on union officials who violated the law, compared to those for members. This intensified the pressure on union officials to act as agents of social control over their members rather than as their spokespersons and organizers.

The corrosive effects on union democracy of this kind of juridical and ideological structuring were severe. The trade unionism that subsequently developed in Canada bore all the signs of the web of legal restrictions that enveloped it. Its practice and consciousness were highly legalistic and bureaucratic, and therefore its collective strength was limited. These characteristics were reflected in the acceptance by the broader labour movement of greater restrictions on public employees' freedom of association. For the most part, the existing labour movement provided no inspiration or example other than legalism for public-sector unions. This model was particularly debilitating for those public-sector unions that had engaged in little of the mobilization and struggle for recognition that was so much a part of the formation of the early labour movement and that had characterized the industrial unions in the period prior to the postwar settlement. Thus, a union like the Public

Service Alliance of Canada (PSAC), in contrast to the Canadian Union of Postal Workers (CUPW), was one born almost entirely of legalism rather than mobilization and struggle. This is not to suggest that all the newly recognized public-sector unions were content with what had been offered them. For many, the limited rights acquired were seen as a waystation on the road to obtain trade union rights equivalent to those enjoyed in the private sector. As events unfolded, however, this proved to be a naively optimistic view. By the time that the waystation had been reached, by the late 1960s, the roadbed was already crumbling. The state had to contend with the wage pressure of organized workers while adjusting to the constraints placed upon it by the emerging crisis of capitalism.

CHAPTER THREE

Permanent Exceptionalism:
The Turn to Coercion

Chapter Summary: This chapter explores the tumultuous decade of the 1970s, a time characterized by both employer and state militancy in their efforts to subdue labour and reconstitute the class power of capital. It was also a decade characterized by global macroeconomic instability, organizational restructuring in the manufacturing heartlands of North America and Europe, and widespread worker discontent. Where workers fought to protect their standards of living, Canadian governments of all political parties responded with wage controls and back-to-work legislation. In this regard, the 1970s can be characterized as the beginning of the end of the postwar social compact.

INTRODUCTION

The wave of industrial militancy that arose in the mid-1960s continued into the early seventies, reaching its crescendo with newly unionized public-sector workers often taking the lead in protesting the assault against working-class standards of living. The heightened degree of industrial conflict reflected both greater militancy on the part of workers and more determined resistance by capital and the state, as the economic crisis deepened. The long postwar boom had led to a broadly held view that economic growth was unproblematic; that capitalism's anarchic character had been subdued by governments armed with Keynesian theory.[1] But this boom could not, and did not, last. The seventies were characterized by "stagflation": growth rates below the level necessary for full employment, combined with severe inflationary tendencies. In such conditions, the margin for concessions to secure labour's consent no longer existed; indeed, capital increasingly required concessions. Faced with stagnant or shrinking markets, rising resource prices, increased foreign competition, and a labour movement ready to defend its living standards, capital experienced reduced profit margins on existing investments and few profitable new opportunities.

One response to this situation by governments, in Canada and elsewhere, involved new subsidies to capital in the form of loans, grants, and tax concessions, thus underwriting investment and shifting the cost of the welfare state onto employed workers.[2] These initiatives had little impact on growth and tended to exacerbate inflation, since organized workers responded militantly to preserve their real incomes. Government deficits ballooned as expenditures rose on corporate subsidies, the unemployed, and public-sector wages. The other major response by the state was to restrict the bargaining power of organized labour. One way governments tried this was by obtaining the "voluntary" agreement of union leaders to limit members' wage demands to a "moderate" level in exchange for a union role in state economic decision-making and a promise of reforms enhancing union security, marginal extensions of the welfare state, or both.[3] Governments' other strategy was to deploy the state's coercive powers against the labour movement with increasing vigour. These two strategies should not be seen as mutually exclusive. Coercive measures, intentionally or otherwise, prompted unions to rethink their opposition to "voluntary" restraint. On the other hand, the inability of the state to deliver an agreement in the form of a "social wage," because of the growing economic crisis, undermined the viability of the voluntary restraint option and forced the state to adopt more coercive measures.

Initially, government policy at the federal and provincial levels reflected both strategies.[4] In 1969/1970, and again in 1974/1975, the federal government held discussions with the Canadian Labour Congress (CLC) aimed at securing voluntary wage restraint. In a number of jurisdictions, there were reforms enhancing union security and workers' collective rights. Among these were a relaxation of the restrictions on secondary picketing in British Columbia; expansion of the rights to refuse unsafe work in Ontario, Saskatchewan, and at the federal level; provisions for imposing "first agreements" on recalcitrant employers in British Columbia, Ontario, and Quebec; and in Quebec, extensive limitations on the use of strikebreakers by the Parti Québécois (PQ) government elected in 1976. Nonetheless, as the decade of the 1970s wore on, the shift towards new coercive measures was particularly obvious.

This shift was above all reflected in the rising incidence of ad hoc back-to-work legislation at both federal and provincial levels. In the first 15 years after 1950, there were only six instances of back-to-work legislation in total; there were 51 such instances in the following decade and a half, with half of these from 1975 to 1979 alone. Yet another 22 such measures were to follow in the 1980–1984 period. The first postwar instance of such legislation in 1950 was used by the federal government against railway workers, striking for a 40-hour workweek and a pay increase. The justification for the legislation, to quote Prime Minister St. Laurent, was that "the welfare and security of the nation are imperilled."[5] Not surprisingly, St. Laurent insisted that it was "not designed to establish precedents or procedures for subsequent bargaining negotiations."[6] Events were to prove otherwise, as railway workers were threatened with similar legislation in 1954, and actually subjected to it again in 1960 and 1966. The increased frequency and wider application of back-to-work legislation that followed were not the only notable trends in the state's use of this weapon. Over time, governments have, after the onset of a dispute, introduced such legislation with greater dispatch and less parliamentary debate, including increasingly onerous penalties for defiance of the law.

This new reliance on back-to-work legislation was part of a broader pattern of developments characterizing a new era in state policy towards labour. What marked this transformation was a shift from the generalized rule-of-law form of coercion (whereby an overall legal framework both establishes and constrains the rights and powers of all unions), towards a form of selective, ad hoc, discretionary state coercion (whereby the state removes for a specific purpose and period the rights contained in labour legislation). We began to witness a return to the pre–World War II era of ad hoc suspension of hostilities. This time, however, the "ad hoc" policy was not designed to avoid or delay the establishment of freedom of association; rather, it sought to contain or repress manifestations of class conflict as practised within the institutionalized freedom of association. Actions legal under general legislation increasingly were declared unlawful for particular groups of workers, or for all workers for a particular period of time. When it becomes common to resort to rhetoric and emergency powers to override the general framework of freedoms, there is clearly a crisis in the old form of rule.

A NEW IDEOLOGY FOR THE 1970s: THE FEDERAL GOVERNMENT LEADS

The treatment accorded to CUPW by the federal government in 1978 illustrated this crisis. At that time, the government publicly stated it would not tolerate the union's exercise of its legal right to strike. Once the strike began, the government immediately invoked back-to-work legislation, the Postal Services Continuation Act, Bill C-8, which revived the previous collective agreement and overrode the relatively small penalties in the Public Service Staff Relations Act (PSSRA) so as to establish potentially unlimited penalties. The government also charged the union's leader, J.C. Parrot, not for encouraging his members to defy the back-to-work law but for remaining silent – that is, for not publicly urging them to obey the law.[7] Similar requirements for union leaders, specified in previous back-to-work legislation, had escaped notice because they were either obeyed or, if not, disregarded by the government. In charging Mr. Parrot, and in granting him bail only on the condition that he tell CUPW members what the law required, the state set aside not only the general legal provisions for the union's right to strike but also the protection of free speech contained in the Bill of Rights.

The use of back-to-work legislation primarily concerned public-sector workers, although the **statutory incomes policy** of the federal Anti-Inflation Program of 1975–1978 suspended free collective bargaining for all workers. It was initiated by the government and upheld by the courts based on an elastic definition of economic emergency. Once again, the rules of the game established in the postwar settlement were set aside through special legislation. This empowered the Anti-Inflation Board to examine newly negotiated agreements and roll back wage increases exceeding the government's guidelines. The Act created an "administrator" to enforce a board report or cabinet order, backed by onerous penalties of unlimited fines and five years' imprisonment. The new spirit of the era was adequately expressed by Prime Minister Pierre Trudeau when he cynically told a radio interviewer immediately after the initiation of the Anti-Inflation Program, "We'll put a few union leaders in jail for three years and others will get the message."[8]

Despite the government's rhetoric about equivalent wage, price, dividend, and profit restraint under the Anti-Inflation Program, the substantive aspect of the policy entailed only wage controls. Prime Minister Pierre Trudeau, in an October 1982 CBC broadcast, referred to a comprehensive but temporary statutory prices and incomes policy of the type in force from 1975 to 1978 as follows: "what controls are for is to place the coercive use of government power between Canadians, like a referee who pushes boxers apart and forces them to their corners to rest up so that they can hit each other again."[9] A more appropriate metaphor for the 1975–1978 case would have the referee holding the arms of one of the boxers while the other flailed away. The 1975 wage controls coincided with the inauguration of **monetarism** – inflation targeting by central banks – as the guiding practice of monetary policy in Canada. Fiscal policy in the last years of the 1970s also showed a tendency towards austerity and restraint in public expenditures. Although defeated in the 1979 election, the Trudeau Liberals swept back to office nine months later as "born again" reformers, clothing themselves with all the themes first raised in the late 1960s: a patriated Constitution; enhanced civil liberties; income redistribution through tax reform; and a program of economic nationalism.

The new government was able to make good on the first two themes through the Constitution Act 1982, including the new Charter of Rights and Freedoms. But the 1981 reform budget was aborted in the face of vociferous capitalist opposition, backed by threats of a capital strike. And although the ambitious National Energy Program was introduced and kept in place until it was dismantled by the Mulroney government, the anger it aroused from Washington to Alberta ensured it was not only the first but also the last effective shot across the bow of continentalism. In all of this, the impact of the sharp 1981–1982 recession played a crucial contributory role. Striving to prove their respectability in the face of the crisis, the Liberals found themselves engulfed. As inflation and unemployment levels reached unprecedented postwar highs, and as business confidence fell to corresponding lows, the second Pierre Trudeau government turned from a policy of enhancing civil liberties and controls on American capital to instead enforcing legislation on Canadian workers that severely restricted their liberties. In so doing, a critical new phase in the turn to coercion was inaugurated.

The federal government's 1982 "6 and 5" program was not a "bolt out of the blue" – an isolated blemish on an otherwise impeccable record of liberal reformism. But its significance lay in the fact that it served as the opening shot in a broad-based assault on trade union freedoms by federal and provincial governments in the 1980s. It made explicit the ad hoc, selective, "temporary" use of coercion, not merely directed at the particular groups of workers affected or at the particular issue of "emergency" at hand, but rather designed to set an example for what was considered to be appropriate behaviour throughout the industrial relations system.[10] The suspension, in 1982, of public-sector workers' rights was not proclaimed or defended in terms of what it would directly accomplish to stem inflation and reinvigorate Canadian capitalism; rather, it was an example of what other workers had to voluntarily do if these objectives were to be attained.

What characterized the new policy was not only the unprecedented severity of ad hoc coercive measures by the state, but also the construction of a new ideology generalizing the state's new coercive orientation towards the working class as a whole. Because this new ideology was not legally codified in the manner of the postwar settlement, since it did not universally remove the right to strike and to "free collective bargaining," the new state coercion was, paradoxically, capable of being ideologically portrayed as "voluntary." Thus, Prime Minister Pierre Trudeau could emphatically declare that the government had explicitly rejected the option of the "coercive use of government power":

> Controls could not create the trust in each other and belief in our country that alone would serve our future. Controls would declare, with the force of the law, that Canadians cannot trust Canadians.... To choose to fight inflation, as a free people acting together – that is the course we chose.

The presentation of increased state coercion in this confusing way was conditional upon three elements. The first was a form of ideological excommunication regarding the rights of public-sector workers as Canadian citizens. The draconian controls established over them in 1982 were hidden amidst careful phrases asserting that only "comprehensive controls" were coercive and contrary to the principle of a "free people acting together." The controls were rather "examples" for other workers' "voluntarism." That this sleight of hand could even be attempted rested upon the fact that, for a decade, state employees had been presented as parasites, and state services – not long ago understood as essential to the community and social justice – were denigrated as wasteful and unproductive.

The second element necessary to this "voluntarist" depiction of coercion was that the specific coercive acts, such as back-to-work legislation, designation, and statutory incomes policies, had to be continually portrayed as exceptional, temporary, or emergency-related, regardless of how frequently they occurred, regardless of the number of workers who fell within their scope or were threatened by their "example." Since the terminology of emergency and crisis can be made elastic enough to cover a whole era rather than just specific events, months, or even years, measures presented as temporary can characterize an entire historical period.

Finally, and perhaps most importantly, the voluntary ideological veneer rested upon the construction of a new set of norms to justify labour's subordinate role within capitalism. The postwar settlement sought to maintain the dominant position of capital by establishing legal rights for organized labour to protect workers' immediate material interests in a capitalist system. The ideology of the new era, however, reversed this earlier logic – it placed the onus on labour to maintain capitalism as a viable economic system by acquiescing to capital's demand for the restriction or suspension of workers' previously recognized rights and freedoms, as well as sacrificing their immediate material interests. Whereas the "question of social justice" was key to the construction of the **hegemony** of the 1940s, Pierre Trudeau's appeal to "trust and belief" became the key phrase in the effort to reconstitute it in the 1980s. In other words, labour should eschew efforts to defend its economic interests directly and instead entrust its future to capital.

The coercive assault of 1982–1984 comprised three movements: first, the generalization of the federal government's "6 and 5" wage restraint legislation, as well as temporary removal of the right to strike from most public-sector workers in Canada; second, the partial extension of these restraints to the private sector; and third, the increasing frequency of permanent legislation restricting trade union rights. The Public Sector Compensation Restraint Act (Bill C-124), introduced in June 1982, was not as comprehensive as the Anti-Inflation Act of 1975–1978, which covered both public- and private-sector workers. However, what it lacked in comprehensiveness, it more than made up in the severity of treatment of the workers it covered. Bill C-124 abrogated the right to strike and bargain collectively by extending existing collective agreements for two years. Since strikes during agreements were prohibited under the earlier legislation, the new Act cynically used the same legislation that had established it to deny free collective bargaining for two to three years. This denial went so far as to "roll back" signed agreements with increases above the "6 and 5" during the life of the Act. The Act also gave sweeping powers to the Treasury Board to enforce compliance and designate affected employees.

All wage increases were to be determined by the government and awarded to public-sector employees without negotiation. For employees earning over $49,000, no merit increment or performance payments were allowed. Significantly, the largest rollback of a negotiated contract – from 12.25 percent to 6 percent – affected the lowest-paid employees in the federal government, the largely female clerical and regulatory groups earning an average of $18,000 annually. The government began phasing out the "6 and 5" program on 30 June 1984, with the exit period for some employees lasting until December 1985. The Lalonde Budget of 15 February 1984 announced that the government would persist with public-sector wage restraint, with no catch-up payments compensating for losses during the controls period. In addition, all settlements had to be based on total package comparisons with, and not exceeding, the private sector. Settlements should continue contributing to lower inflation. Finally, any return to free collective bargaining was qualified by Lalonde's declaration of his intention to amend the PSSRA and impose wage changes through legislation if "reasonable wage settlements cannot be obtained."

The "6 and 5" program was never intended to affect federal public-sector workers alone. Not only were the provinces expected to – and largely did – subject their employees to similar measures, but capital was also to be "inspired." This inspiration was primarily pursued at the ideological level; however, the Trudeau government also offered a more "practical" lead in the summer of 1983. After a settlement in the Nova Scotia construction industry that summer, which exceeded the "6 and 5" ceilings, Finance Minister Marc Lalonde, responding to business fears of a construction-led union wage spiral, reacted swiftly. The minister requested an immediate meeting with Canadian Construction Association (CCA) officials to discuss measures to prevent "excessive" settlements, with the CCA in turn calling for Lalonde to meet with all provincial finance and labour ministers "to examine the grossly unfair monopoly unions hold over employers in the unionized sector of the industry."[11] The contractors' association clearly saw this as an opportunity to push their opposition to the federal Fair Wages and Hours of Labour Act.

This Act came into force in 1938 to prevent unscrupulous contractors from winning bids on federally financed construction projects at the expense of unorganized, low-paid, and overworked tradesmen. Over the 1970s, because of increasing competition in the private sector from non-unionized firms, the CCA had taken a firm position against rigid enforcement of the Act, pressing it upon successive federal ministers of labour. Lalonde called a meeting with provincial finance ministers to discuss a coordinated approach on 27 July 1983. He sent a letter to his provincial counterparts announcing that the Act would be suspended in those provinces where wage settlements in the construction industry exceeded "6 and 5," beginning with Nova Scotia and Ontario, and applying through 1983–1984. This action, subsequently applied to Prince Edward Island and lifted only in Ontario in August 1984 during the federal election campaign, was the prelude, perhaps even the signal, to the anti-union stances taken by the British Columbia and Alberta governments in the construction industry. The disputes over this action predominated the labour scene in those provinces in 1984.

Even more significant was the novel use of designations to remove the right to strike from public-sector workers. Under the 1967 legislation extending collective bargaining to federal public employees, the government had reserved the right to designate certain jobs as "essential for the safety and security of the public" and hence to deny the workers performing these jobs the right to strike. The Public Service Staff Relations Board defined "safety and security" rather narrowly, so that the right to strike could not be vitiated by the indiscriminate use of designations, and the government had accepted the Board's definition. This practice was shattered in 1982 when the government, intent on designating away the right to strike of virtually the whole air traffic controllers' group, successfully challenged the Board's definition of "safety and security" in the Supreme Court.[12] As a result, the government was free to designate anyone whose normal work activities, in the government's own view, affected the safety and security of the public.

... AND THE PROVINCES FOLLOW

While "6 and 5" provided a lead for the provinces, their responses varied in significant respects. However, all cases unleashed an unprecedented degree of government intervention into collective bargaining. Not only were wages restrained but the right to engage in collective bargaining was effectively suspended, and in several cases the entire legislative framework for labour relations and worker protections was restructured. In Ontario and the Maritime provinces, the focus was on constraining public-sector compensation. However, in Quebec, British Columbia, Alberta, Saskatchewan, and Newfoundland and Labrador, governments sought to redesign the entire legislative framework of labour relations and other labour protections to limit trade union and worker rights. Ontario, too, amended its Labour Relations Act to prohibit "illegal strikes." Only Manitoba, which had elected a New Democratic Party government in 1981, did not follow the most aggressive features of this pan-Canadian provincial restructuring of not just labour relations legislative frameworks but class relations.

In Ontario, a series of legislative interventions fundamentally transformed the collective bargaining framework that had existed since the end of World War II. Ontario's Inflation Restraint Act (Bill 179) initiated a process of rewriting the key elements of the capital-labour accord of the postwar period, with the legislation unilaterally extending existing collective agreements for one year, with a 5 percent maximum on compensation increases effective 21 September 1982. This legislation covered 565,000 workers employed in Ontario's broader public sector (core public service, municipalities, hospitals, schools, universities, colleges, and government agencies, boards, and commissions). The Act established a Restraint Board with substantial powers to issue orders restricting public-sector compensation increases. Following the expiry of this legislation, the Ontario government passed Bill 111, Public Sector Prices and Compensation Review Act, on 13 December 1983, which effectively maintained many of the restraints imposed earlier for an additional year. While returning to the form of constrained "free" collective bargaining, the government's objective was to limit compensation increases to 5 percent for the broader public sector. The legislation required arbitrators to take into account the employer's "ability to pay in light of existing fiscal policy" when making awards.

Nova Scotia introduced its wage restraint program following the 1982 federal program. A guideline of 6 percent was made compulsory for non-unionized employees and established a cap for negotiations with unionized public employees. In the other Atlantic provinces, Prince Edward Island enacted the Compensation Review Act (Bill 39) in June 1983. It restricted total compensation increases over two years, beginning 1 April 1983, to a maximum of 5 percent of the prior period's straight-time average hourly rate. In addition, all settlements had to be submitted to a compensation review commissioner and were decided based on certain criteria, such as the precedent established by past settlements, employers' ability to pay, unemployment levels, and impact on inflation. Thus, Bill 39 maintained a facade of "free collective bargaining," but, through the sweeping powers of the commissioner, could arbitrarily impose settlements or break negotiated ones. New Brunswick and Newfoundland limited themselves to guidelines following "6 and 5," but in the case of Newfoundland, the initial two-year program was followed in 1984 by a two-year wage freeze for all broader public-sector employees.

Quebec generally did not follow the federal government's initiative, but the parallel actions of the Parti Québécois government spoke to the essential unity of the Canadian state. In April 1982, the PQ asked public-sector employees to forego impending salary increases in their existing agreements, due to expire in December 1982. As was their right under collective bargaining law, Quebec's Common Front public-sector employees in the Quebec Teachers' Federation (CEQ), the Confederation of National Trade Unions (Confédération des syndicats nationaux, CSN), and the Quebec Federation of Labour (Fédération des travailleurs et travailleuses du Québec, FTQ) offered to open up the entire collective agreement. The government refused and in June 1982 legislated Bill 70, An Act Respecting Remuneration in the Public Sector, which decreed pay reductions averaging 19.5 percent for 300,000 provincial public-sector workers from 1 January 1983 to 31 March 1983. In effect, the government had removed the right to strike and extended collective agreements at lower salary levels. An Act to Amend the Quebec Labour Code, the Code of Civil Procedures and Other Legislation (Bill 72), restricting strikes in "essential services," was passed the same day as Bill 70. The Act required public-sector unions and employers to maintain **essential services**, primarily health and social services, during a strike. The onus was placed on the striking unions to assure a proper level of service. However, under the Act, the government was the final arbiter as to a sufficient level of service and could outlaw the strike altogether if it believed this level of service was not being maintained.

Subsequently, the introduction of Bill 105, An Act Respecting the Conditions of Employment in the Public Sector, unilaterally decreed collective agreements for public-sector workers for three years, to December 1985. The Bill not only covered the same provincial employees as Bill 70, but it also included previously exempt groups of public employees. Its restraint package kept annual increases equal to the **Consumer Price Index (CPI)** minus 1.5 percent. Hourly employees received increases equal to the CPI, with many affected workers earning less at the end of 1985 than in 1982. Bill 105 represented even more than restraint and abrogation of collective agreement processes. The Bill's accompanying 109 decrees, covering 80,000 pages of text, significantly rewrote collective agreement terms regarding job security and working conditions. For example, in the severely hit education sector, there were cutbacks in staff, increases in workloads, enhanced administrative control over teacher distribution, changes in seniority clauses and the ability to obtain "permanent" status, and departmental policy. The severity of the legislation invited a response from Quebec workers. The illegal walkout of Common Front public-sector employees in late January 1983 led to more draconian back-to-work legislation. In passing Bill 111 in February 1983, An Act to Ensure the Resumption of Services in the Public Sector, the PQ government ordered fines, imprisonment, and decertification of bargaining agents if the strike did not end immediately. The Bill exempted Quebec from the Canadian Charter of Rights and Freedoms and suspended sections of the Quebec Charter of Human Rights. Opposed by the Bar Association and civil liberties and human rights groups, Bill 111 represented an unprecedented attack on trade union rights and civil liberties.

Quebec was not alone among the provinces in moving beyond wage restraint and turning to a more fundamental rewriting of the entire framework governing work and labour. British Columbia, Alberta, Saskatchewan, and Newfoundland all embraced the opportunity to shift legislative rights and protections away from labour through a particularly virulent turn to coercion. In February 1982, with industrial settlements averaging 15 percent, the BC government announced public-sector wage guidelines of 10 percent for the first year and 9 percent for the second. These guidelines were quickly succeeded by more onerous controls through the Compensation Stabilization Act (Bill 28) on 25 June 1982, made retroactive to February. The Bill imposed compensation limits – 6 percent in the first year and 5 percent in the second – on 220,000 workers employed in the broader public sector. Moreover, these limits could be lowered depending upon historical relationships or special circumstances. Settlements had to meet employers' ability to pay and consider such factors as productivity, private-sector wage levels, unemployment levels, and cost of living. A compensation stabilization commissioner, appointed to review settlements, had the authority to make the final decision on acceptable agreements. The Bill provided cabinet with the authority to amend compensation guidelines, prohibit increases, identify what compensation is and how increases are divided, and prohibit reclassifications.

The budget of 1983 also introduced 26 regressive bills on what became known as "Black Thursday." The Compensation Stabilization Amendment Act (Bill 11) added new restraint guidelines that limited increases to a range of –5 to +5 percent for an indefinite period. Additionally, the Bill made "the employer's ability to pay" the paramount consideration, effectively allowing cabinet to set anyone's wages by adjusting the public sector's ability to pay.[13] The Bill also specifically allowed the government to unilaterally reduce compensation. In effect, Bill 11 vitiated collective bargaining for public-sector employees by setting up permanent wage controls under strict government authority; the proposed changes would, among other things, permit public-sector employers to terminate employees essentially at will, empower the government to prohibit strikes and/or picketing at any site deemed an "economic development project," and allow minimum standards of work to be overridden by private agreements between employer and employee.

The legislative assault of "Black Thursday" did not go unchallenged;[14] it was met by opposition of unprecedented scope and determination, which came together under the Solidarity Coalition. In essence, this umbrella organization comprised two groupings: the Lower Mainland Solidarity Coalition, an amalgam of several hundred popular organizations, and the British Columbia Federation of Labour's Operation Solidarity, which also included independent unions like the Hospital Employees' Union and Confederation of Canadian Union affiliates. Countless imaginative local protests, as well as a series of massive demonstrations, effectively one-day general strikes of public-sector workers, were held. On 1 November, the BC General Employees Union went out on strike, joined a week later by unions in the education sector, as part of a plan for a phased escalation towards a general strike. This escalation was abruptly halted on 13 November by the infamous agreement struck in Kelowna between the Woodworkers' Jack Munro, on behalf of the British Columbia Federation of Labour and Premier Bill Bennett.

This "deal," despite some retreats by the government, did not deflect the thrust of the government's initiative. The mass dismissal policy and the other "non-labour" budget measures that entailed sharply reduced education standards, together with the wholesale dismantling of civil rights protection and social services, especially for women, went ahead. By March 1984, the government was claiming victory in its attempt to cut the civil service by 25 percent.[15] While this claim entailed no little sleight of hand, it nevertheless was true that the job shifting that took place involved some civil service functions being transferred to non-union status or to more precarious situations in the non-profit sector. The legislative onslaught did not let up in British Columbia. On 16 May 1984, the long-awaited Labour Code Amendment Act (Bill 28) substantially broadened the attack on trade union rights, especially in the private sector. The Bill's main features expressed "right-to-work" principles, extending the ability of employers to fight organizing drives and of employees to engage in decertification action, limiting the right to strike by banning political strikes and restricting secondary picketing. The Bill also empowered cabinet to suspend collective agreements and ban strikes and walkouts. On 25 August 1984, this Bill was invoked on Vancouver's Expo 86 site, forcing unionized construction workers to work beside unorganized labour, notwithstanding a clause in their collective agreement that allowed them to refuse to do so.

In Saskatchewan, as in BC, the overhaul of basic labour legislation was far more significant than the temporary wage restraint measures. Following the NDP government's use of back-to-work legislation against hospital workers, the new Tory government announced guidelines limiting wage increases for public-sector workers to 1 percent below the rate of inflation. Immediately after its election in April 1982, the government had also introduced Bill 104, the Trade Union Amendment Act, passed on 17 June 1983. The many dramatic alterations introduced to the provincial industrial relations system included widening the definition of employees considered management and weakening the ability of unions to discipline members who crossed picket lines or carried out anti-union activities. As well, the Bill made unions legal entities capable of suing or being sued. This was quite important, as the amendments included an obligation for unions to provide a "duty of fair representation" and allow "for the application of the principles of natural justice" in disputes between employees and trade unions.

Unlike British Columbia and Saskatchewan, which had elected social democratic governments, Alberta never provided a legislative framework very favourable to labour and largely bypassed the extension of collective bargaining rights to public employees in the 1960s. Nonetheless, an already repressive situation took a sharp turn for the worse, in line with trends in Alberta's bordering provinces. What was in the wind was first revealed in Bill 11, the Health Services Continuation Act in March 1982, ordering striking Alberta nurses back to work. Dealing with some of the lowest-paid workers in the province, the government not only imposed binding arbitration but provided for union decertification and a prohibition on union members from union activity for a period of two years if the strike was not immediately stopped. A year later, on 6 June 1983, the Labour Statutes Amendment Act (Bill 44) was passed, permanently banning strikes by nurses and hospital workers and restricting the right to strike for other affected groups, notably those (few) members of the Alberta Union of Public Employees (AUPE) who enjoyed this right. Under this Act, arbitrated collective agreements had to be submitted to a government-appointed tribunal that was required to consider government fiscal policy and general economic conditions in making awards, thereby enabling continual public-sector restraint.

Under Bill 44, arbitrators themselves now had to consider factors such as government guidelines, the employer's ability to pay, and non-union wages. The Bill effectively removed any pretence of fairness in the arbitration process: management was under no compulsion "to bargain in good faith," for it could refer the "collective bargaining" process to the arbitration board and it was the minister, not the parties involved, who determined the items in dispute. Besides the compensation restraint and strike restrictions, Bill 44 had other sections of some importance. Similar to Quebec, employers could then suspend the deduction of union dues if a strike occurred. However, there were no penalties set for employers in lockouts. The wide-ranging attacks on trade union rights, which went well beyond the "temporary" aspect of wage restraint legislation, were not confined to western Canada. Newfoundland introduced restrictions on the rights of public-sector employees patterned after US-style "right-to-work" legislation. Bill 59, An Act to Amend the Public Service (Collective Bargaining) Act, denied 2,000 workers the right to join a union by broadening the basis for "managerial" exclusions. Besides making it more difficult to organize in the public sector, the Bill restricted union rights by placing new limits on collective action, including the prohibition of rotating strikes in the health sector.

It is perhaps indicative of how casual governments were becoming regarding restrictive changes in labour legislation that An Act to Amend the Labour Relations Act (Bill 75) passed through the Ontario legislature in 1984 with scarcely any debate. The amendments empowered the Ontario Labour Relations Board (OLRB), in the case of illegal strikes, to act not only against trade unions and union officials but also "any person who has done or is threatening to do an act that the person knows or ought to know that, as a probably or reasonable consequence of the act, another person or persons will engage in an unlawful strike." The government explained to the legislature that the amendment was introduced to clarify the OLRB's authority in the construction industry, permitting it to disallow one group of construction workers engaged in a dispute from closing down an entire site through "selective picketing." Without, however, explaining that it had done so, the government had amended the sections of the Act pertaining to the Board's powers in general, in the case of illegal strikes. By explicitly extending the Board's purview beyond union officials to activist rank-and-file members or to those who support them in illegal strikes, it not only made unofficial union groups (such as the health workers' council that helped organize the hospital workers' strikes in Ontario in 1980) subject to the Board's penalties, but also anyone who offered financial, verbal, or picketing encouragement or support.

CONCLUSION: A TRANSITIONARY DECADE

The 1970s (and the 1980s that followed) marked a transition from two distinct eras in the history of postwar capitalism. Democratic capitalism, where **social democracy** was its most progressive form, had its roots in the class battles of the 1930s and in the mass mobilization to fight fascism in World War II. In the Canadian context, as a dimension of the Congress of Industrial Organizations (CIO) organizing campaigns of the late 1930s and into the 1940s, trade union rights were won and embedded in law. It was a victory, indeed, but a victory where the class struggle in the workplace would be subject to strict regulation by the state. In addition, the period from 1945 into the late 1960s would see significant expansion in a range of public goods and services that, at least partially, served to increase access to health care, post-secondary education, housing, and various social services. This version of democratic capitalism was sustainable as long as the virtuous cycle of increasing productivity and profit aligned with redistributional public policies and predictable collective bargaining. That economic paradigm unravelled as worker militancy took a greater share of profits. Capital went on the offensive and secured the support of the state to defeat the insurgency, and the ascent of neoliberalism was the result as it marched forward to become the "most successful ideology in world history."[16]

The Canadian state's struggle to quell the economic and political crises of the period had its paradoxes and contradictions; the onward march of neoliberalism in Canada did not follow a straight line. Coercion and consent are not mutually exclusive state strategies; a minor chord of reformism could still be heard in the controls period. As the next chapter shows, the newly elected NDP government in Manitoba passed amendments to the Labour Relations Act in 1982 – which introduced extensive reforms, bringing Manitoba into line with other jurisdictions – and began a process of revamping the Act. In 1983, Ontario passed legislation imposing some limited restrictions on the use of "professional" strikebreakers. And at the federal level, the Liberal government, in its dying days in office, introduced several amendments to the Canada Labour Code, enhancing minimum employment standards, individual worker rights, and union recognition, specifying that the Rand formula be included in collective agreements. As we examine in the following chapter, these reforms, while progressive and a welcome contrast to the overall repressiveness of the period, were neither extensive nor path breaking. Indeed, the federal legislation, save for the amendments enhancing union security, were not even proclaimed. As such, they can hardly be said to have muffled the coercive theme orchestrated by the state through the 1980s and into the 1990s. Those who thought the controls period was a temporary interruption of "free collective bargaining" were sadly mistaken.

CHAPTER FOUR

Freeing Trade, Coercing Labour

Chapter Summary: The post-1945 model of economic management and labour-capital compromises began to unravel in the
1970s and was incrementally displaced by an ascendant neoliberalism. Through the 1980s, this model was consolidated. This
ideological turn would by the end of the decade facilitate the
embrace of free trade and competitiveness as the anchors of
Canadian political and economic policy. Advancing these policies required that the assault on trade union freedoms and
worker protections be continued and accelerated.

INTRODUCTION

The 1980s was the decade of paradigm shift.[1] The wobbling of the post-1945
Keynesian world order was in this new decade incapable of withstanding the
forces of neoliberalism. Giving expression in both form and substance to this
transitional decade were the elections of archetypal governments of the New
Right lead by Margaret Thatcher in the United Kingdom and Ronald Reagan
in the United States. A new world was being born out of the ashes of the old,
and Canada would not be exceptional in this historic period. If Canada did
not experience the same rise of neo-conservative ideology as Britain and the

United States, it hardly escaped the "strong state and free market" practice evidenced in those countries and elsewhere. Whereas the Trudeau government's central concern was to break the back of wage militancy in the context of double-digit inflation, the Mulroney government's main concern was to attune the state more directly and fundamentally to the broader business agenda of the 1980s.

The Trudeau government's wage controls were not inconsistent with an enhanced regulatory role for the state in the economy generally. Since the late 1970s, the pace of capitalist restructuring at the level of the firm, and internationally, had accelerated. It became clear that this had to entail, insofar as capital was concerned, extensive restructuring of the state itself: it was a process of deregulation, privatization, and the commodification of public services. It also entailed a restructuring of the labour process in the firm and the state, central to which was the extraction of significant concessions in the terms and conditions of employment entrenched in existing collective agreements. In this context, the Trudeau government's freezing of collective agreements in the public sector was hardly sufficient. Integral to the strong state so necessary to create a "free" market was the consolidation of the assault on trade union rights and freedoms.

THE MULRONEY YEARS: FREEING TRADE, UNFREEING LABOUR

The Mulroney government's intrusions on labour's rights involved further constraints on the right to strike in the federal public sector via the spurious designation of workers as "essential"; overseeing elaborate strikebreaking schemes, including the use of scabs in Crown corporations; and introducing back-to-work legislation of a particularly draconian kind, which intervened directly in the most basic aspects of freedom of association. The Mulroney government thereby not only carried the assault on federal public employees to unprecedented levels but continued to provide an "example" for the private sector and provincial governments.

Most provincial governments hardly needed encouragement. Between 1985 and 1989, there were 22 instances of suspensions of the right to strike via back-to-work measures at the provincial level. Together with five federal measures, this amounted to an annual rate higher than in any previous period, which largely continued into the following decade. This abrogation of the right to strike became more frequent through the 1980s but was also accompanied by additional coercive measures. The penalties on workers and unions specified in the legislation were dramatically escalated. All the more troubling was the willingness of governments to arm themselves with executive powers to remove democratic union rights without reference to legislative approval and public debate before the implementation of such acts. At the same time, the trend continued towards the permanent restrictions noted in Chapter 3. This increasingly entailed rewriting labour codes to undermine workers' rights in the private as well as the public sectors. Direct interventions in the internal conduct of union affairs became an element in this process, and in a number of instances, back-to-work legislation actually went so far against freedom of association as to intrude on the rights of union members to elect their own leaders.

The Mulroney government's own resort to coercion in labour relations was virtually inevitable once bargaining was resumed in the wake of Trudeau's controls, but centre stage was now given to a state strategy of securing concessions from those state workers who most stood in the way of capitalist restructuring and the privatization and deregulation this entailed. These were the workers who always lay at the heart of the Canadian state's productive activities – who, in other words, provided the public infrastructure for private capital accumulation. This shifted state practice vis-à-vis strikes, and the terms of back-to-work legislation, in a direction that carried the assault on workers' trade union rights to unprecedented levels.

In early 1987, the Mulroney government took up this tactic of concession bargaining directly, sweepingly applying it to employees of federal Crown corporations, and ultimately using its powers of coercion to impose it unilaterally in most cases. By the spring of 1987, 100,000 workers in three federal industries (the seaway, railway, and postal sectors) were facing similar demands by Crown corporations for concessions involving work rules, job security, and wages. Informed observers saw the federal government actively pushing the unions concerned into taking strike action just to defend their current collective agreements. Even Bill Kelly, Labour Canada's omnipresent mediator, predicted, "We have the makings of real trouble in some of the company demands…. It certainly could be a long, hot summer."[2]

By the time the inevitable confrontations occurred, the government was well armed with new back-to-work legislation and more. It was hardly unprecedented for striking railway workers to be ordered back to work, as they were in the summer of 1987 and as every rail strike since 1950 had been dealt with. Arguably, the leaders of the railway unions had come to view such leg-islation as an avenue to arbitrated settlements yielding sufficient returns to satisfy members. But the 1987 back-to-work legislation (Bill C-85) would be different. The Bill ignored a conciliation report that had dismissed the rail-road workers' key demands for the unfettered right to contract out work and a two-tiered wage system. Furthermore, unlike the 1973 legislation ending the last rail strike, there was no provision for an interim wage settlement. Nor was there any stipulation that an arbitrator preserve existing job security provisions, let alone one stating that union concerns regarding the adequacy of these provisions be taken seriously.

The federal government's willingness to transgress workers' rights was most evident in the case of Canada Post employees. Having earlier set a two-year deadline for eliminating Canada Post's deficit and having staffed the corpo-ration with aggressive managers brought in from the private sector, the gov-ernment, urged on by the business community, was quite prepared to break CUPW's resistance to management's subsequent demands for massive con-cessions.[3] For a Crown corporation to undertake, and the federal government to endorse, plans that involved mass hiring of strikebreaking workers (also re-ferred to as scabs) and transporting them through picket lines in preparation for a strike was a shocking departure from conventional practice.

The use of private security agents to spy on pickets, including following them home once the strike began, added a particularly ugly dimension to the use of state coercion against workers. In the case of the letter carriers' strike in August 1987, these tactics, and the picket line violence they produced, yielded substantial popular revulsion (to which the media contributed by exposing the chaos that the initial use of these tactics created for the postal service). This caused the government to back off and support a negotiated settlement. However, both the government and Canada Post were determined that this would not happen with the inside workers. From the outset, the government's clear alternative for CUPW was capitulation or back-to-work legislation, even while it stepped up the strikebreaking tactics employed earlier. Despite CUPW's strategy – limiting disruption to rotating strikes and obvious efforts to minimize picket-line violence – in the face of Canada Post's provocative use of scab labour, back-to-work legislation (Bill C-86) came only seven days after the strike began.

To appreciate the government's extremism, it is necessary to review the issues involved in the strike. At the dispute's heart was job security: CUPW was essentially defending itself against management's efforts to reduce the workforce, not least through its "franchising" program, which would contract out some 4,000 clerk positions. In defending these positions, the union argued that Canada Post's plan would harm the community by extending the scope of casual and low-paid employment and changing the post office from a public service to that of a profit-maximizing business. Hundreds of thousands of workers in years past have bargained, and gone on strike, over similar issues. For the government, the issue was the union. Consumer Minister Harvie Andre saw Bill C-86 as the only way to correct an intolerable situation in which "total excess labour cost … is between $460 and 800 million a year. This situation exists not because the workers are lazy, but because of acquiescence to union demands. The present work rules are impossible."[4] The back-to-work legislation was designed not merely to end the strike but to rectify this situation. In particular, the arbitrator was required in the original version of the Bill to take "due cognizance" of the conciliator's report released prior to the strike. This report, praised by Canada Post and the government, strongly supported Canada Post's franchise program.

Finally, the possibility of a union as solidaristic and democratic as CUPW refusing to obey Bill C-86 – despite massive financial penalties – brought to full public light just how far the assault on worker's rights had gone by the fall of 1987. Not only did Bill C-86 bar any union officer or representative convicted of violating the act from employment by Canada Post for five years, it also went on to ban any officer or representative so convicted from holding any union office for five years. This state suppression of the freedom of a private association's members to elect their own representatives transgressed the most basic element of freedom of association. Even the most conservative Supreme Court justices could not contemplate this as possible in "democratic" Canada. The publicity surrounding this dispute, and its draconian resolution, revealed that this was not just an ad hoc action directed at J.C. Parrot, in view of his previous defiance of back-to-work legislation, or even at CUPW, given its militant history. Minister Andre revealed that the Department of Labour was already routinely including such a clause in back-to-work legislation, having sought and obtained assurance as to its constitutionality from Department of Justice lawyers.[5]

The Mulroney government's various anti-labour actions led even centrist observers of labour relations at the federal level to suggest that the government's "longer range game plan appears to call for the gradual elimination of the strike option in federal dealings."[6] This appeared to be confirmed by a package of proposed amendments to the PSSRA unveiled in early 1987. These included new powers for the Public Service Staff Relations Board (PSSRB), enabling it to delay strikes; empowering the Treasury Board to lay off and lock out employees; substantially expanding the definitions of "management" and "essential" in the Act; and requiring arbitrators to consider Ottawa's economic and fiscal policies when making awards. Furthermore, this package included a proposal to empower the cabinet to end strikes by Orders-in-Council when Parliament was not in session. Thus, a strike allowed for by parliamentary legislation could be declared illegal without recourse to Parliament (which is why we have back-to-work legislation) but by mere executive order. As has so often been the case historically, the pruning of workers' fundamental freedoms tends to atrophy liberal democratic freedoms within the state as well.

According to then-PSAC president Daryl Bean, if these amendments were introduced, it "would destroy collective bargaining in the public service."[7] Certainly it was clear that the object of the exercise was to at least hang the threat of these kinds of amendments over the union's head so that it would voluntarily accept arbitrations that would yield lower wage increases.[8] As one industrial relations observer noted at the time, this was connected with the government's free trade strategy: "The debate on free-trade in Canada is already underway, and when free-trade becomes a reality in Canada, the requirement to be increasingly competitive in world markets will have one major policy implication for public-sector compensation – namely that governments will pursue and apply even more vigorously a public policy that compensation levels in the public sector must follow and not lead the private sector."[9] These turned out to be prophetic words.

The 1988 election intervened before the proposed amendments to the PSSRA could be enacted. An unprecedented alliance of labour, women's, and other popular groups, in which public employee unions played an important role, turned the election into a virtual referendum on the Free Trade Agreement (FTA) with the United States. The Tories were re-elected, although a majority of Canadians voted for parties opposed to the FTA, revealing that the centrepiece of the government's agenda was hanging by a very slender thread. Under these circumstances, the government made some slight conciliatory gestures towards its employees in the immediate aftermath of the election. For example, it agreed to "negotiate" its decisions with PSAC regarding the use of designations ("designations" refers to the tactic of declaring more workers as essential and therefore unable to strike), giving the PSSRA a mediating role in the case of disagreements, a procedure that reduced somewhat the percentage of designations in several bargaining groups. However, it must be noted that the threat of the proposed amendments to the PSSRA very much remained in the air and that threat was far from an idle one.

In December 1989, back-to-work legislation was passed against two PSAC bargaining units. In the same month, the government unveiled a broad-ranging attempt to reform the management and organization of the federal government, called "PS 2000." Notwithstanding the rhetoric of concern with improving federal workers' morale and the quality of service, the nature of the exercise was described by John Carson, appointed to oversee PS 2000, as "an unabashedly management-driven exercise."[10] The evident priority attached to strengthening the freedom and discretion of management led federal unions to fear that their members were more likely to be its victims rather than its beneficiaries, and that PS 2000 was the new vehicle for carrying forward the attack on collective bargaining foreshadowed in the proposed changes to the PSSRA before the election.

The ink on the FTA was barely dry when the Canadian economy slid back into recession. If the coincidence of this recession with the FTA created the impression that the latter was the principal cause of the former, in fact it only accelerated the impact of what was quickly to become an acute global economic downturn. And with this came a further stage in the assault on federal public employees. In its budget of February 1991, the federal government announced yet another wage restraint measure for federal employees. Pay would be frozen for the 1991–1992 fiscal year, with a 3 percent limit on wage increases for the following two years. The timing of this announcement was hardly an accident, coinciding with the opening of serious negotiations with PSAC over a renewed collective agreement. The government did not introduce legislation to give effect to its wage restraint pronouncement; its intention was to achieve restraint through "negotiation," banking on PSAC lacking the will or ability to offer serious resistance. To this end, the Treasury Board simply made any progress in negotiations towards a new collective agreement contingent upon the union first acquiescing to the government's wage freeze pronouncement. As events would have it, the government sorely miscalculated both the leadership and membership of PSAC.

PSAC had never managed to recoup from the assaults suffered over the preceding decade. From 1985 to 1990, federal workers secured the lowest wage increase of any bargaining jurisdiction in the private or public sector, and in five of the six years, negotiated increases were below the rate of inflation. Further, despite rising service demands, the number of federal employees in non-managerial positions (i.e., administrative support, technical, and operational), who form the bulk of PSAC's membership, fell by roughly 10 percent.[11] Were they to have capitulated after all this to another draconian wage freeze at the beginning of the 1990s, PSAC would have rendered incredible any claim that the union still had to protecting its membership. Responding to pressure from the core of activists that had developed over the past decade, the union sought a strike mandate to back its negotiators' efforts to secure a wage increase, pay equity adjustments, and increased job security at the bargaining table. The leadership's determination was reinforced by the introduction in June 1991 of Bill C-26, the Public Service Reform Act. The disdain shown by the government for serious contract negotiations with PSAC in 1991 had already revealed just how empty had been its rhetoric on the promised "empowerment" of federal employees under the rubric of the PS 2000 exercise.

The omnibus legislation introduced in June 1991 that grew out of this exercise made this fully apparent. Bill C-26 incorporated some of the changes proposed in 1987, notably expanding the definition of "management," and empowering the cabinet to suspend strikes by Orders-in-Council, albeit only during an election period. Instead of undermining union bargaining power by continuing to unilaterally expand designations, the new legislation once again allowed unions and the PSSRB a role in defining "essential" services. However, the new changes were mainly designed to make the employment status of public employees more precarious. It greatly expanded management's scope and incentive for contracting out work and for using part-time and casual workers. At the same time, it regrouped occupational structures to allow managers much greater discretion in shifting workers from one job to another. This latter change would, in all likelihood, effectively block progress on equal pay for women in the federal public sector.[12]

PSAC's call for a "general strike" involving the vast majority of federal public employees, most of whom had never been on strike, was unprecedented in the history of the Canadian state. As the Mulroney government remained resolute through the summer, the question remained whether, with a vote of 62 percent in favour of striking, the membership would display sufficient solidarity to mount an effective strike on such a mammoth scale. Although the government's whole strategy was clearly premised on the traditional absence of such solidarity, on 9 September 1991, tens of thousands of PSAC members joined picket lines across the country, surprising themselves and the rest of Canada by their overwhelming support for the strike. With support for the strike growing day by day, the government once again resorted to back-to-work legislation. But on 16 September, just as the legislation was rushed through second reading and with 20,000 public-sector workers and their supporters amassed on Parliament Hill, the PSSRB came out with a ruling that found the government guilty of bad faith bargaining. Under these embarrassing circumstances, the government agreed to a deal brokered by the NDP, whereby the legislation was stayed and the strike suspended while genuine negotiations finally commenced.[13] In fact, the government's stance remained unaltered, and 12 days later the union opted to resume the strike. It is difficult, even in unions with a long tradition of militancy, to get members to come back out after a strike has been suspended, yet PSAC succeeded even in this. A decade of attack on their democratic rights as workers had finally generated a culture of struggle (including the traditional working-class disdain for and abuse of "scabs") among federal public employees, reminiscent of class formation among industrial workers in an earlier era.

The strike ended on 2 October, when the government passed the Public Sector Compensation Act (Bill C-29). Having been unable to impose a wage restraint policy through an ingenuine collective bargaining strategy, the Mulroney government finally had to resort to the same measures as the Trudeau Liberals in 1982, once again criminalizing the otherwise legal behaviour of public employees by extending pre-existing collective agreements. The Act extended for 24 months all compensation plans in effect on 21 February 1991, in all federal departments, boards, commissions, agencies, designated Crown corporations as well as the Senate, House of Commons, Library of Parliament, armed forces, and the RCMP, providing no wage increase in the first year and 3 percent in the second.

The failure of PSAC to defeat the government's wage restraints should not lead to the conclusion that the strike was in vain. By defending their rights, PSAC members gained a real measure of self-respect and went a long way towards establishing their credibility in the eyes of the broader labour movement. Further, they succeeded in garnering considerable public sympathy, calling into question the image held by many Canadians that federal employees were a pampered lot and that the postal workers stood alone in their militancy as a unique bunch of cranks and malcontents. Indeed, CUPW's own series of rotating strikes in the fall of 1991 was put in a much more balanced perspective for Canadians. This was partly due to the union's effective tactics (it offered to deliver pension and welfare cheques, which the Post Office refused to allow them to do until their own efforts to use scabs failed miserably). However, it was also in good part due to the PSAC strike simultaneously making it clear just how general were the problems of federal public employees, especially as the key issues in the postal dispute, as in 1987, centred on job security. CUPW was a leader among unions in trying to convert insecure casual and part-time jobs into regular ones, particularly benefiting women workers (who by this time comprised almost half of inside postal workers).[14] The Post Office's continuing efforts to defeat the union on this was particularly significant in the era of free trade, for it would have broken a strategic attempt to counter the growth of a two-tiered workforce, whereby the majority of women and new labour force entrants are generally barred from full-time work, job security, and the pay and benefits appropriate to a decent existence.

BRITISH COLUMBIA AND THE PRAIRIE PROVINCES

Coercive developments at the provincial level were particularly, albeit not exclusively, evident with governments that were explicitly neoliberal in orientation, although ideology alone was not a determinant. Highly resource dependent economies were severely squeezed throughout the 1980s as falling international commodity prices and declining markets limited their participation in the temporary recovery of the mid- to late 1980s. The ensuing pressure to resolve this problem at the cost of workers' rights was intimately connected to government strategies of inducing private investment amid the globalization of capital and free trade. Such competition strategies presumed that the economic crisis that began in the 1970s and resulted in the severe recession that opened the 1980s was a thing of the past. The speculative real estate recovery could not last, and the 1990s opened with a new prolonged and severe recession. In this context, yet another wave of "temporary" abrogations of collective bargaining rights broke over public and para-public employees in Canada, while workers in the private sector experienced unprecedented job loss.

It is important to keep in mind that to speak of the consolidation of an era of coercion does not mean that class struggle ceases: the historical record surveyed in this chapter demonstrates that further restrictions on labour rights were often prompted by workers' continuing struggles and resistance. Nor does it mean that such struggles cannot produce state concessions. Just as the reforms of the previous era were enmeshed in a web of juridical restrictions, and just as the old era developed unevenly, it should not be surprising that instances of reform are found in the new context. The most significant legislative reform of the 1980s was, without doubt, "pay equity," which was a product of feminist struggles both inside and outside the labour movement. The consolidation of coercion at the provincial level did not simply follow the federal lead, but in a number of cases broke new ground. Nowhere was this more evident than in British Columbia. The deal Jack Munro struck at Kelowna with Bill Bennett (see Chapter 3) proved to be anything but a durable truce and came unstuck as soon as the **Social Credit** government won re-election. The government's first priority involved significantly extending the legislative assault begun earlier in the decade in order "to increase our labour stability."[15] Bill 19, the Industrial Relations Reform Act passed in June 1987, sought to secure the twin goals of "cost containment and international competitiveness"[16] for business by eroding further the organizational security of workers in the province.

This new legislation's severity was testament to the powerful economic and political forces pushing for a complete overhaul of the province's industrial relations. With union membership and nominal wage increases at a virtual standstill – the result of continued high unemployment, public-sector wage controls, and the 1984 Labour Code revisions – even the Business Council of BC conceded in 1985 that "[t]here is a trend toward increases in wages and benefit costs being related to the profitability of individual firms and not to industry-wide, union-wide or national patterns or other external indices such as the consumer price index or inflation."[17]

Nonetheless, it was the renewed resistance of labour in BC, symbolized by the Industrial, Wood and Allied Workers union's (IWA's) successful seven-month strike against contracting out that set the stage for the new phase.[18] Drafted behind the labour minister's back by private management lawyers, Bill 19 was described by the former deputy minister of labour, Graham Leslie, as "the product of too few and too narrow minds."[19] While employer representatives at first expressed concern over its radical interventionist aspects, they were pleased with the legislation's general thrust, which addressed many of their complaints about "inflexible" labour relations. By changing existing successor rights provisions, the definition of a related employer, and rules regarding the rights of unions to include non-affiliation clauses in their agreements (forbidding contracting out to non-union firms), this Bill promised to weaken enormously workers' power to prevent employers from escaping collective bargaining.[20]

Most notable was the Bill's provision for an unprecedented level of state intervention restricting union powers. Through the Industrial Relations

Council (IRC), chaired by a government-appointed commissioner, the government, for the first time, wielded the power to declare workers in the private as well as public sector "essential." If the labour minister considered "that the dispute poses a threat to the economy of the Province or to the health, safety or welfare of its residents or to the provision of education services," the minister could order a 40-day cooling-off period and/or direct the IRC to "designate" any number of workers it considered necessary to ensure the provision of "essential" services. Failure to respect a back-to-work order constituted "just and reasonable cause" for disciplinary action (i.e., dismissal) by the employer; a provision requiring the IRC to file its orders in the Supreme Court of British Columbia, upon request, was aimed at guaranteeing further union compliance.

At the same time, workers' strike capacity and rank-and-file solidarity were threatened by the IRC's power to prohibit secondary boycott agreements and restrict picketing "in such a manner that it affects only the operation of an employer causing the lockout or whose employees are lawfully on strike, or an operation of an ally of that employer." The BC Federation of Labour organized a series of regional protests and a very successful one-day general strike on 1 June 1987, when no less than 300,000 workers brought the province to a halt and did so with widespread public sympathy. The government responded and sought an injunction before the BC Supreme Court, claiming that further industrial action organized by the unions would be tantamount to sedition as defined in the Criminal Code. While hardly questioning Social Credit's fitness to govern by displaying such tendencies, most establishment opinions saw the government's claim as hysterical, and the Court endorsed the unions' request that the action be dismissed.

In Alberta, a pattern similar to that of BC was seen, although it developed somewhat more circuitously. Alberta was subjected to particularly harsh criticism by the ILO mission to Canada, which declared that the restrictions on public-sector workers' right to strike imposed by Bill 44 in 1983 went "beyond acceptable limits which are recognized in Convention No. 87."[21] The Alberta government's contempt for this ruling was shown in its refusal to offer any improvements to the legislation governing state employees. Indeed, a 1985 amendment to the Public Service Employee Relations Act (Bill 30) actually broadened the power of the Public Service Employee Relations Board to exclude persons from a bargaining unit. The collapse of energy prices in the early to mid-1980s reinforced the trend towards intensifying and generalizing the assault on trade union rights already underway. But this was, at the same time, a response to the determined resistance by Alberta workers, made even more remarkable by the province's reputation over the past half-century for its allegedly monolithic right-wing populism.

Confronted by the threat of continued labour unrest in the wake of the Gainers' strike in the meat packing industry, a strike that drew national media attention and popular support among Albertan workers, the newly elected premier, Don Getty, agreed to a formal review of the province's labour legislation. Tellingly, the review committee's report completely evaded issues of key concern to the unions. Instead, the committee sought major changes to collective bargaining aimed at increasing government intervention, while further restricting workers' use of the strike weapon. After two years of deliberation, the Labour Code was amended in June 1988.[22] The new Labour Code also embodied a dramatic and qualitative shift in the role of the executive vis-à-vis the right to strike. The cabinet was empowered to declare an emergency to end any dispute in which "damage to health or property is caused or is likely to be caused" as a result of a reduction in municipal or health services, or in any case where "unreasonable hardship" may result to a third party.

This legislation was an unmistakable expression of "class struggle from above," but it failed to stem the continuing current of struggle from below among Alberta workers. A remarkable 19-day strike by Alberta nurses in the winter of 1988 immediately revealed the limits of the new coercion. The well-organized and militant nurses' union, which had defied back-to-work legislation in the early 1980s and, along with other hospital employees, had their right to strike abrogated through Bill 44 in 1983, proclaimed they would not accept an arbitrated settlement as prescribed in the legislation. When the Labour Board hastily intervened to declare even a strike vote illegal, this had the perverse effect of getting more nurses to vote for strike action. So strong and confident was the nurse's leadership that, when the strike ended with a negotiated settlement, they would still not take their members back to work until the six-month freeze on union dues imposed by the Labour Board under the new Labour Code was rescinded.

The structural erosion of workers' collective rights within the "post-controls" collective bargaining system was also clearly evidenced in Saskatchewan, which was the first province to revise its Labour Code along the lines of the new era. Here, the 1983 legislation had already undermined the integrity of existing bargaining units while allowing employers, particularly in the construction industry, to operate free of unions entirely. In just three years, an estimated 85 percent of work governing the construction sector was being performed at non-union rates.[23] In early 1986, legislation ended a strike by 12,000 public employees, including a provision allowing for the dismissal of anyone disobeying the back-to-work order. The Saskatchewan Government Employees Union Dispute Settlement Act (Bill 144) contained the infamous clause exempting it from Section 2(d) – "freedom of association" – of the Charter of Rights and Freedoms, as well as from similar provisions in the Saskatchewan Human Rights Code. The government's invocation of the Charter's "notwithstanding" clause was a response to a decision by the Saskatchewan Court of Appeal ruling as unconstitutional the back-to-work legislation passed in 1983–1984. The marked deterioration of industrial jurisprudence in the province was accompanied by what was described as "a complete loss of confidence" by unions in the Department of Labour, especially "because of the unions' perception of an anti-union bias."[24]

Manitoba was the only province in which an NDP government was in office through most of the 1980s. The NDP, which was elected in 1981, introduced a number of significant reform measures. During the controls period, the Labour Relations Act was significantly amended by Bill 22, which came into effect on 1 January 1985. In addition to revamping the Labour Board, simplifying and expediting the grievance arbitration process, the amendments made unionizing easier and extended the legal protections afforded strikers. In particular, the use of "professional" strikebreakers was prohibited and striking workers' right to reinstatement after the conclusion of a dispute was reinforced. The Pay Equity Act (Bill 53) was passed in 1985, and the government also amended the Employment Standards Act (Bill 74) that same year, providing paternity leave and increased notice in the case of mass layoffs. Nevertheless, even in this case, the limits of reform in this era were clearly visible. What at first glance looked like a glowing record, at least in comparison with what was going on in other jurisdictions, lost much of its shine upon closer inspection. The amendments relating to certification, when compared to the Canada Labour Relations Act or even the Ontario Act prior to the defeat of the Conservative regime, can hardly be said to have broken new ground. This aspect of the Manitoba record became even more pronounced with the 1987 amendment to the Labour Relations Act (Bill 61) allowing for **final offer selection (FOS)**. FOS is a form of binding arbitration where management and the union each present a "final" proposal to an arbitrator, who chooses one of them to be the new collective agreement. FOS selectors had to take into account "the employer's ability to pay" in making their choice. Second, it gave employers the right to demand a vote by workers, thus allowing employers to sidestep union representatives. The Manitoba reform experience in the mid-1980s, in this respect, provided a telling example of the impact of the new coercive measures in redrawing the limits of reform.

When the Conservatives were elected in 1988, they turned attention towards public employees. In July 1991, workers in the civil service, hospitals, personal care homes, child and family services agencies, and Crown corporations were subjected to a one-year wage freeze under the Public Sector Compensation Management Act (Bill 70). The Conservative government, with opposition Liberal support for its anti-labour position, felt confident enough in this context to announce in January 1992 plans to cut 300 civil service positions, which together with an earlier cut of 1,000 positions announced in the 1991 budget, brought the number of positions in the Manitoba civil service down by 6 percent. In the summer of 1992, the government turned its attention back to the Labour Code, passing amendments (Bill 85) that opened considerable space for employer interference during union organizing drives while it made certification more difficult. Although the labour movement was unable to effectively counter this assault, it did prove increasingly willing to align itself with radical forces in Manitoba that formed the social justice coalition Cho!ces to oppose the right-wing agenda in particularly creative new ways, from street theatre to alternate budgets that captured extensive media and popular attention.[25]

QUEBEC'S TURN TO PERMANENT EXCEPTIONALISM

The trend towards "permanently temporary" coercive legislation was especially evident in Quebec. In 1985, the PQ government followed the welter of "temporary" restrictions imposed during the controls period with Bill 37, which institutionalized and extended these restrictions. The government's powers to restrict the extent of work stoppages were broadened significantly; its control over the actual content of any agreement in the area of monetary issues became almost absolute and provided for a fundamental restructuring of the collective bargaining relationship.

Within the public and para-public sectors, Bill 37 designated as "essential" anywhere from 55 percent of workers in the social services to 90 percent in special health care centres. Exact numbers in any specific situation were to be negotiated by the union and the Essential Services Council; however, the Council could increase or modify required levels of service "if the situation of the establishment justifies it." Under the Act, bargaining was split into two levels, with monetary issues determined at the provincial level while most other job conditions were subject to local negotiations. At the provincial level, wage and salary scales were not subject to mediation, nor could the parties be bound to any third-party recommendations. Strikes during the second or third year of provincial-level agreements, or respecting matters negotiated at the local or regional level, were prohibited absolutely. In fact, the state took the power to set wages and salaries during the last two years of an agreement. Bill 37 simply required that the president of the Treasury table annually to draft regulation fixing the salaries and salary scales for the current year and that these should subsequently form part of the existing collective agreement.

While Bill 37 weakened unions through severe restrictions on their right to strike, it also hobbled their efforts at concerted bargaining by splitting negotiations into numerous subdivisions. The consequences of this reorganization of bargaining structures were significant. For the first time since 1972, the three largest public-sector groups were now unable to form a Common Front for negotiations. Undoubtedly, this failure was due, in large part, to tensions among the three federations, stemming from the refusal of the CSN and FTQ to back the CEQ's demand to restore wage levels eroded under the 1982 restraint legislation. However, by allowing the government to avoid negotiating at a central table, the new bargaining framework exacerbated existing divisions within union ranks.[26] The Liberal government that succeeded the PQ made ready use of the restrictive negotiating framework they had inherited. In addition, the new government introduced in 1986 alone no less than six back-to-work measures, two of which were actually Orders-in-Council, removing the right to strike from particular groups of workers. The harshest legislation, passed in November 1986, ended a rotating strike by Quebec nurses. Described by one union representative as "the most severe law Quebec has had in the last twenty years," Bill 160 applied to all health, hospital, and social services establishments and councils, and it was extended in 1988 to include ambulance services.[27] Ostensibly a piece of back-to-work legislation, it terminated the nurses' strike by requiring that as of midnight, 12 November 1986, every employee had to "perform all duties attached to his functions in accordance with the conditions of employment that are attached to him, without stoppage, slowdown, reduction or alteration in his usual activities." Bill 160 epitomized permanent exceptionalism by not specifying when the legislation would cease to have effect or even the particular dispute to which it applied.

This allowed it to be invoked at any time in the future for any dispute in the health and social service sectors that the government chose to prohibit under Order-in-Council as permitted in the changes the PQ had already made to the Labour Code. The penalties that thereby came into play as soon as a slowdown or strike was declared illegal by the cabinet were merciless. In addition to heavy fines and the suspension of dues check-off for 12 weeks for every day of a strike, it provided for a salary reduction upon the conclusion of the strike by an amount equal to that foregone during the strike and the loss of one year's seniority for every day on strike. It must be stressed again that this remarkable degree of arbitrary state intervention against workers should be seen not simply as a reflection of the more "politicized" nature of labour relations in Quebec under the Liberals. It is also the consequence of the PQ's earlier Labour Code changes, which facilitated such interventions. In granting the Essential Services Council power to order individuals or groups of workers back to work, the PQ's Bill 37, further supplemented by the Liberals' Bill 160 four years later, forced Quebec's public-sector unions to confront a state apparatus ever more able and willing to intervene in disputes it deemed threatening to the "public interest."

At the end of the decade, there was an eruption of unexpected militancy in a strike of 300,000 public-sector – primarily female education, social service, and health – workers organized by the CSN, the CEQ, and a newly formed independent nurses' union. Pay equity, contracting out, part-time work, and restoring adequate funding and service levels were the central issues in a dispute that came to a head at the same time as the 1989 provincial election. The government reacted by bringing the full weight of Bill 160 to bear. It unilaterally modified collective agreements to facilitate the hiring of strikebreakers, deducted two days' wages for every day the workers were on strike, and reduced seniority to the extent that some nurses lost no less than seven years' credit, while the unions faced million-dollar fines and the loss of up to 60 weeks in dues check-offs. The squeeze on public revenues in the recession of the 1990s moved the Quebec Liberals, like other provincial governments, towards public-sector wage restraint.[28] The mechanism for this involved, once again, the extension of existing collective agreements, alongside a six-month wage freeze followed by a 3 percent increase, plus a 1 percent lump sum payment. What was now very different from the early 1980s in Quebec, however, was that the unions in the public sector assented to this program of statutory wage restraint after consultations with the government in 1991, thus following the **corporatist** lead of private-sector unions.[29]

Legislation passed in July 1991 gave the agreement statutory effect by extending collective agreements from January to June 1992, but by February 1992, the government was already seeking a new agreement from the unions to extend the term of collective agreements for two more years and to spread over that two-year period the 3 percent increase previously promised at the end of the original six-month freeze. The unions refused to go along with this and led massive protest marches to the National Assembly.[30] Both the Conseil du patronat and backbencher Liberals felt the government was going too far in breaking an agreement with a union leadership that had proved so anxious to cooperate, and the government relented, striking a further set of agreements with the unions that paid most of what was due in June 1992 while securing union compliance for a further year of restraint (two years in the case of the Quebec teachers). In May 1993, much to the chagrin of the union leadership, legislation imposing yet a further statutory collective agreement extension for two more years was introduced entailing wage rollbacks. Its implementation was held in abeyance until September in the hopes that union assent might again be forthcoming.[31] The effects of the draconian legislation passed in Quebec in the 1980s were contradictory. Governments now had at their fingertips massive arbitrary powers to use against striking workers. They rarely used these powers, however, for when they did so the consequences were troublesome for employers and full of potential for further enflaming class struggle. Yet the fact that these powers hung over public-sector negotiations could not but intrude into the strategic choices made by the unions. Rather than run the risk that these powers may be invoked if they exercise the right to strike, unions were drawn towards accommodation if not collaboration, from an increasingly weakened bargaining position.[32]

THE ATLANTIC PROVINCES AND ONTARIO

Severe restrictions on trade union rights characterized the whole postwar era in Atlantic Canada. The fact that the New Brunswick Labour Relations Act provided for decertification of any union that violated a "cease and desist" order regarding an illegal strike from the Labour Board is illustrative of the general backwardness of existing labour legislation in the area. The widespread dissatisfaction with this state of affairs was exacerbated by the wage restraint measures introduced under the wing of Trudeau's controls and also by the new, permanent restrictions of Newfoundland's Bill 59, which led trade unionists there to increasingly demand fundamental reforms. The New Brunswick Federation of Labour, for example, voted unanimously in May 1985 to cease all further participation in the government's Industrial Relations Council to back its long-standing demands for reforms such as a full-time labour board, first-contract legislation, limitations on "designations," and anti-scab legislation like Quebec's.

What transpired in the ensuing years was certainly remarkable but bore little correspondence to the aspirations of trade unionists. Apart from the adoption of pay equity legislation in all four Atlantic provinces between 1986 and 1990 – which in no case broke new ground – and a couple of minor legislative changes in New Brunswick and Newfoundland, reform was confined to PEI. Following a decision by that province's Labour Relations Board in the fall of 1985, which stated that employers were under no obligation to rehire striking employees, the newly elected Liberal government led by Joe Ghiz pledged his party's support for reforms. After some delay, the government did make good on this promise by passing an amendment (Bill 55) to the Labour Act in May 1987. This Bill, guaranteeing the reinstatement of any striking employees following the termination of job action and the immediate layoff of any replacement workers, essentially did no more than restore the 1985 status quo. One year later, another amendment to the Labour Act, Bill 65, extended collective bargaining rights to nurses, hospital employees, and non-instructional school personnel. However, these rights did not include the right to strike – a right enjoyed by many of their counterparts in other provinces – but rather imposed binding arbitration as the ultimate dispute resolution mechanism. Finally, in 1990, Bill 2 was passed, which modestly broadened the jurisdiction of the Labour Relations Board with respect to unfair labour practices by employers.

In Nova Scotia, the only major legislative change in the immediate post-wage controls period was regressive. Introduced in 1986, Bill 91 paralleled the restrictions imposed on private-sector construction workers in Alberta and Saskatchewan. It required a vote on the employer's final offer before a strike could be called and narrowed permissible strike tactics while imposing no limits on employers' ability to establish non-union spinoff firms.[33] By far the most important development of the mid-1980s took place in Newfoundland, where an illegal strike against Bill 59 by the Newfoundland and Labrador Association of Public and Private Employees (NAPE) constituted the most serious labour conflict in the Maritimes since the 1970 Canso strike in Nova Scotia. The context for this strike was set in April 1983, when the

Newfoundland legislature debated and passed – in 19 minutes – Bill 59, which, among other things, required public-sector unions to designate up to 49 percent of their members "essential" and thereby ineligible to strike. Bill 59 merely added to the growing pressure for long overdue reform. The existing labour relations regime was such that no legislative changes were needed for 60–90 percent of the construction industry to go non-union in the 1980s, through the incorporation of new "general contracting companies" to evade unionized workers.[34] Further fuel arose out of a Labour Standards Tribunal ruling that a majority of Newfoundland companies owed almost $100 million in back wages for ignoring since 1978 the required notice period regarding layoffs. While this was obviously a progressive ruling, it led to the perverse consequence of the government promptly exempting them by special retroactive legislation forced through by closure. Justifying the government's action, the labour minister stated that "[n]obody in his right mind wants to make legislation retroactive. Anyone with a sense of fairness wouldn't want to do it, but there was no other way. Either the companies paid, in which case a lot of them would have gone bankrupt, or government paid, and we went bankrupt. Neither of these were in the public interest." The president of the Newfoundland Teachers' Federation responded that "[t]his legislation is the last message that has finally convinced people that Peckford has lost his vision for the common man and has succumbed to the interests of the traditional power brokers in Newfoundland – the large corporations."[35]

Ontario workers were largely spared the consolidation of coercion in the latter half of the 1980s. After four unbroken decades of Conservative rule, a minority Liberal government was elected in May 1985 and formed a political accord with the NDP, which kept it in office until a majority was secured two years later. This changing of the political guard in Ontario touched off some significant changes in the labour relations regime. At the Ministry of Labour, a number of senior bureaucrats, including long-time Deputy Minister Tim Armstrong, were effectively forced out.[36] A former law partner of David Lewis and leading legal adviser for the UAW, Armstrong had developed a good working relationship with provincial labour leaders. Over the postwar decades, the latter had obtained a voice in departmental affairs, including appointments to various public bodies, in exchange for muted opposition to government policy, particularly in the area of workplace health and safety but also with respect to the denial of the right to strike to public-sector workers. In other words, the industrial unions' considerable political influence within the Ontario Ministry of Labour was purchased at the cost of ignoring and at times suppressing rank-and-file challenges to managerial prerogatives. Nor did they, despite all the rhetoric about solidarity, attempt to overcome Premier Davis's implacable refusal to even countenance discussions about Ontario civil servants or hospital workers obtaining the right to strike, even after the Ontario Public Service Employees Union (OPSEU) and the hospital unions made this a priority.

The defeat of the short-lived Miller government suggested that the terms of this relationship would be renegotiated under the aegis of the Liberals' Bill Wrye as the new minister of labour. Given the growing pressure from the rank and file and the press, a cleanup in the area of health and safety was clearly on the political agenda. So was first contract legislation. Armstrong had strongly opposed reforms in both these areas. Ultimately, it became a matter of either Wrye or Armstrong leaving; it was certainly significant that it was Armstrong who went. Nevertheless, as in the case of the Manitoba NDP government, the limits of reform were clearly visible under the Ontario Liberals. Conspicuous in its absence from the reform agenda was the most outstanding issue of all – the blanket denial of the right to strike, under any circumstances, for provincial government employees and hospital workers. Like other provincial governments, even with explicitly different ideological predispositions, the Liberals were apparently unmoved by the ILO's ruling that this proscription violated its Convention 87 on freedom of association, to which Canada is a signatory.

On the positive side, in addition to pay equity legislation (Bill 154), severance pay, and pension reforms, the Peterson government also passed Bill 65, amending the Labour Relations Act to provide for the imposition of first agreements by the Labour Relations Board. Moreover, the actual terms and conditions under which first agreements were to be imposed met with strong approval from organized labour.[37] However, given the limits of first agreement legislation, other developments were arguably more important. For instance, Ontario Labour Relations Board rulings in this period supported union demands for broader-based bargaining as a means of redressing weakness due to fragmented bargaining unit structures and extended striking workers' right to return to their jobs beyond the old six-month limit.

The most important legislative initiative was probably Bill 208, which extensively revised the Occupational Health and Safety Act. This came in response to a series of rank-and-file struggles, including plant sit-ins, which were all the more remarkable in that they occurred in the context of widespread job insecurity. The Bill extended bipartite structures for monitoring and regulating health and safety, including education and training, right down to the shop floor. The extension of worker involvement was, however, limited when the government withdrew from the final draft of the legislation a provision allowing certified worker inspectors to unilaterally shut down production in dangerous conditions.

The legislation clearly had contradictory implications, despite it being favoured by the labour leadership. This was partly because it attenuated the responsibility of government in the setting and enforcement of standards and partly because it also attenuated the growing autonomy of shop floor activists in health and safety matters.[38] Even under the Liberal-NDP accord, coercion remained present alongside reform. As if not to be outdone by the preceding Conservative government – which, in its last days, passed two pieces of back-to-work legislation, one of which, in honour of the Pope's visit, pre-emptively denied Toronto Transit Commission workers the right to strike – the Liberals, in their first year in office, also passed such legislation on two occasions. The Peterson government's own use of back-to-work legislation, not surprisingly, signalled to some that little would change under the Liberals. Its common use throughout Canada over the decade of the 1980s had to be seen not only in terms of workers whose rights it directly suspended, but also in terms of its indirect effects of intimidating other workers who feared its application. It made many managers in the public sector much less prepared to engage in serious bargaining in the expectation that a long public-sector strike would elicit a back-to-work measure from governments.

It is certainly significant that the core private-sector industrial unions in Ontario were spared the kind of restrictive state legislation visited on others through the 1980s. Apart from the differing ideological dispositions of a Peterson-style as opposed to a Vander Zalm-style provincial government, the reason for this relates to the specific material conditions of the Ontario economy, particularly the central role of manufacturing and financial capital. The importance of manufacturing in Ontario means that the overall tone of government policies vis-à-vis labour is determined more by considerations pertaining to the industrial unions than in other provinces, where public-sector or resource unions are core to the labour movement. Restrictive legislation against public employees in Ontario does not itself provide the signal to capital that the government "means business"; however, subjecting the core industrial unions in Ontario to restrictive legislation is more fraught with problems than taking on public employees.

In any case, the Peterson government had more room to manoeuvre by virtue of the manufacturing industry's temporary recovery after 1982, aided by the labour cost advantage yielded by a low Canadian dollar relative to the

American dollar as well as by Toronto, specifically, benefiting from financial capital's speculative romp through the 1980s. At the same time, the leading role industrial unions themselves played in collective bargaining in the earlier era had been much constrained in a new era of capitalist restructuring and the heightened competition that produced it. Operating under the old legal framework and in the context of Ontario's relatively robust economy, real wages, even among the historically militant autoworkers, hardly went up through the 1980s. This does not mean that these unions were rendered ineffectual. Insofar as workers maintained living standards, this itself indicated that there was still power in the union. Moreover, in the context of international capitalist competition, the existence of solid shop-floor organization posed a barrier to attempts at restructuring.

CONCLUSION: NEOLIBERALISM MOVES CENTRE STAGE

In significant respects, the 1970s and early 1980s were years where capital and the state confronted an unfamiliar reality. The stagflation that marked much of the 1970s was an unknown economic phenomenon. However, as the 1980s unfolded, the momentum of capital and its political allies intensified and consolidated the neoliberal counter-revolution, but not without resistance from trade unions, which rallied against free trade. The anti–free trade movement was spearheaded by labour and allied social movements. It was a clear second mass mobilization, after the fight against wage controls, marking a resurgent left nationalism.

It is for this reason, in large measure, that manufacturing capital supported free trade. It obviously suited capitalists, who profit directly from Canada's resource exports and fit with financial capital's worldwide drive to subjugate national governments' economic policies. Free trade endangers manufacturing industries in Canada by rendering them more open to competition. But capital hoped to achieve, through enhanced flexibility regarding plant locations and sourcing of inputs, the breaking of union power that had occurred in the United States. It is not only the immediate protection of jobs but the protection of workers' basic democratic freedoms that hung in the balance in the context of free trade. As the following chapter shows, the situation grew much worse in the severe recession that opened the 1990s. As with any period of intense conflict, the political terrain was uneven and resulted in certain outcomes that served to if not stall, then mitigate the worst effects of the neoliberal project. The results of this would be short-lived as Canada moved into a new era.

CHAPTER FIVE

Consolidating Neoliberalism

Chapter Summary: The 1990s was a volatile decade in both economic and political terms. If in the 1980s neoliberalism consolidated its hold, it became outright hegemonic in the 1990s. Even the remaining space left to social democracy was to some greater extent eviscerated, and the experiences of the NDP and PQ provincial governments was a testament to this reality. In 1994, the North American Free Trade Agreement came into effect. The agenda of trade and investment liberalization was now entrenched and, together with the deep recession of the early 1990s, contributed to a broad restructuring of the Canadian economy and its workers. Public-sector austerity was a common feature of fiscal policy regardless of which party held government. Consequently, workers across the country engaged in varying forms of resistance.

INTRODUCTION

The extension of a global neoliberal order, the ascendancy of financial capital, and the spread of commodification into every aspect of social life led to even greater pressures on organized labour through the 1990s. In the private sector, the turn to "lean" production methods to meet the growing demands of competitiveness in the global economy dramatically altered the relationship that workers had both to their jobs and to each other.[1] Combined with contracting out and part-time work, these changes produced a so-called "flexible" workforce beset by job insecurity at the very time governments considerably reduced the eligibility for and funding of Unemployment Insurance and social assistance. Consequently, many workers were forced to accept part-time employment for low pay, while others were required to work more overtime or go deeper into debt to maintain the same levels of income.[2] For public-sector workers, these same pressures coincided with a severe downsizing trend by federal and provincial governments. This trend partly reflected old-fashioned business pressures to reduce social expenditures, but it was also part of a broader ideological shift centred on the notion that state intervention in the economy led to inefficiency and waste.[3]

Equally significant, it was also a reflection of the state's embrace of neoliberalism itself as the operations of government were altered to reflect market dependency and to engage the private sector as never before in the direct provision of public services. Wage settlements through the 1990s ran considerably lower than the 1980s in both public and private sectors. It was only through increased hours of work that real wages, which had stagnated over the preceding decade, rose somewhat. The difficulty in securing workers' consent to this economic trajectory ensured that federal and provincial governments would continue the assault on trade union rights and freedoms into the twenty-first century, as illustrated with the ever-growing use of back-to-work legislation. There were many instances of such legislation in the provinces in the 1990s, and as the wage freezes finally expired at the end of the decade, the use of back-to-work laws by provincial governments reached unprecedented heights.

The 1990s began with the second major recession in ten years and the deepest recession since the Great Depression of the 1930s. The downturn was reinforced by the Bank of Canada's anti-inflationary policies of high interest rates and a high dollar, as well as by the implementation of the North American Free Trade Agreement (NAFTA) between Canada, the US, and Mexico. What was occurring across North America went beyond the sectoral decline of the so-called "Fordist" mass production industries, like steel and auto. The service and high-tech sectors that fuelled the boom of the mid-1980s were also severely affected. The European economy followed a similar trajectory, with unemployment in Europe exceeding 10 percent by early 1993, virtually matching the level experienced by Canadian workers. Even Japan, with huge excess capacity in so many industrial sectors globally, from semi-conductors to autos, had not escaped.[4] The recession of the 1990s needs to be understood in the context of the crisis that the capitalist order entered into over two decades earlier. What is referred to as **globalization** – the effective subjugation of even advanced capitalist countries to the competitive logic and contradictions of production and finance on a world scale – was both a cause and a consequence of this crisis of the post-1945 world order.[5] Social democracy everywhere – and particularly in Ontario, Saskatchewan, and BC – was overwhelmed by this.

THE FEDERAL GOVERNMENTS OF CHRÉTIEN AND MARTIN

The 1993 general election was a disaster for the Progressive Conservative Party. Anger with the Tories ran deep among Canadians, and Brian Mulroney's departure could not save the party from being reduced to two seats in the House of Commons. Given the paralleled unpopularity of the NDP in Ontario and the regional politics of both the Reform/Alliance Party and the Bloc Québécois, it is not surprising that the Liberals won a majority government (albeit with only 41 percent of the popular vote). The Liberals' campaign document, dubbed the Red Book, had outlined a vision of Canada that was very different from the previous nine years of Tory rule. The party promised to renegotiate the impending NAFTA deal to include effective protections for labour and the environment, to scrap the GST, and to abandon the previous government's monetary policies. The Red Book included a commitment to protect social programs and, perhaps more importantly, to take an active role in job creation.

Once in government, the Liberals did not take long to stray from their election platform and to fully embrace an emerging global neoliberal consensus. NAFTA was ratified almost immediately, with no substantive changes to the deal. And with only a slight push from the international bond-rating agencies, Finance Minister Paul Martin was allowed to place the deficit issue at the top of the government's agenda.[6] His first budget contained measures that prolonged the 1991 wage freeze for federal public-sector workers that had been due to end in 1995 for two additional years by extending the life of contracts until 1997, thus unilaterally foreclosing on collective bargaining in the federal public sector. Under the rubric of New Public Management, fiscal restraint was accompanied by downsizing, contracting out, and new private-sector management techniques. Minister Martin's draconian 1995 budget slashed spending in virtually every federal department and reduced government expenditures by more than $25 billion over the next three years – representing a 40 percent reduction in federal social program spending, compared to Mulroney's 25 percent cut. In announcing the cuts, he boasted: "Relative to the size of our economy, program spending will be lower in 1996–97 than at any time since 1951."[7] Martin and Chrétien's decision to end the Canada Assistance Plan released provincial and territorial governments from any federal conditions in order to receive financial support. The new Canada Health and Social Transfer (CHST) allowed for greater variation and private-sector provisioning, paving the way for the decentralization of financing and delivery.[8]

In the realm of labour relations, the Liberals moved quickly to set the tone for what was to come when 3,500 workers at the Port of Vancouver, having been without a contract for over a year, went on strike in the last week of January 1994.[9] By 1 February, the federal government had appointed a mediator, with back-to-work legislation tabled a week later. Then in 1995, having been without a contract since 1992, 500 foremen went on strike at the ports represented by the International Longshoremen's and Warehousemen's Union. Within two days, the government had stepped in with back-to-work legislation. On 8 March 1995, Brotherhood of Maintenance of Way Employees in northern Ontario and southern British Columbia launched one-day strikes at Canadian Pacific (CP) Rail. Management responded by locking the workers out and suspending all pay and benefits. The decision by the union to extend the strike nationally was bound to provoke back-to-work legislation. The Canadian Auto Workers (CAW), which, as a result of recent mergers, then represented 4,500 shop craft workers at CP, felt that calling a national strike would, as Buzz Hargrove put it, "be playing into the company's hands." The rift between the unions would last for the duration of the strike and grew more dramatic as the dispute spilled over to CN and to VIA, directly involving 10,000 more CAW members. The strike threatened to spill over further to Ford and General Motors due to the lack of parts the plants needed for just-in-time production. The rail companies were initially divided on the issue of a legislated end to the dispute, but the government soon made clear its intentions not only to go ahead with legislation but to impose a settlement that leaned towards the employer position on the key issue of job and income security. Legislation ending the strike was passed on 26 March 1995, supported by the NDP after certain demands for impartiality in arbitration were met.

Given the history of struggle for and against the right to strike over the previous two decades, it was perhaps inevitable that postal workers would be drawn into a confrontation with the Chrétien government. When, during negotiations, Canada Post announced plans to cut 4,000 jobs, CUPW president Darrell Tingley saw the plan as an attempt to force a strike in order to push the government to use back-to-work legislation. The Alliance of Manufacturers and Exporters jumped in to call for the permanent removal of the right to strike for postal workers since they performed an "essential service." Lack of progress in negotiations led the union to walk on 20 November 1997, one day after the corporation laid off 15,000 workers. Less than a month later, the government had introduced back-to-work legislation and imposed a wage settlement with an increase less than that already agreed to by Canada Post.

By 1998, Martin and Chrétien had erased the $42 billion deficit they had inherited just a few years earlier. The decade reached a climax in a strike by PSAC blue-collar workers in 1999. Because of the Mulroney government's 1991 wage freeze and its three-year extension by the Chrétien government, PSAC members had gone nearly a decade without a raise that would keep up with inflation. Rotating strikes began in mid-January 1999. In a classic example of what we have called permanent exceptionalism, the Treasury Board suggested that the union was violating the 1991 Public Sector Compensation Act. The strategy of rotating strikes continued for several weeks as PSAC sought to avoid calling a full strike, which it believed would lead to back-to-work-legislation. Some two months into the rotating strikes, PSAC organized a demonstration in Ottawa, bringing in 500 support pickets from Montreal. They were met with an abundance of riot police, clubs, and pepper spray, foreshadowing the intolerance of the democratic right to protest that was soon to be seen at anti-poverty and anti-globalization demonstrations. With the looming possibility of disruptions to the delivery of tax returns and grain shipments, the government introduced back-to-work legislation (Bill C-76). The bill opportunistically included provisions that would allow the government to order an end to a strike of prison guards represented by PSAC that had not even started yet.[10] By the end of the decade, the Chrétien government had actually gone further than the Tories in its pursuit of a neoliberal downsizing, providing well over 50,000 federal employees with pink slips.

Consecutive budget surpluses paved the way for the Liberals to win re-election in 2000. Hypocrisy was indeed a badge that the Liberal government seemed to wear proudly as it reneged on virtually every promise contained in the Red Book. The Liberals used these budget surpluses to dramatically cut taxes by $100 billion over five years, with 77 percent of the personal benefits going to the wealthiest 8 percent of the population. They also moved to constrain the scope of bargaining with the 2003 passing of the Public Service Modernization Act, which broadened the definition of essential services by giving the employer the exclusive right to determine the level and frequency of service during a strike. In practice, this meant that the right to strike could be severely curtailed, if not removed, in addition to excluding fundamental workplace issues such as staffing and classification from collective bargaining.

With the Liberal government besieged by accusations of corruption connected to the Quebec sponsorship scandal, Martin was on the verge of resigning when, on 2 June 2002, Chrétien fired him.[11] Martin continued to sit as an MP and, following Chrétien's resignation, was elected leader of the Liberals, succeeding Chrétien as prime minister in December 2003. An election was held a year later, with the Liberals reduced to a minority government with NDP support. Although the Liberals remained mired in the sponsorship scandal, this did not stop them from passing the Railway Continuation Act in 2007, which ended a strike by railway workers and imposed a final offer selection process to resolve matters remaining in dispute between the parties. By this point the damage had been done. Provincial governments, if they needed any encouragement, could point to the Chrétien and Martin government's actions in extending the era of coercion to the twenty-first century.

FROM SOCIAL CONTRACT TO COMMON SENSE IN ONTARIO

Insofar as the labour movement had any strategy to combat the repeated intrusions on trade union rights over the previous two decades, the election of NDP governments was its centrepiece. Unfortunately, the party born in the Depression of the 1930s that insisted **fiscal orthodoxy** was no answer to the anarchy of capitalist competition gave rise to a government in the 1990s that not only embraced the goal of competitiveness but assumed the mantle of fiscal orthodoxy. What distinguished the NDP's attack on trade union rights was the particularly perverse and dangerous fashion in which it attempted to conceal coercion as consent with the passing of the Social Contract Act (Bill 48) in 1993.[12] The NDP had initially viewed the economy as merely being in a normal cyclical downturn for which the appropriate remedy was deficit financing. Its first budgetary deficit of $10 billion was explicitly presented as a counterweight to the recession. This deficit was less the product of active job-creation measures than of mere passivity in the face of declining government revenues brought on by a severe economic recession – the worst, up to that point, since the 1930s. Bankruptcies and layoffs hit record levels, and automatic increases in social assistance expenditures, which many of the long-term unemployed were forced to rely upon, all converged to deepen Ontario's budget deficit.

In fall 1991, the government brought forward a considerable package of reforms. Amendments to the Employment Standards Act (Bill 70) helped workers recover unpaid wages when their employer went bankrupt, while amendments to the legislation governing the construction industry (Bill 158) were designed to enhance provincewide collective bargaining. More ambitious were amendments to the Pay Equity Act to provide for additional methods of determining whether a particular female-dominated job class was suffering pay discrimination. The central pillar of the government's labour reforms was the overhaul of the Ontario Labour Relations Act, which contained a considerable package: the right to organize was extended to some domestic, agricultural, and professional workers; provisions for secondary organizing and picketing were extended; petitions from dissenting employees after the date of a certification application were banned; just cause was required by employers for all disciplinary actions against employees once a union was certified; automatic access was provided to first contract arbitration after 30 days of a strike or lockout; broad restrictions were placed on the use of replacement workers in strikes undertaken on the basis of a 60 percent strike vote; the right of workers to return to their jobs in the event of lengthy strikes was extended; and the OLRB was empowered to combine bargaining units for workers at the same company represented by the same union.

The business community mobilized in unprecedented ways, launching vicious advertising campaigns comparing Rae with Joseph Stalin (former leader of the Soviet Union) and forecasting the loss of hundreds of thousands of jobs and billions of dollars in investment. It became clear that the government's forecasts of substantial deficit reduction had been premised on an otherworldly underestimation of the severity of the global recession. The NDP now turned their previous tactics upside down and, rather than underestimate the deficit, they grossly exaggerated it to justify austerity measures to their own supporters. In 1993, the government unveiled a three-pronged strategy to get the deficit under control. First, a series of income and other tax increases worth some $2 billion were planned. Notably absent were increases in corporate taxes or the imposition of a wealth tax. Second was an Expenditure

Control Plan that would cut expenditures by roughly $4 billion and eliminate 11,000 public-sector jobs. Third, the government would seek $2 billion in annual reductions through a Social Contract Act (Bill 48) with public-sector workers, which required that over 900,000 people employed in the broader public sector accept a three-year wage freeze and an effective 5 percent wage reduction through 12 days of unpaid leave each year.

The tremendous discretion the legislation left to the state executive concealed coercion behind the facade of attempts to secure consent. On the same day the Social Contract Act was tabled, the government also tabled Bill 49, An Act Respecting the Collective Bargaining of Employees of the Crown, designed to finally extend the right to strike to provincial employees in Ontario. The cynical conjunction of tabling legislation that recognized collective bargaining rights while on the same day statutorily removing them for a three-year period symbolized the accommodation of the NDP to the transformation that had taken place in the labour relations regime throughout Canada: the shift from consent to coercion that had rendered the right to strike so tenuous.

As the Ontario NDP trudged to its final hours in office, it had lost any vision that it might have once had. The aggressive strategies of capital and a significant part of the bureaucratic apparatus of government had beaten the party into being a conventional manager of the state. The government continued to administer the Social Contract, rolling back existing collective agreements with public-sector workers and using back-to-work legislation three times to end teachers' strikes.[13] The most tragic legacy of this alienation was that it paved the way for the NDP's collapse in the 1995 election and for the success of Mike Harris's Common Sense Revolution.

The Conservatives promised to cut welfare payments, end employment equity, balance the budget, cut taxes, reduce the size of the public-sector labour force, and implement business-friendly, anti-union measures. They infamously started by immediately cutting welfare benefits by 21.6 percent, followed up quickly by Bill 7, the Labour Relations and Employment Statute Law Amendment Act, in 1995, which repealed the progressive sections of the NDP's labour relations reforms.[14] By the end of 1995, the Conservatives had also repealed the law that allowed for farm labourers to unionize, ended the employment equity program introduced under the NDP, and introduced the notorious Savings and Restructuring Act (Bill 26). The latter was an omnibus bill that involved drastic cuts to public expenditures, including cutting 13,000 public-sector workers' jobs, sweeping new powers that allowed Queen's Park

to unilaterally restructure municipalities and hospitals, and special requirements that arbitrators respect government concerns in adjudicating disputes
with firefighters, police, health workers, and others who did not have the legal
right to strike.[15]

The first sign that "Common Sense" would require considerable coercion to
implement came on the day of the Tories' first throne speech when riot police
were let loose on demonstrators on the steps of Queen's Park.[16] This conflict
helped inspire additional resistance, which soon took shape in an imaginative
series of one-day strikes (Days of Action) in cities across Ontario organized
by the Ontario Federation of Labour with networks of social justice groups.[17]
It seemed like the strategy had a great deal of potential insofar as it went beyond legislative politics or even the next election to mobilize public support
for social rights, build a movement, and challenge the power of capital.[18] But
the movement eventually broke down, in no small part due to divisions over
strategy.[19] In 1998, the government moved to prohibit people on social assistance who had been forced into "workfare" programs from unionizing on the
grounds that workfare participants were volunteers. The same year, the Tories
introduced the Prevention of Unionization Act, and so-called Economic Development and Workplace Democracy Act, which inserted further barriers to
certification, made it easier to decertify unions, and empowered the government to ban strikes at certain large industrial construction sites in the name of
boosting investor confidence. Automatic certification rights were also eliminated when the Labour Board found that an employer had used intimidation
to sway workers away from unionization drives.

Following the Harris government's re-election in June 1999, the Labour
Relations Amendment Act in 2000 made it mandatory for employers in unionized workplaces to post procedures for decertification, provided for a
one-year cooling-off period, and fast-tracked applications to decertify a new
union. These changes to the Ontario Labour Relations Act (OLRA) were cou-
pled with changes to the Employment Standards Act (ESA), which allowed
employers to require employees to work up to 60 hours per week without
receiving overtime, if the average workweek over a four-week period did not
exceed 44 hours.[20] This disdain for labour rights was reflected in the government's dealings with its own employees. Using its one positive legacy from
the NDP, OPSEU launched the first-ever legal provincewide strike in Ontario
on 26 February 1996. The government seemed quite willing to face down the
strike with the expectation that it would severely damage the union, given
that not all members had been keen on getting the legal right to strike and

that the union had achieved a relatively weak strike vote. On 18 March 1996, demonstrators at a massive rally staged at Queen's Park were met with riot police wielding clubs, ending in a violent confrontation where two people were injured. The violence only helped to stiffen the resolve of the pickets and fuelled support from the broader labour movement. When the strike finally ended on 31 March, the union had shown that it was indeed capable of pulling off a strike relatively successfully, and it actually won an agreement that gave at least some protection against privatization, improved "bumping" rights – where an employee under threat of layoff would have greater opportunities of being placed in a vacant position – and increased benefits for those employees who eventually lost their jobs through downsizing.[21]

Up next were the province's teachers. The Harris government moved quickly to massively restructure the education system by centralizing control of funding and curriculum and reducing the number and autonomy of local school boards. Bill 160 effectively removed 8,000 principals and vice-principals from bargaining units and eliminated teachers' right to bargain over preparation time, class sizes, teacher-to-student ratios, the length of the workday and the school year.[22] For teachers' unions, it was a full-frontal assault, leading to an unprecedented show of unity among all the teachers' unions when over 125,000 teachers walked off the job on 27 October 1997. The government immediately sought an injunction on the grounds that the strike was illegal, since it took place during the term of existing collective agreements, while also claiming that the education of the province's children was being irreparably damaged and that working parents were being inconvenienced by the strike.[23]

Although initially unsuccessful, there were fears that a second attempted injunction may succeed, which led several teachers' unions to return to work by the end of the second week, with other unions soon following. By the end of the year, Bill 160 was passed with all of the objectionable sections intact. Bill 160 came back to haunt the government the next year by virtue of its having set a common end of 31 August 1998 to all teachers' contracts. Efforts across the province to negotiate a new collective agreement led to a series of strikes beginning in September 1998. Some high school teachers had not received a raise in eight years but were being required to do 20 percent more work as a result of the new provisions. The strikes lasted throughout the month and were only ended by back-to-work legislation applied to strikes in eight separate boards.

The growing unpopularity of the government led the Conservatives to choose Ernie Eves to succeed Mike Harris as premier in early 2002. It was significant that the transition took place in the middle of a second OPSEU strike, with one of the central issues being the government's proposal to re-move from workers the ability to control their own pension surplus. Although the government initially responded to the strike by going to the courts (suc-cessfully) for injunctions to limit picketing, and to the Labour Board (largely unsuccessfully) to try to restrict the number of OPSEU members who could legally be on strike, Eves attempted to distance himself from the unpopular Harris by taking a somewhat more conciliatory approach. Eves' approach led to a deal that included a wage hike of 8.45 percent over three years and agreement by the government to allow the union to control the pension sur-plus. However, this more conciliatory approach did not last long as more than 24,000 striking civic workers at the City of Toronto were legislated back to work less than two weeks after exercising their right to strike, which cemented the turn to permanent exceptionalism.[24]

THE ATLANTIC PROVINCES AND QUEBEC: CONSOLIDATION AND CONFRONTATION

In all four Atlantic provinces, Liberal governments continued the assault on trade union rights and freedoms through the 1990s. In Newfoundland and Labrador, amendments to the Labour Relations Act in 1994 removed auto-matic certification and made strike votes mandatory. In the same year, the Liberal government in New Brunswick also amended its Labour Relations Act and Public Service Relations Act, making it easier for employers to obtain forced ratification votes. The latter Bill appeared more even-handed as it re-tracted the old provision for automatic decertification of unions that engaged in illegal strike activity, but it left the Public Service Labour Relations Board with the discretionary power to decertify a union for this action.

Meanwhile, in Prince Edward Island, the Liberal government's strict pro-gram of fiscal austerity prompted the largest labour demonstration ever in the province in 1994 as 5,000 Island residents demanded that the Liberals put the brakes on their proposed Public Sector Pay Reduction Act. The demonstra-tion convinced the government to slightly soften its proposed 7.5 percent pay cut so that public-sector workers making less than $28,000 would only be re-quired to take a 3.75 percent reduction. The Liberals never recovered from the debacle over their austerity program and were soundly defeated by the Tories in the 1996 provincial election. The most sparks were to fly in Nova Scotia, though, when the Liberal government passed the Public Sector Unpaid Leave Act in November 1993, followed by the Public Sector Compensation Act in April 1994. The former forced public-sector workers to take a 2 percent wage cut through unpaid leave, while the latter froze all collective agreements, prohibited most wage increases until 1 November 1997, reduced wages by 3 percent, and removed the right to strike, mediate, or arbitrate.[25]

In Nova Scotia, Russell McLelland's minority Liberal government was forced to call an election the next year, at which point the Tories were able to secure a majority government. The new premier, John Hamm, picked up where the Liberals left off. He began by legislating striking ambulance workers back to work in the fall of 1999. The Financial Measures Act of 2000 completely withdrew government funding from the arbitration process, and amendments to the Teachers' Collective Bargaining Act in 2001 narrowed the range of items that could be put on the bargaining table. The Hamm government then introduced the Act to Continue Health Care Services, sparking a bout of labour militancy in Atlantic Canada. The bitter negotiation process between the Capital District Health Authority and the nurses ended on 13 June 2001 with a mediated settlement. But before members of the Nova Scotia Government Employees Union (NSGEU), representing nurses, were able to cast ballots in a ratification vote, the government intervened by introducing legislation to suspend the right to strike for nurses and allowed cabinet to impose a settlement.

The government's move incensed nurses, who then used the ratification vote as an opportunity to send the government a clear message, rejecting the tentative settlement and voting instead to strike. A series of large demonstrations at the Nova Scotia legislature did not deter the government from pushing the Bill through. However, a mass resignation threat from the provincial nurses' unions and talk of a provincewide general strike prompted the government to announce that the changes would not be brought into force. Both sides agreed to end the dispute by sending all outstanding issues to final offer selection. Amid all the defeats suffered by the labour movement in Atlantic Canada, trade unionists in Nova Scotia pointed to their successful stand as proof that organized labour was alive and well. Only in an era of permanent exceptionalism can a union concession be considered a victory. Throughout Atlantic Canada, the mere threat of back-to-work legislation has been as effective as the actual use of such legislation. Workers in the health care sector in Newfoundland and Labrador also found themselves to be the target of anti-union legislation. Members of the Registered Nurses' Union of

Newfoundland and Labrador were ordered back to work on 1 April 1999. The government followed up in May 2001 with an amendment to the Labour Relations Act, which increased fines for illegal strikes and lockouts. Also, in March 2001, striking hospital workers in New Brunswick went back to work for fear that Premier Bernard Lord would make good on a promise to impose a substandard contract and stiff fines. Four months later, the Lord government essentially suspended the right to strike for nursing home workers. Under the new regulation, no worker was permitted to reduce or withdraw services unless or until the government found alternate living arrangements for nursing home residents.

The squeeze on public revenues in the recession of the 1990s moved the Quebec Liberals, like other provincial governments, towards public-sector wage restraint. Very differently from the early 1980s in Quebec, the unions in the public sector assented to this program of statutory wage restraint after consultations with the government in 1991, thus following the corporatist lead of their private-sector counterparts. As discussed in the previous chapter, as a result of the draconian legislation passed in Quebec years earlier, governments now had at their fingertips massive arbitrary powers to suspend, renege, and use against striking workers. They rarely used these powers, however, for fear that it would further enflame class struggle.

Corporatist arrangements between the state, business, and the Quebec labour movement were initially a product of the Quiet Revolution but became particularly embedded in the PQ's version of social democracy. The Quebec labour movement's determination to accommodate the government arguably reached its peak under PQ premier Jacques Parizeau, a self-described social democrat. Labour leaders and the PQ closed ranks around a nation-building strategy that would lay the groundwork for a sovereign Quebec. However, the referendum loss in 1995, followed by Parizeau's resignation and Lucien Bouchard's succession as premier, signalled a return to the permanently exceptional coercive legislation that was so prevalent a decade earlier. While the labour movement's nation-building project was always based loosely on social democratic principles, the PQ's vision of a sovereign Quebec was transformed under Bouchard. The Bouchard government arbitrarily reopened collective agreements and slashed salaries in specific areas of the provincial and municipal public sector. And in the spring of 1998, the PQ government severely restricted the bargaining power of thousands of workers, limiting their right to strike by broadening the definition of essential public services to include the storage of gas; the transportation, collection, and distribution of blood products; and forest fire protection activities. In 1999, the PQ also suspended the right to strike for workers at the municipal housing office in Montreal by making the office an essential public service. A month later, the PQ ordered striking nurses back to work, but the nurses refused and walked the picket lines illegally for 23 days. The government fined the union roughly half a million dollars for the infraction.[26]

The provincial election of 1999 offered little hope for workers who were tired of the PQ's anti-labour offensive. Given a choice between two former Mulroney cabinet ministers (Bouchard and Quebec Liberal leader Jean Charest), Quebeckers stuck with the devil they knew. Bouchard's eventual retirement certainly did nothing to shift Quebec politics to the left. Instead, it sent the PQ into a tailspin and opened up room for the right-wing Action Dèmocratique du Québec (ADQ) to make its presence felt in provincial politics. The growth in popularity of the ADQ over the following years would shift the political spectrum right as the Quebec labour movement continued to struggle with the limitations of corporatism.

A TURNING POINT: THE PRAIRIE PROVINCES AND BRITISH COLUMBIA

The 1990s marked a significant turning point in the political and economic history of the prairie provinces with the emergence of the regionally based Reform/Alliance Party at the federal level. Its skill at using populist rhetoric ("The West Wants In") to advance a neoliberal agenda had been especially well developed in Alberta when the 21-year Tory dynasty was handed over to Ralph Klein in late 1992. Unionized public-sector workers were a particular target for the Klein government, whose determination to balance the provincial budget while also lowering taxes led it to privatize, contract out, and outsource many of the traditional services performed by public-sector workers. By 1997, the provincial workforce had been reduced by 23.5 percent, the single largest decline of public employees across Canada. Public employees were also asked to take a "voluntary" 5 percent wage reduction, followed by a two-year wage freeze, with the government giving employers the authority to lay off workers if the wage rollbacks were not agreed to.[27]

Several administrative acts opened the door for greater privatization and contracting out of public services, with the added bonus for potential contractors to not have to pay full union wages. The government also changed the structure and powers of the Labour Relations Board, as well as the rules for certification, bargaining rights, and grievance arbitration in ways that disadvantaged unions.[28] In 2001, a dispute between the City of Edmonton and the ambulance drivers of CUPE Local 3197 threatened to disrupt emergency services in the city. In response, the government passed an amendment to the Labour Relations Code, giving the government the power to declare emergency procedures in any labour dispute it deemed might cause undue harm, hardship, or damage to health or property; it then went on to prohibit any strike or lockout for ambulance drivers.

After a series of rotating job actions and strikes by the Alberta Teachers' Association in 2002, the Klein government passed the Education Services Settlement Act, which legislated the legally striking teachers back to work, imposed severe fines on teachers and their union in the event of a continued strike, and stripped the ATA from any reasonable form of collective bargaining. Notably, the Tories took the unusual step of changing the normal parliamentary rules in order to prevent extended discussion or debate in the legislature, so as to speed the passage of Bill 12. For its part, organized labour failed to build on the mobilizations during the Gainers meat packers' strike, and again during the nurses' strike at the beginning of the decade, never posing a serious challenge to the Klein cuts. On the few occasions when workers did strike or attempt to challenge the government, they were dealt with harshly.[29]

The continued erosion of union rights was not limited to Alberta or the Klein revolution. In Saskatchewan, the NDP's throne speech of 27 April 1992 announced an agenda of labour reform, promising changes to occupational health and safety, the construction industry, workers' compensation, and reviews of the Trade Union Act and the Labour Standards Act. The government moved very slowly in pursuing this agenda and insisted that provincial employees accept a two-year wage freeze, even though their real wages had fallen by some 10 percent since 1982. The government's refusal to move from this position led to a series of rotating strikes by the SGEU in 1992–1993, and eventually to a ruling by the Labour Board that the government had failed to bargain in good faith. Ignoring the ruling, the government was ultimately successful in bludgeoning the SGEU to accede to the freeze but in the process alienated virtually the whole of the Saskatchewan labour movement.[30]

While not moving as aggressively on the neoliberal austerity policies introduced in Alberta, Roy Romanow's government was revealing the limits that social democracy evinced elsewhere and was quick to reassure the Saskatchewan business community that increased public spending was not on the political or economic agenda.[31] The government introduced its long-awaited legislative package for trade unions in 1994, with the passing of the Trade Union Amendment Act. Its concern to strike a balance between the rights of organized labour and the perceived stability of the business environment meant that long-standing union expectations for anti-scab measures and pay equity legislation were not addressed. The changes did, however, ease restrictions on collective bargaining and dispute resolution by handing more power to the Labour Relations Board to rule in unfair bargaining practices, loosening restrictions on first contract arbitration and on the administration of collective agreements, and making it more difficult for employers to terminate workers during a legal strike.

With a weak opposition split between Liberals and Conservatives, the NDP secured a second majority government in the 1995 election. This victory allowed it to continue with limited reform measures to the province's labour laws by introducing the Health Labour Relations Reorganization Act, which provided for significant trade union participation in the reorganization of labour relations in the health sector. But it also passed the Balanced Budget Act that capped public-sector wages at 2 percent per year, aggressively cut taxes, closed rural hospitals, and increasingly turned to costly public-private partnerships as a means to deliver public services. Perhaps the most telling example of the demise of the Saskatchewan NDP as a progressive pole was its handling of two strikes in 1998 and 1999. The first involved members of the International Brotherhood of Electrical Workers Local 2067 who, having reached a bargaining impasse with the Saskatchewan Power Corporation, had taken legal strike action. Fearing a shutdown of the province's power supply, the Romanow government introduced back-to-work legislation, which ended the strike by extending the previous collective agreement for two years.

The government then showed even greater contempt for the collective bargaining rights of workers when it quickly moved to end a nurses' strike through the passage of back-to-work legislation in 1999. Despite being faced with $50,000 fines on the union and $2,000 a day for individual workers, the nurses vowed to resist and defied a court order to return to work. With overwhelming support from the public, the nurses won, securing a collective agreement with a 13.7 percent wage increase over three years. If the New Democrats had ever expected these confrontations with public-sector unions would be electorally helpful, they were sadly mistaken. In the 1999 election, the party lost 13 seats and fell to 38 percent of the popular vote, forcing it into a coalition government with the Liberals. While the NDP would take a more moderate course, particularly under the leadership of Lorne Calvert after 2003, it nevertheless remained committed to the politics of austerity. The NDP's last two budgets drove a final stake into any remaining prospects of forming government in the near future – it drastically reduced corporate and individual taxes; reduced royalty rates on oil, gas, potash, coal, and uranium; and massively expanded private-sector development in the province's natural resource sectors.

In Manitoba, the Filmon Tories' majority re-election in 1995 pushed further the radical neoliberal agenda it had been pursuing. Its inelegantly named Balanced Budget, Debt Repayment and Taxpayer's Protection and Consequential Amendments Act made individual ministers responsible for balancing the budget of their departments and stipulated that any increase in taxes had to go before a provincial referendum.[32] The Act paved the way for decentralized public services, hospital closures, and the sale of the Manitoba Telephone System. The cutbacks meant major reductions in public service employment and continued the reductions in real wages and benefits that had taken place each year after 1990. The government then turned its attention to the province's labour laws. In 1956, Manitoba teachers had voluntarily given up the right to strike in exchange for a system of binding arbitration. The Public Schools Amendment Act, passed exactly 40 years later, removed what few bargaining rights remained regarding teacher selection and appointment, length of the school day, the scheduling of professional development days, classroom size, and the provisions for layoffs. Salary, benefits, preparation time, and pensions were also withdrawn from the traditional form of collective bargaining as union members were arbitrarily subject to a form of concessionary bargaining by local school boards who were able to base financial compensation on the district's ability to pay.

Then, at the beginning of 1997, the government passed Bill 26, amending the Labour Relations Act. The Bill subjected Manitoba unions to the most restrictive measures in Canada on the use of members' dues for political purposes. It also stripped the unions of automatic certification rights and gave employers new tools to resist union drives in the workplace, eased restrictions on employers' unfair bargaining practices, and strengthened their ability to dismiss employees who had been on legal strike. Collective bargaining rights and the right to strike were further weakened when Bill 17 amended the Essential Services Act, giving the government greater unilateral ability to determine what public services were deemed essential, which workers fell outside of a collective agreement, and the conditions by which public-sector workers could strike. By 1997, the Manitoba Government and General Employees Union (MGEU) had lost 22 percent of its members.

In 1999, the labour movement's resistance to these changes contributed to the election of the NDP under Gary Doer. Within a year, the new government moved quickly to pass Bill 44, which repealed many of the restrictive measures of the Filmon government, including the provisions to allow employers to dismiss workers for picket-line activity, to restrict the use of union dues for political purposes, and to eliminate teachers' rights to collective bargaining. The Manitoba Federation of Labour was still understandably disappointed, however, that the NDP failed to repeal all the restrictive provisions of Bill 26, most notably those on certification rights and the continued refusal of previous Manitoba NDP governments to pass anti-scab legislation.[33]

Like Saskatchewan and Ontario, British Columbia was governed by an NDP government throughout the 1990s. Elected in 1991, the Mike Harcourt government promised to reverse a decade of legislated restrictions imposed by the former Social Credit government. Beyond repealing the notoriously misnamed Compensation Fairness Act that had so severely undermined public-sector collective bargaining in the province, the NDP government's major legislative initiative was Bill 84, reforming the Labour Relations Code. But while it re-established many rights previously taken away by Social Credit and particularly workers' rights to engage in secondary picketing, common-site picketing, and boycotts as well as successor rights in the event of ownership changes, Bill 84 preserved many of the restrictions on the right to strike introduced a decade earlier. The Bill maintained the broad definition of a strike introduced by Social Credit so that political strikes remained illegal; a vote by secret ballot (valid only for three months) was still necessary to conduct a legal strike; employers still had to be given 72 hours' written notice of any strike; and the Labour Board could order a vote on the employer's last offer even during a strike. Moreover, the Bill enabled the government to appoint a special officer who could issue orders delaying a strike for 30 days.

Among the new reforms introduced by the Bill, the most important were restrictions on the use of replacement workers, automatic access to first contract arbitration, and the removal of the prohibition on strikes during the life of a collective agreement in certain circumstances, notably where the health and safety of workers was at stake. The main advance involved restrictions on the use of replacement workers, but the minister and/or the Labour Board were given very broad discretion to designate any facility, production, or service as essential. Essential services, moreover, had to be provided "in full

measure" by the union, meaning that, unlike in Ontario where essential services were merely exempted from the restrictions on the use of replacement
workers, providers of these services in BC lost their right to strike.

The NDP government did not shirk from using back-to-work legislation
under this rubric. Bill 31 ended a strike by Vancouver teachers in 1993 even
though the teachers had accepted the proposals of an independent mediator.
This was an important testament to the role that coercion continued to oc-
cupy even within the framework of NDP reforms. The government did enact
several reform amendments to the 1994 Employment Standards Act, including the introduction of more flexible arrangements in the scheduling of work,
which they hoped would address many of the earlier limitations and their fal-
tering relationship with many public-sector unions. It also passed the Public
Education Labour Relations Act (Bill 52), which restructured the collective
bargaining process for teachers so that all major decisions involving monetary
compensation, classroom size, and pensions were bargained at the provincial
level rather than with local school boards.

The BC NDP appeared to put its best foot forward in the process of overseeing what it called a social contract with three unions in the health sector. The
accord was struck in March 1993, with the hope of gaining the cooperation of
health care workers to shift away from acute-care institutions and towards community-based care; the proposal provided employment security and a modest
wage increase alongside a government pledge to maintain the existing balance
between public and private facilities. In addition, the accord specified considerable new rights and procedures for the active involvement of workers' representatives in developing proposals for new community health programs, as well as in
certain areas of management and expenditure planning at local and provincial
levels. The government's short-term interest in the deal was very much bound up
with securing the minimal 1.5 percent wage increase and three-year extension of
contracts that the three unions had agreed to, thereby undercutting a 3 percent
deal the BC nurses had earlier negotiated. This lower-level increase immediately
became the definition of realistic expectations for other public-sector unions in
their negotiations with the government. In this context, the main impetus towards community-based health care, as far as the government was concerned,
was cheaper delivery. Yet the principal reason health care is cheaper when it is
community-based is that community health care wages are very low. The government's objective was clearly one of downsizing the costs of the acute-care sector.

The health care unions in BC certainly thought that they were buy-
ing into new labour relations, especially by obtaining much more input in

decision-making on a cooperative basis. But the employers' resistance at first left the NDP government paralyzed, and the entire process of health sector reform was stalled for many months after the unions signed on. In the ensuing conflicts of interpretation and implementation, the government repeatedly sided with the employers and took positions largely indistinguishable from them. The best that could be said is that the BC social contract in this sector provided a more favourable framework for strategic union manoeuvring than was on offer at any point from the NDP in Ontario.[34]

Under new leader Glen Clark, the NDP was reduced to a bare majority in the 1996 legislature. Despite his left-wing reputation and union background, Clark moved quickly to reduce fiscal expenditures, and balancing the budget became a key component of the government's discourse. The British Columbia Government Employees' Union (BCGEU) was able to bargain around an early Clark government attempt to lay off 3,500 workers. From here out, the BC government's long-term restructuring plans did not include massive lay-offs or the radical downsizing of public-sector employment as was the case in Saskatchewan, but the continuing signal from the government was that its highest priority was the reduction of costs in the public sector. The Clark government also did not shy away from coercion when collective bargaining measures reached an impasse. In 1998, when teachers threatened to strike over a new contract, the government passed the Public Education Collective Agreement Act, which effectively limited the collective bargaining rights of teachers. In the wake of a number of scandals surrounding Glen Clark, the party elected Ujjal Dosanjh as leader and quickly turned against many of its key supporters in the labour movement. In 2000 it passed the Public Education Support Staff Collective Bargaining Assistance Act, which imposed a collective agreement to end a CUPE strike of support workers and cleaning staff in public schools. Besides alienating many in the labour movement, the passage of Bill 7 also revealed deeper splits within the Dosanjh caucus – and legislating CUPE workers back to work was a nail in the coffin for the party's key labour supporters.

CONCLUSION: THE DEMISE OF SOCIAL DEMOCRACY

The experiences of social democracy across the provinces through the 1990s shattered the labour movement's principal strategy of electing NDP governments. Insofar as trade union leaders and activists saw the NDP as part of the labour movement, the contradictions between the unions and the party took a tremendous emotional toll. Had this experience been confined to Ontario, its strategic implications might not have been so profound. Unfortunately, NDP governments in BC and Saskatchewan, and even the PQ in Quebec, as well as the party's poor performance federally, did not evince a sufficiently different practice to deflect a general sense of crisis in political strategy pervading the whole labour movement.

What had become clear by the end of the decade was that the NDP did not just fall short in terms of the degree of reform needed and expected by the unions, but it had actively undermined union power. One cannot underestimate the political significance of an NDP government joining in the general attack against workers and marginalized groups. What had made the Canadian labour movement distinctive in the 1980s was its strategy of opposition to, or at least refusal to legitimate, concessionary bargaining. But by the 1990s, it was no longer clear what path lay ahead. For the first time in half a century, a major debate took place on how to challenge the limited parameters of electoral politics in Canada. The importance of being openly critical of the NDP, even at possible short-term electoral cost, was particularly clear.

Also raised was the longer-term strategic necessity for putting substantial union efforts and resources into movement-building political activities outside of electoral politics. For all too long, the labour movement in this period had barely begun to confront, let alone resolve, its crisis of political strategy. The need for autonomous political mobilization butted up against the NDP's **electoralism** and **parliamentarism**, which had saturated the labour movement's definition of politics for decades. Although links with new social movements began to move the unions some way towards greater independence from the NDP, the social movements themselves had for the most part suspended popular mobilization vis-à-vis NDP governments. No less than the unions, they tended to see the main cause of such problems they faced as residing in the practices of the Liberal or Conservative governments of the day. Even without the organic ties and burdens of loyalty that labour had with the NDP, they had not come to terms with or been prepared for the utter conventionality of the party.

What also constrained mobilization against the NDP was some sense of truth in the claim that, however disappointing NDP practice was, the alternatives of the other parties were worse. To be sure, there was no immediate electoral alternative. Nor was there any ready-made package of alternative policies that could be quickly implemented. The strategic crisis confronting the labour movement was not about policies but instead a more fundamental crisis of politics. It bespoke the exhaustion of the social democratic reformism that had characterized labour's overall political strategy since World War II. The strategy had once made a certain sense, but it no longer did so in the new era of global neoliberalism. The challenge confronting the labour movement entering the twenty-first century was to develop a political strategy appropriate to the new era. Insofar as it failed to do so, it could only gird itself for repeated assaults, which is exactly what it faced over the following decade.

CHAPTER SIX

Austerity and Authoritarianism

Chapter Summary: The first decade of the 2000s continued the public-sector fiscal austerity that had marked the previous decade. Although some modest additional public spending was unevenly implemented by provincial and federal governments, when the global financial crisis struck in 2008, governments moved (rather reluctantly, in the case of the federal government) to apply significant fiscal stimulus to avert economic catastrophe. For workers and trade unions, the defeats of the 1990s now weighed on them as militancy declined and new right-wing governments were elected in several provinces and at the national level that immediately renewed the direct assault on trade unions and legislated worker protections. What remained of social democracy, as typified by NDP governments in Manitoba and Nova Scotia, offered only modest reforms as they otherwise settled into managing the status quo.

INTRODUCTION

The arrival of the twenty-first century continued the prior decade's permanent exceptionalism. There were few signs that workers might use the right to strike to regain some of their losses or resist further ones. As discussed in the previous chapter, the Canadian fiscal "miracle" of the 1990s was grounded upon the destruction of 50–50 cost-sharing programs created in the 1960s to support health care, social services, income maintenance, and post-secondary education. This program spending was offloaded onto the provinces, which, in turn, restrained expenditures and, following the same logic of displacement, shifted as much as they could onto municipalities. The Chrétien-Martin governments, like their provincial counterparts, consolidated this remaking of the welfare state through an aggressive program of labour coercion, which crushed trade union and broader working-class militancy that had been a hallmark of earlier decades.

Into the early 2000s, a Canadian strategy of punitive austerity established a pattern of federal and provincial government surpluses. In coming to power in 2006, the hard right Conservative government of Stephen Harper had only to build on this fiscal legacy. It shaped both the "rescue" and "exit" strategies to the financial crisis that would define the decade. Whether social democratic, Liberal, or Conservative, each of the provinces shared a fidelity to ensuring the cost of the crisis was borne by workers via tax shifting, declining levels and quality of public services, and regressive user fees. Over the decade, all provinces presented budgets that sought to keep program expenditure growth at or below 2 percent per year, cut or froze operational budgets, and introduced constraints on public-sector hiring and compensation. It was a decade in which governments of all partisan stripes finally shed any remaining vestiges of consent, extending the era of austerity and coercion.

THE HARPER DECADE

In 2006, the Stephen Harper Conservatives formed a minority government. In coming to power, Harper's victory had been the culmination of efforts by right-wing conservatives for over 20 years.[1] An uncompromising adherent of *laissez-faire* capitalism, Harper's party platform, titled Stand Up for Canada, touted smaller government, reduced taxes, a shrinking of the welfare state, limited government spending, and strict separation of federal and provincial powers. Having inherited a $10 billion surplus, among the government's first acts was to reduce the Goods and Services Tax (GST) from 7 to 6 and later 5 percent over the course of two years. This reduced government revenue by some $13 billion annually, which, by 2009, had lowered total public spending to 36 percent of the economy, its lowest since 1974. Total government revenues from taxes also fell to 32 percent of all revenue sources, their lowest since 1985.

The Harper government wasted little time in continuing the assault on trade union rights and freedoms. In February 2007, 2,800 train conductors and yard workers organized with the United Transportation Union (UTU) went out on strike against CN's poor safety record, plans to reduce breaks, and eroding wages and benefits. As the government readied back-to-work legislation, tensions rang high within the UTU as US-based representatives argued alongside the company in trying to get the strike declared illegal at the Canada Industrial Relations Board (CIRB). The UTU head office would sack the Canadian leadership and install a new bargaining team, which soon reached an agreement. However, it was rejected by more than 80 percent of the membership, with CN then moving to lock out workers. On 17 April 2007, the government, supported by the Liberals, passed Bill C-46, the Railway Continuation Act, which ended the strike and imposed a final offer selection process on outstanding issues. The following year, rail workers would join Teamsters Canada.[2]

Little more than a year into the Conservatives' mandate, things would change dramatically as the global financial crisis unleashed the largest and longest recession since the 1930s. In the face of a deteriorating economy, Harper called a snap election in 2008. In the midst of the election, Finance Minister Flaherty insisted that Canada would not run a deficit. Six months later the deficit was estimated to be roughly $54 billion. While no party was able to secure a majority, the Conservatives saw their minority government strengthened by 16 seats. In his ensuing Economic and Fiscal Update, Minister Flaherty announced that Bill C-10, which included both the Expenditure Restraint Act and the Public Sector Equitable Compensation Act, would suspend the right to strike for federal public employees. In addition, wages would be constrained for four years at 2.3 percent in the first year and 1.5 percent for the subsequent three years. In several cases, the legislation overrode previously negotiated collective agreements containing wage increases above the imposed salary caps. In an effort to undermine the success of pay equity complaints filed against the federal government, Flaherty introduced changes that removed adjudication by the Canadian Human Rights Commission and instead required that they be dealt with only through the collective bargaining process – a process that could itself be uprooted at any time, as he had just demonstrated.[3]

Rarely does fiscal policy become the source of high drama, but that is exactly what unfolded nationally between November 2008 and January 2009. Within that short timeframe, the Harper government's fiscal policy lurched from an uncompromising commitment to balanced budget orthodoxy to Keynesian-style emergency stimulus. The two forces behind the fiscal policy reversal were the severity of the economic crisis and Washington's call for a coordinated global stimulus package led by the G20, along with the possibility that a vote of non-confidence would see the minority Conservative government replaced by a coalition of the Liberals and NDP backed by the Bloc Québécois (BQ). In the face of a united parliamentary accord, Harper immediately sought a prorogation of Parliament, which essentially put an end to the accord.[4]

The government's new Speech from the Throne in January 2009 signalled that the Harper government was now going to set a more conciliatory tone and a budgetary U-turn. At the core of "Canada's Economic Action Plan" was an emergency fiscal stimulus built on a budgetary deficit of $34 billion and then $30 billion over two years. Emergency stimulus measures were then to be eliminated, with deficit spending steadily reduced. Other measures included a $20 billion cut to personal income taxes, $50 billion to expand a government program to purchase mortgages from banks, and $13 billion in additional financing for several state-owned agencies concerned with insuring mortgages, export marketing, and business loans.

Buried in the omnibus budget, Bill C-60 allowed federal cabinet, via the Treasury Board, to intervene and direct collective bargaining for 48 Crown corporations. The legislation also allowed cabinet to unilaterally define any employee's work as essential, preventing those workers from taking job action. Likewise, Bill C-4 replaced health and safety officers with those appointed by the government, increased the threshold required to refuse unsafe work, and restricted the human rights remedies that an adjudicator can award by removing the power of the adjudicator to order an employer to cease a discriminatory practice.[5] By this point, it was becoming increasingly clear that such legislation was in violation of the Charter of Rights and Freedoms (see Chapter 8), but that did little to deter the government from violating basic labour rights. With the possibility of a Liberal-NDP coalition all but gone, and with Michael Ignatieff, a reluctant supporter of the accord replacing Stéphane Dion as leader, the Liberals decided to support the budget with an amendment that held the government to a regimen of three updates on the implementation of the budget.

The recession set a postwar record for the most consecutive months (eight) of uninterrupted decline. From October 2008 to October 2009, Canada lost 400,000 jobs as national unemployment swelled to 8.6 percent. In January 2009 alone, 129,000 jobs were lost – the single-largest monthly job loss on record – as 5 percent of employment in manufacturing disappeared. These pressures intensified longer-term patterns of labour market restructuring as Canadian employment in manufacturing fell by nearly 556,000 between 2004 and 2009.[6] Despite the significant job losses, however, the Conservative government continued along the path of austerity and coercion as demonstrated in their hands-on approach to negotiations between the CAW and General Motors. In order to help both companies qualify for aid, the CAW agreed to reopen the three-year collective agreements reached with GM and Chrysler in 2007. Despite a faint commitment to "no concessions" bargaining, the union and GM eventually reached a new deal that would extend the existing agreement for an additional year, to September 2012, and preserve the average assembly-worker base wage of roughly $34 per hour. However, the new deal eliminated a $1,700 annual bonus, reduced paid absences from two to one week per year, and introduced monthly payments by members towards their health benefits. In total, GM would save $1 billion annually through salaried workforce cuts in Canada, as well as $1 billion in future legacy costs – mainly pension and health care payments.

It is important to note that these concessions built on earlier ones made by the CAW in 2007 that were estimated to save the Big Three automakers $900 million over three years by freezing wages and implementing lower salaries for new hires.[7] Not only did Chrysler (and Ford) reject the new deal, saying that parity with non-unionized automakers was required, but the deal was also rejected in stunning fashion by both the federal Conservatives and Ontario Liberals for not going far enough to cut labour costs.[8] Two months later, the CAW agreed to more concessions, putting the company's labour costs on par with those at Toyota Canada's non-unionized plants. With further concessions secured, General Motors (GM) finally received $10.5 billion from the federal government and an additional $3.5 billion from Ontario for an 18 percent stake in the company and a promise by GM to keep at least 16 percent of its North American production in Canada. Chrysler received $1.25 billion each from Ottawa and Ontario for a 2 percent stake in the company and a non-voting seat on the board of directors.[9] With 86 percent of members voting to ratify the labour pact, the concession-filled deal was a decisive blow to the CAW and labour movement as a whole.[10]

Jim Flaherty's fifth budget contrasted sharply with the previous year's reluctant "rescue" budget. Budget 2010 assumed the corner had been turned on the economic crisis and presented a plan for "exit" from deficit financing and a return to balanced budget orthodoxy. A crisis firmly rooted in the recklessness of the private sector was redefined as a crisis of public finances. A range of constraint measures were deployed, including a three-year freeze on federal program spending that saw 11,000 public-service jobs eliminated. The 2010 federal budget cut another $17.6 billion over five years through operating and administrative reductions. This is on top of four previous strategic reviews and a personnel expenditure freeze totalling close to $8 billion. While executing a program for aggressively shrinking public expenditures, Minister Flaherty boasted that Canada's federal tax-to-GDP ratio had dropped to its lowest level since 1961 as Canada now had the lowest statutory corporate income tax rate in the G7. Within the span of just 12 years, Liberals and Conservatives had nearly halved corporate taxes. It would not be too far off to describe the evolution of Canadian fiscal strategy as a turn to permanent austerity, particularly when the constraints on provincial budgetary policies are also considered.

On 25 March 2011, Harper's Conservative government was found in contempt of Parliament for their refusal to share information with parliamentarians on the transfer of Afghan prisoners. The non-confidence motion triggered the fourth election in seven years. On 2 May 2011, the Harper Conservatives achieved a majority government (albeit with 39.6 percent of the vote), while the NDP made a historic breakthrough, catapulting them to the Official Opposition.[11] The Conservatives immediately set sight on shifting the burden of responsibility for debt repayment away from capital and onto workers. Resorting to back-to-work legislation became the preferred negotiating tactic, and this was vividly demonstrated with its handling of negotiations between Canada Post and CUPW. Despite 15 consecutive years of profitability, Canada Post entered negotiations with the aim of using the economic slump as a justification to extract concessions from workers. This included increasing the volume of mail carried by each carrier; cutting well-paying, full-time positions and replacing them with more part-time work; introducing more evening and overnight shift work; replacing sick leave rights with an inferior short-term disability plan; and, most contentiously, introducing a lower pay scale and replacing the defined-benefit pension plan with a defined-contribution plan.[12]

After seven months of negotiations, on 2 June 2011, nearly 50,000 CUPW members took job action. Rather than launch a full strike, CUPW implemented rotating strikes, while continuing to deliver pension and social assistance cheques. After 12 days, Canada Post locked out its workers. The next day, Labour Minister Lisa Raitt forced them back to work with the Restoring Mail Delivery for Canadians Act, 2011. Not only did the Conservatives impose a wage scale that was lower than Canada Post's last offer, but the new collective agreement was to be determined by final offer selection. CUPW twice successfully challenged the Conservatives in court for their selection of partisan arbitrators, eventually reaching an agreement without the use of one.[13] The agreement introduced two-tier wages as well as a hybrid pension plan.

Like Canada Post workers, on 14 June 2011, 3,800 call-centre staff and check-in workers unionized with the CAW at Air Canada took job action against Air Canada's efforts to implement a two-tiered wage system, increase the minimum retirement age by five years and, like Canada Post, impose a defined-contribution pension plan. Workers' wages had largely been frozen since 2003 amidst bankruptcy proceedings and the elimination of more than 2,000 jobs. Just two hours into the strike, Labour Minister Lisa Raitt once again motioned that back-to-work legislation would be forthcoming. With the threat looming large, Air Canada and the CAW were able to reach an agreement just as the minster tabled legislation forcing strikers back to work. The new four-year agreement saw wages rise with inflation, re-established a 30-minute paid lunch break, and limited the use of part-time labour, with guaranteed full-time positions at Chorus (formerly Jazz Air). However, binding arbitration resulted in lower pay scales and a hybrid pension plan for new hires.[14]

In February 2012, 8,600 baggage handlers, mechanics, and ground crew with the International Association of Machinists (IAM) rejected a contract offer from Air Canada that would see wages and benefits stagnate. Around the same time, 3,000 pilots also rejected Air Canada's final offer. In response, the company threatened to lock workers out. Both unions announced plans to legally strike in early March; however, the Conservatives pre-emptively passed An Act to Provide for the Continuation and Resumption of Air Service Operations, thwarting the strikes before they began. The legislation sent these cases to binding arbitration, while the government awaited a ruling by the CIRB to determine if air travel was an essential service. In the wake of three Air Canada workers' suspension for heckling Minister Raitt at Pearson Airport, 150 baggage handlers and ground crew walked off the job in Toronto. They were joined by ground crews in Montreal, Quebec City, and Vancouver.

Consequently, over 100 flights were cancelled. A CIRB arbitrator issued an injunction putting an end to the wildcat strike.

With their return to work, 37 employees were initially fired but were soon reinstated after negotiations with the IAM. Although the union did not condone the action, a CIRB arbitrator ruled that eight employees were found to have used Facebook to organize the Toronto wildcat. Only two of those eight were reinstated and four resigned. In a similar act of trade union militancy, on 13 April 2012, 150 pilots called in sick, leading to the cancellation of 75 flights. This sick-out was staged by pilots frustrated with the use of back-to-work legislation and final offer arbitration. The CIRB also ruled this job action to be illegal. In both cases, federal arbitrators sided with Air Canada and imposed five-year agreements that would see more than 1,000 jobs eliminated, increased contracting out of domestic and international flying, reduced pension funding obligations through 2024, and new hires moved to a cheaper defined-contribution pension plan.[15]

Just a month later, the Conservatives would once again flex their majority muscle in legislating striking locomotive engineers, conductors, and rail traffic controllers at CP back to work. Canadian Pacific Railway was seeking to increase the length of a shift from 10 to 12 hours, introduce a defined-contribution plan for new hires, and reduce pension obligations for existing employees to the same level as those as their competitor, CN Rail. The strike began 23 May 2012, and lasted nine days before Bill C-39, An Act to Provide for the Continuation and Resumption of Rail Service Operations, put an end to the strike and sent close to 5,000 strikers back to work. The legislation gave an arbitrator the power to impose a settlement and prohibited either the company or the union from challenging it.[16] As the examples of rail, postal, airline, and other workers show, state power often led to capital leading an assault against trade union rights in an indeterminate period of austerity (or created the conditions to do so).

Not content with merely coercing workers back to work, the Harper Conservatives set their sights on the most regressive revisions to the laws, regulations, and policies governing trade unions at any point in the postwar period. Bill C-525, the Employees' Voting Rights Act, 2014, removed card-check certification in federally regulated industries and instituted a secret ballot once 45 percent (up from 35 percent) of a proposed bargaining unit signed union cards. The Bill also allowed a decertification vote to occur when only 40 percent (down from 51 percent) of the membership requested one. Any worker who did not participate in the vote was counted as a "no" ballot. These new and stricter requirements made it more difficult for workers to organize, created longer delays between the beginning of an organizing drive and its conclusion, and allowed the employer significantly more time to undertake anti-union initiatives.[17]

Likewise, Bill C-377, An Act to Amend the Income Tax Act, forced unions to submit 24 different detailed statements of their finances, including any transaction over $5,000, salaries over $100,000, health benefits, and legal costs. Any labour organization that failed to comply could be fined $1,000 a day and up to $25,000 a year. The new law went far beyond any public financial disclosure requirements from business and professional associations, amounting to an attack on legitimate union rights and freedom of association and expression, through the back door of income tax legislation. The Canadian Bar Association noted that the Bill also endangered political rights, rights to personal and commercial privacy, confidentiality, and solicitor-client privilege.[18]

Before the Harper Conservatives were ousted from government, they initiated changes to the Employment Insurance program – already diminished by Chrétien-Martin era reforms in the 1990s – that reduced eligibility yet again and helped to create a "surplus" in the program that the Tories raided to the tune of nearly $2 billion to help balance their last budget. The changes to EI compelled unemployed workers to commute up to an hour or more for a job and accept pay cuts amounting to 30 percent of their previous income. They also significantly ramped up a series of temporary foreign worker programs before public pressure forced them to back off.[19] The assault on labour rights that developed in the wake of the global financial crisis cemented the permanent shift towards greater reliance on coercion to subordinate workers to the exigencies of capital accumulation. In this regard, the federal government's assault was echoed in several provinces.

THE "NEW" RIGHT IN BRITISH COLUMBIA AND THE PRAIRIE PROVINCES

British Columbia's 2001 election proved to be devastating to the NDP government, which was reduced to two seats in the legislature, while Gordon Campbell's Liberals were able to secure a majority government. Corporate and personal taxes were reduced immediately, including an across-the-board cut of 25 percent to personal income taxes.[20] The new government then undertook a massive legislative assault against labour. After imposing a cool-ing off period for striking nurses, it released the Health Care Services Col-lective Agreements Act, forcing an end to the nurses' strike and imposing a collective agreement that a majority had earlier rejected.[21] The Greater Van-couver transit strike in 2001 by CAW Local 111 was similarly ended by back-to-work legislation. The government then introduced major changes to the Skills Development and Labour Statutes Amendment Act. The reforms out-lawed any form of sectoral bargaining in the province, changed the certifica-tion procedure in favour of the employer, and eliminated the right of teachers to strike by declaring teaching an essential service. This was followed by the Skills Development and Fair Wage Repeal Act, which removed the require-ment for construction industry employers performing public works to hire trade union labour. In a stunning act of contempt, the government passed the Miscellaneous Statutes Amendment Act, which repealed amendments to the British Columbia Human Rights Code by the previous NDP government concerning discrimination in the payment of wages.

Recalling the worst days of Social Credit rule in the 1980s, the new year brought a stepped-up attack on the rights of public-sector unions. On 27 January 2002, the government invoked closure to pass the Education Services Collective Agreement Act, the Public Education Flexibility and Choice Act, and the Health and Social Services Delivery Improvement Act. Under the terms imposed by these Bills, the BC Teachers' Federation's existing contract was repealed and replaced by one imposed by a government-appointed arbi-trator. Nurses also saw their agreements reopened and a new contract imposed that rolled back the wages of 100,000 workers in the health sector, giving the government greater flexibility to contract out the provision of health care, close hospitals, and lay off workers.[22]

The government then turned its attention in May 2002 to a comprehensive overhaul of employment standards in the province. The changes reduced pro-visions for overtime benefits and the protections provided against employer abuse of overtime, removed a requirement to obtain permission to employ a child under 15 years of age, and even removed the requirement for farm pro-ducers to retain copies of payroll records of farm labour contractors. It went so far against basic democratic rights as to remove a general requirement to post a statement of employees' rights under the Labour Relations Act in a work-place. A series of anti-austerity and anti-privatization demonstrations erupted in 2002, organized by the Hospital Employees' Union (HEU), BC Federation of Labour, and other groups around the province. The HEU even erected a blockade to thwart the transportation of contracted-out linen services running from Chilliwack, BC, to Calgary, Alberta. But the government did not relent. On 31 March 2003, changes to the Human Rights Code Amendment Act came into force that eliminated the BC Human Rights Commission and replaced it with a tribunal headed by a politically appointed chair who controls procedures and serves as judge and jury. Also in 2003, the government ordered striking BC Ferries staff back to work and followed this up a year later with similar legislation ending a strike by 43,000 workers in long-term care facilities. The Liberals then introduced sweeping changes that prioritized using for-profit public-private partnerships to design, build, finance, operate, and/or maintain public infrastructure assets such as hospitals, highways, bridges, and transit projects.

A series of expenditure restraint measures for hospitals and health authorities resulted in a number of service cuts (e.g., cancelling elective surgeries), fee hikes (e.g., parking lot rates and private hospital rooms), and reductions to labour costs (e.g., freezes on hiring and overtime, layoffs).[23] While negotiations were taking place between unions and the Liberals to come up with an agreement around wage concessions, vacation time, job losses, and other items, a 2003 tentative agreement was swiftly rejected by 57 percent of HEU members. In a bizarre arrangement, the Industrial, Wood and Allied Workers (IWA) union signed "partnership agreements" in July 2003 to take on the now contracted-out positions under the employ of multinational corporations Sodexo, Aramark, and Compass. An HEU strike vote, held in March 2004, was endorsed by 90 percent. The provincial government quickly passed back-to-work legislation and imposed a new collective agreement. Wildcat solidarity strikes, protests, and new picket lines soon followed, culminating in a 40,000-strong protest in May 2004.[24] However, just as solidarity and union resistance reached their apogee in spring 2004, union negotiators and the Liberals were able to reach an agreement. Within the span of a few years, more than 9,000 HEU members had lost their jobs, wages had been slashed in half, and benefits were eliminated in newly contracted-out positions.[25]

In the fall of 2005, as negotiations with the school board association once again reached an impasse, BC teachers threatened an illegal strike. BC teachers were seeking three things: improved learning conditions, a fair salary increase, and restoration of bargaining rights after they had been declared an essential service. In coercive fashion, the Liberals responded by immediately imposing a wage freeze that extended the contract until June 2006. Teachers followed through with their threat of an illegal strike on 7 October, defying a court order to return to work as well as one forbidding the union to provide strike pay to its members.[26] The teachers' defiance compelled the government to appoint a mediator, who brokered an agreement ending the strike on 24 October. This was one of the few instances in which workers actually fought repressive legislation through direct action. Overwhelmingly, the union officials' response had been to comply and then appeal to the courts and/or work to change the government in the next election.

After attempts to challenge the government orders through the lower courts had failed, the case was brought before the Supreme Court of Canada. As will be discussed more fully in Chapter 8, in 2007, in a 6–1 ruling, three sections of the legislation were found to be constitutionally invalid – Sections 6.2 (no restrictions on contracting out), 6.4 (no requirement of consultation prior to contracting out), and 9 (relating to layoffs and bumping). The Court also instructed the government to compensate workers for their losses, but it did not terminate the contracts that had been struck with Sodexo, Aramark, and Compass. The HEU reached a settlement with the government in 2008, and this has provided some measure of compensation, retraining, and expanded rights for workers affected by contracting out. Collective bargaining has also led to an improvement in pay and benefits, but nominal wages for some occupations barely kept pace with what they were in 2002.

With the onset of the global financial crisis, the Liberals were forced to introduce a stimulus package to deal with the recession. The Campbell government imposed a contract on paramedics, who had been on strike for seven months. Represented by CUPE Local 873, 3,500 paramedics were seeking wage parity with other first responders, which would mean a 7 percent raise every year for three years. The Ambulance Services Collective Agreement Act, 2009, marked the first time in Canadian history that back-to-work legislation was passed in the midst of a contract vote. The wage increase was less than what BC Ambulance Services was offering, with the government stepping in to prevent a higher wage.[27] Budgets 2008–2011 included $20 billion for infrastructure spending on roads, transit, schools, and hospitals, $3.9 billion for health care spending, as well as tax relief for small businesses and cuts to personal income tax. The deep cuts to revenue-raising capacities, preceding but accelerated by the Liberals, exacerbated budgetary deficits as real provincial GDP contracted, setting the stage for a renewed bout of austerity and retrenchment that will be the focus of the next chapter.

Like BC, the assault against worker rights and social protections would reach new heights with the election of the Saskatchewan Party (SP) in 2007.

Established in 1997, the party arose as a coalition of disgruntled Liberal, Reform, and Conservative MLAs, positioning itself as a populist alternative to the NDP. Despite the non-ideological sounding name, the new party was an amalgam of pro-business and right-wing forces catering to business elites and social and fiscal conservatives drawn largely from rural areas in the province.[28] The party quickly rose to prominence, attracting urban business elites and, in particular, working- and middle-class supporters from the province's (largely male) natural resources sector. Upon forming government, Brad Wall's SP vowed to lower business and personal taxes, reduce royalty rents, "rebalance" labour laws, and get the province's books under control. These changes, however, were done less in the spirit of Mike Harris's "slash-and-burn" policies and more in the spirit of incrementalism – a series of small-scale reforms that actively expanded private market power. These changes were systematically transformative.[29]

The prairie provinces, in a sense, did not experience the severity of the 2007–2008 market downturn like much of the rest of Canada, and the party took power during an unprecedented global commodities boom. Increasing world demand from emerging markets for natural resources and food commodities helped maintain revenues, contributing to steady economic growth and job creation. This created the conditions for the SP to rapidly implement its free-market agenda of lower taxes, weakened labour laws, and reduced social services provisioning. Its first term in office prioritized spending restraint in most areas outside of public health.[30] This included reducing the size of the public service by 15 percent, as well as the restructuring and sale of a number of the province's Crown corporations under the SP's "SaskFirst" policy. The SP also moved to remake the province's education funding formula in ways that limited school board autonomy in budgeting and programming, redirecting the "surplus" to paying down provincial debt.

It was in the field of labour relations that the SP would cement the turn to exceptionalism and permanent austerity with the passing of Bill 5, the Public Service Essential Services Act (PSESA), and Bill 6, the Trade Union Amendment Act.[31] The PSESA created what was likely the broadest definition of "essential services" across the country. By effectively curtailing, if not eliminating, the right to strike for public-sector workers, the Act severely diminished the bargaining power of a wide range of workers employed by the provincial government, Crown corporations, regional health authorities, post-secondary institutions, and municipalities. So wide was the definition of essential service that any collective decision to, say, refuse overtime or engage in work-to-rule actions could be deemed illegal and subject to significant fines. Similarly, the Trade Union Amendment Act made it more difficult for workers to organize into new unions by expanding employers' ability to wage anti-union campaigns in the workplace through weakening legal protections that prevented threats and intimidation against union supporters. Bill 6 also abolished card-check certification by making certification votes mandatory and raising the threshold to obtain certification to 50 percent plus one of those in the new bargaining unit (rather than a simple majority of those voting), as any non-voter is counted against the union.[32]

Near the end of their first term, the SP passed into law Bill 80, An Act to Amend the Construction Industry Labour Relations Act, 2010, which ended the mandatory craft-based union representation model that had been in place since 1992. Bill 80 introduced union competition and allowed any trade union to organize a company on a multi-trade basis. Previously, employers had to be members of a representative employers' organization (REO). The REO would then bargain with each union representing a specific trade to set a provincewide collective agreement for that trade. Bill 80 did away with the REO requirement. Construction industry groups and employers supported the legislation, while labour organizations feared that Bill 80 was simply a means of allowing pro-business unions, like the Christian Labour Association of Canada (CLAC), access to the building trades.[33] For unions, this was another parallel with the 1980s Grant Devine government, which had crippled the building trades three decades earlier through legislative "reforms."[34]

Unlike Saskatchewan, Alberta has long been a province dominated by Conservative rule.[35] In office since 1971, questions of leadership and factional rivalries would besiege the Alberta Progressive Conservatives into the early 2000s. Despite maintaining a grip over provincial politics, the far-right Wildrose-Alliance Party was rapidly gaining ground in jurisdictions once thought of as PC strongholds. Between 2006 and 2014, the PCs had five different premiers and seven ministers of finance.[36] With the onset of the global financial crisis, provincial revenues collapsed, as royalties and fees from the oil and natural gas sector fell from a high of more than 40 percent of provincial revenues in 2005–2006 to just shy of 18 percent in 2014–2015. Rather than retreat from neoliberal dogma and using the recession as an opportunity to rethink fiscal and economic policy, the PCs responded to the decline by withdrawing billions from the Sustainability Fund and maintaining a program of austerity lite.[37]

Unlike the Klein Revolution of the mid-1990s, there were no across-the-board funding cuts to programs; instead, they nibbled away at the margins.

The PCs were willing to borrow for infrastructure improvements, but this deficit financing was otherwise matched by spending cuts of 2–4 percent factoring in inflation. Aside from some minor increases to user fees for several provincial services, tax increases and changes to revenue streams were not considered. Provincial income and corporate taxes were frozen at the "flat" rate of 10 percent, as were taxes on tobacco and alcohol. The government initiated a comprehensive review of the more than 800 provincially run programs, then rapidly transitioned to a program of zero-based budgeting as a way to reduce and eventually eliminate the provincial deficit in the same way that the Klein government had used performance-based budgeting to justify its austerity program of the mid-1990s.

Despite the instability in the PC party, austerity and coercion worked hand in hand to restrict trade union rights and freedoms and quash any inklings of working-class organization. Bill 26, the Labour Relations Amendment Act, 2008, eliminated the right of ambulance workers to strike if a new agreement could not be reached in bargaining. Instead, binding arbitration would be imposed. The new Act also affected the ability of construction workers to organize. New hires who had been employed for less than 30 days and employees who quit between the time of the application for certification and the secret ballot vote were no longer eligible to participate in the certification vote. And if certification is ratified in favour of the members, they have 90 days to decertify the union if they wish to do so through a vote. These changes were designed to prevent the practice of "salting" by unions – that is, having a few strategically placed union activists within the workplace spearhead a union drive. The creation of market enhancement recovery funds (MERFs), which were used by union contractors to submit more competitive bids for projects in relation to non-union contractors, was also restricted. The idea behind MERFs is that they would act as a pool of funds that would then be used as wage subsidies to make a union contractor's bid more competitive when compared to a non-union contractor.[38]

Like Saskatchewan and, to a lesser extent, Alberta, the Great Recession was milder and shorter for Manitoba compared with central and eastern Canada. Part of the explanation for this lies in the province's generally diversified economy and slightly larger proportion of public-sector employment compared with most regions. As noted in the previous chapter, the neoliberal turn in Manitoba was made by the PC government of Gary Filmon (1988–1999), which mandated balanced budget legislation, required a public referendum to raise any of the province's major taxes, and made it more difficult for workers to unionize. The considerable pushback against these measures subsequently led to 17 years of NDP rule. Rather than retreat from the neoliberal project, the NDP largely embedded it, reversing some but not all of the PCs changes. In many ways, the Manitoba NDP's time in government demonstrated a general alignment with twenty-first-century neoliberalism consistent with the interests of Manitoba capital in keeping alternative voices from mobilizing politically against the NDP.[39]

Upon forming government, the Doer NDP brought back card-based certification, albeit with a 65 threshold rather than the 55 when Filmon took office. Health care and education funding was increased, but the government stopped short of reversing the draconian cuts to social assistance and housing. As Errol Black and Jim Silver have noted, over time, the Doer governments largely abandoned the idea of challenging dominant ideas and powerful forces.[40] But unlike the PCs' widespread cuts to public services and privatizations in the 1990s, the NDP proceeded with selective restraint measures that trimmed rather than slashed spending. In 2010, the government amended the balanced budget legislation to allow deficits during an economic recovery period lasting from April 2010 to March 2014. The government's five-year economic plan devoted the majority of new spending to health care, with half of all government departments seeing spending reduced.[41] The budget also announced the elimination of the general corporation capital tax and a range of other boutique tax cuts, leading Finance Minister Rosann Wowchuk to boast: "In total, the tax cuts delivered by our government since 1999 will save Manitoba families and businesses more than $1.1 billion each year including $455 million in personal tax savings, $269 million in property tax reductions and $422 million in business tax cuts."[42] Successive NDP governments have managed to avoid outright class conflict, taking a corporatist approach that integrates and negotiates austerity. However, as time would tell, the NDP was merely preparing the ground for the assault that was to come.

ATLANTIC CANADA: AUSTERITY AND A LABOUR MOVEMENT BECALMED

As discussed in earlier chapters, the four provinces that make up Atlantic Canada share a modern history of economic and fiscal crisis brought on by economic underdevelopment, dependence upon a few resource extractive industries, and small but powerful regional elites. In mainstream media accounts, Atlantic Canada is routinely characterized as a "have-not" region. What is less familiar is its history of class struggle, which has exploded at different points. From the 1970s fishers' strike in Nova Scotia to organizing the fishing industry in Newfoundland, all examples underscore a "strong culture of resistance ... symptomatic of an economy focused on export-based resource extraction."[43] Economies based on resource extraction are prone to the boom-and-bust cycles of the commodities produced, so when the natural resources are depleted or fall in value, the jobs disappear or wages are pushed lower. And that history has informed episodes of government boom-and-bust fiscal policy, with an increasing emphasis on the bust. Various standard metrics underscore how Atlantic provincial governments have embraced structural adjustment policies, to the detriment of workers.[44] One real effect of this restructuring and the attendant government policies to subdue trade unions in the region was a marked decline in strike action in both the public and private sectors. The reduction in strikes and lockouts between 1980 and 2000 is particularly telling, dropping 84 percent in New Brunswick, 80 percent in Nova Scotia, more than 67 percent in Newfoundland, and PEI – where the history of labour relations was rather placid, save for a hot period in the early 1980s, where nine private-sector strikes took place – had by 2000 become significant if only for its total absence of strike action. Turning to public-sector strikes specifically, 1981 was a high water mark, where there were 64 public-sector strikes (but none in PEI). In 2000, the total sum of strikes in the Atlantic provinces' public sectors was ten.[45] Thom Workman suggests this quietude was the result of workers' fear of job loss and they thus "strategically pulled back."[46] The real unemployment rate across the region (meaning the unemployment rate that includes not only those formally unemployed and looking for work but also discouraged workers who have given up on searching, those waiting for recall, and workers not working the number of hours they wish) was in 2000 markedly higher than the Canadian rate of 9.9 percent. In Newfoundland the rate was 26.8 percent, Nova Scotia was 13.7 percent, PEI was 16.6 percent, and New Brunswick was 14.9 percent.[47]

One consequence of the decline in militancy was a measurable decline in real wages in three of the four provinces between 1992 and 2001. Nova Scotia led the decline through this period with a 7.7 percent drop, followed by Newfoundland, where the decline was 5.8 percent. The story in Prince Edward Island was uneven as the Confederation Bridge construction project raised overall wages between 1992 and 1997, but once complete, real wages declined by 7.7 percent between 1997 and 2001. Only in New Brunswick, despite fluctuations, did real wages remain stable but flat.[48]

The political and tactical conservatism of Atlantic Canada's trade unions from the late 1990s into the first two decades of the twenty-first century can be partially explained by the foregoing economic context – reversion to what former British Labour Party leader Neil Kinnock labelled a "dented shield" strategy. In other words, a protected retreat from the battlefield. And as we will see, the reliance by unions on legal mechanisms to challenge the legislative assaults by governments suggests that more political, mass mobilization strategies are seen as too risky with uncertain outcomes. And here is the conundrum facing trade unions and their various allies. The hard-fought-and-won array of labour laws regulating the employment relationship – including hours of work, minimum wages, collective bargaining, health, and safety – also "undermine any further evolution in the class struggle against capital."[49] The second paradox is that class struggle in Atlantic Canada is weak, and thus serious progressive reform and upgrading of labour protections are simply not on the agenda. The effective depoliticization/demobilization of the Atlantic Canadian working class concretely has meant that what labour protections exist tend to be relatively weak in comparison to those in other provinces and so a class power imbalance is locked in that heavily privileges capital.

The other key dimension in Atlantic Canada is the relative size of the provincial public sector. In each of the four provinces, public-sector employment accounts for 25 to 28 percent of total workforce. In other words, public expenditures provide not just important public services but jobs for the workers who produce and deliver these services. The fiscal health of each province at any given period, regardless of the party holding governmental power, is of central importance. And federal transfers, given the noted underdevelopment of the Atlantic provinces, have historically been critical to ensuring fiscal stability. In that respect, a key destabilizing event was the 1995 federal budget during the government of Jean Chrétien and his finance minister, Paul Martin, where transfer payments were dramatically cut, which in turn "forced provincial governments to cut expenditures."[50]

While the global economy reeled from the 2008 financial crisis and its aftershocks, Canada generally and specifically the Atlantic provinces fared relatively well compared to other jurisdictions. That is not to say they were unscathed. Between 2008 and 2010, job losses in the region were uneven, totalling for Newfoundland a loss of 5.6 percent, Nova Scotia lost 4.4 percent, and New Brunswick lost 1.3 percent. PEI broke the pattern by posting a

1.6 percent increase in employment.[51] Already scarred by the 1995 loss of
federal transfer monies, these provinces were left with the challenge of attempting to design and implement policies to facilitate economic growth
while tightly managing public expenditures.

Into the first decade of the twenty-first century, austerity generally prevailed over the fiscal policy and politics of each province. The notable exception is, of course, Newfoundland and Labrador, where the windfall of offshore
oil royalties gave that province considerable fiscal capacity to reinvest in public services. For other provinces, the new century would be one of continued austerity. Paradoxically, in Nova Scotia, the turn to an aggressive form
of austerity and attacks on public-sector workers began with the unexpected
2009 victory of the NDP.[52] Prior to the NDP's ascent to government, budgets from 2002 to 2008 all posted surpluses, which enabled the government
to reduce various tax rates rather than invest in public services or roll back
previous cuts. The NDP government confronted a deficit of $592 million that
they chose to address with a spending cut of $772 million over four years.
It was estimated that the NDP budget cuts cost the province 10,000 jobs.[53]
Nothing so dramatic would prevail in New Brunswick, but it did enter the
first decade of the twenty-first century as the growth of the 1990s faded.[54]
Both the Liberals and Conservatives would alternate in government and do
so frequently. Indeed, from 2007 forward, New Brunswick was home to the
highest rate of government turnover in Canada. One consequence of this
instability was that the province confronted unrelenting demands for fiscal
discipline from both provincial business interests and from the federal government, as well as American credit rating agencies.[55] New Brunswick fiscal
policy from 2000 to 2009, as captured in the government's annual budgets,
was a conservative exercise for a poor province. A string of budget surpluses
was converted to tax cuts for small business and corporations alike. In 2004,
the budget took a nastier turn, with the elimination of 750 public-sector jobs
although via attrition. But here again, reflecting the Janus-like approach to
budget policy, health spending was increased 5.2 percent. A string of surpluses running from 2005 through to 2008 returned to a mix of business tax
cuts and additional spending on health care, education, and infrastructure.
The impact of the 2008 crisis was reflected in the ensuing budgets of 2009 to
2013, where significant deficits ranged from a low of $183 million in 2012 to
a high of $754 million in 2010. The government responded to this fiscal stress
with a mix of budget and tax cuts and, at certain points, modest increases in
expenditures. The unrelenting fiscal stress meant that public-sector workers

and their unions would face various general and specific interventions by the province to limit their rights. In this respect, a notable intervention took place in 2009 when the Liberal government of Sean Graham introduced Bill 41, the Essential Services in Nursing Homes Act. This legislation empowered support worker and homecare employers to propose to the Labour Board which nursing home employees should be declared essential in the event of a strike at one of the province's private nursing homes.

In Newfoundland, the fiscal context was initially similar, as budgets from 2000 to 2002 all ran deficits, but no major cuts and no significant new expenditures were made. However, in 2003, with an election in the offing, the province increased spending on health and education while cutting corporate taxes. The smoke and mirrors disappeared post-election with the Conservatives now in government, confronting a deficit of $840 million. To address this, the government turned to austerity, with a commitment to cut 4,000 public-sector jobs, representing 12.5 percent of the public-sector total workforce. In addition, the salaries of public-sector workers were frozen for two years. However, unlike other Atlantic provinces, Newfoundland was about to reap the fiscal benefits of both higher prices for offshore oil and increased federal transfers. While Premier Danny Williams' government's cuts fuelled conflict with public-sector workers, the growth in revenues provided the fiscal capacity to address a range of issues confronting those workers. This included the government's surprise decision to fund pay equity demands (in 2006) and increase the minimum wage (in 2007), which would continually increase for several years to become the highest in Canada. The Williams government also agreed to significant wage increases for public-sector workers totalling 20 percent over four years (2008), and settled a high-stakes conflict with the province's nurses' union, which had militantly pursued their members' interests to the point of a strike (2009).[56]

In late 2010, Kathy Dunderdale replaced Williams as premier and she made efforts to keep relations with public-sector unions positive. She went on to win the 2011 election, in part because of this strategy, and there was "little reason to believe that the labour movement" was "dissatisfied overall with the Progressive Conservatives' new version of neoliberalism."[57] However, this did not mean that unions had an ally in the premier's office. In 2012, she introduced Bill 38, An Act to Amend the Public Service Collective Bargaining Act. This legislation permitted the government to direct the Labour Relations Board to submit the final offer of government, as the employer, to a vote of bargaining unit members. The end result was that it was possible that there could be a situation where the union has spent considerable time engaging members in order to obtain a strike mandate from the membership, only to find the government forcing members to vote again, bargaining unit by bargaining unit.[58] With Dunderdale's resignation in 2014, Tom Marshall became interim party leader and premier. His government introduced Bill 22, An Act to Amend the Labour Relations Act, in 2014. This legislation reintroduced secret ballot union certification when 65 percent or more members of a proposed bargaining unit signed a union card, even if card-check certification existed. It further stipulated that during a union certification vote, 50 percent plus one of all bargaining unit members must vote in favour of unionization (meaning that not voting was in effect a vote against unionization).[59] In sum, the later Williams (despite a rough start) and Dunderdale governments marked something of a break from the assaults on public-sector workers' rights that had stretched back to the 1980s Peckford government.

Through the first decade of the twenty-first century, PEI continued to have the lowest incomes in Canada and a chronically high unemployment rate, oscillating between 12 and 19 percent.[60] As a result, the province remained largely dependent upon federal transfer programs, such as regional development grants, equalization disbursements, and health and social transfers equivalent to some 40 percent of provincial government revenues.[61] As noted earlier, Premier Joe Ghiz's Liberal government was largely accommodating of modest improvements to labour policy. Strategic interventions to roll back worker rights were simply not necessary. The exception to this was Bill 35, An Act to Amend the Labour Act, which came into effect 1 January 2011.[62] This legislation added employees of ambulance service providers as well as dispatchers for police, fire, and ambulance services to the list of essential workers who were denied the right to strike, forcing them to rely on binding arbitration if bargaining failed.

The Atlantic Accord of 2005, struck between the federal government and Nova Scotia/Newfoundland and Labrador, provided these oil- and natural gas-producing provinces with new fiscal capacity. For Nova Scotia, this meant several years of budget surpluses until the 2008 crisis struck. In 2006, Hamm resigned from the premiership and was replaced by Rodney Macdonald. Macdonald was not particularly committed to austerity and indeed moved to rescind the Hamm budget constraints in 2009, but his government was defeated in the legislature vote to do exactly that. The ensuing election surprised everyone in delivering an Atlantic Canada first – an NDP victory, wherein Darrell Dexter became the province's first social democratic premier. The party's election platform proposed several modest initiatives. This included the creation of 2,200 jobs; a 50 percent rebate on the provincial sales tax on new homes; a commitment to reduce wait times for medical procedures; a plan to stem the out-migration of young workers and professionals; removal of the 8 percent harmonized sales tax (HST) on electricity consumption; upgrading rural roads; and a commitment to expanding home care for seniors. These new initiatives would be pursued within a context of public expenditure restraint.

Upon forming government, the NDP moved quickly to appoint an independent auditor to review the province's public finances. The platform did not raise a single standard social democratic policy commitment.[63] The media thus came to characterize the NS NDP as a "party focused on tweaking government – and pursuing cautious change."[64] The promised financial review concluded that Nova Scotia's public finances were seriously out of balance and projected ongoing deficits of $1.3 billion.[65] The 2010 budget centred on shrinking the deficit. A turn to austerity was announced, where $1.1 billion in public expenditures was to be cut. Practically, this meant public-sector wage restraint, cutting the public service workforce by 10 percent, and the public service pension plan was to be deindexed with increases limited to 1.25 percent per annum for five years.[66] Despite the restraint, deficits continued. While the NDP did not engage in an all-out assault with public-sector unions, towards the end of its first and only term, it forced paramedics back to work (Bill 86, the Ambulance Services Continuation Act) after they voted to reject the employer's offer. Not only did the legislation bar the paramedics from striking but it required final offer selection.[67] The 2013 election would see the NDP returned to third-party status and replaced in government by the Liberals, led by Stephen McNeil.

ONTARIO AND QUEBEC: THE MYTH OF "PROGRESSIVE" LIBERALISM

Through the provincial election of 2 October 2003, the Common Sense Revolution came to a formal end, with Dalton McGuinty leading the "third-way" Liberals into a majority government. The Liberals sought to create a distinct inclusionary and pragmatic centrist brand in contrast to the polarizing actions of the Common Sense Revolution, speaking of the need to reinvest in public services. This commitment to repair the damage done to public services over the previous eight years came with a platform committed to "keeping taxes down."[68] Between 2003 and 2010, the Liberals increased expenditures in the five main social program portfolios of health, education, post-secondary, social services, and children's services in the range of 6 to 8 percent. Despite the increases, the new investments still failed to put these services where they would have been if they had grown at the rate of inflation preceding the Harris Conservatives. Centrist intimations notwithstanding, the Liberals also privatized services formerly covered under the Ontario Health Insurance Plan, such as eye examinations, chiropractic therapy, and physical rehabilitation; they also spearheaded the expansion of private health care clinics and imposed a staggered health premium ranging between $60 and $900 per year.[69]

Despite these new investments, the Liberals had no desire to abandon the tax cuts implemented through the course of the Common Sense Revolution. Although public expenditures increased, the revenue side of the ledger was largely ignored, and corporate tax rates were cut in the 2008 budget, adding to the $18 billion in lost revenue attributable to the 1995 deep tax cuts.[70] Further expression of continuity with important aspects of the Common Sense Revolution centred on labour policy. In this respect, the Liberals demonstrated no interest in reversing the Conservatives' rollback of NDP improvements to worker protection and collective bargaining rights, changes to employment standards, workers' compensation, and the Occupational Health and Safety Act.[71] By 2008, however, the Liberals' centrist rhetoric and political strategy began unravelling, with public-sector workers and their unions specifically coming under attack. At the request of social democratic Toronto mayor David Miller, the Liberals legislated striking transit employees back to work and followed this up by putting an end to an 85-day strike by contract faculty and teaching assistants at York University in 2009. As the tailwinds of the Great Recession swept across Ontario, the Liberal government responded by calling for a decade of austerity. The major policy plank of this program was the Open Ontario Plan (OOP), which called for tax relief, a wage freeze for public-sector workers, the privatization of public assets, and regressive reforms to employment standards legislation.[72]

The OOP signalled a new era of austerity and coercion that deepened and extended the neoliberal remaking of the province. The general corporate income tax (CIT) rate was reduced from 14 to 10 percent, along with the elimination of the small-business deduction surtax. The tax rate on the first $37,106 of personal taxable income was also reduced by more than 16 percent, from 6.05 to 5.05 percent, while those earning up to $80,000 per year saw a tax cut of 10 percent. This made Ontario's tax regime among the lowest of countries belonging to the Organisation for Economic Co-operation and Development (OECD). The OOP also cut the marginal effective tax rate in half by 2018, equivalent to some $4.6 billion in tax cuts on income and capital.

The omnibus Open for Business Act marked the revival of state coercion in the form of a legislative assault that introduced over a hundred amendments to legislation across ten ministries, and its stated objective was to create a more competitive business climate. The climate of restraint was further amplified through engaging the province's largest unions in less-than-genuine consultative negotiations, which sought to develop an austerity "framework agreement" that would see private- and public-sector unions moderate their bargaining demands.[73] This dynamic stifled free collective bargaining by using the recession as a rationale to extract concessions while extending new forms of corporate welfare and furthering the neoliberal remaking of the province. The Liberals also enacted the Public Sector Compensation Restraint to Protect Public Services Act and Broader Public Sector Accountability Act. The Acts imposed a two-year wage freeze for 350,000 non-unionized public-sector workers while also indirectly affecting 710,000 unionized public-sector workers through a proposed "voluntary" two-year wage freeze and concentrating new powers in the Management Board of the Cabinet. The Liberals clearly stated that they would not fund net compensation increases to operational costs associated with collective agreements. Throughout the consultations, they maintained that all options were on the table, including legislated wage freezes and furloughs, as well as a 5 percent reduction to local transfers if municipalities failed to hold the line on expenditures. Following the two-year freeze, wage increases were to be kept below inflation and not exceed the province's 1.9 percent cap on expenditure growth.

The Liberals also solicited CIBC World Markets and Goldman Sachs to come up with a plan to privatize the province's $60 billion worth of public assets. The idea behind "SuperCorp" was to combine Ontario's Crown assets, including nuclear power plants, power generation facilities, 29,000 kilometres of electrical transmission and distribution lines, and over 600 liquor stores and gaming operations. As Chapter 7 discusses more fully, the politically sensitive task of liquidating Ontario's assets was temporarily put on hold, however, to deal with the more immediate issue of reducing the deficit through public-sector service and employment cuts. As part of the OOP, Bill 68 replicated Alberta's and British Columbia's "self-help" model for complaints and enforcement under the Employment Standards Act (ESA). Under the changes, employees were required to address employment grievances directly with their employer in advance of government intervention – in other words, employees were expected to make all "reasonable efforts" to resolve the dispute individually on a case-by-case basis. The implications of this amendment to the ESA were twofold. First, it promoted voluntarism by creating the potential for employers to resist the process if they felt it would not work in their favour. Second, it privileged a mediated settlement over an actual award, which may expedite the claims process but could reduce the value of the settlement achieved by a worker. Regardless of the outcome of individual settlements, this orientation represents a transformation in the role of employment standards officers from those who make judgments based on fact-finding to mediators in a process that assumes two equal parties when, in fact, the parties are far from equal.[74] It is likewise telling to review what the McGuinty government chose not to do. Avoiding the question of raising taxes meant explicitly agreeing to allow Ontario's public economy to shrink. Without the slightest hint of irony, by the end of the decade the Liberals had come full circle back to the Common Sense Revolution.

In Quebec, austerity was legislatively embedded with the 1996 Act Respecting the Elimination of the Deficit and a Balanced Budget. Deficits were essentially prohibited with this legislation, and it further established that deficits, if incurred, were to be eliminated within five years. The objective was to constrain future governments' range of fiscal manoeuvre.[75] The fiscal table was thus set. The general election of 1998 saw the PQ re-elected with a majority government now led by Lucien Bouchard. Immediately, the new premier confronted pressure from the business sector to cut public expenditures. Politically, while Bouchard shared with business a similar economic vision for the province, the PQ's electoral success was tied to a broad coalition composed of labour and social movements. To engineer a political accord to bridge this divide, the Bouchard government turned to a strategy of social concertation to engage all of Quebec's key social and economic actors. The end result was a commitment to eliminate the deficit in two years without raising taxes and to reduce unemployment.[76] However, business representatives rejected proposals that imposed costs on their constituents. Indeed, the PQ government's allies in the labour and social movements had come to the view that "the PQ had made too many accommodations with neoliberalism and had exhausted much of the progressive energy that had surrounded its societal project a decade earlier."[77] Several legislative interventions by the PQ government into collective bargaining and social service delivery contributed to the growing rift.

The first of these was Bill 72, An Act Respecting the Provision of Nursing Services and Pharmaceutical Services, tabled in July 1999. The government was committed to its debt reduction goals and maintained that wage increases would be capped at 5 percent for three years. In addition, issues of work insecurity and higher expenditures for public services were not to be considered. Nursing union (Fédération des infirmières et infirmiers du Québec – FIIQ) demands included a 15 percent increase and the creation of permanent jobs in the health care system. In mid-June, 47,500 nurses commenced an illegal strike. The collection of union dues was suspended while the attorney general initiated legal proceedings against the 22 locals, seeking fines of $125,000 per day. In order to increase the pressure on strikers, the government proceeded to adopt Bill 72, which added new penalties for the union, including fines for union leadership and the suspension of the Rand formula for 12 weeks for every day the strike continued. The back-to work order was made effective 3 July 1999.

Despite this, the strike continued illegally with strong support from union members and in public opinion. The union proposed that a 48-hour truce be agreed to with a view to restarting negotiations. The result was an agreement in principle that did not include raising wages. The agreement was rejected by the members, but the strength of the movement was seriously undermined by the pause in the strike and the severity of the penalties now in play. After 23 days of strike action, the FIIQ agreed to mediation; this resulted in a new collective agreement containing a wage increase of 3 percent and a provision for the creation of 1,500 permanent jobs.[78] The Bouchard government's second intervention into labour relations came in November 2000. In this case, Port of Montreal truck drivers were attempting to unionize. The truckers were considered independent contractors as they were contracted by 51 different companies. The union seeking to represent the drivers, the National Road Transport Union (Syndicat National du Transport Routier, or SNTR), sought to have all the accreditations dealt with as a bloc by the Canada Industrial Relations Board (CIRB). However, employers and the Board wanted to evaluate each on a case-by-case basis. On 22 October, frustrated truckers initiated an illegal strike, thus paralyzing the movement of long-haul goods.[79]

In response, the government introduced Bill 157, An Act to Order the Resumption of Certain Road Freight Transport Services. One week later, the CIRB announced that it had rejected union accreditation in 33 of 51 claims. In response, and in defiance of the back-to-work legislation, the strike continued. However, on 19 November, the strikers capitulated and returned to work without substantive gains. The PQ government was defeated in the general election of 14 April 2003 and replaced by Jean Charest's Liberal Party. Wasting no time, the new government quickly unrolled a series of bills restricting labour rights (Bill 30 and Bill 31). Through 2003, the union movement mobilized against the government. The Common Front, composed of Quebec's trade union confederations, united around shared key bargaining points, including a purchasing power catchup (12.5 percent in three years), restrictions on precarious work, and a massive reinvestment in public services.

The Charest government's war on public-sector workers was officially launched on 17 June 2003 with the tabling of Bill 7, An Act to Amend the Act Respecting Health Services and Social Services. The Act decertified existing unions in facilities for people with disabilities and the elderly whose needs are lower than those residing in long-term care facilities and other health and social service agencies providing residential care. The Act decreed that workers in such facilities were independent contractors, not employees of the public institutions with which they were associated. In addition, the Ministry of Health and Social Services was empowered to negotiate with associations representing the facilities, not the workers, to establish service rates. Bill 30, An Act to Respecting Bargaining Units in the Social Affairs Sector and amending the Act respecting the process of negotiation of the collective agreements in the Public and Parapublic Sectors, followed on 11 November 2003. This legislation sought nothing less than to restructure the Quebec public sector with the primary aim of restricting public spending. To do so, the legislation empowered public-sector employers with the legal means to flexibilize their workforce.[80] Bill 30 was passed on 17 December 2003, establishing a ceiling of four bargaining units per health care employer, eliminating the right to strike, and instead stipulating mandatory arbitration. All affected unions challenged the legislation in a complaint to the ILO, and the ILO requested the government amend the legislation. While the Bill was declared invalid by the Quebec Superior Court on 30 November 2007, the government's successful appeal reversed that decision.[81] A mere two days after the tabling of Bill 30, on 13 November, the Charest government introduced Bill 31: An Act to Amend the Labour Code of Quebec. This legislation amended the Quebec Labour Code to allow employers to subcontract work with no guarantee of successor rights for their immediate employees. It was passed on 17 December 2003. Casting off any allusions to consent, the objective was plainly coercive: to flexibilize workers by facilitating non-standard and precarious employment arrangements.[82]

A fourth major intervention by the Charest government was Bill 142, An Act Respecting Conditions of Employment in the Public Sector, passed in 2005. The context for this case was the previous PQ government's initial negotiations with its 500,000 public-sector workers where the parties had agreed to extend the collective agreement for one year with a wage increase of 2 percent.[83] However, in June 2004, the new and now Liberal president of the Treasury Board declared that wage increases would be capped at a cumulative total of 12.6 percent over six years. The public-sector unions were incensed, particularly so because the government included within this cap any compensation increases arrived at through the implementation of the pay equity act.[84] The government was intransigent with respect to wages, and thus the Common Front opted to stage a four-day rotating strike. In response, on 18 November, the government tabled an ultimatum whereby collective agreements were to be signed by Christmas Day. The unions, however, continued to resist and on 14 December, 150,000 health and education workers went on a one-day strike.

A second one-day strike was planned for the following day, but the government convened an emergency session of the National Assembly, where Bill 142 was passed into law, thus forcing strikers back to work. Bill 142 was unique in the history of Quebec as it decreed the working conditions for 500,000 public-sector employees. However, unlike previous eras, this legislation was adopted in the absence of a general economic crisis.[85] Coercion was now part and parcel of the everyday makeup of neoliberal governance arrangements. The unions challenged the Bill at the Superior Court, which recognized that the government had not negotiated in good faith as required by the Quebec Labour Code. However, the Court confirmed the constitutionality of Bill 142, stating that budgets are a matter for the legislature to decide; decisions to restrain public expenditures are not to be considered an impediment to the collective bargaining process even if such fiscal restraints inform negotiations with respect to compensation. The turbulent Charest era came to an end in August 2012 when the PQ, under the leadership of Pauline Marois, returned to government having campaigned on a modestly progressive platform.

CONCLUSION: A DEEPENING DIVIDE

Canada's ten provinces have been likened to laboratories – places where diverse social and economic policy experiments can take place. That may have been more accurate through the post-1945 period of economic growth, expansion of social programs, and the modest state-led version of a mixed economy than it was through the neoliberal era. The application of coercive interventions and policies in the ten provinces (and, to a lesser extent, territories) and the federal state through the first decade and a half of the twenty-first century reveals a multilevel consistency in politics and policy in contrast to an earlier era of diverse responses. Before the 2008 crisis struck, every jurisdiction, federal and provincial, irrespective of governing party, rolled out public-sector austerity through legislative interventions to constrain public-sector wages, suspend collective bargaining, and command striking private-sector workers back to work. These interventions differed in detail and focus by jurisdiction, but all shared a common objective in stifling both trade union rights and public expenditures.

As the 2008 global financial crisis morphed into a general economic crisis, it provided something of an interregnum between two periods of austerity as Canadian governments responded with emergency monetary stimulus. But as the crisis wound down, a more aggressively interventionist approach would return. Taken as a whole, the period revealed the extent to which organized labour, including its community-based allies, had been weakened through the previous three decades of ideological and political assault by the Canadian state. It also vividly demonstrated that Canadian social democracy, whether housed in the NDP or PQ, had reached its limits politically in its inability to defend working-class interests.

CHAPTER SEVEN

From Great Recession to COVID-19 Crisis

Chapter Summary: The second decade of the twenty-first century saw the post-2008 fiscal consolidations observed in most Canadian provinces take an authoritarian turn. This included not only a repudiation of the most basic parliamentary principles of legislative debate and public scrutiny, but also a remarkable multiplication of both new constraints on collective bargaining and the right to strike, as well as legalized restrictions on trade union and community-based groups' right to assembly and protest. Although the defeat of the Harper Conservatives in the 2015 federal election rolled back some of the most draconian aspects of the former government, the election of the Justin Trudeau-led Liberals was more a return to the status quo than a progressive leap forward. At the same time, the provinces sought to make permanent the "austerity state" while eroding the remaining vestiges of the postwar social compact. Where the 2008 financial crisis had defined the previous decade, this second decade would be defined by the shock of the first global pandemic in more than a century. Among the many morbid symptoms revealed by the pandemic – particularly the weakening of organized labour as a social and political force – was the breadth and depth of inequality in Canadian society.

INTRODUCTION

On 19 October 2015, the federal Liberals, led by Justin Trudeau, were pro-
pelled from third-party status to form a majority government. The election
of the Liberals was as much a repudiation of the Harper Decade – its social
conservatism, lean welfare state, weakened regulatory agencies, and general
disdain for a strong public investments and unions – as it was of an NDP
devoid of any remaining vestiges of social democracy. Whereas the Liberals
moved left on a platform of deficit-financed investment and infrastructure
spending, the NDP under Thomas Mulcair moved right, pledging to balance
the budget in their first term. Through the election, the Trudeau Liberals actively courted labour, promising improved relations and greater legislative
input. However, the 2015 federal election was less transformative than it was
a "return to normal" – the quiet consolidation of neoliberalism in the context of a defeated working-class opposition. In this regard, while the Trudeau
Liberals rescinded the most contentious aspects of the previous government's
approach to labour relations, they largely maintained the status quo – albeit
with select "progressive" interventions – in order to secure the broader subordination of labour consistent with what the state and capital would accommodate in an era of permanent exceptionalism.

It was in the provinces where coercion would take centre stage, particularly among Conservative parties in the Prairies, as every step previously
taken forward resulted in two back. The assault included not only a barrage of
regressive work and labour laws, but rollbacks to a range of income supports
and broader social services. The second decade of the twenty-first century
saw not only an ongoing austerity regime but the acceleration of authoritarian
tendencies that repudiated the most basic parliamentary principles of legislative debate and public scrutiny. It also held a remarkable multiplication of
legalized restrictions on trade union and community-based groups' right to
assembly and protest.

TRUDEAU PART TWO

Through their first term (2015–2019), the Liberals made good on their promise to repeal Bills C-377 and C-525, saying that doing so was necessary to restore a "fair and balanced approach" to federal labour relations. As a result of
a recent Supreme Court decision, to be discussed further in the next chapter,

they followed this up with the enactment of Bill C-7, which extended collective bargaining rights to the Royal Canadian Mounted Police. Central to the Liberals' labour reforms were changes to the Canada Labour Code, and they introduced Bill C-65, An Act to Amend the Canada Labour Code, which extended protections for workers in federally regulated industries such as banking, broadcasting, and aviation, as well as Crown corporations and agencies, against harassment and violence. The Act also extended some protections to Parliament Hill staff, including Commons and Senate employees, and political staffers in the offices of individual MPs and senators. Bills C-63 and C-86 introduced a suite of changes for workers in federally regulated industries, including increased vacation and holiday pay entitlements based on years of service; enhanced leaves, breaks, and rest periods; improved requirements for work scheduling and overtime; strengthened protections against employee misclassification; and a requirement to consult with employees that request flexible work arrangements.

With about 10 percent of the total workforce subject to the Canada Labour Code, these changes were certainly in the spirit of an earlier era of consent where the predominant view was that the federal government should lead rather than follow that of the private sector. However, the Liberals stopped short of fundamental change, including support for an NDP private members' bill that introduced an amendment to the Canada Labour Code preventing the use of scabs during a lockout or a strike – like in British Columbia and Quebec – as it would "upset the balance in labour relations."[1] When it came to legislating workers back to work, however, the Liberals did not exhibit the same reluctance. After more than a year of unsuccessful negotiations, on 22 October 2018, CUPW workers staged a series of rotating strikes in Victoria, Edmonton, and Windsor. The main issues in bargaining revolved around job security and pay equity between urban and suburban/rural mail carriers, as well as health and safety issues related to increased parcel delivery and the use of forced overtime. Consistent with long-term patterns (see Table 7.1), within a month, Bill C-89, the Postal Services Resumption and Continuation Act, legislated employees back to work and granted a mediator-arbitrator the power to enact their own ruling or resort to final offer selection. To get around court rulings that invalidated the previous Conservative government's Bill C-6, the legislation did not mandate particular constraints but rather that a solution be reached within 90 days. After both parties agreed to an extension, a final ruling was reached a year later that saw both urban and suburban/rural letter carriers receive 2 percent pay increases, improved job security for urban

Table 7.1. Back-to-Work Measures, 1950–2021

Year	Federal	Provincial	Total	Annual Average
1950–1959	2	1	3	0.3
1960–1969	4	9	13	0.6
1970–1979	10	31	41	4.5
1980–1989	6	43	49	5.4
1990–1999	9	16	25	2.7
2000–2009	2	23	25	2.7
2010–2021	6	6	12	0.9

carriers, and a new committee to study the workloads of rural and suburban mail carriers.[2]

Though the Trudeau Liberals' first term in government did not see a repeat of the outright class war reminiscent of the Harper era, it did see the Liberals use coercion when consent failed to achieve its desired outcomes. While much has been made of the Liberals' willingness to use deficit spending, this was not, as has been frequently claimed, an outright repudiation of neoliberalism and austerity as it was a deepening of commodity relations linking institutional structures to the totality of capitalism. The Liberals have done little to address rising income and wealth inequality, even extending tax breaks for corporations to the tune of $10.5 billion to remain "competitive" with the Trump administration in the United States.[3] With regard to revenue-raising capacities, here too the Liberals have largely continued along the path established by the Harper regime, despite introducing a small personal income tax rate increase for those earning $200,000 or more. Instead, the Liberals rebuked earlier campaign promises to cap the tax deduction available for stock options and to take on corporate tax avoidance by digital giants.[4] As a percentage of Canada's national GDP, federal revenues stood at 15 percent in 2019 – three points lower than where federal revenues stood in 1992, before three decades of tax cuts for the wealthy.[5] The Liberals also established the Canada Infrastructure Bank (CIB), with $35 billion in public money to help finance infrastructure. However, as a condition of receiving grant monies, the new agency must mandate public-private partnerships (P3s). The CIB is the brainchild of Wall Street titan Larry Fink, head of the world's largest investment firm, BlackRock, with input from key figures central to Canada's business and financial community.[6] Corporate and pension-fund backers have already announced they expect returns of 8 to 10 percent on their investments. A growing mountain of evidence from

Canada and abroad has found P3s to be more costly and less transparent than traditional public procurement.[7]

The Trudeau Liberals were re-elected in 2019, though they were reduced to a minority government. This did not deter them from driving through back-to-work legislation, however. On 10 August 2020, 1,500 Port of Montreal dock workers with CUPE Local 375 walked off the job after having tried in vain for two years to negotiate a new contract. At the urging of business groups, the governments of François Legault in Quebec and Doug Ford in Ontario pressed the federal government to intervene to force the strikers to return to their jobs.[8] At the time, Labour Minister Filomena Tassi wrote, "Our government has faith in the collective bargaining process, as we know the best deals are made at the table," which the Mining Association of Canada (MAC) called "incomprehensible."[9] In response, the Maritime Employers Association announced its intention to hire scabs to unload the sitting containers. However, on 21 August, a truce was called as the two sides agreed to resume negotiations.[10]

After eight more months of fruitless deliberation, job actions resumed on 19 April 2021, in response to the employers' unilateral alteration of working conditions, including enhanced management rights to alter schedules and an end to job security for workers. A day later, Labour Minister Tassi introduced back-to-work legislation ending the one-day-old strike, saying the economic and health toll is too high to let the dispute continue. Bill C-29, An Act to Provide for the Resumption and Continuation of Operations at the Port of Montreal, allowed for arbitration to be imposed in matters that cannot be resolved through mediation. There was a cruel irony in that the legislation was introduced on the National Day of Mourning for workers who have been injured or lost their lives on the job. One year after the federal government adopted back-to-work legislation to force an end to the strike, longshore workers denounced what it called "bad faith" at the negotiating table from the Maritime Employers Association, including failing to be available for talks.[11]

In the context of continued coercive measures, working-class Canadians continued to struggle, with nearly half of the country's population estimated to be some $200 away from insolvency at the end of each month.[12] In fact, since the Liberals came to office, the amount of money stashed away in tax havens by the richest Canadians has nearly doubled to $353 billion. Journalist Martin Lukacs has referred to the Liberals' ability to implement modest reforms on the one hand – better representation of women and racialized persons in cabinet, tinkering with labour legislation, incremental measures to reduce carbon emissions – and, on the other, its commitment to free-market orthodoxy – expansion of extractive industries, ongoing maltreatment of Indigenous communities in Canada, increased military spending, growing inequality – as "changeless-change." In other words, the Trudeau Formula utilizes grand virtue-signalling that helps dissuade movements from leading more aggressive challenges to government actions even when those actions represent the maintenance of the status quo.[13]

With the onset of the COVID-19 pandemic, the Liberals responded with a number of relief programs both for individuals and businesses. While an in-depth examination is not possible here, some points are worth noting. Key measures included $60 billion (2.7 percent of GDP) for the health system to support increased testing, vaccine development, medical supplies, and mitigation efforts; $290 billion (13 percent of GDP) in direct aid to households and firms, including wage subsidies, payments to workers without sick leave, and enhanced access to Employment Insurance, as well as an increase in existing GST tax credits and child care benefits; and approximately $85 billion (3.9 percent of GDP) in liquidity support through tax deferrals.[14] For individuals, the Canada Emergency Response Benefit (CERB) was one of the government's signature COVID-19 supports, providing a 75 percent wage subsidy between March and October 2020 that was equal to roughly $80 billion for 9 million people who had lost income as a result of the pandemic. Eligible recipients – those 15 years of age and older and who had earned a minimum of $5,000 in 2019 or in the 12 months prior to the date of their application – received a taxable benefit of $2,000 for up to 28 weeks.[15]

In autumn of 2020, the Liberals transitioned CERB beneficiaries to an expanded EI program and three new benefits called the Canada Recovery Benefit (CRB), the Canada Recovery Sickness Benefit (CRSB), and the Canada Recovery Caregiving Benefit (CRCB). Designed for self-employed workers or those who are not eligible for EI but still requiring support, the CRB provided $500 for 54 weeks to those who saw their income drop by at least 50 percent. The CRSB provided $500 per week for those who could not work due to illness or having to self-isolate in the pandemic, up to a maximum of four weeks. The CRCB provided income support to employed and self-employed individuals who were unable to work for at least 50 percent of the week because they needed to care for their child under 12 years of age or a family member who needed supervised care. Recipients received $500 for a one-week period and were required to reapply each week to continue receiving the benefit, up to a maximum of 42 weeks per household.

The Canada Child Benefit (CCB) provided temporary additional support in 2021 of up to three payments of $1,200 to families with children under the age of six. The Canada Workers Benefit (CWB) provided a refundable tax credit ranging from $1,400 for individuals and those without children to $2,400 for workers with families to help people who were working and earning a low income.[16] The Liberals also passed Bill C-30, the Budget Implementation Act, in 2021. This legislation introduced some changes impacting federally regulated workplaces, including increasing the federal minimum wage to $15 per hour at the end of 2021 and tying it to inflation; extended COVID-19–related leave from 38 weeks to 42 weeks; extended medical leave from 17 to 27 weeks; and an increase to maximum EI sickness benefits from 15 to 26 weeks.

For businesses, the largest of these programs was the Canada Emergency Wage Subsidy (CEWS) with an estimated cost of $86 billion and a further $26 billion in the fiscal year 2021–2022.[17] The program covered up to 75 percent of payroll costs for businesses that have seen revenue declines as a result of COVID-19. The Canada Emergency Rent Subsidy (CERS) provided support to tenants and property owners through a subsidy for their rent or property ownership costs estimated to total $8.4 billion. Finally, the Canada Recovery Hiring Program (CRHP) provided eligible employers with a subsidy of up to 50 percent of the incremental remuneration paid to eligible employees, up to a maximum of $1,129/week per employee, between 6 June and 20 November 2021. The program, worth an estimated $600 million, was intended to offset a portion of the additional costs that employers take on as they reopen, by increasing wages, hours worked, or by hiring more staff.

While it is still too early to determine what the longer-term impacts of these combined measures will be, early indications suggest that hundreds of millions intended to preserve jobs instead went to bolstering the profit margins of some of Canada's largest employers. An analysis by the *Globe and Mail* found that the median CEO pay at the 100 largest Toronto Stock Exchange-listed Canadian companies was up nearly 1.4 percent in 2020–2021 to $7.65 million; one-third of the CEOs made at least $10 million, and six made $20 million or more – both higher proportions than in 2019.[18] Likewise, after negotiating a $5 billion support package from the federal government, Air Canada sparked outrage when it revealed it had previously paid a total of $10 million in bonuses in early 2021.[19] And in cases of salary reductions for Canada's top earners, these were more than compensated through cash bonuses, stock options, and awards. In fact, 50 of Canada's largest companies made record profits, growing their margins by more than 50 percent during the COVID-19 pandemic, while another 50 increased their historical profit margins all the while paying effectively lower tax rates.[20] In the face of public outcry, Bill C-30 introduced a CEWS repayment framework for certain publicly listed companies if the total executive compensation in 2021 exceeded the amount paid in 2019, but this remains to be seen. Deficit spending rarely reveals much about the character of state intervention. But in this case, far from a second coming of Keynesianism, the broad thrust of the Liberals' efforts has been conservative – to ensure that neoliberal capitalism remains intact, lest "Canadians eventually begin to entertain more radical options," as Justin Trudeau himself once quipped.[21] In this regard: plus ça change, plus c'est la même chose!

BRITISH COLUMBIA AND THE PRAIRIE PROVINCES: AN AUTHORITARIAN TURN?

In 2011, the BC Liberals were re-elected with a majority government. The previous decade of Liberal rule had resulted in severe austerity and labour coercion, leaving very little "waste" to cut in the context of the global financial crisis. With Christy Clark replacing unpopular leader Gordon Campbell, the Liberals would set upon their first task of maintaining the province's AAA rating by focusing on eliminating the provincial deficit. Rather than address the province's recurring revenue constraints, the Liberals sought to maintain existing commitments to health care, education, and social services through the sale of public assets and temporary increases to personal income taxes for those earning over $150,000. Together, these one-time fiscal injections were estimated to raise $625 million over two years. The Clark government also increased premiums for the province's medical services plan by 4 percent, generating some $2.4 billion by 2015–2016, even as health care spending fell year over year as a percentage of GDP.[22] While the cuts were minor compared with the draconian austerity of the 1980s, there was not much left to cut given earlier rounds of restraint that saw public-sector employment as a proportion of total employment shrink to the smallest of all provinces by 2011.

In 2012, the Liberals took away the right to strike from BC's 41,000 public school teachers, imposed a wage freeze, and sent the remaining unresolved issues to a government-appointed mediator. Mirroring legislation passed a decade earlier, Bill 22, the Education Improvement Act, prohibited bargaining on class size, class composition, and teacher-student ratios. Any salary increase would have to be offset by concessions elsewhere. Teachers initially responded with a work-to-rule campaign, which progressed to a full strike, but they were swiftly ordered back to work. Soon after, the government announced a "managed staffing strategy," which saw an across-the-board hiring freeze for the public sector, leading to cuts equal to $100 million between 2009 to 2014. During this time, BC's employment level dropped year after year, reaching a new low in 2013.

By 2014, the BC Supreme Court had struck down Bill 22, but a year later the BC Court of Appeal upheld the Act. It was challenged again at the Supreme Court of Canada, which, in its 2016 decision, struck down Bill 22, recognizing the right to strike and the obligation to negotiate in good faith (see Chapter 8). By this time, public-sector employment as a proportion of total employment was the smallest of all provinces, while spending as a percentage of GDP was 2.3 percent lower, or roughly $5 billion less, compared with a decade earlier.[23] The remainder of the Liberals' time in office was spent maintaining the freeze on public-sector hiring, expenditures, and tax cuts.[24] If 15 years of Liberal rule in BC showed anything, it was that the province's role in securing a more flexibilized and market-dependent workforce was no less important today than it was at any point previously.

The 9 May 2017 BC general election saw the governing Liberals finish with 43 seats, while the NDP were left with 41, leaving the balance of power in the hands of three Green MLAs. Although Green leader Andrew Weaver offered potential support to both the Liberals and NDP, they were eventually able to come to a power-sharing agreement with the John Horgan-led NDP, resulting in BCs first minority government in over six decades. The NDP ran on a platform promising to improve housing affordability, end bridge tolls, create a $10-a-day daycare program, and boost school funding. The NDP also vowed to launch a review of the BC Labour Code, including a return to card-check unionization, as well as a fair wages commission to look into raising the minimum wage.

Within its first two years, the NDP administration had stuck to a number of its promises, including the removal of bridge tolls in Metro Vancouver, the reintroduction of a provincial human rights commissioner, a commitment to increase the minimum wage to $15 by 2021, and increases to social welfare and education spending. The Horgan NDP also tied rent increases to the Consumer Price Index, made small increases to corporate tax rates, including a surtax on properties valued over $3 million, eliminated medicare premiums, and received wide-ranging praise for its handling of COVID-19 health and safety restrictions.[25] However, the government's approval in late 2017 of the Site C dam – a 1,100 megawatt hydro dam first proposed in the 1970s and currently under construction on the Peace River in northeastern BC – appears to have been a turning point for the premier and his administration.[26] At a cost of $16 billion, Site C is both the costliest dam in Canadian history and the most expensive publicly funded infrastructure project in BC history. The NDP moved forward with $6 billion worth of tax breaks to attract LNG Canada, a consortium of oil and gas companies, to build a $40 billion liquefied natural gas terminal in Kitimat. In reflecting on the NDP's decision to move forward with Site C and LNG Canada, Horgan remarked, "If we're going to be a government that governs for all BCers, we have to set aside our activism and start being better administrators."[27]

On 24 October 2020, the NDP was able to secure a majority with 57 seats. The seat differential was the largest margin of victory for the NDP in BC history, with Horgan also becoming the first NDP premier in BC to win a second term. A year into its new term, the NDP kept its promise to amend the BC Labour Code, the first amendment in 30 years, including the removal of public education as an essential service; new restrictions on contract flipping that grant successor rights protections for workers in food, janitorial, security, transportation, and non-clinical health services; raising the minimum age a child may work from 12 to 16, with some exemptions for younger workers; improvements to unpaid job-protected leave for workers escaping domestic violence and those caring for critically ill children; new restrictions on employers withholding or deducting tips; and the elimination of the province's "self-help" requirement that forced workers to first confront employers about Employment Standards Act violations before an investigation could occur.[28]

At the request of the Green Party, however, the government stopped short of reinstating card-check union certification. Following months of pressure and after more than a year into the COVID-19 pandemic, the NDP also announced plans to introduce a permanent paid sick leave program to cover the gaps in the federal government's Canada Recovery Sickness Benefit (CRSB).[29] There is little denying that the BC NDP has taken important steps in the right direction, though they have for the most part been slow to move on issues of inequality, reconciliation, and climate change, preferring to tinker, not alter, the economic and environmental plans set in motion by their predecessors. The NDP has also been slow to adopt more ambitious proposals, such as sectoral bargaining, a "living wage," and broader reforms that reverse occupational health and safety changes made by the Liberals.[30] In June 2022, Premier

Horgan announced he would be stepping down as premier and leader of the BC NDP. Leadership front-runner David Eby succeeded Horgan on 20 October 2022 and is expected to continue along Horgan's cautious path.

In Saskatchewan, following the Saskatchewan Party's re-election in 2011, austerity was incrementally embedded across major program expenditures, such as education and social assistance, including experimentation with private, for-profit health care delivery for services like magnetic resonance imaging (MRI). The SP's second term would see the government double down on its efforts to gut labour and employment laws and weaken collective bargaining rights, picking up where Bills 5 and 6 (see Chapter 6) left off. Bill 85, the Saskatchewan Employment Act, 2013, consolidated more than 12 labour statutes and, like their then-federal Conservative counterparts, expanded the statutory definition of supervisor to include more members in a bargaining unit, imposed mandatory conciliation and a further 14-day cooling-off period, restricted unions' ability to collect fines from members crossing a picket line, and created a new definition of "confidential worker" that stripped hundreds, if not thousands, of workers of collective bargaining rights altogether. The Act also erodes workers' rights to reasonable work hours, overtime pay, meal breaks, holiday pay, and weekends off; it grants employers the right to unilaterally impose a ten-hour day and four-day workweek; and it created new rules that individualize health and safety responsibility, including fines of up to $500,000 for individual workers.[31] Together, these changes strip both unionized and non-unionized workers of their rights and protections, leaving them less equipped to contest austerity and coercion down the road.

Where the government eroded labour and employment rights, it increased tax breaks for capital, reducing the business tax rate from 12 to 10 percent. The government also sought to reduce public-sector employment by 15 percent and embraced P3s, with the creation of SaskBuilds.[32] In the face of Bills 5, 6, and 85, labour largely acquiesced, shedding what remained of any trade union militancy or broader efforts to mobilize working-class discontent. Instead, the province's labour leaders chose to challenge the Bills in court, alleging that Bills 5 and 6 violated the Charter's guarantee of freedom of association. What transpired over the next seven years would lend a lifeline to the constitutionally protected rights of labour unions vis-à-vis government intervention. After winning their constitutional challenge before the Court of Queen's Bench then losing at the Saskatchewan Court of Appeal, the Saskatchewan Federation of Labour (SFL), along with 18 other unions, would try their case before the Supreme Court of Canada (SCC). The SCC ruling in

January 2015 struck down numerous sections of the PSESA but upheld the government's amendments to the Trade Union Act (see Chapter 8 for a fuller discussion). Though not a complete legal victory for the province's unions, the decision constitutionally protected the right to strike as part of a process of meaningful collective bargaining. After backing away from the threat to use the notwithstanding clause to override the SCC's decision, the SP passed the Saskatchewan Employment Amendment Act (Essential Services) later that year, which required that workers and management collectively determine what is essential in their sectors.

By 2015, a sharp downturn in the oil and gas sector led to a wider slump across the province. The downturn compounded successive rounds of revenue erosion, resulting in decreased growth and budgetary deficits. The 2016 budget responded with a provincewide austerity plan that included spending cuts equal to $64 million in health care, as well as $9 million each in education and social services.[33] By 2017, it had been estimated that the SP government had sold over $1.1 billion in public assets and eliminated at least 1,200 public-sector jobs via privatization and outsourcing.[34] With the onset of COVID-19, the SP government of Scott Moe came under fire for ineffectively allocating provincial dollars to fund the type of income and workplace supports required to mitigate the worst effects of the pandemic. An analysis by CCPA Saskatchewan found that the vast majority of COVID-19–related spending has been exclusively from the federal government, with the provincial government contributing about 10 percent towards new income supports, 2 percent towards new health spending, and 8 percent towards school and child care centre adaptation initiatives. The province did not provide any additional supports to municipal operating or transit budgets.[35]

What is more, the SP government has left unspent millions in federal aid, including $18 million for child care, $13 million to help train early childhood workers, $42 million for job training for workers in hard-hit sectors, $50 million for the essential workers wage top-up, $31 million from the Safe Long-Term Care fund, and $12 million for the purchase of hotels and motels for rapid housing. Through the pandemic, the Moe government has committed to balancing the budget by the 2024 election, boasting of lower deficits than expected, while providing working people with little in the form of new supports. Reflecting on the SP's time in power, Simon Enoch noted, "during the worst public health crisis in 100 years, failure to spend and access every available dollar to protect us from the ravages of this pandemic looks a lot less like financial caution and a lot more like callous recklessness."

On 23 April 2012, the Alberta PCs, now led by Alison Redford, secured their twelfth majority government – and, for the first time, the Wildrose Party won 17 seats to become the Official Opposition. The PCs quickly picked up where they left off, continuing their assault not only against trade union rights and freedoms but also workers across the province. Adding insult to the already severely curtailed rights of public-sector workers, Bill 45, the Public Sector Services Continuation Act, 2013, expanded the definition of strike to include any slowdown or any activity that has the effect of restricting or disrupting production or services. Bill 45 must be seen in the context of growing working-class discontent – as seen in the 2012 wildcat strike by hospital support staff and, in 2013, of correctional officers over safety concerns.[36] Affecting over 100,000 unionized provincial public-sector workers who already were denied the right to strike, the new Act created, for the first time in Canadian labour law, the idea of a "strike threat" that made it illegal for the union to solicit opinions from their members about their desire to strike or for the unions to advocate for one.

Shortly thereafter, the Redford PCs passed Bill 46, the Public Service Salary Restraint Act, 2013, which eliminated the option of binding arbitration for 21,000 AUPE members when a collective agreement cannot be reached through bargaining. It was also set to impose a new four-year contract of 2 percent wage increases over four years if the AUPE refused to accept the employer's last offer. However, in February 2014, the Alberta Court of Queen's Bench issued an injunction. With the resignation of Alison Redford as premier in March 2014, interim premier Dave Hancock reached a deal with AUPE that saw wages rise 6.75 percent over three years, including a $1,850 lump sum payment. In subsequent negotiations, Alberta teachers saw their salaries frozen for three years, to be followed by an increase of 2 percent in 2015 and a one-time lump sum payment, while physicians approved a seven-year deal retroactive to 2011 that saw a total 5 percent increase and cost of living adjustment. Following the reveal of a 2015 budget that slashed social spending and raised general taxes, interim premier Jim Prentice called an election. The tumult in the PC party signalled both the end and beginning of a new political realignment in Alberta that brought rapid electoral swings across the political spectrum over a remarkably short period of time.

On 5 May 2015, Rachel Notley led the NDP to a majority government, its first victory in the province, ending more than four decades of Tory rule in Alberta. It also marked the first time in nearly 80 years that an explicitly social democratic party had formed government in Alberta since the defeat of the

United Farmers of Alberta in 1935. Hopes were high that an NDP government in Alberta would present real opportunities for the labour movement and wider working class to make substantial gains. Their platform consisted of pledges to raise the minimum wage to $15 an hour, increase taxes on the wealthy and corporations, launch a review of royalty rates from the oil and gas sector, and increase health care spending. In government, the NDP moved quickly to implement a number of campaign promises, increasing spending on health care and education, as well as an increase in corporate taxes from 10 to 12 percent, and progressive increases of 2–5 percent for those making over $125,000 (about 7 percent of Albertans). Together, these changes were estimated to raise revenues approximately $1.5 billion annually.[37]

The Notley government also repealed Bill 45 and incrementally raised the minimum wage from $10.20 an hour in 2015 to $15 an hour in 2018, which benefited about one-eighth of employed Albertans. However, the New Democrats refused to move on a provincial sales tax, continuing the 3 percent tax rate for small business as well as the lowest fuel surtax in Canada. While the NDP followed through on their promise to conduct a review of the energy industry, this resulted in marginal adjustments rather than wholesale changes to the royalty regime.[38] Fiscally, Notley operated within neoliberal parameters to manage government expenditures and keep tax levels low, while avoiding the harsh austerity measures other provinces adopted after the 2008 recession. While the NDP passed a new carbon tax, it pushed for more pipelines, with Notley going as far to call for the abandonment of the national climate action plan.

Bill 17, the Fair and Family-Friendly Workplaces Act, 2017, brought maternity and compassionate leave up to federal standards and set new rules for overtime and vacation pay. The new legislation introduced some of the longest periods of unpaid, job-protected leave in the country; introduced workplace protections for farm workers; granted employment standards officers new enforcement rights and administrative powers to levy fines; raised group termination requirements from four to eight weeks; expanded the period in which union drives could occur from 90 to 180 days; introduced a hybrid card-check union certification process; expanded the definition of dependent contractors, and introduced first contract arbitration provisions and a compulsory dues check-off regime; repealed anti-salting provisions; and limited the use of market-enhancement recovery funds, particularly by unionized construction contractors to submit more competitive project bids.[39]

The majority of the changes set out in Bill 17 focused on improving the lives of non-unionized workers, who comprise about 80 percent of the Alberta workforce. In the wake of the Notley NDP expanding private, for-profit long-term care and freezing hiring as well as the wages of teachers and nurses, the labour movement neither challenged the NDP nor mobilized their members behind more ambitious reforms, such as anti-scab provisions. As Bob Barnetson has noted, "Limiting the bargaining power of unions in continuing care will encourage unions to reduce their demands, thereby transferring the cost of senior care onto workers in the form of substandard wages and working conditions. This, in turn, perpetuates the financial advantage (to government) of privately operated long-term care facilities, where pay is as much as 30% less than in publicly operated facilities. This dynamic also impedes unions (like AUPE) from negotiating higher staffing ratios (which improve patient care). The effect of this policy (which may have been unintentional) sits uneasily with many union activists, in part because the New Democrats' record on labour disputes on continuing care is looking much like the Tories' record."[40] The governing NDP called an election for 16 April 2019. By this time, the opposition Wildrose Party and long-governing PCs had merged, further shifting the policy spectrum right, creating the United Conservative Party (UCP).

On election day, the UCP, led by former Harper minister and PC leader Jason Kenney, was able to secure a majority government with roughly 55 percent of the popular vote. Significant losses in Calgary and rural Alberta reduced the NDP to the Official Opposition. It did not take long for the UCP to begin implementing their far-right program. Bill 1, the Critical Infrastructure Defence Act, expanded police and prosecutorial power to hand out penalties for disrupting any infrastructure the government deemed essential. The new law came into force in the context of the solidarity protests and blockades, led by Indigenous and environmental groups, that erupted throughout much of Canada in late 2019.[41] The passage of this Bill, supported by the NDP, led the *Edmonton Journal* to concede that this new law criminalizes the constitutionally protected right to free speech and assembly.

The UCP's embrace of authoritarianism included "highly partisan referendums designed to diminish representative democracy; unilateral possession of workers' pensions without their approval or consent; the appointment of hyper-conservative partisans to the courts; targeting organized labour; using provincial government resources to harass members of civil society on social media; making it illegal to protest or dissent; retaining prejudiced staff members; firing Alberta's elections watchdog while he was in the midst of investigating the premier; and setting up a war room to persecute Indigenous activists and environmentalists."[42] The UCP have also shown a blatant disregard for the most basic procedures of accountability, using the COVID-19 public health crisis as a pretext to subvert parliamentary debate.

The government also introduced Bill 2, An Act to Make Alberta Open for Business, 2019, which reversed many of the changes to employment standards and labour relations implemented by the NDP. Changes to the Occupational Health and Safety Act and Workers' Compensation Act lowered compensation rates for injuries and limited psychological and disease claims, appeal systems, and Ministry of Labour reinstatement powers.[43] Bill 9, the Public Sector Arbitration Deferral Act, 2019, passed by the legislature on 20 June 2019 and suspended the 24 collective agreements of 180,000 employees until 31 October 2019, when a government report on public-sector spending would be released. Chaired by former Saskatchewan finance minister Janice MacKinnon, who had long advocated for public-sector spending cuts, the report recommended that the Alberta government mandate wages and benefits for the public sector using legislation and that, in the event of a strike, the government utilize back-to-work legislation. On 30 July 2019, the Alberta Court of Queen's Bench ordered an injunction to apply to Bill 9 in a case brought forward by AUPE. However, on 6 September 2019, the Alberta Court of Appeal overturned the injunction. On 12 March 2020, the Supreme Court of Canada declined to hear the case on the constitutionality of Bill 9.[44] In early 2020, arbitrators awarded a 1 percent increase to some AUPE members and instituted a wage freeze for others, but refused compensation reductions sought by public-sector employers.

In an accelerated assault against both trade union and broader working-class rights, Bill 32, the Restoring Balance in Alberta's Workplaces Act, and Bill 47, the Ensuring Safety and Cutting Red Tape Act, imposed limits on where unions could picket during strikes or lockouts; constrained secondary picketing; made it easier for employers to impose overtime averaging agreements; and expanded variances that enabled employers to avoid statutory entitlements.[45] Bill 32 also made Alberta the only jurisdiction in Canada to require union members to opt in to having a portion of their dues go to "political activities" and required that unions share with employers how members voted on particular issues. The Act also grants provincial cabinet the power to set the "time and frequency" of when unions can make changes to their due structures.[46]

Bill 22, the Reform of Agencies, Boards and Commissions and Government Enterprises Act, required the Alberta Teachers' Retirement Fund to hand over its $18 billion pension fund to the Alberta Investment Management Corporation. As the COVID-19 pandemic accelerated, the UCP government unilaterally cancelled and imposed reduced compensation agreements with physicians and the Alberta Medical Association.[47] The Kenney government also laid off 11,000 hospital support staff, lab technicians, licensed practical nurses, laundry and cafeteria workers, outsourcing future work to private contractors. In response to this, and ongoing concerns related to short staffing, overwork, and exhaustion, roughly 800 health care workers engaged in a wildcat strike across several hospitals. They were ordered back to work a day later by the Labour Relations Board, with dozens of workers receiving suspensions.[48] If the first two years of the UCP showed anything, it is that labour movements and working people cannot rely on "progressive" governments and the courts to build and sustain long-term change. The UCP project has been so intertwined with de-democratization and authoritarian measures that it is impossible to separate them in practice. This claim is based, in part, on the further strengthening of executive power and insulation of economic policy from parliamentary accountability that we noted above. But it also arises from the incredible multiplication of legalized restrictions for the disciplining of labour and dissent by the austerity state.

In Manitoba, Gary Doer stepped down as premier and leader of the NDP in 2009. He was replaced by Greg Selinger, who announced a wage freeze for public-sector workers in the 2010 budget. In subsequent negotiations, most public-sector unions agreed to four-year settlements with no wage increases in the first two years, followed by 2.9 percent over the next two.[49] An exception was the provincial workers with the MGEU, who rejected a similar tentative agreement by a vote of 54 percent. The "no" vote came as a surprise given the relative absence in MGEU history of any rank-and-file militancy or activist organization. Negotiators returned to the bargaining table and while the government did not move on its wage policy, it did agree to extend layoff protection to non-seasonal departmental employees over the life of the agreement, extending some dental benefits and mileage reimbursement increases.[50] The largest exception to the wage freeze were teachers who, lacking the right to strike, reached settlements containing 3 percent increases in 2010–2011 and 2 percent in each of the following three years. City of Winnipeg workers, represented by CUPE Local 500, managed to get 1 percent for 2012 and 2.5 percent for the following two years.

In the face of a higher-than-expected deficit for 2011–2012, the government merged six regional health authorities into five, raised gas and tobacco taxes, and broadened the provincial sales tax to include insurance and cosmetic and hair services. The NDP also merged the Manitoba Liquor Control Commission with the Manitoba Lotteries Corporation and directed all departments to cut costs, with energy, mines, agriculture, and conservation taking the biggest hits. Core government spending was held at 2 percent annual increases over the next five years and public-sector wages were frozen. Efforts were also made to restrain labour costs in the civil service through leaving vacancies unfilled and, in 2012, the NDP announced plans to privatize the province's property registry.[51] Budget 2013 reduced the ranks of the provincial public service by 600 positions over three years and amalgamated a range of departments, while raising the PST from 7 to 8 percent and dedicating the revenue to infrastructure spending. The government also imposed a retroactive 4 percent cut, worth $3.1 million, on social services agencies for 2013–2014.

The 2014 and 2015 budgets reflected continuity in the direction of fiscal policy, including selective investments in health care and education spending, but encased in a web of balanced budget orthodoxy and ongoing restrictions on workers' rights to organize and strike.[52] In many ways, NDP governments did not implement significant spending cuts or outright conflict with public servants, but this was not due to altruism or an abrupt policy shift. Rather, the heavy lifting of austerity had been done a decade earlier, leaving the NDP to quietly consolidate neoliberalism across provincial policies and institutions. Consider, for instance, that from 2000 to 2015, personal income tax cuts added up to $881 million annually in foregone revenue. In response to the tepid social democratic practice of the NDP, Errol Black and Jim Silver suggested that "mobilizing workers for extra-parliamentary action against this government would prepare the labour movement to take on the next Conservative government." Little could they imagine that their words would take on new meaning as NDP popularity sank, leading to the election of the PC party in 2016, which swiftly launched a new wave of aggressive austerity and labour restrictions.

The Brian Pallister-led PCs attack against labour got its start early with the passage of Bill 7, the Labour Relations Amendment Act, 2017, which ended card-check union certification, and Bill 28, the Public Services Sustainability Act, which froze the wages of 120,000 public-sector workers for two years and limited increases for another two years to 0.75 and 1 percent. The government went so far as to send a letter to University of Manitoba administrators instructing them to rescind wage freezes that it had offered the University of Manitoba Faculty Association (UMFA) during bargaining. In response,

UMFA struck for three weeks, after which they were able to come to an agreement with administrators. The one-year deal saw no wage increases but it did see improvements to workload protection, instructor assessments, collegial governance, and a letter from the university committing to no librarian or instructor layoffs.[53]

Manitoba unions launched a court challenge to Bill 28, arguing that it took away their Charter-protected rights to collectively bargain and, on 11 June 2020, the Manitoba Court of Queen's Bench agreed, striking down the Bill. In her ruling, Justice Joan McKelvey noted the Act "operates as a draconian measure that has inhibited and dramatically reduced the unions' bargaining power and violates associational rights."[54] At the same time, the Manitoba Labour Board ruled that the university had engaged in an unfair labour practice by withdrawing a salary offer and implementing a wage freeze at the behest of government. In May 2018, the university apologized and paid the maximum fine of $2,000 per member.[55] However, with regard to Bill 28, the government challenged the lower court's decision, which the Manitoba Court of Appeal eventually overturned, dealing a significant blow to labour. The Pallister government continued along its aggressive austerity agenda, contracting out road work, French translation services, and buying out 800 workers at Manitoba Hydro. In 2019, the PCs instructed Crown corporations to cut their workforces by 8 percent, which built on a 15 percent reduction in 2016.[56]

The government expanded its attack against labour with a number of bills that undermine workers' rights and protections. Bill 11, the Workplace Safety and Health Amendment Act 2020, undermined health and safety protections by eliminating the position of chief prevention officer; granted new powers to the Workplace Health and Safety Branch to dismiss worker appeals without a hearing; and imposed a time limit on workers' ability to defend themselves in serious cases where workers face illegal retaliation from their employer for asserting their health and safety rights. Bill 18, the Workers' Compensation Amendment Act, 2020, removed psychological injuries and illness from the category of occupational disease and reinstated a cap on maximum insurable earnings. Bill 26, the Human Rights Code Amendment Act, 2020, introduced a new maximum amount of $25,000 in damages that may be awarded to complainants for injury to dignity, feelings, or self-respect, significantly limiting an employer's potential liability for general damages that were previously uncapped.

In a similar vein, Bill 51, the Limitations Act, 2020, reduced from six to two years the period in which a former employee may file a claim for breach of contract (such as a wrongful dismissal or constructive dismissal claim) after the termination of their employment, dramatically reducing the civil liability of employers. Finally, Bill 16, the Labour Relations Amendment Act, 2021, made it easier to terminate an employee for "strike-related misconduct"; it also lowered the threshold to trigger a decertification vote from 50 to 40 percent; granted the Labour Board new powers to review the appropriateness of a bargaining unit even after certification has occurred; increased financial reporting transparency rules for unions; removed a requirement that employers give 90 days' notice to workers of new technology that could significantly change the kind of work they do or displace their jobs; prohibited employers from paying the salary of workers on leave as full-time union executives; constrained successor rights; and eliminated binding arbitration for strikes and lockouts lasting more than two months. In addition to the draconian labour reforms, the marketization and erosion of public services and assets has been a hallmark of the Pallister regime.

With regard to housing and social supports, the PCs raised the income threshold to receive rental assistance from 25 to 28 and then 30 percent of household income, while freezing it for single low-income adults. The PC government also cut a $25/month allowance for people on Employment and Income Assistance, sold off low-income rental housing, slashed maintenance of funding for housing stock threefold, and replaced a graduated child welfare funding formula with a block funding arrangement. In the arena of education, the PCs have increased class sizes while limiting funding increases to 0.5 percent, which, given inflation and population growth, means real cuts. Between 2016–2021, provincial funding for K–12 education declined in real dollars by 7.6 percent on a compounded basis. The Education Property Tax Reduction Act, 2021, means a loss of approximately $384 million of income for the Manitoba government annually by 2022. And if the government follows through on its planned full phase-out of education property taxes, it will mean a loss of nearly $900 million annually.[57] Post-secondary education fees have also risen, on average, 5 percent annually plus inflation, while the government eliminated rebates that encouraged graduates to remain in Manitoba.[58] The PCs also cut Manitoba's sales tax from 8 to 7 percent, at a cost of $325 million annually, which returned government revenue relative to the size of the economy back to 2006–2007 levels, equal to a loss of $1.9 billion in annual revenue for program expenditures.[59]

In the years preceding the COVID-19 outbreak, the PCs cut $119 million from the Winnipeg Regional Health Authority and scrapped capital funding to six proposed health care facilities, including $300 million for Cancer Care Manitoba expansion.[60] The Pallister government also privatized outpatient physio and occupational therapy and air ambulance services, introduced prescription co-payment fees, and closed three of six emergency rooms in Winnipeg and converted them into urgent care centres. The closures resulted in a significant increase to mandatory overtime worked by nurses, which rose from 328 mandated shifts in 2017 to 511 mandated shifts by the midway point of 2018. In total, overtime hours increased by 32 percent for nurses and 71 percent for critical care nurses over 2017–2018, with the total number of nurses falling by more than 500. In response, several rallies demanding an end to the cuts were hosted by nurses and labour supporters outside the Manitoba legislature, but they were unable to transform this into a broader movement for change.[61]

As the COVID-19 crisis grew, the Pallister government only matched 5 percent of total federal essential worker wage top-ups, which was meant to be cost shared 25–75 percent. Some 90 percent of COVID-19 relief spending has been footed by the federal government, while the provincial measures that were enacted disproportionately benefited Saskatchewan businesses, particularly in the oil, gas, and agricultural sectors.[62] As party support plummeted in the polls, Pallister announced he would resign as premier 1 September 2021. Just five years of PC rule in Manitoba dramatically transformed an already weakened labour and employment regulatory framework, eroding public services and insulating executive power from parliamentary and public scrutiny. Politics is generally equated with elections won and lost, but if the transition from NDP to PC rule shows anything, it is that labour and wider social movements cannot pin their hopes on electoral or legislative changes from above. Rather, building union density and class organizing has been workers' best shot at securing long-term, full-time employment with benefits and wages that rise steadily over time that provide the chance for a "decent" life.

ATLANTIC CANADA: EMBEDDED AUSTERITY

The period 2013 to 2020 saw deficits return to each Atlantic province, but the root cause for the erosion of fiscal health varied. In Newfoundland, it was the decline in oil royalties. In Nova Scotia, it was the result of long-standing structural and demographic problems stemming back to the deindustrialization of the 1970s. For New Brunswick, it was a function of a province that has been locked into a trajectory of decline for far too long. And PEI, with the help of federal transfers and a large public sector, was able to muddle through without need of forcing major battles with its public-sector workers. Each province had a somewhat different strategy to deal with this new but familiar fiscal reality. However, the differences were a matter of how intensely the public sector, and those working to deliver public services, would be attacked to return to fiscal balance.

In Nova Scotia, a new Liberal government took the most aggressive approach of the four Atlantic provinces, with the elimination of the deficit within three years as the chief priority. Their argument was that "budgetary deficits hamper the province's growth prospects" and so the 2015 budget stated the government would "hold the line on spending, restructure and reduce the size of government, and continue to clear the way for private sector growth."[63] However, the magnitude of the deficit problem was exaggerated when placed in historical and jurisdictional context. Regardless, the end result was shrinking of the size of the core public service as jobs were cut and public-sector wage restraint implemented. By 2016, budgets had returned to a surplus, lasting through to 2020. These surpluses were accompanied by increases in public expenditure from 2017 forward after the three previous years of restraint. In 2017, overall program spending increased by 4.3 percent but certain priority areas were allocated funds well beyond this level. For example, business development increased by 49 percent and early childhood development by 10 percent. Health care was held to below the average, at 3 percent. The subsequent 2018 budget restricted overall increases in expenditures to 1.8 percent but education and health care were given particular priority; these spending envelopes were increased by 5.5 and 2.4 percent, respectively. The prioritization of health care continued into 2019, where that year's budget allocated an additional 4.3 percent to that envelope, above overall program increases of 3.1 percent. In 2020 spending on health care slowed to 2.3 percent but education increased by 3.4 percent.[64] In sum, while these years marked a break with the previous period of austerity, the overall increases in expenditures to finance public services was modest.

Given that Nova Scotia's public sector was, as in other Atlantic provinces, comparatively large, composing 28 percent of the total workforce and 70 percent of those unionized, a policy regime of that type would be difficult to sustain politically. This, combined with the province's reliance on federal transfers for fiscal sustainability, has meant for Nova Scotia a history of "fiscal experimentation" and, for the most part, the dominance of government controls on public-sector wages since the early 1990s. Other forces informing the McNeil government's fiscal policy included the continued fallout from the 2008 crisis, as well as the 2014 Ivany Report (commissioned by the NDP in 2012), which argued that the province was on the precipice of long-term economic decline and recommended fiscal restraint.[65]

In response, the McNeil-led Liberal government implemented an array of legislative changes that impacted public-sector workers in every corner of the province. In this respect, the government continued the austerity initiated by the NDP but adopted a much more aggressive approach to public-sector labour relations, particularly for health and education workers. While the NDP government had earlier agreed to public-sector wage increases of 2 percent, 2.5 percent, and 3 percent, the Liberals now argued for public-sector wage restraint, citing the claim that nearly 60 percent of provincial budget expenditures went to compensation.[66] The first of what would be several interventions to roll out over 2014 and 2015 was Bill 30, the Essential Home-support Services Act. This legislation was the government's response to a strike by 400 home-support workers that began 28 February 2014. A further 670 home-support workers employed with the Victorian Order of Nurses were eligible to go on strike the following week, but the legislation declared their work an essential service and ordered them all to return to work. This was the beginning of a contentious relationship between the McNeil government and public-sector workers, especially in health care.[67] It was also, importantly, an expression of the ongoing struggle for care workers, primarily women, to win decent pay and working conditions.[68]

Bill 37, the Essential Health and Community Services Act, followed shortly thereafter. The legislation deemed 2,400 nurses working in the Halifax area as essential workers with no right to strike. The nurses, represented by NSGEU Local 97, sought to slow down the passage of the legislation by staging a one-day wildcat strike, followed by a legal strike on 3 April. The passage of Bill 37 the next day forced an end to the strike, legislating as essential more than 35,000 nurses, home care and hospital workers, 911 operators, and paramedics.[69] This was followed with the passage of the Health Authorities Act (Bill 1). The passage of Bill 1 was intended as a pre-emptive action to foreclose any possibility for wildcat strikes aimed at disrupting the legislative process as had been the experience with Bill 37. In scope, the legislation captured over 21,000 health care workers by limiting the number of bargaining units in the health care sector from 50 provincewide units to just four. It further required that each of the four unions in the health care sector – the NSGEU, the Nova Scotia Nurses Union (NSNU), CUPE, and Unifor – could only represent one of the four new bargaining units. In this way, not only did the government remove the democratic right of workers to determine which union would represent them, but it also made coordinated action more difficult.[70] Next on the Liberals' agenda would be a remaking of the education sector.

Universities were the first target, with the tabling of Bill 100, the Universities Accountability and Sustainability Act in 2015. This legislation empowered university administrations to declare a "revitalization period" if they projected a significant operational deficit over a five-year period. The revitalization period could be in place for 12 to 18 months and in this period, strikes would be prohibited and new collective agreements could not be negotiated during that time. The government imposed its own priorities upon the universities by requiring that research and funding be aligned with the economic priorities of the government. A university could decline the revitalization process, but the government would not come to its aid should it find itself in financial difficulty. A contentious section provided that all grievances would be suspended, but this was removed from the Bill at the legislative committee stage.[71] These measures aligned with the government's attempts to strongly limit workers' ability to engage in collective bargaining and to impose a "marketability" agenda on the broader public sector. More generally, it is an early expression of the deepening of this trend among Canada's universities.[72] The Canadian Association of University Teachers was alarmed at the prospect of seeing collective bargaining rights suspended and the empowering of government to abrogate university autonomy in such areas as research and teaching. Ultimately, the powers granted by Bill 100 were never used by other universities, as it was an ex-post response to the earlier budget crisis at Acadia University and NSCAD and its provisions were designed for exceptionally dire situations.[73]

In 2017, the government set its sights on primary and secondary schooling. Nova Scotia teachers had rejected three tentative agreements reached between 2015 and 2017, beginning a work-to-rule campaign in December 2016. In response, the government passed Bill 75, the Teachers' Professional Agreement and Classroom Improvements Act, on 21 February 2017. The teachers responded with a one-day strike but to no effect. The legislation imposed a four-year contract that was based on the first two rejected tentative agreements. The details included a two-year wage freeze followed by a 1 percent increase in year three, a 1.5 percent increase at the start of year four, and an extra 0.5 percent increase on the last day of the contract. Accrual of long service for new hires was terminated and capped at ten years for current members.[74] In

November 2017, the teachers launched a Charter challenge with the NS Supreme Court. In June 2022, the Court ruled the legislation invalid. The teachers' union was successful in compelling the government to release internal documents that the government claimed were confidential advice to cabinet. The Supreme Court of Nova Scotia, however, ruled the province could not withhold internal government documents related to Bill 75. The Court decisions stated that these documents were "relevant to the determination of the NSTU's Charter litigation" and there was "a strong public interest in having that resolved without the relevant information kept secret."[75] In June 2022, a Nova Scotia court ruled Bill 75 unconstitutional.

The Nova Scotia Liberals' most significant public intervention was Bill 148, the Public Service Sustainability Act, 2015. This legislation applied to 75,000 unionized and non-unionized public-sector workers. Bill 148 imposed a four-year deal where the cumulative wage increase was restricted to 3 percent. Long service awards at retirement were terminated for all post-2014 hires. The Act sparked a wave of protests from unionized workers across the province. The affected unions elected to follow a legal challenge rather than intensify political mobilization against the legislation. In August 2017, the NSGEU launched a Charter challenge against Bill 148, alleging the Bill contravenes the right to freedom of association. The case was sent by the province to the Nova Scotia Court of Appeal for a constitutional reference. Seven unions (CUPE, NSGEU, NSNU, SEIU, NSTU, CUPW, and Unifor) representing workers affected by the legislation were granted Intervener Status in January 2018. The unions sought permission to present their own evidence regarding the constitutionality of Bill 148. This bid was ultimately rejected at both the provincial Court of Appeal and at the Supreme Court of Canada.[76]

In September 2019, following the NSTU's success in forcing the government to release documents related to Bill 75, the unions pushed to have similar cabinet minutes and documents released to the court that the government claimed were privileged. The government objected and thus further delayed the court case by making the Court of Appeal rule whether or not they have the ability to force the government to produce these documents. "The Court has issued a decision that said it does have the power to do this under the right circumstances."[77] The pandemic further slowed the legal process, and the union alleged the government was purposefully delaying the constitutional reference on Bill 148. In the meantime, Manitoba's Court of Queen's Bench had struck down legislation modelled after Bill 148, though the Manitoba government appealed that decision.[78] In sum, the McNeil Liberal government had done more to curtail the right of public-sector workers at any point since the Savage Liberals of the 1990s. The affected unions organized rallies to voice their opposition to the various interventions and chose legal strategies to oppose government rather than turn to mass political mobilization. As the record states, the legal interventions had mixed effect but, to date, have not succeeded in forcing the government to retreat. It is an outstanding question at this point as to whether a strategy of mobilization could have achieved more and, today, whether or not decades of setbacks have made a more militant and mass-based resistance untenable.

Budget deficits had become the norm in PEI. In 2012, public-sector compensation was frozen, 300 public-sector jobs were eliminated over three years, and cuts of 2.6 percent made to all program areas, with the exception of health and education. In 2014, 900 more public-sector jobs were cut as expenditures across all programs (again, except health care and education) were reduced by 1.3 percent. The Liberals, now under new leader Wade MacLauchlan, were elected to a third consecutive term in 2015. As with previous PEI governments, coercion, as a means of imposing austerity on public-sector workers, was held in check. Indeed, a series of modest, though not unimportant, reforms were made to enhance labour protections for workers generally, thus deviating from the more general pattern of restricting trade union rights witnessed in the post-2008 crisis period. From 2015–2018, the MacLauchlan Liberals passed four amendments to the Employment Standards Act providing for a diverse range of benefits and protections, including provisions for leave to care for ill children or for bereavement leave in the event of a child's death; enhanced access to holiday pay; and wage replacement in the event of wage theft by an employer. A private members' bill was passed unanimously in 2018, which provided for paid leave where a worker has been a victim of domestic or sexual violence. But these modestly progressive amendments were not near enough to prevent the defeat of the Liberal government. The results of the 2019 provincial election marked a sharp departure from PEI's electoral history. The Progressive Conservatives, led by Dennis King, were elected in a minority government, the first minority government in PEI since 1890, and the Green Party formed the Official Opposition. The Liberals, with six seats, were relegated to third-party status, which was unprecedented. However, the Conservatives maintained a moderate course with respect to labour policy and introduced only one piece of labour legislation (Bill 38) in 2020 to align labour law with COVID-19 protocols.

More than any other Atlantic province, the politics of Newfoundland and Labrador has been defined by the fate of the province's resource extraction sector, in particular its offshore oil and gas industry. Despite the boom provided by newfound oil wealth, unemployment and inequality remained high, but it did provide new revenue streams for the provincial government that papered over the worst of the financial crisis.[79] Unlike Nova Scotia, where public-sector austerity had been a constant, in Newfoundland and Labrador public-sector wage negotiations during this period oscillated between austere and reasonable, where the latter was enabled as a result of oil revenues. There were elements of consensus on some issues as well as several instances of modest but not unimportant improvements to workers' rights and protections. Despite signalling a more collaborative approach to public-sector labour relations, the PC government unveiled an austerity budget in 2013 that cut $300 million and eliminated 1,500 jobs.

In 2015, the Dwight Ball-led Liberals formed a majority government, inheriting a $1.1 and $1.8 billion deficit for 2015 and 2016 from their PC predecessors. The Ball Liberals amended the Labour Standards Act in 2016 and 2018, which established unpaid leave for workers to assist a dying family member, extended parental leave and established leaves to allow for care of ill children, and provided critical illness leave. This was followed by amendments to the Workplace Health, Safety and Compensation Act in 2018 that modestly improved compensation rates and established new paid and unpaid leaves for workers who had been victims of domestic violence. In 2018, austerity returned with the passage of Bill 24, the Salary Restraint and Extinguishment of Severance Pay Act. This legislation imposed a two-year wage freeze on non-union public-sector employees, and severance pay entitlements were eliminated. In response to the cuts, CUPE launched an anti-austerity ad campaign across all media platforms. The campaign messaging warned that the austerity measures affecting non-union employees would, at some point, be applied to the entire public sector.[80]

In the context of protracted austerity and the absence of new revenue-raising tools, New Brunswick, like other Atlantic provinces, struggled with how to deal with rising deficits. The government approached the fiscal imbalance with a mix of business tax cuts and modest increases in overall expenditures but did not pursue any major restructuring as witnessed elsewhere. New Brunswick's 2014 election saw the Liberals defeat the single-term Progressive Conservative government. The Liberals, led by Brian Gallant, began their single term in government by announcing they would undertake an across-the-board austerity drive but, in reality, did very little to cut public expenditures to reduce the deficit. It should be noted that the economic and fiscal context was difficult, with among the lowest levels of economic growth on record and one of the highest net debts per capita. Despite this, the Liberals would approach labour policy and labour relations in much the same way as other Atlantic provinces, with some modest reforms.[81] These included extending and broadening leave for care of ill children or family members, leave for victims of domestic and sexual violence, and broadening leave provision for adoptive parents. An element of coercion did appear in 2017 with an amendment to the Industrial Relations Act that eased the ability of either workplace party to refer collective bargaining proceedings to binding arbitration – which was clearly of more benefit to employers.

The 2018 election resulted in a narrow win for the Conservatives but with a minority, as the Green won three seats as did the right-wing People's Alliance. The Conservatives would govern through to the 2020 election, where they then won a majority government. Between 2018 and 2020, they introduced several pieces of legislation which, while very particular in terms of focus, were clearly a coercive departure. These various legislative changes included a narrowing of workplace injuries and illnesses eligible for compensation through the provincial workers' compensation legislation; legislation (pre-pandemic) declaring nursing-home work as essential and therefore severely restricting the ability of unions within the sector to strike; and a further amendment of the Workers' Compensation Act to empower the government to determine a workers' fitness to return to work.

ONTARIO AND QUEBEC: THE THIRD WAY FALTERS

As discussed in the previous chapter, by the 2011 budget the Ontario Liberals had come full circle back to the Common Sense Revolution, with pledges to restrain expenditure growth to 2 percent annually. The budget also vowed not to raise taxes and to freeze non-priority program spending by reining in union wages. Tax cuts amounted to the second largest platform item in their 2011 budget, costing the Treasury $327 million by 2015–2016. The McGuinty government also established the Commission on the Reform of Ontario's Public Services, headed by former TD Bank chief economist Don Drummond. The Commission argued that without new forms of revenue generation (their mandate explicitly prevented them from exploring these options), program spending would need to be cut "more deeply on a real per capita basis, and over a much longer period of time, than the Harris government did in the 1990s."[82] The Liberals' budgetary emphasis on balanced budgets reinforced pressures for "competitive austerity" and seems to confirm Hackworth's contention that "soft edge" neoliberal governments may actually be able to go further than their most aggressive proponents.[83]

In 2012, the Liberals implemented a range of austerity measures: Children's Aid societies were restructured and wages frozen in order to find $9 million in "efficiencies"; social assistance and disability payments were reduced by $200 million over three years, resulting in benefits that were less in real dollars in 2015 than they were in 1986; correctional services and legal aid were cut by 1.6 percent every year until 2017–2018; municipal and local infrastructure funding was cut by $48 million from 2011 levels; hospitals lost $1 billion and OHIP another $1.5 billion in cuts and wage freezes, despite having the highest out-of-pocket health care costs and fewest hospital beds per person compared with any other province; K–12 school funding was cut by $660 million over three years, while post-secondary education transfers stagnated and fees rose 3 percent annually. From 2010 to 2012, Ontario fell from seventh to last place among Canada's ten provinces in total social program spending.[84] The crowning irony of McGuinty's ninth budget was that it completed the job of cutting government down to the size it was during Harris's tenure. In total, the budget cut $10.7 billion (equal to 1.5 percent of GDP) from expenditures. With inflation, by 2012–2013 social assistance had lost 5.5 percent of funding and disability lost some $200 million compared with when Harris left government. The budget also legislated a pay freeze for 1.2 million broader public-sector workers, nullifying some 4,000 collective agreements.[85] All said, the 2012 budget took $17.7 billion out of the economy over the next three years.

The 2013–2014 budget further reduced expenditure growth to 1.5 percent and backend loaded austerity measures, with each year of restraint being more aggressive than the last. From 2014–2016, program spending growth was held to 1.1 and 0.4 percent. On 3 January 2013, the Liberals imposed concessionary contracts on the province's teachers, which followed 2012 legislation restraining spending in the education system. This included wage controls, layoffs, and the freezing of pension contributions for five years. Teachers responded with a number of one-day strikes, work-to-rule campaigns, the withdrawal of extracurricular activities, and mass protests. Despite the labour discontent, the job actions did not see a repeat of the Harris-era confrontations.[86] Amid a barrage of scandals, both Premier McGuinty and Finance Minister Dwight

Duncan stepped down in what was portrayed as a period of renewal.[87] Kathleen Wynne emerged as new party leader and premier of Ontario, positioning herself as the "social justice" and "activist" premier against the old guard. In power, however, much of the McGuinty (and Harris) legacy continued.

The Liberals launched the largest expansion of public-private partnerships (P3s) in Ontario history. In a review of value for money, Siemiatycki and Farooqi found P3s to be 16 percent more expensive than traditional public procurement.[88] Likewise, a major report undertaken by the auditor general found that of the 74 completed P3 projects between 2003 and 2014, Ontario could have saved up to $8 billion through traditional public procurement. In June 2013, the Liberals launched a panel headed by president and former CEO of TD Bank, Ed Clark, to advise the government how to get more than $3 billion through the "recycling" of public assets. The panel suggested selling off Ontario's estimated $3.3 billion lottery, which brought in close to $1 billion annually in public revenue. Following the panel's recommendations, lottery and provincial liquor store lands were put on sale, as was Hydro One Brampton and Hydro One Networks' distribution arm, worth some $2–3 billion in one-off monies, although the government retained a 40 percent majority stake. In doing so, the Wynne Liberals went further than the Harris Conservatives in the privatization of public hydro.

The Liberal minority government fell on 2 May 2014, as the NDP and Conservatives voted against the budget. The election saw the NDP move sharply right, while the Conservatives raised the spectre of "right-to-work" laws and cutbacks to the public service. The Liberals were not only re-elected but unexpectedly regained a majority in the legislature. The Liberals' 2014 budget cut total public spending to 14.6 percent of total GDP, equivalent to roughly $20 billion in public spending cuts, as compared with 2010–2011, where total public program spending represented 17.9 percent of GDP in Ontario. Likewise, the share of Ontario's public health care paid by employers through the Employer Health Tax dropped, having decreased from 17.2 percent in 1991 to 12.4 percent in 2014. Welfare incomes adjusted for inflation dropped by 34 percent and disability support payments by 14 percent between 2003–2014. With population growth and inflation factored in, the 2017 Liberal budget decreased total program spending by the largest amount per person since 1995 – a per capita spending reduction of $179 compared with 2013 levels. The Liberals continued a "net zero" policy in public-sector labour negotiations, meaning that no budget would be allotted to departments for increased wages. In a report examining the fiscal impacts of the Hydro One sell-off,

Ontario's former financial accountability officer Andre Leclerq noted: "In years following the sale of 60% of Hydro One, the Province's budget balance would be worse than it would have been without the sale. The Province's net debt would initially be reduced, but will eventually be higher than it would have been without the sale."[89] The report noted how Hydro One brought in close to $750 million annually, making its sale roughly equivalent to five years of continued public ownership.

As the Wynne government entered what would turn out to be its final two years, it would intervene with back-to-work legislation in 2017 to end what had become Ontario's longest strike in the colleges sector. Bill 178, the Colleges of Applied Arts and Technology Labour Dispute Resolution Act, was passed on 16 November 2017 and directed the parties to arbitration.[90] Before defeat in the 2018 election, Wynne revived the "one Ontario" politics that had characterized the early McGuinty years. From 2017 to the end of their term in office, the Wynne Liberals initiated a comprehensive review of labour policy. The ambitious *Changing Workplace Review* was tabled in May of 2017 after a full two years of research and stakeholder consultation. This process concluded with legislation, Bill 148, the Fair Workplaces, Better Jobs Act, which was tabled on 1 June 2017. This was the most significant improvement of worker rights and protections since the NDP government's overhaul of the Labour Relations Act in 1991 and among the most far-reaching reform of the Employment Standards Act since 1969. Notable changes included increasing the minimum wage from $11.40 to $14.00, with another bump to $15 on 1 January 2019; an 18-month parental leave (12 months of EI parental leave payments over 18 months); all employees provided with two paid days of leave and eight unpaid days for illness/emergency; workers with at least five years' seniority entitled to a minimum of three weeks' vacation; equal compensation, including benefit coverage, for part-time employees performing substantially the same work as full-time equivalents; placing the onus on the employer to prove a person is a contractor, not an employee; allowing unions to obtain lists of employees from employer; and switching to card-based union certification in building services, home care, community services, and temp-help industries.[91]

Predictably, Bill 148 provoked a strong and negative response from Ontario's business sector, including umbrella organizations like the Ontario Chamber of Commerce (OCC) and the Canadian Federation of Independent Businesses (CFIB), which quickly mobilized their opposition to Bill 148 and released several reports on the supposed detrimental economic consequences of the minimum wage hike as well as aggressively lobbying Queen's Park for its repeal. The OCC claimed that 185,000 jobs would be at risk, while TD Bank and the CFIB predicted 90,000 and 125,000 losses. Even the Ontario Financial Accountability Office predicted 50,000 job losses. Fast-forward a year and Ontario added 78,000 new jobs, bringing the unemployment rate down to the lowest it had been in nearly 20 years. Some employers, such as Tim Hortons franchise owners, of course did retaliate against workers by cutting shifts, breaks, and even jobs. They were met with a significant public backlash and even threats to boycott the very profitable company (even Tim Hortons' parent company, RBI, lashed out at "rogue" franchises).[92] Despite this very open class war, jobs grew across the labour market as a whole, in particular full-time work, while total hours worked in the food and accommodation services industry actually increased year over year. In the end, the big business lobby's predictions turned out to be a canard – a totally misleading attack against living wages.[93] And after 15 years of "third-wayish" government, it was continuity, not change, that defined the Liberals' time in power.

On 7 June 2018, Liberal support collapsed, leading to a majority Conservative government and the NDP forming the Official Opposition. The Doug Ford-led Conservatives moved rapidly on several labour issues. The first intervention in a legal strike came with Bill 2, the Back to Class Act (2018) passed in July, just weeks after their election. The Act legislated an end to the 2018 York University strike that had begun the previous March. Lasting 143 days, the strike was the longest in the history of the Canadian post-secondary sector.[94] The dispute was largely defined by a bargaining stalemate between the union, CUPE 3903, and the university. The employer abandoned most attempts at bargaining early on in the process, essentially waiting for back-to-work legislation and binding arbitration to resolve the impasse, and the strike ended in early August 2018.

The Ford government made its move to undo Wynne's Bill 148 in November 2018 with the tabling and passage of Bill 47, the Making Ontario Open for Business Act. The legislation repealed major provisions of Bill 148, including the $15 minimum wage that was to kick in January 2019. Moreover, the minimum wage was to be frozen for two years, after which it would again be tied to inflation. Bill 47 also repealed provisions relating to increased penalties for employers contravening ESA regulations; the extension of card-based certification into home care, building services, and temporary help agencies; mandatory sick days; and the restriction of binding arbitration in labour disputes.[95] Unlike Bill 148, which undertook two years of consultation and research,

Ford's Bill 47 was preceded by little consultation with stakeholders outside of the business community and represented an unabashedly pro-business perspective.[96] The reaction to Bill 47 was a mirror image to that which greeted Bill 148. Business organizations applauded the Ford government's efforts to "reverse most of the employment standards and labour reforms of Bill 148," which were "hastily implemented before the last election without any economic analysis or understanding of the potential negative impacts on job creation and the economy."[97] The Ontario Federation of Labour (OFL) called the Bill "unconscionable" and argued that the "government has shown again that it is governing for the few, making decisions without sufficient consultation and research that will drive millions of working Ontarians into poverty."[98]

The Ford government's second intervention into a legal strike came in December 2018 with Bill 67, the Labour Relations Amendment Act. Bill 67 was pre-emptive back-to-work legislation aimed at Power Workers' Union (PWU) members at Ontario Power Generation (OPG) who had voted to take strike action. As the legislature had adjourned for the winter break, the government called it back into session early to pass the back-to-work ruling, claiming the move was necessary to prevent power outages over the holidays. The central issue in the dispute was the refusal of the employer to grant contract workers at the Darlington and Pickering nuclear power plants equivalent rights to full-time workers. The legislation prohibited both strikes and lockouts, and the dispute was sent to binding arbitration for resolution. The NDP, Greens, and OFL criticized the move from the government, which once again removed the statutory right to bargain collectively and strike.[99]

The Ford government's most far-reaching intervention into public-sector collective bargaining arrived in November 2019 with the tabling and passage of Bill 124, the Protecting a Sustainable Public Sector for Future Generations Act. This legislation, which applied to nearly one million unionized and non-union public-sector workers, ordered a three-year public-sector wage freeze (increases limited to 1 percent) on any collective agreements or arbitration awards occurring on or after 6 June. Further, the Act prohibited any retro- or proactive compensatory wage increases before or after the legislation came into effect, and it ensured the wage freeze implementation by removing the jurisdiction of both the Ontario Labour Relations Board and labour arbitrators to enquire into the constitutionality of the Act or its congruence with the Ontario Human Rights Code. To make doubly certain that full compliance would be achieved, the minister of labour was given the discretion to void any agreement or award that did not conform to Bill 124. It should be noted that several exemptions were written into the legislation, including police and firefighters, leading some nurses' union to criticize, among other things, the gendered nature of the Bill.[100]

Public-sector unions were sharply critical of this intervention and claimed the legislation was unconstitutional, like similar legislation passed in Manitoba was found to be in 2020 (see Chapter 8).[101] The OFL spearheaded a Charter challenge against Bill 124 in December of 2019 that brought together several public- and private-sector unions, including CUPE, OPSEU, Unifor, and the United Food and Commercial Workers (UFCW).[102] The unions argued that Bill 124 undermined the right to free collective bargaining under the freedom of association guarantee in Section 2(d) of the Canadian Charter of Rights and Freedoms.[103] It is expected the Supreme Court will make a ruling in 2022.

In Quebec, the Marois-led PQ were able to secure a minority government and replace the outgoing Liberals in September 2012. Having campaigned on a moderately progressive platform, among the PQ's first acts was to cancel the tuition hikes that had sparked the 2012 student strikes.[104] The PQ also appointed well-known activists to the environment and natural resources portfolios in cabinet and announced it would replace the payroll-based health premiums with a new tax on high-income earners. A year into its mandate, however, the government's progressive tinge waned as back-to-work legislation and austerity returned.[105] The PQ intervened in the construction sector in 2013 with Bill 54, An Act Respecting the Resumption of Work in the Construction Industry, which ordered 77,000 construction workers back to work under threat of fines for non-compliance. The election of April 2014 returned the Quebec Liberals, led by Philippe Couillard, to power, with a clear majority. The Couillard Liberals would reprise the policy of public expenditure restraint established by the previous Liberal government and intervene in collective bargaining several times, rewriting key elements of labour policy.

The first intervention came in October 2014 with the introduction of Bill 8, An Act to Amend the Labour Code with Respect to Certain Employees of Farming Businesses. This legislation sought to reverse a previous Quebec Superior Court ruling making it easier for farm workers, including migrant farm workers, to organize a union. Bill 8 amended the Labour Code to stipulate that migrant workers were prohibited from forming a union and further required that an agricultural enterprise must employ a minimum of three full-time workers year round in order to be eligible to organize a union. It was modelled after the Ontario Agricultural Employees' Protection Act, which was found not to violate Canada's Charter of Rights and Freedoms in the controversial Supreme Court of Canada Fraser decision released in April 2011. The adoption of Bill 8 was greeted by the Union of Agricultural Producers (Union des producteurs agricoles, UPA), the main farming and forestry business lobby, as a way to preserve the sustainability of small agricultural production.[106] The labour movement denounced Bill 8 as discriminatory because it excluded workers from the right of association due to their migration status. The legislation, it was rightly argued, reproduced and institutionalized racialized discrimination between citizens and temporary migrant workers.[107]

Over the next four years, the Couillard Liberals would intervene or threaten to intervene on six further occasions in a diverse range of collective bargaining and labour disputes. These included imposing arbitration in the case of striking automotive mechanics in the Saguenay-Lac-Saint Jean region (2015); legislation to deregulate the taxi industry and create room for Uber ride-share services (2016); back-to-work legislation to force striking Quebec government lawyers back to their jobs (2016); and passing back-to-work legislation to end a strike in the construction sector (2017). Electoral politics in Quebec had, since the 2008 recession, become increasingly volatile. And the election of 2018 would again demonstrate that the province's voters had become increasingly unglued from traditional partisan loyalties. The Liberals were defeated and replaced by the conservative and autonomist Coalition for Quebec's Future (CAQ), which had only formed seven years earlier. While the CAQ government was not supportive of unions in any respect, it recognized in pragmatic terms that full-on assaults had proven to be a losing tactic for previous governments.

In the face of recalcitrant worker militancy, however, they did not hesitate to flex their coercive muscle. In January 2018, 1,000 aluminum smelter workers organized with the United Steelworkers were locked out by Alco/Rio Tinto. For 18 months, workers waged a courageous battle against not only a global mining giant with a long history of environmental and labour rights abuses but also a new government threatening to impose arbitration if an agreement was not swiftly concluded.[108] With the full weight of the state behind them, Alco/Rio Tinto made a final offer to the union which, if not accepted, would lead to the closing of the plant. While the union recommended rejecting the offer, roughly 80 percent accepted the concession-laden agreement that included the replacement of a defined-benefit plan with a defined-contribution plan, a 10 percent reduction in the workforce, and changes to seniority rights and the organization of work. The strike would go down as one of the longest in Quebec history. It also demonstrated in dramatic fashion the profundity of a labour movement becalmed.[109] For whatever it is worth, in the aftermath of public threats by the premier and labour minister, the union filed a complaint with the ILO. In its decision, the ILO refused to point a finger, amounting to little more than a collective shrug.[110]

For a conservative party, the CAQ's approach to fiscal policy was not particularly austere. All four CAQ budgets increased public spending, especially in health care, education, and social services.[111] In its first pre-pandemic budget of 2019, overall program expenditures increased an average of 5 to 7 percent, with spending on health care and education increased by 5 percent. This continued into the 2021 and 2022 budgets as the pandemic wore on. In the 2021 budget, higher education funding was boosted by 8.2 percent while health care increased 5.8 percent. Across the board, program spending had increased 14.5 percent year over year. The 2022 budget, the final one before the next election, saw program spending increase by a robust 5 percent. Polling in mid-2022 suggested the CAQ enjoyed wide-ranging support and would easily win re-election.

However, the fiscal policy of the CAQ government is not to be construed as an expression of progressive Keynesianism. Obviously, the onset of the COVID-19 pandemic in March 2020 pressed all governments, irrespective of partisan hue, to ramp up public spending to meet the public health and associated economic crises. With collective agreements across the public sector set to expire in March 2023, Quebec's three major trade union confederations – the Confédération des syndicats nationaux (CSN), the Fédération des travailleurs et travailleuses du Québec (FTQ), and the Centrale des syndicats du Québec (CSQ) – representing 355,000 public-sector workers, formed a common front to coordinate their bargaining efforts. The shared bargaining priorities were increases in wages to match the 7-plus percent inflation of the time and "improving working conditions that have deteriorated" through the pandemic.[112] Moreover, the CAQ centred its politics on a conservative nationalism that amplified the protection of the French language; it did so, in part, by demanding greater control over immigration and further limiting the use of English in the workplace.

CONCLUSION: PERMANENT EXCEPTIONALISM AND AUTHORITARIANISM

Through the 2008 crisis, Canadian media punditry was awash in self-congratulatory assessments of Canada's exceptionalism in escaping the worst of the economic fallout experienced by so many other countries. The post-crisis period of fiscal cleanup, particularly in Canada's provinces, suggests a rather different reality. While Canada did not endure the severity of crisis as did the United States, Greece, Ireland, or Spain, the historical record demonstrates that if there was "exceptionalism" of any kind, it was that of the permanent austerity and suspension of workers' rights to bargain collectively and strike, as detailed in this book. At the most legalistic level of analysis, the specific characteristics of Canadian federalism and the constitutional allocation of responsibilities entailed therein is one key element to understanding how the crisis impacted Canadian workers.

The second decade of the twenty-first century is one where the immediate post-crisis fiscal consolidations observed in most Canadian provinces largely took a distinctly authoritarian turn. The exit strategies from deficit financing, including cutbacks in redistributional programs and public services more generally, were augmented by suspension of collective bargaining and legislatively deeming a growing number of workers as essential. These were all the elements necessary to institutionalize austerity into the operational policy framework of provinces. In other words, workers across the occupational spectrum were called upon to pay for the enduring economic legacy of the 2008 crisis. The result normed cutback management into the routine work of provincial and federal governments. Where no government of any partisan hue was prepared or capable of countering embedded austerity, the result was, not inevitably, an ongoing assault on trade union rights and freedoms.

What also looms large through this period is the obvious inability of unions, save for some specific sectional struggles, to mount effective campaigns of resistance. Protest events, media campaigns, and lobbying only went so far – and that was often to no avail. The primary weapon of defence was legal challenge, with the courts as the terrain of struggle. Whether these were effective or not is another serious question to which the following chapter turns, but it is telling that broad mobilization of members and allies was no longer in the political arsenal.

CHAPTER EIGHT

The Right to Strike: Freedom of Association and the Charter

Chapter Summary: For 40 years, Canadian trade unions have come to rely on legalistic strategies – reverting to the law and courts – to sustain and advance their rights and freedoms. Within any liberal democracy, the legal system is a foundational pillar to maintaining legitimacy and order. However, the laws and the institutions that uphold them are deeply embedded within institutional structures and capitalist power relations that reflect the relative balance of class forces. The International Labour Organization (ILO) provided an early forum through which to contest the actions of Canadian governments, but this was of limited effectiveness. The adoption of the Charter of Rights and Freedoms in 1982 opened up new avenues, but these have evolved unevenly and with limited success. In some instances, the courts have reprimanded governments for overreaching, while in others they have given their stamp of approval. In nearly all of these cases, they have done little to extend rights to non-unionized workers, let alone contribute to a reinvigorated and confident labour movement. While knowledge of the law can be a powerful tool, it rarely translates into bargaining power; only politics does, and in this regard, the turn to legalism has been an ineffectual tool for organizing workers and wider working-class communities.

INTRODUCTION

The liberal democratic legal principles of capitalist social relations in Canada were given their most internally coherent expression with the constitutional entrenchment of the Charter of Rights and Freedoms in 1982. Section 2 of the Constitution Act, 1982 listed the fundamental freedoms: freedom of conscience and religion; freedom of thought, belief, opinion, and expression; freedom of peaceful assembly; and freedom of association. These rights were guaranteed to everyone, except so far as Section 1 made them "subject only to such reasonable limits as can be demonstrably justified in a free and democratic society."

The framing of the Charter was removed from the actually existing conditions of class relations and struggle in the early 1980s, a mark of the abstract, and to some extent cosmetic, nature of such an **a priori** guarantee of freedom of association. The freedom of association it guaranteed was, at the time, abstract, as its specific application to collective bargaining and trade unions was unclear to say the least. As we have shown, by the time the Charter was proclaimed, the process of ad hoc state actions that arbitrarily undermined the exercise of freedom of association by large groups of workers was already well advanced – the harmonious system of constitutional law that the Charter established at an abstract level was already being denied. In practice, what had come to the fore was the disjuncture between the guarantee of freedom of association enunciated in the Charter and the increasing state incursions against this freedom, at least as exercised by workers.

In promulgating the fundamental freedom of thought, belief, opinion, and expression, the Charter included freedom of the press and other communication media. Notably, it was silent on whether freedom of association similarly included the essential means of making that freedom effective for working people – that is, the associated rights to bargain and strike. Certain group rights were recognized in the Charter, above all the language and educational rights of French and English linguistic minorities and, albeit undefined, the rights and freedoms of Indigenous peoples. To be sure, the coinage of liberal-democratic constitutional discourse uses a universal language of rights that obscures the class nature of capitalist societies. These conventions largely account for the general absence of the collective rights of subordinate classes from declarations of rights. A mark of the Charter's conventional nature was that it did not advance the limits of liberal discourse regarding trade union rights.

For the rights of labour to bargain and strike to be considered an essential component of Canadian liberal democracy, it would require that the judiciary construe them as essential to freedom of association for workers. Despite certain equivocations during the constitutional debate, the actual practice of governments to increasingly restrict the right to strike could hardly instill confidence that the framers of the courts would interpret the Charter in a manner that would constitutionally guarantee Canadian workers' rights to bargain collectively or strike. Even the social justice ideology, which Rand's famous ruling in 1946 had enunciated to sustain and elaborate the legal enactments of the 1940s, clearly corresponded with the dominant ideological orientations of political elites at the time. Rand had accepted that "the predominance of capital over labour" was "unquestionable"; but he had interpreted the legislation of the 1940s to mean that the Canadian state had acknowledged that "the power of organized labour ... must be available to redress the balance of what is called social justice." In contrast, the ideology of neoliberalism that governments rapidly adopted from the 1980s onwards inevitably raised the question: since trust and belief in capital and the state rather than social justice were the immediate order of the day, what was the point of freedom of association for workers at all? For all its ringing of abstract phrases, the Charter gave no positive guidance to answer this question.

Had it expressly included the right to strike, the Charter would have served to limit the judicial and legislative room to manoeuvre. In any case, there was a loophole, cynically crafted by the attorneys general of Saskatchewan, Ontario, and the federal government in their infamous middle-of-the-night meeting in the kitchen of the Ottawa Conference Centre: the notwithstanding clause (Section 33) at the tail end of the Charter allows governments to pass legislation that specifically declares that an act is not subject to the fundamental freedoms or equality rights provisions. Such a declaration ceases to have effect after a five-year period, but the notwithstanding declaration can be re-enacted indefinitely. Thus, even if the Canadian courts were to give a broad and generous interpretation to freedom of association, it was by no means guaranteed that governments determined to restrict the rights of labour would necessarily adhere to the interpretation. The freedom of association provision incorporated in the Charter of Rights and Freedoms lay cheek by jowl with legislation that effectively removed the right to strike and to free collective bargaining for unionized workers. The legal confusion immediately threw the responsibility for re-establishing a semblance of coherence to the rule of law in Canada in the sphere of labour relations into the lap of the courts.

THE FIRST LABOUR TRILOGY

Until the Charter was entrenched in the Canadian Constitution, the most common avenue of juridical appeal by Canadian unions was to the ILO. The ILO is a United Nations tripartite agency composed of business, labour, and government representatives of which Canada has been a member since 1919. Canada has never had a particularly sterling record in terms of ratifying ILO conventions, having to date ratified only 37 of 190 conventions.[1] Ratification requires unanimous provincial consent, and it is questionable how much priority federal governments have assigned to securing such assent. The Canadian state's shift towards legislative interventions against labour rights has led to increasing complaints by Canadian unions to the ILO's Committee on Freedom of Association (CFOA). As Table 8.1 shows, Canada has become the cause of more complaints than any other ILO member country, despite its much smaller population. Since the 1980s, more than 90 complaints have been filed against federal and provincial governments, with the CFOA finding a violation to have occurred in more than 90 percent of these cases. In bringing these complaints to the ILO, however, Canadian unions had to be aware that the tactic could only have demonstrative effects, since the federal and provincial governments had already made it clear that any endorsement of union complaints by the CFOA would be effectively ignored.

Still, one must be very careful with these comparisons: they must not be taken on their own to show that any one government restricts union freedoms more than another. Such complaints reflect a dialectic between state behaviours and the inclinations of trade unions in particular countries to make use of the ILO's capacity for moral suasion against governments. An inclination to appeal to the ILO will depend on a given labour movement's attitude to that body, its general approach to litigation, as well as the availability of other juridical avenues of appeal regarding incursions against freedom of association. A growing number of complaints to the ILO is only suggestive of discontent felt by the country's labour movement, particularly on the friction between labour and the state. The ILO is certainly not a body quick to condemn its member states. It keeps a very close eye on retaining the membership of those many regimes that by no stretch of the imagination could be designated as anything other than authoritarian. In fact, the ILO has been inclined to give governments the benefit of the doubt with respect to temporary measures, such as statutory incomes policy programs, that restrict the right to bargain and strike. It has also accepted that the right to strike for workers in essential

Table 8.1. Complaints of Violations of Trade Union Rights Filed with the ILO against the Group of Seven Capitalist Countries, 1954–2019

Countries	1954–1973		1974–1991		1992–2001		2002–2019	
	No.	%	No.	%	No.	%	No.	%
Canada	5	6	37	39	33	70	37	54
France	20	22	6	6	2	4	9	13
Italy	3	3	2	2	0	0	1	1
Japan	3	3	17	18	4	9	8	12
United Kingdom	41	46	17	18	5	11	4	6
United States	12	14	14	15	1	2	9	13
Germany	5	6	2	2	2	4	1	1
Total	89	100	95	100	47	100	69	100

Note: Percentages rounded.

services can be prohibited on the grounds that strike activity might endanger public health and safety.

ILO decisions have generally been ignored by Canadian governments, a sorry testament to the gap between Canada's willingness to sign international declarations and its adherence to them in practice. What of the guarantee of freedom of association now established in the Canadian Constitution itself? Canadian governments could hardly ignore this so readily. As governmental transgressions of the right to strike and to bargain collectively followed one after the other, Canadian unions, despite their initial disdain for involving themselves in Charter debates, increasingly appealed to the Canadian courts, hoping to secure the guarantee of freedom of association that the Charter now constitutionally established on grounds similar to those that Justice Rand had offered 40 years earlier.

Despite the ideological and juridical importance of Rand's 1946 ruling, the pro-employer biases of most judges could hardly be missed over the ensuing decades. Often enough, they found ways to employ their own judge-made doctrines to invent or manipulate restrictions on labour and used non-constitutional juridical review to fashion expansive interpretations of the law to benefit employers, above all through the ready use of injunctions. However, freedom of association was not within their constitutional frame of reference as a means of limiting government actions until 1982. It was never clear whether this judicial bias extended, on their part, to challenging the fundamentals. The legislative assault on unions that accompanied the Charter's introduction en-sured that the answer would not be too long in coming. However unlikely it was that the courts would interpret the Charter generously for workers, the effect of judicial review in a liberal democracy should never be minimized.

Whether the courts – ultimately responsible for overseeing the coherence of a legal system – would sustain a legislative assault on free collective bargaining in the face of the embodiment of freedom of association in the Constitution was crucial; a great deal depended on the outcome. It was a measure of the dissonance in Canada's constitutional labour law that the judiciary, far from immediately providing a semblance of coherence, was revealed to be in a state of confusion itself for some time. From 1983 to 1987, the courts did not resolve, but rather mirrored and reproduced, that discord through a cacophony of contradictory judgments. As an initial example, the Divisional Court of the Ontario Superior Court ruled in 1983 (in the *Broadway Manor* case testing the constitutionality of Ontario's Inflation Restraint Act) that legislative disposal of collective bargaining rights and of the right to strike, by cynically extending collective agreements beyond their termination, was unconstitutional. The three judges of the High Court unanimously held that the Charter guarantee of freedom of association extended to the activities of trade unions, a ruling that overturned a decision by the Ontario Labour Relations Board endorsing the practice. As Justice Galligan put it: "Freedom of association must include freedom to engage in conduct which is reasonably consonant with the lawful objectives of the association. The purpose of an association of workers in a union is to advance their common interests. If they are not free to take such lawful steps that they see as reasonable to advance those interests, including bargaining and striking, then as a practical matter their association is barren and useless."[2]

Even if this argument only recalled a long-established principle (going back in Canada to 1872), these were still heady words, reflecting what Justice Galligan termed the need for "a large and liberal construction" of freedom of association judicially. It seemed to suggest the reality and the importance of a degree of relative autonomy the courts had from both government and capital. Despite the strong message, the ruling itself had little strength. It is not unusual for judges to award one side a win in principle, while giving the other the substantive victory. The Court only narrowed the range of permanent exceptionalism. It found that the Inflation Restraint Act as a whole could stand on the grounds that the imposition of temporary, statutory wage restraint was a political judgment consonant with the exceptional infringements of the fundamental freedoms allowed for under Section 1 of the Charter. Thus, given that statutory wage controls had been in effect in Ontario, as in most

Canadian jurisdictions, for more years than not since 1975, the Court put its stamp on permanent exceptionalism by endorsing the primacy of political judgments over freedom of association when it came to wage restraint.

Still, the judgment's restrictions on the range of permanent exceptionalism, applying only to temporary wage restraint, was significant. It not only challenged the much broader nature of the existing shift to coercion, but it also implicitly challenged such special restrictions for public servants on the right to bargain and strike as had been applied in most Canadian jurisdictions. However, the strength of the judgment was further vitiated as the Alberta government immediately displayed the utility of Section 33 of the Charter for governments that would not brook the relative autonomy of the courts with respect to positive interpretations of labour's rights. In the wake of the *Broadway Manor* judgment, Premier Lougheed declared that his government would use the notwithstanding clause to ensure that Alberta's public-sector workers could still be denied the right to strike. The Alberta government immediately initiated a reference to the Alberta Court of Appeal whereby an advisory opinion was sought on the constitutionality of those provisions of the province's labour laws that denied the right to strike and imposed a system of compulsory arbitration. The majority of the Alberta Court of Appeal responded with a judgment that directly contradicted the *Broadway Manor* ruling in Ontario.

The provisions of the Charter had to be interpreted in a "broad and liberal" manner, but not in an "extreme or extravagant" way, either. The Court was not persuaded that prohibition of strikes and the imposition of compulsory arbitration limited public employees' freedom of association or ability to bargain collectively in a meaningful manner. In any case, a measure of restraint was required in judicial review. The arbitrariness of this interpretation should not be overlooked. The issue at stake was crucial, not only for the Alberta government, but for virtually the whole Canadian state at the time. The attorney general of Canada and attorneys general of no less than seven other provinces intervened on the side of Alberta when this judgment was appealed to the Supreme Court of Canada by the Alberta Union of Provincial Employees, the Alberta Fire Fighters' Association, and the Canadian Union of Public Employees. Manitoba, where the NDP was in office, intervened on the side of the unions; New Brunswick alone stayed out of this juridical fracas.

It took until April of 1987 for the Supreme Court's long-delayed judgment to be rendered, and by this time, an even broader array of lower court judgments had accumulated. A clear inflection towards an interpretation that disadvantaged trade union freedoms appeared in these court decisions, but it is important to emphasize that they only sustained what governments were doing to disadvantage labour. It was not a matter of the courts versus the attorneys general and their legislatures; it was the attorneys general, the legislatures, and the courts versus labour. Nevertheless, the Ontario Court of Appeal, in October 1984, without striking down the judgment of the Divisional Court the year before, completely sidestepped the constitutional issue and argued that the lower Court had been wrong to base its decision on the constitutional grounds of freedom of association. Yet in 1985, the Saskatchewan Court of Appeal, in examining a case of back-to-work legislation, rejected in very strong terms these interpretations (the *Dairy Workers* case). The majority ruling broadly returned to the reasoning that underlined the initial *Broadway Manor* judgment in Ontario and emphasized the connection between freedom of association for workers and the freedom to bargain collectively and to strike.

The Saskatchewan government took note. Not deterred from legislating its public employees back to work in a dispute in 1986, it invoked the notwithstanding clause of the Charter to override the expansive interpretation of its guarantee of freedom of association. It was left to the Supreme Court to provide coherence to all this juridical discord. An important sign of the way the wind was blowing on the Supreme Court appeared in December 1986, when it dismissed an appeal of the *Dolphin Delivery* ruling on picketing. The case involved a challenge by the Retail, Wholesale and Department Store Union (RWDSU) of a court injunction prohibiting secondary picketing on the grounds that the injunction violated the union's freedom of expression. While the Court ruled that picketing did involve an element of expression, it also held that the Charter was unavailable to review an order of the Court in a dispute between private litigants (insofar as Section 32 of the Charter limits its scope to governments). Given that the courts have always provided a mechanism by which employers seek to restrict the scope of picketing and the success of strike action by workers, the exemption from the Charter that this ruling established for court decisions preserved the Court's capacity to review and limit the collective action of workers. It appeared that the labour movement was in for a difficult time in pressing their constitutional claims before the Supreme Court.

The issues of freedom of association and the rights to collectively bargain and to strike were only directly addressed on 9 April 1987, when the Supreme Court finally offered a set of simultaneous judgments on appeals for the *Alberta Reference*, the PSAC challenge to the "6 and 5" legislation (see Chapter 3), and the *Dairy Workers* case. The judgment rendered in *Alberta Reference*, since the Alberta legislation provided the broadest and most permanent example of the denial of the rights to strike and bargain collectively, took centre stage. The decision in this case would frame the response given by the Court to the question of the validity of more ad hoc and temporary restrictions of the kind involved in the back-to-work legislation case and temporary statutory wage-restraint cases. The majority judgment was a shockingly brief one, running only three substantive paragraphs, with the reasoning as short in elegance as it was in social justice: the constitutional guarantee of freedom of association in Section 2(d) of the Canadian Charter of Rights and Freedoms does not include, in the case of a trade union, a guarantee of the right to bargain collectively and the right to strike.

In considering the meaning that must be given to freedom of association in Section 2(d) of the Charter, it is essential to keep in mind that this concept must be applied to a wide range of associations or organizations of a political, religious, social, or economic nature, with a very wide variety of objectives, as well as activity by which these objectives may be pursued. It is in this larger perspective, and not simply with regard to the perceived requirements of a trade union, however important they may be, that one must consider the implications of extending the concept of freedom of association to the right to engage in particular activity on the ground that the activity is essential to give an association meaningful existence. In considering whether it is reasonable to ascribe such a sweeping intention to the Charter, the premise that without such additional constitutional protection the guarantee of freedom of association would be a meaningless and empty one must be rejected. Freedom of association is particularly important for the exercise of other fundamental freedoms, such as freedom of expression and freedom of conscience and religion. These afford a wide scope for protected activity in association. Moreover, the freedom to work for the establishment of an association, to belong to an association, to maintain it, and to participate in its lawful activity without penalty is not to be taken for granted. That is indicated by its express recognition and protection in labour relations legislation.

What is at issue is not the importance of freedom of association in this sense but whether particular activity of an association in pursuit of its objectives is to be constitutionally protected or left to be regulated by legislative policy. The rights for which constitutional protection is sought – the modern rights to bargain collectively and to strike, involving correlative duties or obligations resting on an employer – are not fundamental rights or freedoms. They involve the creation of legislation and balancing competing interests in a field that has been recognized by the courts as requiring special expertise. It is surprising that in an area in which this Court has affirmed a principle of judicial restraint in the review of administrative action, this Court should be considering the substitution of its judgment for that of the legislature by constitutionalizing in general and abstract terms rights that the legislature has found it necessary to define and qualify in various ways according to the particular field of labour relations involved. The resulting necessity of applying Section 1 of the Charter to a review of particular legislation in this field demonstrates the extent to which the courts become involved in a review of legislative policy for which they are not really fitted. Thus, the constitutional issue of the right to strike and bargain was collectively disposed.

Note that there were but three reasons offered. The first involved an equation of working-class association with all other associations, adopting a haunting silence on the capitalist and class-based nature of Canadian society. The second explicitly denied that freedom of association involves a distinct and separate conception of freedom from the others enumerated in the Charter, despite the fact that the Charter specifically recognizes it as such. The Court had rendered it an adjunct to the other fundamental freedoms, such as freedom of expression or belief. The constitutional guarantee of freedom of association was reduced to what you can say or think, omitting what is necessary for workers to do about their subordinate status vis-à-vis their employers. Finally, the Court reasoned – with no little dissimulation regarding judicial activism that benefited employers before the Charter, and despite its rulings in other contexts that affirmed its new activist role under the Charter – that what the legislature granted, the legislature can take away.

All this was done without so much as a bow to the fact that for a century the courts had recognized that workers could legally use their collective economic power in certain circumstances. Nor, extremely unconventionally, was any reference made to the international conventions to which Canada is a signatory. Having rendered this blunt judgment, the Court felt no need to comment on specific exceptional abrogations of the right to strike and bargain collectively, such as were on appeal before it. Indeed, the ruling did not even deign to address one of the important questions raised by the *Alberta Reference* itself, which pertained to Section 2(2) of the Police Officers' Act, which explicitly forbade police officers from becoming members of a trade union or of an organization directly or indirectly affiliated with a trade union.

As we have already recalled, Justice Rand had cited "the history of the past century" as demonstrating "that the power of organized labour had to be available to redress the balance of what is called social justice." The struggles by workers to organize at that time were seen by Rand to connect with the statist notions of reformist **gradualism** of his day, sanctioning labour laws designed to harmonize the capital-labour relationship so as to secure social order in a class-based society. Rand had recognized as a fundamental condition of capitalist society that the power of employers lay in their ownership and/ or control of the means of labour, whereas the power of those who sold their labour lay in their collective organization, and he regarded labour legislation as a historic institutionalization of working-class rights in a capitalist democracy. However, in 1987 the Supreme Court of Canada grimly refused the opportunity opened by the Charter to constitutionally sanction this notion.

The primary reason advanced by the SCC for rejecting the position that freedom of association for workers necessarily entailed the right to bargain and strike was that guarantees in the Charter were individual rather than group rights. Collective bargaining is a group concern, a group activity, but the group can exercise only the constitutional right of its individual members on behalf of those members. If the right asserted is not found in the Charter for the individual, it cannot be implied for the group merely by the fact of association. It follows as well that the rights of the individual members of the group cannot be enlarged merely by the fact of association. Justice Rand openly recognized that capital was the structurally dominant and labour the subordinate force in "a society whose economic life has private enterprise as its dynamic." Justice McIntyre, in the *Alberta Reference*, by contrast, referred to capital merely as the "employers" and treated capital and labour as "two equally powerful" socio-economic forces. McIntyre, no less than Rand, certainly recognized that the evolution of labour legislation reflected delicate shifts in the balance between capital and labour. But what McIntyre did was to make more explicit the effect of the Court's majority ruling – providing a judicial rationale for a state now concerned less with securing social harmony in labour relations and more with undoing the collective power of labour organization in the context of the global and domestic capitalist restructuring of the time.

If McIntyre's judgment was more obscure than Rand's, it was perhaps not only due to personal factors, but also to the ideological effects of postwar collective bargaining in concealing the class relationships and private profit-driven dynamics of a capitalist society. Moreover, such is the relative autonomy of the judiciary in a liberal democracy that it cannot be said that this particular decision by the Supreme Court was inevitable. Chief Justice Dickson and Justice Bertha Wilson presented two dissenting opinions, as carefully reasoned and exhaustive as the majority judgment was pre-emptory. They cited foreign jurisprudential authorities in a balanced and considered fashion and included experts in international law. The chief justice came to a chilling, and in our view incontrovertible, conclusion: "If freedom of association only protects the joining together of persons for common purposes, but not the pursuit of the very activities for which the association was formed, then the freedom is indeed legalistic, ungenerous, indeed vapid." In the chief justice's view, the majority judgment had rendered the Charter's explicit and independent guarantee of freedom of association superfluous: "the express conferral of a freedom of association is unnecessary if all that is intended is to give effect to the collective enjoyment of other freedoms." Nor was it only individual political rights that were protected by the Charter.[3]

The role of association has always been vital as a means of protecting the essential needs and interests of working people. Throughout history, workers have associated to overcome their vulnerability as individuals to the strength of their employers. The capacity to bargain collectively has long been recognized as one of the integral and primary functions of associations of working people. While trade unions also fulfil other important social and political functions, collective bargaining remains vital to the capacity of individual employees to participate in ensuring fair wages, health and safety precautions, and equitable and humane working conditions. The impact of McIntyre's decision was thus immediate: the putative grounds for union court challenges to restrictive legislation had been undermined, all the more dangerous as it took place within a climate of renewed employer hostility towards collective bargaining itself.

In the context outlined above, the Court had provided juridical and ideological space for a broader assault on private- and public-sector collective bargaining by virtue of the breadth of its ruling that freedom of association did not constitutionally protect workers' rights to bargain collectively and strike. The general inclination of the Court was to defend restrictive governmental actions. However, while it established that the right to strike would not be protected under the Charter, the decision had not so definitively ruled out the possibility of constitutional protection for some aspects of the collective bargaining relationship. No clear majority was expressed on the question of collective bargaining, and principles of judicial interpretation dictated that the issue was left unresolved by the Court, although the implications of the Court's ruling certainly did not give much cause for optimism. Indeed, the overwhelming tendency of the courts was for quite some time to follow the Supreme Court's lead and to deny Charter protection for collective bargaining.

The real test of precisely how much protection would be afforded to collective bargaining under the Charter came before the Supreme Court of Canada in a challenge by the Professional Institute of the Public Service of Canada (PIPSC) to Section 42 of the Northwest Territories Public Sector Act, which authorized the government to legislatively determine who will represent employees in bargaining. The case arose when responsibility for health care services in the area was transferred by the federal to territorial government. PIPSC applied to the territorial government for incorporation as the bargaining agent for the nurses but was refused. It then challenged the restrictions contained in the Public Sector Act on the grounds that it contravened the Charter's guarantee of free association. A shift in the SCC's composition since 1987 offered some grounds for optimism. Among those judges who had heard the trilogy, only Dickson and Wilson, who had both written strong dissenting opinions, and LaForest, who had concurred with the majority, remained. In a 4–3 decision, however, the Court rejected the union's claim, categorically ruling that collective bargaining warrants no constitutional protection.

Ironically, the swing vote in the case fell to Chief Justice Dickson, who this time displayed none of the courage or insight that characterized his dissents in the labour trilogy. Feeling constrained by principles of judicial precedent, Dickson "reluctantly" and with "considerable hesitation" accepted the position of the majority, for to do otherwise would be to overrule the labour trilogy. By characterizing the case as involving only the interests of the union, Dickson ignored the representative function of unions and the relationship between a union and its members. To echo his own words from the labour trilogy, Dickson, through the PIPSC judgment, helped to ensure that for trade unions and workers the right to freedom of association remained indeed legalistic, ungenerous, and vapid.

The majority decision in the PIPSC case endorsed the broad propositions of the labour trilogy that had denied any protection for the activities of an association, no matter how essential those activities might be to the very purpose and existence of the organization. However, the decision also extended the scope of freedom of association to protect some group activities, so long as they could be pursued legally on an individual basis. Although the effect was to extend the scope of Section 2(d) protections to include the actual activities of a group, it appeared impossible to reconcile the denial of protection for foundational or essential activities of a group with the granting of protection for individual activities pursued on a group basis. This news appeared to be good for trade unions seeking to establish protection for collective bargaining. However, in a perverse twist, the ruling held that the extension of Section 2(d) was not to benefit trade unions, since collective bargaining legislation itself had displaced the individual employment contract, thereby rendering bargaining illegal on an individual basis. The result was that PIPSC could only argue for the protection of collective bargaining as a foundational or essential activity for the existence of the group, the very argument that was precluded by the labour trilogy.

The ruling went on to hold that the legislation did not at all impair the ability of PIPSC to exist or to maintain itself, since employees were free to be members of PIPSC, even if it could not bargain or represent them. Consequently, the Court dismissed the argument that the legislation's failure to provide a mechanism for certification violated the principles of freedom of association. Since the activity of bargaining was not constitutionally protected, there could be no protection for "voluntary recognition." It is indeed a strange form of voluntary recognition in which the employer determines with whom it will bargain but is free to ignore the employees' choice of bargaining agent. The PIPSC decision was not unanimous, but it nevertheless demonstrated the Court's unwillingness to extend constitutional protection for the democratic rights of trade unions and their members, along with its insistence that the collective bargaining regime is a matter of legislative, rather than judicial, concern.[4] This attitude was reflected in a long line of cases that stretched to the end of the 1990s as the courts refused to grant constitutional protections to workers, and employers sought to utilize the Charter to further undermine and erode collective bargaining rights; such was the case in compulsory multi-employer bargaining in the construction industry – on the grounds that it violated employer freedom of association – and in the case of union security clauses – on the grounds that they violated employees' freedom to not associate. In virtually all these cases, the employer's challenge was dismissed by the courts.

This tendency reached its zenith with the SCC decision in *Lavigne v. OPSEU*, which showed that while the Court was not willing to protect unions and workers from legislative attacks, it was willing to protect them from attacks by employers and others who ideologically objected to unionism. Francis Merv Lavigne was a community college teacher who had refused to become a member of OPSEU, crossed picket lines when his fellow workers were on strike, and objected to paying union dues because they were used for a variety of "political" purposes with which he disagreed. Some of the expenditures to which he took exception included the support of the NDP, disarmament campaigns, pro-choice groups, and striking coal miners in Britain. The case was financed by the National Citizens' Coalition, a right-wing lobby group, and struck at the heart of the Rand formula and the preservation of free collective bargaining. Initiated in 1986, the case was finally decided by the SCC in 1991.

At trial, Justice White found that Lavigne's constitutional right to not associate had been violated by the forced payment of dues. In assessing whether the Rand formula constituted a reasonable limit on Lavigne's rights, Justice White ruled that only those payments related to collective bargaining could be justified. In a second, remedial decision, White ordered that the union keep detailed records of its expenditures for review by dissenting employees and that an opt-out mechanism be established so that workers could reclaim that portion of their dues spent on non-collective bargaining purposes to which they objected. With regard to the specific expenditures challenged by Lavigne, White found most to be impermissible, including payments to the NDP. Only payments to other unions were considered legitimate expenditures within the scope of collective bargaining, in that they helped to foster union solidarity. The Ontario Court of Appeal overturned White's decision, on the basis that the collective agreement negotiated between OPSEU and the colleges' governing body was a private matter to which the Charter did not apply. The Court, however, went on to say that even if the Charter did apply, the Rand formula did not constitute a violation of Lavigne's right to free association since nothing prevented him from opposing the union and associating with those of his own choosing.

At the Supreme Court, four judgments were issued. While the justices disagreed as to the correct approach to Section 2(d) and the question of whether Lavigne's rights had been violated, a majority held that the Rand formula did not contravene the Charter, and all agreed that the Rand formula would pass the Charter's Section 1 reasonable limits test. In dismissing Lavigne's claim, the Court pointed to the hypocrisy that would be involved if the Court – having refused to grant constitutional protection to the objectives of trade unions under Section 2(d) – permitted individuals to utilize the same rights to undermine unions. While the *Lavigne* case represented an exception to the general trend of Charter jurisprudence dealing with unions, it did not offer much hope for a judicial strategy of resisting the turn to coercion. Union democracy was permitted only so long as it operated within the context prescribed by the state. Collective bargaining was treated as a legislative policy that the Court found "reasonably justified" but that did not deserve constitutional protection in its own right.

THE INTERVENING YEARS: A JUDICIAL LIFELINE

Decisions by the Canadian judiciary could not be ignored by federal and provincial governments, but given the Supreme Court's endorsement of governmental restrictions on the right to bargain and strike in the first labour trilogy, and other decisions in the same vein, unions had little hope or reason to take similar restrictions back to the courts. The unions did indeed finally get some protection from the SCC in four cases it heard between 1999–2002. By this point, the unions were in a much weaker political and economic position than at the time of the 1987 trilogy, and the language that the judges chose to describe the situation of labour organizations in this conjuncture, and the protections that they offered, reflected this weakness. The famous Rand ruling after World War II had interpreted union rights in terms of balancing the interests of the great social forces of labour and capital in light of the latter's "long-term dominant position." In the 1987 trilogy, even with the freedom of association now listed in the Charter, the Supreme Court refused to find the legislative assault perfectly legal. However myopic such a view was in the 1980s, by the end of the 1990s not even a Supreme Court justice could expect it to be seen as credible. And indeed, the Supreme Court was now prepared to recognize that workers' rights in Canada needed to be offered certain protections under the Charter. This view, however, did not imply that the Court was overturning its trilogy stance. For the Court, freedom of association still did not include the rights to bargain and to strike. Further, insofar as the Court thought that a particular group of workers had, by virtue of their place in Canadian society, some degree of collective strength, there was not necessarily any right to even associate in a union. It was only insofar as they were members of a disadvantaged or vulnerable group that this right was to be given some protection.

In *Dunmore v. Ontario* (2001), the Court was asked to rule on whether the Ontario government's exclusion of agricultural workers from the province's collective bargaining regime was consistent with the Charter's guarantee of freedom of association. Until the NDP's Agricultural Labour Relations Act (ALRA), farm workers in Ontario had always been excluded from the law that protects union organizing. Their inclusion in collective bargaining legislation by the ALRA in 1994 (albeit only with a system of final offer settlement rather than the right to strike) was immediately undone in 1995 by the Harris Conservatives through its repeal of the ALRA and its further amendments to the province's Labour Relations Act to prohibit farm workers from forming unions (see Chapter 5). The UFCW, which had organized a few hundred mushroom and poultry workers in Leamington, brought an application challenging the amendments to the OLRA on the basis that it infringed their rights under Sections 2(d) and 15(1) (equality rights) of the Charter. The CLC intervened and urged the Supreme Court to reconsider the labour trilogy and read freedom of association to include collective bargaining and striking. The UFCW's position was narrower, however, only arguing that the exclusion of agricultural workers from labour relations legislation violated their right to associate and participate in unions.

The Ontario government maintained before the Court that the protection of the family farm was of primary importance in repealing the ALRA in order to ensure that the labour relationship remained a private action between individual farmers and employees. How discriminatory this position was could be seen from the Supreme Court's comment that it had never before been asked to review the complete exclusion of an occupational group, other than essential public-sector workers, from collective bargaining legislation. In finding for the union, Justice Bastarache, writing for seven of his colleagues, held that there was a positive freedom to collectively associate, at the same time reaffirming that this freedom did not include the rights to bargain and strike. The Court also asked whether in the age of expanding Charter values a positive obligation existed for the province to enact protective legislation for vulnerable groups in the context of labour relations. The Court determined that agricultural workers represented a vulnerable section of the workforce that had been unable to associate without state protection. It also implicated the government in the failure of agricultural workers to associate. According to Bastarache, "by extending statutory protection to just about every class of worker in Ontario, the legislature has essentially discredited the organizing efforts of agricultural workers. This is especially true given the relative status of agricultural workers in Canadian society."

The majority decision in *Dunmore* acknowledged that vulnerable workers have a right to associate with a union and that the state has a certain obligation not to restrict that right. It said little, however, about the limitations imposed by the state on the ability and restrictions to organize per se. In this sense, rights to collective bargaining and to strike remained clearly off the table. The fundamental basis of the Court ruling (without using the group-rights provision of Section 15(1) of the Charter, as only Justice Claire L'Heureux-Dubé wanted to do) held that the vulnerability of agricultural workers in the labour market undermined their Section 2(d) freedom of association rights under the Charter. By extension, were these workers able to maintain a lasting social or economic strength, the Court would not be willing to extend Charter protection to them. For farm workers, the Court was only willing to extend Section 2(d) to the organizational aspect of union activity rather than to the full ambit of labour relations rights that would include the collective rights to bargain and to strike. Their decision therefore still left vulnerable workers in a weak legal position vis-à-vis the employer and the state.

Building on this contradiction, the Ontario government responded to the *Dunmore* decision through the introduction in 2002 of Bill 187, the Agricultural Employees Protection Act. Although the government acknowledged the Supreme Court's recognition that farm workers have a legal right to associate, it stressed that those rights were not extended to the collective bargaining and strike rights enshrined in the OLRA. Bill 187 maintained the spirit of the *Dunmore* decision (freedom of association) but did not expressly give agricultural workers the same rights guaranteed to other unionized workers under the OLRA, including the rights to bargain and strike.

The logic of vulnerability as the basis for the protection of workers' rights had already surfaced in a 1999 Supreme Court ruling in a case involving freedom of expression. During a labour dispute with two K-Mart stores in British Columbia in which the mostly part-time women workers had been locked out for six months, the UFCW local involved had distributed leaflets at various other non-unionized K-Mart stores. The leaflets contained information on the unfair labour practices of K-Mart Ltd., informed shoppers of the labour dispute, and encouraged them to shop elsewhere. When K-Mart appealed this action to the BC Labour Relations Board, the tribunal found that the union action had constituted secondary picketing and was illegal per se. The union claimed that the legislated definition of picketing was too broad and grouping picketing, leafleting, and boycotts in the same legal definition violated both workers' freedom of association and freedom of expression rights.

In reviewing this case, the Supreme Court agreed with the union that the definition of picketing outlined in the BC labour code was too expansive and did infringe on freedom of association rights. The Court concluded that there was a distinction between picketing, which produces a signal effect to individuals, and social protest, which is a political right of all individuals in Canada. In striking this balance, however, the Court did not challenge the long-standing presumption in Canadian jurisprudence that secondary picketing was illegal per se. In finding for the workers, the Court came to the conclusion that K-Mart employees were vulnerable workers who needed to be protected alongside other disadvantaged social groups. The Court came to this conclusion through a comparison of the vulnerability of retail workers to many other non-labour groups, including new Canadians, which also address infringements in human rights actions through the use of leafleting and consumer boycotts. The Court's decision rested on a delicate balance between the individual rights of vulnerable workers to political speech, and their ability to politically engage their employer through the use of a strike. Despite the narrowness of this ruling, which avoided the issue of secondary picketing being illegal per se, the UFCW expressed relief that the decision at least acknowledged the traditional right of workers to communicate their message to their communities, implying that union members have the same right to bring their issues to a public forum as everyone else.

Similar to the *Lavigne* case a decade earlier, in 2002 the freedom to *not* associate was once again brought to the SCC. Especially important in this case was the freedom for provincial governments to legislate mandatory union membership within the construction industry, but it had wider implications in terms of whether courts in Canada would find "right to work" legislation to be constitutional.[5] Andre Gareau, owner of Advance Cutting and Coring Ltd., challenged the Quebec government's law that required workers in the construction industry to belong to one of five unions sanctioned by the province. Against this ruling, the attorney general of Quebec argued that the construction act incorporates legal rules that answer the need to set up an efficient and stable collective bargaining system in the Quebec construction industry. In a 5–4 ruling, the Court concluded that it did not and, like *Lavigne*, there was profound disagreement on why. In writing the decision, the newest member of the Court from Quebec, Louis Lebel, argued that in the past 20 years of Charter jurisprudence and labour relations, the Court had generally maintained that the judiciary was not the best arbiter of the conflicting interests at play in the field of labour relations.

The Court acknowledged that the construction industry in Quebec was heavily regulated by the state in an effort to retain the best interests of both organized labour and the industry itself, and it expressed its reluctance to question this regulation. Although the Quebec legislation did create a form of union shop, the Court saw this as justified by the Quebec government's attempt to create stability in the job market. Given the contentious labour history in Quebec, the community as well as individual workers would benefit from the balance in the construction industry. Most importantly, the Court argued that the Construction Code did not create any mechanism to enforce an ideological conformity on union members and also pointed out that individual workers are given the choice of five different unions to join. With four judges dissenting, the decision went the way it did only because of the swing vote of Justice Iacobucci, who agreed with the dissenters that there was a powerful right not to associate, but he was prepared to accept that the Section 2(d) protection of that right could be overridden by a Section 1 definition of what was permissible for the common good in a free and democratic society.

The legality of secondary picketing came back to the Court in a similar case brought against Pepsi-Cola in 2002. The case arose when a RWDSU local in Saskatoon was locked out, leading to a bitter strike in which Pepsi brought in replacement workers. The union began picketing retail outlets that did business with the employer, dissuading the store staff from accepting Pepsi deliveries, and they also picketed outside the homes of some of the management personnel. The employer argued before the Court that this form of secondary picketing was illegal in common law, even though there was no legislative prohibition against it. The union countered this argument, claiming that secondary picketing is a fundamental right under Section 2(d) of the Charter. The Court now finally addressed this issue directly in terms of the constitutionality of secondary picketing, asking itself two essential questions: 1) Do the courts have the power to make the changes to the common law and rule in the secondary picketing manner in which the union advocated? 2) If so, how has the Charter affected the development of the common law?

On both questions, the Court argued yes, they had the jurisdiction and, more importantly, the Charter does enshrine certain values that have a fundamental influence in the extension of the common law. The Court deemed that the value of freedom of expression was of such fundamental importance to Canadian democracy that it could take primacy over common law principles developed before the implementation of the Charter. By linking this approach to the collective action of striking workers, the Court affirmed that the postwar compromise – in which Rand's formula was entrenched within the modern forms of labour law – was an important point of departure. Such a compromise recognized that certain legal rights for organized workers have entrenched "good faith negotiation as the primary engine of industrial peace and economic efficiency." Workers are free to withdraw their labour and to legally picket, while employers are free, the Court reasoned, to hire replacement workers. In this regard, the Court defined picketing as an organized effort of people carrying placards in a public place or near a business premises. The effect of this decision was that, instead of resting with Rand's class model of the centrality of labour and capital in capitalist society, the Court inflected its defence of labour picketing towards a distinctly pluralist group model of society.

The next big crack in the first labour trilogy occurred in 2007 when the SCC released its decision on *Health Services and Support (Facilities subsector Bargaining Association) v. British Columbia*, the *BC Health Services* ruling. By removing protections against contracting out from collective agreements in order to privatize health services, the SCC, in building on *Dunmore*, ruled that the reasoning of the majority in the first labour trilogy that excluded collective bargaining from Charter protections could no longer stand. A majority ruling found that in 1987, the SCC had failed to adopt a contextual approach to the interpretation of Section 2(d) and therefore valued the associational aspect of collective bargaining as merely a constitutive right. In reversing its earlier decision, the SCC extended the scope of freedom of association to include protection of the right to engage in collective bargaining on fundamental workplace issues and a concomitant obligation on employers to bargain in good faith.[6]

Just as constitutional protections seemed to be picking up steam, however, the 2011 SCC case of *Ontario (Attorney General) v. Fraser* ground things to a halt. In responding to the *Dunmore* decision, the Ontario government passed the Agricultural Employees Protection Act (AEPA). AEPA provided protections against unfair labour practices and the ability to make "collective representations," but did not include an expressed obligation to bargain in good faith or provide protections for strike action or alternative methods of dispute resolution. In other words, as long as employers listen and consider collective bargaining representation, they had met their legal obligations. The *Fraser* decision ultimately established a legal requirement to negotiate in good faith but stopped short of mandating any statutory duties to do so, essentially endorsing surface-level bargaining.[7] If *Fraser* hit the brakes on the constitutional right to collectively bargain after *BC Health Services*, the second labour trilogy would once again shift hopes into high gear.

THE SECOND LABOUR TRILOGY: REAL HOPE OR FALSE PROMISE?

In 2015, three cases, collectively known as the second labour trilogy, would broaden and reaffirm Section 2(d) rights as encompassed in the *Dunmore* and *BC Health Services* rulings. The first, *Mounted Police Association of Ontario (MPAO) v. Canada (Attorney General)*, arose in response to prohibitions on the rights of Royal Canadian Mounted Police (RCMP) to unionize and engage in collective bargaining independent of RCMP management. Consistent with the precedent established in the *BC Health Services* decision, the SCC asserted that freedom of association entailed both the freedom to create an independent employee association and the right to engage in meaningful collective bargaining though an association of their choosing. The Court ruled that the "associational rights protected by Section 2(d) are not merely a bundle of individual rights, but collective rights that inhere in associations." The decision continued: "The guarantee functions to protect individuals against more powerful entities. By banding together in the pursuit of common goals, individuals are able to prevent more powerful entities from thwarting their legitimate goals and desires. In this way, the guarantee of freedom of association empowers vulnerable groups and helps them work to right imbalances in society. It protects marginalized groups and makes possible a more equal society."[8] While the decision was a reaffirming step forward, it was not a complete victory. The Court's decision only went so far as to guarantee a process, rather than an outcome or access to a particular model of labour relations. The end result was to simultaneously extend collective bargaining rights to RCMP officers who were previously denied them – but it did little to substantively extend these same rights to countless others.[9]

Some weeks later, in *Saskatchewan Federation of Labour (SFL) v. Saskatchewan*, the SCC made another landmark ruling that upended the first labour trilogy when it declared that the right to strike was constitutionally protected. At issue was the passage of the Public Service Essential Services Act (see Chapter 6), which prohibited essential services employees from striking. The Act also did not provide for a neutral substitute mechanism for determining bargaining disputes in the event of an impasse. The SFL argued that the denial of the right to strike weakened the union's position at the bargaining table, thus undermining their right to bargain collectively. In a 5–2 ruling, the Court agreed, writing: "The right to strike is an essential part of a meaningful collective bargaining process in our system of labour relations. The right to strike is not merely derivative of collective bargaining, it is an indispensable component of that right. Where good faith negotiations break down, the ability to engage in the collective withdrawal of services is a necessary component of the process through which workers can continue to participate meaningfully in the pursuit of their collective workplace goals. This crucial role in collective bargaining is why the right to strike is constitutionally protected by s.2(d)."[10]

In rendering their decision, the SCC ruled that the Saskatchewan legislation violated Section 2(d) of the Charter by banning the right to strike at the conclusion of a collective agreement because it went further than was needed to ensure the continuation of essential services. In indiscriminately labelling all workers "essential," the legislation unduly prevented workers from participating in any strike action and removed any processes for appealing. Moreover, the legislation failed to provide any meaningful alternative mechanism for resolving bargaining impasses, such as interest arbitration. While the decision is to be lauded as a symbolic buffer recognizing trade union rights, as Walchuck has noted, "It remains difficult to see how this facilitates growth and expansion for the labour movement. Union density has remained relatively stable since the decision, and the right to strike applies only to those who belong to an existing union. The legal strategy here has proven to be defensive and does not contribute to a strategy based on organizing and mobilizing."[11] Ultimately, a "right" that can be so easily taken away is no right at all. Knowledge of the law seldom helps workers because knowledge rarely effectively translates to bargaining power, only politics does, and that requires an approach to organizing that prioritizes the urgent task of rebuilding and renewing socialist politics – of getting people to think ambitiously again and of meeting new challenges through unique solutions left of social democracy (see Chapter 9).

The final decision in the second labour trilogy, *Meredith v. Canada (Attorney General)*, poured cold water on the expanding terrain of Section 2(d) rights. The trial division of the SCC found that the Expenditure Restraint Act infringed on the rights of RCMP officers when it had rolled back scheduled pay increases across the federal public sector. However, in reviewing the case, the SCC held that the legislation was not a violation of the Charter.[12] Three factors account for the SCC's about-face. First, unlike in *BC Health Services*, where the legislation altered significant terms of the collective agreement, the Act imposed wages generally in line with wage rates bargained elsewhere in the federal public service. Second, the imposed wage rates were time limited and, third, left room for the RCMP members to negotiate additional allowances.

Although the SCC affirmed that Section 2(d) protects both a right to strike and a right to engage in a process of collective bargaining through an independent representative chosen by the employees, the Court found that when a group of employees who have no right to strike actually reach an agreement, and then the state rescinds that agreement, no violation had occurred.[13] Such a decision clearly suggests that there are permissible instances for legislatures to infringe upon rights in ways that the courts will likely continue to find to be consistent with the Charter. While the SCC has provided some constitutional protection to freedom of association and collective bargaining, it has stopped short of guaranteeing the substantive outcomes of collective bargaining. In fact, as Hurst has argued, there are reasons to be concerned that the second labour trilogy may not live up to expectations. It is important to recall that while sections of the PSESA invalidating strikes were declared unconstitutional, the Court set a precedent that introduced stricter requirements for a union to be certified and loosened the requirements for decertification. In doing so, the Court left room for governments hostile to labour to otherwise continue to coerce, constrain, and erode union power.[14] Far from heralding a new era of Charter protections, the repeated failure of the SCC to defend, let alone extend, freedom of association clearly reveals the need for the labour movement to mobilize and politicize its membership rather than rely on a legalistic approach to defending its interests.[15]

In the wake of the second labour trilogy, there have been a number of new Charter challenges alleging that governments have infringed on Section 2(d) freedom of association rights. While a full overview is not possible here, brief mention is nevertheless worthwhile for illustrative purposes. In the case of the *British Columbia Teachers Federation v. British Columbia* (2016, Supreme Court of Canada), the BC government was found to have violated freedom of association rights when it enacted a law (Bill 22) prohibiting negotiation over class sizes, staffing levels, and teaching loads (see Chapter 7). In *OPSEU v. Ontario* (2016, Ontario Superior Court of Justice), the Court ruled that the provincial government had violated Section 2(d) to engage in meaningful collective bargaining when it restricted five teachers' unions from bargaining terms of employment that were substantially different from those bargained by a single other union, and it then imposed those terms. And in *CUPW v. Canada* (2016, Ontario Superior Court of Justice), the Court found that in resorting to back-to-work legislation, the government had infringed on workers' Charter-protected right to strike. With the government intimating its intention to use the legislation, this was found to have contributed to Canada Post stalling negotiations and not bargaining in good faith.[16]

On the other end of decisions exploring whether wage rollback legislation violated freedom of association, appeal courts in British Columbia, Ontario, and Quebec have ruled that limitations did not violate Section 2(d) because the restrictions were short-term, done in "good faith," and did not amount to "substantial interference." In *CSN (UCCO-SACC-CSN), et al. v. Attorney General of Canada* (2019, Quebec Court of Appeal), a statute prohibiting unions from negotiating over pensions and retirement benefits was found to have violated Section 2(d) by preventing meaningful collective bargaining; however, the violation was saved by Section 1 of the Charter on the grounds that it was "reasonably justified."[17] A number of legislative restrictions on collective bargaining rights, discussed more fully in Chapter 7, including Ontario's Bill 124 (Protecting a Sustainable Public Sector for Future Generations Act, 2019), Alberta's Bill 32 (Restoring Balance in Alberta's Workplaces Act, 2020), and Manitoba's Bill 28 (Public Services Sustainability Act), are currently making their way through the courts and seeking leave at the SCC.

CONCLUSION: THE LAW'S FLAWS

The practical result of the first labour trilogy was such that governments could essentially continue to ban or restrict strikes and to exclude specific groups of workers from collective bargaining with relative impunity. The intermediate years brought a renewed sense of hope and optimism that the courts could be used as an effective vehicle to defend, even extend, the right to strike and bargain collectively. Though the SCC shifted to a broader interpretation of Section 2(d) rights, no particular type of bargaining was protected. The second labour trilogy once again raised expectations that the courts could be used in a manner that challenged state efforts to undermine and weaken collective bargaining rights – but the record here, too, has been mixed. While the courts have in some cases chastised governments for overreaching, in others they have given their stamp of approval. In nearly all of these cases, they have done little to extend rights to non-unionized workers, let alone contribute to a reinvigorated and confident labour movement. Judicial decisions aside, governments retain the "nuclear option" of utilizing the notwithstanding clause, and indeed, in an era characterized by mounting authoritarianism, have been more willing to use or threaten to use it to achieve their desired ends, as seen with governments recently in Saskatchewan, Ontario, Alberta, and Quebec.

The double-edged sword involved in unions' four-decade-long reliance on labour law and the courts reaffirms that unions in Canada are in desperate need of a new strategy to broaden and deepen their connection not only with their members but with working people generally, to build a political class consciousness that alone could stop, even reverse, the continuing assault against union and workers' rights and freedoms more broadly. This makes the task of reorganizing society in more socially just and equitable ways all the more urgent. A pious fidelity to upholding the same practices and politics that have gotten labour to the state where it finds itself today – perennially on the defensive – will not be able to reverse course. For labour and the left, the results of neoliberalism's ability to reinvent itself amid weak constitutional protections have been clearly and consistently tragic. The decade of austerity that has followed in the wake of the Great Recession and then COVID-19 reveals how constituted state powers remain political obstacles requiring strategic address, not legal abstractions. In this regard, criticism of the labour movement should not be seen as divisive, nor as an attempt to undermine solidarity, but rather an attempt to build an empowering politics capable of transcending a Sisyphean-like reliance of organized labour on the courts, a relationship to which we now turn.

CHAPTER NINE

Labour's Last Gasp or Revival? Rebuilding Working-Class Resistance

Chapter Summary: The impasse of organized labour as a social and political force lays bare the need for a new politics. In this regard, if unions are to live up to their potential as transformative workers' organizations, it is necessary to transcend what are often insulated labour and activist subcultures. While trade unions must be a central part of any radical political renewal, their renewal is equally dependent upon a broader revitalization of the socialist left outside of organized labour but which is simultaneously and organically a component of the labour movement. This, in our view, is the only realistic starting point from which to move forward.

INTRODUCTION

In this concluding chapter to the fourth edition, we deepen the political insights raised in earlier versions by highlighting several serious questions of political strategy – in short, how to move beyond the now long-standing impasse of working-class politics. In what follows, we foreground the primacy of politics: how can we develop a political vision, defined as the rebuilding of working-class capacities to engage in class struggle – in our workplaces, communities, and in and through the state? By necessity this entails a withering critique of the dominant political force in working-class politics since the mid-twentieth century – social democracy. And, by extension, it is equally necessary to move on and build a new type of political organization that serves to organize workers politically, ideologically, and culturally in order to engage in effective struggles with both the state and capital. In other words, a party that functions in but, more importantly, beyond the electoral field.

Much of what was achieved through the class struggles from the end of World War II through to the late 1970s has dissolved. Post-1945 democratic capitalism was predicated upon a social pact that accepted organized labour as a junior partner in the management of the political economy. Social democracy, as the major political orientation within working-class politics, was instrumental here. Today, however, social democracy offers no vision of a society beyond capitalism, offering up instead a technocratic managerialism to coordinate the state and economy. The undemocratic and increasingly authoritarian variant of neoliberal capitalism has gradually insulated state institutions from popular pressures through concentrated power in the political executive and central bank "independence," among other transformations within the state. As there is "no going back," these developments raise the question as to whether democratic capitalism has arrived at a dead end.

The claims of neoliberals for a moral life of freedom have been built on individual subordination to market imperatives enforced by the exercise of state coercion in defence of contracts and property. In practice, neoliberalism reinforces the inequalities of social class and dependence on labour markets at the expense of the egalitarian and developmental processes of democracy. Indeed, the neoliberal project has been so intertwined with "de-democratization" and authoritarian measures, as outlined in the preceding chapters, that it is impossible to separate them in practice. Few would not have made the political calculation, especially on the left, that the discrediting of neoliberalism by the global financial crisis and, a decade later, by tepid COVID-19 responses, would not have provided a revitalization of the project to revive social democratic capitalism. But the social democratic parties have provided few – some might say any – political and economic alternatives.

These parties have proven as able in reconstructing the neoliberal policy matrix as they had been in helping assemble it through the Third Way turn of the 1990s. This is a remarkable setback for the democratic capitalist thesis of political organization and social advance. In the early 1980s, as neoliberal policy was struggling to achieve hegemony, Gøsta Esping-Anderson put forward a parallel evolutionary program for a democratic capitalism: "The notion of a social democratic 'road to power' is premised on the assumption that class formation under democratic parliamentary conditions can provide the strength and solidarity needed to transform capitalism. It is also premised on another assumption: that electoral politics and reformist accomplishments will enhance social democratic progress."[1] The record of the past four decades suggests otherwise.

BETWEEN PAST AND PRESENT: THE CONTOURS OF TRADE UNION STRUGGLES

How has the labour movement responded to permanent austerity and authoritarianism? One must never fall into the defeatist perspective of overestimating the dominance of capital and the state. The relations of class power in a capitalist society are asymmetric; nevertheless, the power inherent to labour, through its potential to collectively mobilize, always remains a real force. The legal framework of collective bargaining established in the 1940s – so well described by Rand as "machinery devised to adjust toward increasing harmony" among the interests of labour, capital, and the state – still left capital occupying the "dominant position." As we saw in earlier chapters, this framework had been supplemented by further reforms that have explicitly described labour policy reform as the "means of legitimizing and making more acceptable the superior-subordinate nexus inherent in the employer-employee relationship." Despite these reforms, it still proved no easy task to "domesticate" and "housebreak" the unions and fit "them into the national family as one of the tame cats."

Free collective bargaining was rooted in a material basis of consent given by the expansion of postwar capitalism. As this stage drew to a close in the 1970s, the material basis of consent became more fragile. This prepared the ground for the turn to coercion and, later, authoritarianism, and it also opened space for resistance to such coercion that was determined by organizational, political, and ideological factors as well as economic ones. It is this resistance, actual and potential, that we now want to explore. As we have seen, class struggle has continued, and even increased, through the course of the era of free collective bargaining. Indeed, it could be argued that the fact of ongoing class struggle in a changed economic climate largely prompted attempts to increase capital's hegemony through legalistic coercion. To be sure, this limited and sectionalized struggle was underwritten and institutionalized by the legal and institutional matrix of collective bargaining. This framework certainly limited the mobilizing capacity of unions. It even played a considerable role in marginalizing the kind of socialist vision and purpose that had helped fuel the labour movement's organizational struggles of the 1930s and 1940s.

The Canadian labour movement in the following decades mainly undertook such struggles as could be advanced within the parameters of "actually-existing capitalism." This focus left unchallenged the underlying structural asymmetry of power between capital and labour inherent in capitalism. Thus, the ground always remained in place for capital and the state to carry out an assault on the free collective bargaining that emerged in the new economic, political, and ideological conditions of neoliberalism. The conditions for class struggle against the new era of coercion were not closed off, not least of all because of neoliberalism's own contradictions. If the new economic conditions made workers less secure in their jobs and undermined their confidence to act militantly, it also meant that union organization and rights became more important in order for workers to protect their jobs and material conditions. Moreover, such economic contradictions were overlaid with ideological ones. Capitalism's claim on workers' consent in the Cold War had been sustained, in part, not only by the rising standards of living, but also by the postwar settlement's legal proclamation of workers' democratic rights while pointing to the travesty of democratic rights in so-called communist regimes. Ideological conditions were not entirely propitious for convincingly selling the new coercion to Canadian workers in the name of voluntarism and freedom. Considerable ideological space existed for unions to mobilize workers' struggles against the new coercion.

It should be clear from our account of the transition from consent to coercion that the labour movement did not simply lie down and play dead. Economic crises, employers, and the state all worked together to effectively cripple the capacity of Canadian unions to resist. Canadian workers and the Canadian labour movement have had little to celebrate in terms of conventional workplace gains and collective bargaining victories. As Graph 9.1 shows, the length and breadth of the wage deceleration since 1980 has been unprecedented.

The consolidation of permanent exceptionalism through the 1990s and into the 2000s also coincided with a decline in strike activity Indeed, if the 1970s marked the zenith of labour militancy as measured by the number of strikes, the first two decades of the twenty-first century were its nadir. In 1974,

Graph 9.1. Major Wage Settlements, Public- and Private-Sector Unions, 1977–2020

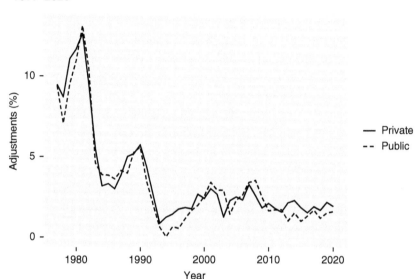

there were 1,218 strikes across Canada, a historic high. From 2006 to 2017, there was not a year with more than 200 such actions, and 2011, with 149 strikes in total, was the historic low point. The main weapon in workers' arsenal has been deployed ever less frequently and confidently. There were strong examples of determined militancy, albeit mostly defensive, designed to prevent massive cutbacks, but clearly, as Graph 9.2 shows, the will of workers to struggle was not completely quashed in Canada.

Nonetheless, it is remarkable just how unchanging the Canadian labour movement has been in the face of each successive blow struck by the state and employers since the turn to permanent exceptionalism and, in particular, authoritarianism. In short, the labour movement has been largely incapable of mounting any meaningful or sustained counter-offensive, appearing largely confused both ideologically and strategically. Major wage settlements, which exceeded 5.5 percent at the beginning of the 1990s, were only half that by the end of the decade, substantially below the rate of productivity increases. Real wages, which had stagnated during the 1980s (and actually fallen for men) increased only marginally, just 0.68 percent between 2000 and 2020.[2] Over the preceding quarter-century, productivity output per employee had risen close to 40 percent, while real wages over the same period generally remained flat.

Graph 9.2. Number of Work Stoppages, Person-Days Not Worked, 1950–2020

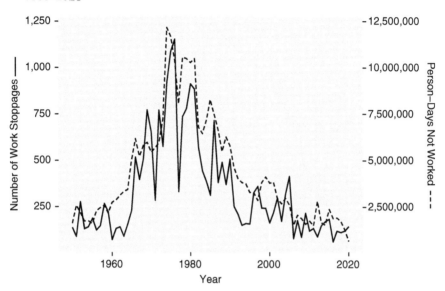

There has been an inverse relationship, then, between productivity growth and real wages as workers increased their hours of work, emptied their savings, added family members to the workforce, and took on debt to maintain modest living standards.

As Graph 9.3 shows, union membership, which had seemed to stabilize at around 37 percent of non-agricultural workers in the early 1990s, fell steadily through the 2000s, reaching a historic low of just above 30 percent in 2016. And as Graph 9.4 shows, while public-sector union density remained rather stable at about 75 percent through the same period, private-sector union density was another story, declining from just over 21 percent in 1997 to roughly 16 percent by 2017 – a level not seen since the mid-1960s.[3] These declines are only part of the picture, though. As discussed earlier, underlying the divisions and confusion among workers is the growing realization that the centrepiece of the labour movement's strategy for defending and advancing its members' rights – securing the election of NDP governments – has been a colossal failure.

Over the past decade, we have again seen determined and courageous acts of resistance, such as the historic political strike by Ontario teachers or the illegal strikes by hospital workers in Alberta, Saskatchewan, Quebec, and Nova

Graph 9.3. Total Union Density, 1951–2020

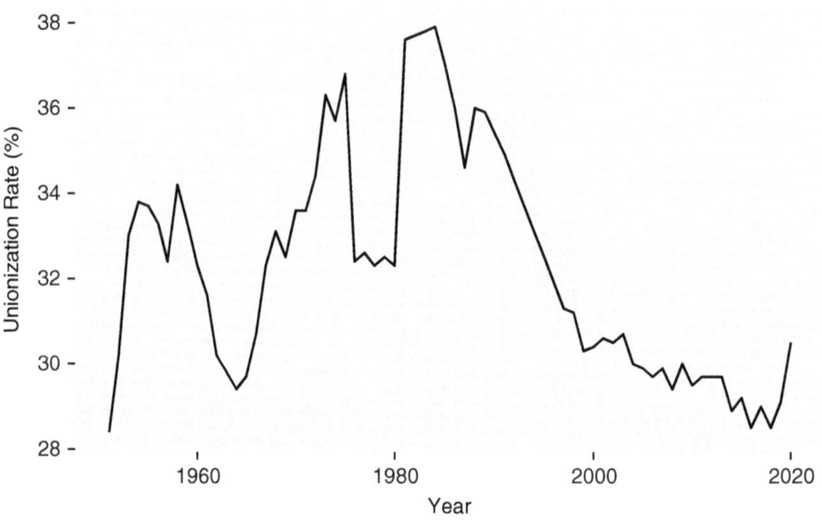

Scotia. Yet workers' backs remain against the wall. The social contract experience that the unions went through with the Rae NDP government turned out to be far from unique. The reforms introduced by NDP governments in other provinces fell far short of what the labour movement had hoped for and failed even to undo the restrictions on trade union rights imposed by their predecessors. In fact, it was not long before they, too, were facing new incursions into those rights. Together, these experiences destroyed the confidence of union leaders in the strategy of support for the NDP. Some parts of the movement continue to cling to the NDP; after all, the alternatives are not any better and, in some cases, far worse. For most, however, it became clear that the NDP was just another party, so that just getting union members to vote for it was no strategy at all. If electing the NDP is not the answer, what is?

For many political activists in Canada and elsewhere, the answer lay in leaving labour to its own devices and turning to new social movements. Yet the need to work towards a new strategy for labour cannot be set aside. The new social movements, with some focused on advocating for and mobilizing non-unionized workers' struggles, are certainly no less important than the labour movement. However, the promise of social movements for social transformation will only be realized if a powerful labour movement – measured in terms of its capacity to halt production as well as its size and organizational

Graph 9.4. Union Density, Public and Private Sector, 1997–2021

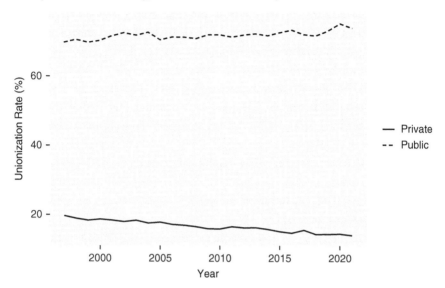

strength – takes on board the key emancipatory themes raised by the other movements. At the same time, social movements can hardly ignore their own need for labour's support.

Experiences of feminist and anti-racist politics in the labour movement are also telling. These considerations suggest that a crucial element in the strategy for all transformative movements must be a strategy for transforming labour movements themselves in fundamental ways. Social movement activists have rightly been wary that many traditional labour attitudes and old strategies are recipes for failure, and the labour movement's clinging to them, even if they are sometimes cloaked in new language, is a major factor in blocking social change. The most favoured labour strategies have indeed turned out to be failures, partly due to changing conditions represented under the symbol of globalization, but also partly due to fundamental flaws in the strategies themselves, limitations that were already visible under the old conditions. The principle old strategic impediments for labour are associated politically with social democratic gradualism and industrially with the service or corporatist models of trade unionism, the former more common in Canada than the latter. Within these frameworks as they evolved after World War II, unions overwhelmingly eschewed any efforts to help their members understand the structure and dynamics of capitalism as a system or to develop the wide range of capacities necessary to challenge that system. Indeed, unions were more concerned, particularly in the context of the Cold War, to marginalize anyone who sought to educate their membership. Aspiring to become partners in managing the "mixed economy," union leaders saw their primary role as representing workers' interests in the broader society, a belief fostered by the regular access of labour representatives to state officials even in the absence of explicit corporatist structures. Unions overwhelmingly focused on the interests of their members as sellers of labour power, limiting themselves to being agents of collectively bargaining the terms and conditions of work with employers. This focus privileged negotiating skills over those of educating and mobilizing, devalued the importance and vitality of democratic forums, and exacerbated the tendency towards a bureaucratic consciousness and practice within the labour movement.

The mobilization that did occur was linked to securing agreements with employers, and it was discontinued, if not discouraged, once that objective was achieved. On its own terms, this strategy worked in the postwar golden age and with various controls on cross-border capital movements. But under increasing pressure from multinational corporations and financial institutions, especially in the context of the fiscal crisis of the state, governments everywhere continue to look for a way out of the postwar class compromise. The shift from consent towards coercion in securing the subordination of labour soon became part of the broader turn to neoliberal globalization through the 1990s and into the 2000s, and such dynamics have taken a decisively authoritarian turn over the last decade or so. Not only were labour movements unprepared for these changes – what's worse is they had also not prepared their members and supporters with the organizational and intellectual resources to readily understand what was happening, nor had they encouraged imagining any alternative. It was in good part because of this inertia that the neoliberal restoration proved possible in the face of the impasse of the Keynesian welfare state. No wonder that capital was once again been able "to make the world in its own image," in what has come to be known as the era of capitalist globalization since then.

The need for a new strategy for labour has been widely recognized over the past quarter-century. Unfortunately, this recognition has generally been tied to a misconceived understanding of globalization as an irreversible economic phenomenon that has undermined the capacity of nation states to manage domestic economic spaces. Moreover, when we examine the principle strategies being advanced, what is striking is their affinity with the failed strategies of the past. One common version, "**progressive competitiveness**," envisions state measures, particularly skills training for labour and research and development support for industry, to promote an export-oriented, high value-added, high-tech economy capable of paying high wages. Labour's role in this strategy is to induce capital to cooperate by offering its help in securing productivity increases that capital is incapable of achieving on its own. The problems with this as a "strategy" for labour have proved manifold. First of all, there were obvious ethical ones. Even Robert Reich, former US president Bill Clinton's labour secretary, who was one of the first to make the case for such a strategy, pointed to the immorality of a strategy that would pit developing countries, with their meagre resources and histories of colonization, in competition with the more developed countries to attract high technology investment. For any economy deemed not successful enough in its exports, the diagnosis and recipe offered by progressive competitiveness was analogous to that offered to the homeless and hungry on the street who are viewed as not motivated enough, entrepreneurial enough, or skilled enough to get a job. What is missing here, of course, is the notion that something may be wrong with the system, and this idea is also missing from what the progressive competitiveness framework says to whole sectors, regions, and economies. Moreover, even if such a strategy of export competitiveness were successful in one country or region, its effect would be to export unemployment to the places that are less successful.

More generally, the progressive competitiveness strategy poses a threat to the moral core at the basis of the labour movement. The fundamental basis of unions is the replacement of competition between workers with solidarity – acting collectively in defence of common class interests. Unions' moral authority is based on their adopting a discourse and practice that extends solidarity to all workers. What then can be the ethical basis of a unionism that would limit competition within the workplace only to recreate it in export competition that defines success in terms of getting investment and jobs at the expense of other workers at home or abroad? Fundamentally, a progressive competitiveness strategy that conceives of unions essentially in terms of what they can do for capital – and at the firm level at that – robs them of any meaningful autonomy and undermines the material basis for their existence. Moreover, the class relations at the base of capitalist production are further obscured as workers increasingly identify as members of the enterprise rather than as workers with interests that are distinct from those who own the productive assets of the firm. The problems with this strategy have also proved to be practical ones. Since establishing the groundwork for success through progressive competitiveness entailed some long-term structural changes in both firms and the state, for instance, to set up a strong training regime, it could offer little in the short term to most governments. Since everything in this strategy hinges on the goal of cooperating with capital to maximize exports and attract capital flows in the meantime, it invariably has led even social democratic NDP governments to embrace neoliberal policies of fiscal austerity and enter into sharp conflicts with the unions supporting them. The ultimate irony has been that these conflicts have encouraged social democracy not to see itself as being involved in developing a strategy for labour at all, but to distance itself from the labour movement. Left social-democratic labour movements are thus left without any political strategy at all. Just as a broadly defined Keynesianism was abandoned by social democracy, the policy surrogate, progressive competitiveness, was also discarded. However, nothing filled this void save for the prescriptions of neoliberal orthodoxy. Thus, social democracy came to be thoroughly emptied of any vestige of political imagination that could pass for even an alternative variant of neoliberalism. Social democracy, save for the odd interruption, became integrated ideologically and practically into neoliberal modalities of governance.

Another broad strategy advanced might be termed partnership internationalism. This strategy envisions re-establishing a variant of the postwar Keynesian order at a supranational level, above all by incorporating provisions for labour and environmental standards into international trade agreements, such as with WTO and "new NAFTA" agreements. Opening international institutions to representatives of civil society resonates well with labour leaders because it fits their understanding of their role as representing workers' interests within state institutions. Such a strategy may have a certain utility for bringing terrible labour conditions and anti-union policies into public discussions of globalization, but this attention is purchased at considerable cost. The very idea of attaching labour rights to international economic treaties means endorsing the free trade and capital flows that these treaties are all about securing, which proposals for a Tobin Tax on currency speculation can do little to stem. And it means endorsing the export-oriented model of development throughout the Global South that has accompanied these flows, creating economies in which employment rests on low-cost exports to the North. Under these circumstances, global labour standards, insofar as they are enforced, inevitably serve a protectionist function for labour in the North and have not surprisingly garnered widespread opposition from union leaders in the South.[4]

What is most disturbing about this response to globalization is how often it has been used both by the International Trade Union Confederation and national union leaders to justify the abandonment of collective action locally, and even nationally, as ineffective or irrelevant. This new strategy of global compromise displaces rather than supports militant worker struggles, making it not only misguided, but positively harmful. Certainly, the institutions of globalization do not have to be engaged by unions; the question is what priority they assign to and what they seek from such engagement. Past experience has shown that getting a seat at the table sometimes places far too much emphasis on representing labour rather than organizing labour. More important is the task of breaking down walls to these behind-the-scenes deals in a way that mobilizes members along with a broader alliance of democratic forces. Clearly this requires a public education and mobilization campaign to achieve what WTO technocrats and multinational corporations do not want – a critical awareness among working people of what is being done to them.

And again, the limits of social democracy in these respects are made evident. There is no social democratic remedy to any of the foregoing. That project is no longer even capable of integrating workers, unionized or not, into the corridors of representation within the state. Witness, as a case in point, the dramatically diminished role of labour departments. Once central to the coordination of political/policy negotiations between labour, capital, and the state, they now serve a residual enforcement function and as centres for labour force training programs. In the absence of class confrontation, there is little over which to deliberate. And thus, the twentieth-century social democratic political economy, which understood the state as a technocratic instrument standing above class relations, has proven increasingly irrelevant to a world of staggering economic inequality brought on by a systematic, public and corporate policy–induced degradation of work and workers. In short, as the state and capital amplified the class war from above, social democracy, with no ideational and ideological means to understand this new political economy, was left in the wilderness without a compass and, more importantly, an electoral base.

THE END OF DEMOCRATIC CAPITALISM: MOVING BEYOND SOCIAL DEMOCRACY

Social democratic theorizing is now as austere as social democratic parties are in practice. Colin Crouch, for one, has moved from a programmatic vision of "competitive corporatism" sustaining egalitarian class compromises in core countries to a dismal reading of the "post-democratic" condition. Against neoliberal austerity and the impossibility of returning to state-directed economic policy (the outmoded confrontation between "state and market"), a crack for reform is open for extra-market institutions providing constraints leveraged by civil society mobilizations. Crouch identifies the possibility not of a democratic project, but of a "comfortable accommodation." This is partly because corporate power makes it its business to bind them all together, but also partly because the only alternative to some kind of accommodation would be a rather wretched society.

Crouch is hardly an isolated theorist in concluding that the project of democratic capitalism is at an impasse, if not dead. The most extreme case is, perhaps, Jürgen Habermas – extreme for the illusions he conjured about the EU as the historical bearer of this project. In a flight to normative theory when concrete analysis is called for, Habermas has suggested that the EU embodies the "transnationalization of democracy" carrying forward the "constitutionalization of political authority." But rather than examine the actual modalities by which the EU works through the European Central Bank – directives on deregulation, austerity, and liberalization of capital movements – Habermas makes the astonishing claim that a central accomplishment of the EU is the constraining of national states and that what is now required is the closing of the "democratic deficit." This is liberal idealism unconstrained by the actual political economy of contemporary capitalism.

This last observation is the starting point for *Politics in the Age of Austerity*, which explores the "social democratic straitjacket." There is, throughout the text, a blunt acceptance that neoliberalism is the policy matrix and social form of the state that has triumphed through crisis. It is not credible to forward projects for social change, Schafer and Streeck counsel, particularly if they are redistributive in nature. The austerity state is a pervasive parameter for political choices, and centre-left parties have come to understand this. A few of the essays confront Habermas's prospects for the EU to revive democratic capitalism. But having averred from his philosophical idealism to focus on the realpolitik of the EU, Schafer and Streeck's conclusion is that this is, at best, "a long shot." Instead, it is the bleak realism that compels confronting the death of party democracy (including social democracy), the fortified hegemony of financial capitalism, and the bind of fiscal constraints well beyond the impact of the crisis tripping up any reflationary plans. In consequence, "governments … have to turn their citizens into a disciplined quasi-workforce who willingly produce market compatible returns on the capital that has been invested in them, both by moderating their demands on the 'social wage' accruing to them as citizens and by continuously improving their productivity."

As shown in previous chapters, social democracy is a protean political entity, one that has sought not to transform capitalism but rather to become integrated into capitalist modes of governing – that is, to be the humane face of capitalism. In this, social democracy both ignores and obfuscates that the problem is capitalism itself. The immediate three decades following the end of World War II provided the material and political conditions that facilitated the golden age of social democracy. This was a historical anomaly, not historical normality. Those geopolitical and macroeconomic conditions have disappeared and along with them the foundations of the "best years" of social democracy. In this regard, there is no going back. The contradiction within social democratic political economy reached its limit with the 2008 crisis, where it became abundantly evident that "social democratic parties ... have no vision of a society beyond capitalism, no ambition beyond administering the existing society a bit more fairly. But capitalism is a social system based on putting the expansion of private capital above everything else, especially the well being of workers, whose potential to make gains can threaten capitalist control and profits. So while social democratic parties ... claim to represent working people, the contradiction is that a party committed to capitalism cannot ultimately defend and advance the needs of working people."[5]

The trajectory of social democracy since World War I can be summed up as one of moving from representing working-class interests within the liberal-democratic political shell of capitalism to one where the purpose is to govern on behalf of capitalism. Party by party, post-1945 social democracy formally dropped Marxism as its theoretical lodestone. Its key programmatic elements then emphasized redistributional policies; de-emphasized nationalization of the means of production; adhered to broadly Keynesian approaches to economic management; and to implement such, turned to constructing a broad, multi-class electoral coalition.[6] The ideological devaluation of ownership is a critical shift in social democracy's reorientation away from class and towards a technocratic-managerialism. Expanding working-class prosperity necessitated capitalist growth, which logically led to the imperative that "socialists must logically applaud the accumulation of private profit."[7] With the ascent of neoliberalism, social democracy again transformed to accommodate the new conditions. Through the 1980s and 1990s, as cases in Ontario, Manitoba, and elsewhere make painfully clear, social democratic parties accepted "the necessity of adapting to international markets and the austerity policies capital has demanded."[8] In the early days of the Great Recession, there was considerable speculation that the neoliberal era was concluding and that a Keynesian-informed classical social democracy would be retrieved and reanimated. One prominent social democrat intellectual declared: "The 2008 crisis marks the end of the Reagan-Thatcher counter-revolution. Neoliberalism and monetarism are dead."[9] It turned out to be a "strange non-death."[10]

Instead, through the post-2008 crisis brought on by austerity, social democrats emerged not as champions of equality and redistribution but rather of austerity. In this context, fault lines began to show within social democracy. In February 2013, the Socialist International (SI), then the organization representing the global family of social democratic parties, met in Cascais, an expensive beach resort town in Portugal. There, the secretary-general of the SI's youth organization, Beatriz Talegon, called out the assemblage of government ministers, parliamentarians, and party professionals for failing to enjoin their parties with the struggles of those resisting the crisis: "When people are taking to the streets in Madrid, in Brussels, in Cairo, in Beirut, they're fighting for what we here, as socialists, defend…. Unfortunately, it has not been we socialists taking enthusiastically to the streets and mobilizing."[11] The 2008 financial crisis presented social democracy with an opportunity to advance an alternative agenda entailing significant public investment, a return to steeply progressive taxation, and centred on a wage-led recovery. Instead, social democratic governments in Canada, no less than abroad, pursued austerity. Why? Larry Elliott, writing for the *Guardian*, framed the problem as one of intellectual bankruptcy. Elliott notes that despite 30 years of market orthodoxy, the social democratic left has failed to develop an "intellectual critique of what has gone wrong and what needs to be done to put things right," and the inevitable result, as we are now witnessing, is that "matters will revert more or less to where they were before."[12] The result is that social democrats simply offer up more of the same policy interventions as parties of the traditional centre-right.

Social democracy transformed as it adapted to the requirements of neoliberal capitalism. Internationally, the Tony Blairs and Gerhard Schröders embraced their role as social democracy's "progressive modernizers," for whom this "often meant deregulation and privatization … that the only way forward is to abandon notions of equality and fraternity … and to weaken the state to the advantage of the forces of capital."[13] In the Europe of 2022, there is something of a social democratic revival. Social democrats now lead governments in Germany, Finland, Denmark, Sweden, Norway, Spain, and Portugal.

However, even in these cases, save for the exception of Portugal, these parties have succeeded in winning elections but with dramatically lower vote shares than the post-1945-to-2000 norm. In the social democratic heartland countries of Scandinavia, this is particularly the case. The Swedish social democrats, the very party that came to epitomize the social democratic approach to governing, cannot garner more than 25 to 30 percent of the popular vote, compared to 40 to 45 percent in the postwar years. As elsewhere, the social democratic welfare states constructed by these parties over decades were eroded through the 1990s and beyond by those same parties that had built them. Large parts of their working-class base responded by withdrawing for the electoral process or finding new partisan homes with parties of the right and far-right. And in the third decade of the twenty-first century, we see some of this political realignment taking place within the Canadian working class.

In Canada, the New Democratic Party has fared no better. Canada's social democratic party has never won governmental power at the national level. In the context of Canadian federalism and the policy and program responsibilities allocated to the provinces, this is a relatively minor fact. Provincial jurisdiction encompasses such core social democratic policy areas as health, labour, and social services. Of course, this is not to diminish the federal role in setting the framework for transfer payments to the provinces, monetary policy, national defence, international relations, and the capacity to use its considerable spending power to incentivize provinces to participate in national programs. New Democrats have formed government in six of Canada's provinces and in one territory. There is a considerable history to draw on here as we have seen, at least partially, in earlier chapters presented in this book.

The main party organizations of Canadian social democracy have been the Co-operative Commonwealth Federation, founded in 1932, which then, in the late 1950s, dissolved and was refounded in 1961 as the New Democratic Party.[14] The national trade union confederation in Canada, the Canadian Labour Congress, played a significant role in the establishment of the new party. In terms of the geopolitical context, the NDP emerged at the height of the Cold War. A key characteristic of the party, shared with its trade union affiliates, was an aggressive anti-communism – which sat comfortably within a broad tent, meaning a shrinking of the political role of the industrial working class within its electoral base, alongside technocratic Keynesianism. The enthusiastic embrace of red-baiting and the attendant raids and campaigns to marginalize the radical left within trade unions sowed the seeds for future defeats of trade unions more generally. With the defeat of the left, both within the unions and outside, including within the CCF and NDP, the "capacities critical to understanding, strategizing, and mobilizing" were also lost.[15]

From day one, the new party expressed an adaptation to the economic conditions of postwar North American capitalism and to the political conditions prevailing through the 1950s and 1960s. In this respect, the political evolution of Canadian social democracy has been characterized as one of a "protest movement becalmed," meaning electoralism, where the goal is exclusively to win elections, which became the central if not singular purpose of the party. To do so required a broad electoral tent, a people's party rather than a working-class party, capable of winning parliamentary majorities. By definition that necessarily would entail an ever-increasing ideological moderation and internal organizational centralization. This was inevitable given that the NDP "had never been a socialist party in the orthodox sense.... The NDP was created as a liberal party."[16] This is not to say there were and are not socialists within the NDP – history suggests otherwise – however, what is important in this framing is how the party would understand, or misunderstand, class power. An informal, but by no means less significant point of refoundation arrived in the 1990s. There was no defining convention or manifesto to mark this turn. Instead, it was a series of fits and starts, here and there, which nonetheless signalled an accommodation with the conditions of neoliberalism. New Democrats, like other members of the global social democratic family of parties, "began to incorporate neoliberal policies into their programmes and rule as neoliberals in power."[17]

Particularly through the first two decades of the twenty-first century, the NDP, at all levels, pursued a strategy of "modernization and moderation" entailing efforts to professionalize the party apparatus and to adopt simple, focused policy positions that aligned well with mainstream sensibilities.[18] For a party ostensibly founded as the political arm of labour, it is remarkably devoid of any class politics. This is, however, simply the expression of yet another contradiction within the political practice and culture of the NDP. As a party that seeks to both protect workers from the worst of what capitalism will hurl at them but at the same time be unequivocally wedded to capitalism as the only viable economic system, it leaves the NDP, and social democracy more generally, with a circle that cannot be squared. Concretely this comes down to an understanding of how social change is to be achieved. One strategy entails the role of mass mobilization in challenging capitalism. Due to their role in the economy and the organizational resources of trade unions, workers must be the central actors in any project of social and economic transformation.

This is, however, beyond the political imagination of the NDP, which does not see workers as capable of "developing the capacities to one day play a leading role in transforming capitalism" and therefore cannot concern itself with "equipping working people with the vision, analysis, ideology, organizational skills and the structures to counteract the power of, and constraints imposed by, capitalism."[19] Obviously, investing in the complex and risky endeavour of building a class-based movement is not the NDP's project. In practice, social democracy seeks class harmony through the social concertation of class interests – something that capitalists do not feel compelled to do, which is a major problem with this model of governance. And class conflict, integral to the logic of capitalism, is to be managed. Instead, politics as the art of the possible is shrunk to the electoral field and specifically to the act of voting and, all importantly, to donating funds. In this respect, social democracy tends towards lowering worker expectations of "what is possible" and, through the practice of transactional politics, "it contributes to the disorganization of workers as a class."[20] So, what is to be done to move beyond this impasse?

For Canadian trade unions, the limitations of electoral politics and social democracy contributed to a gradual ideological shift within the unions. More importantly, unions reverted to a practice of separating politics from economic issues. In other words, economic issues were to be addressed at the bargaining table and political questions at election time by voting for the NDP. Moreover, the accumulated defeats of the past 40 years have transformed the political imagination of Canadian unions rather profoundly. The history of workplace occupations through the 1930s CIO's organizing drive, the remarkable mid-1970s resistance to wage controls culminating in Canada's first, and only, national general political strike on 14 October 1976, the actions of Quebec's Common Front in the 1970s and beyond, the prominent role of trade unions in the anti–free trade campaign of the late 1980s, Ontario's "Days of Action" local political strikes in 1995 and 1996, are now the stuff of nostalgia. The old left, both social democratic and communist, together with the post-1945 model of trade union practice and culture, is gone and it is now necessary to move on and start over.

Imagining the potential for working-class mobilization leading to a more fundamental transformation in class power seems an impossible feat. Canadian social democracy is "becalmed" because, in some serious measure, the most important organizations for working-class mobilization, the trade unions, are not only "disarmed" but are convinced, like their social democratic party (sometime) allies, there is no realistic political project beyond voting for the NDP (and that too is on very wobbly ground) to be undertaken that challenges the prevailing economic order in a fundamental way. In Canada, as elsewhere, the inability of working-class organizations, including formal political parties of the left but also trade unions, to turn the 2008 economic crisis into a general political crisis of the capitalist state is a remarkable case in point.

As multiple crises roll out – the climate catastrophe, the fight for Indigenous and racial justice, gender rights, living wages, the COVID-19 pandemic, geopolitical tensions, an emboldened far right, mounting economic insecurity – it is obvious that social democratic politics and prevailing union practices and strategies of status are inadequate to the challenges now and those to follow. The necessary, and by no means easy, first step is the struggle to fashion a party of a new kind that is socialist and deeply rooted in the working class, together with union renewal informed by those socialist politics.[21] As Marx long ago noted, while trade unions could bargain within the wages system, they could not transcend the political and economic forces that stymied their continued expansion owing to the structural exploitation at the root of capital accumulation.[22] The challenge before unions, then, was to simultaneously improve the working conditions of their members while extending those gains to the non-unionized, un(der)employed, and unwaged as part of generating a socialist class consciousness.

Unless unions made an effort to broaden their aims and advocate on behalf of and in accordance with all of society's oppressed, unions risked degenerating into almost reactionary enclaves of privilege, upholding the manifest divisions of the working class and stunting its political development. Rather than applying palliatives, Marx argued, trade unions must cure the malady: "they must now learn to act deliberately as organizing centres of the working class in the broad interest of its complete emancipation. They must aid every social and political movement tending in that direction."[23] Because the capital-labour relationship extends beyond the realm of paid employment, if organized labour is going to have a progressive future, it will need to be anchored in a politics that orients its struggles towards the emancipation of the working class as a whole, linking trade union activism with socialism as part of a radical politics of universalism. In other words, it will involve identifying the means through which the diversity of the working class could be transformed via a class-based project that recognizes how multiple registers of class oppression are not just abstract particularities, but politically and economically rooted in capitalist social relations.[24] Building a socialist politics inclusive of a party and movement of a new kind dedicated to replacing capitalism will require a new type of union practice informed by the same objective.

CONFRONTING GLOBAL CAPITAL: NATIONAL AND INTERNATIONAL DIMENSIONS

It is, nevertheless, the case that there is no adequate new strategy for labour without addressing globalization. It is first of all necessary to clear up some misconceptions. Globalization is not an objective economic process that labour needs to catch up to. It is a political process advanced by identifiable interests. The failure to see the strategic political nature of globalization reflects an **economism** that needs to be overcome. Nation states are not the victims of globalization, they are its authors. States are not displaced by globalized capital, they represent globalized capital, above all financial capital. Any adequate strategy to challenge globalization must begin at home, precisely because of the key role of states in making globalization happen. There is no sense pretending that, in the South as much as in the North, anything other than class struggles of the most trenchant kind at the level of each state are required to shift the global political terrain.

It is nonsensical to imagine that campaigns to reform the IMF, World Bank, or even the ILO can amount to anything significant without a major shift in the balance of class forces in the leading capitalist states. Hugo Radice is right to note that "the asymmetry between labour and capital in their degree of transnationalisation makes workers more a passive object of globalization than an active contestant."[25] If so, it is mainly because of the asymmetries of power between capital and labour at the national and subnational level, which makes any manner of meaningful reform impossible. As long as labour remains satisfied with being – and capable of being no more than – a subsidiary partner of the national business class, nationalism can be no more progressive than this. Such a partnership is no longer on offer, in any case, given the increasing inability – and with very few exceptions, the increasing lack of interest – on the part of domestic business classes to chart a course of development beyond that determined by globally dominant imperialism in this conjuncture. This is precisely why a new strategy for labour has such importance and promise today.

In this era of globalization, such a shift can be sustained only insofar as local and national struggles in each state learn from struggles elsewhere, gain strength from one another, and support one another internationally. For this, a new labour internationalism is certainly required. But what exactly does internationalism mean for labour in this era of globalization? There is no sense pretending that problems that are deeply embedded in, and that reflect the weaknesses of, each national movement will somehow be resolved through transnational collective bargaining with multinational corporations and international campaigns against the political institutions of globalization. As Sam Gindin points out, international labour bodies can still make constructive contributions to our struggles.[26] They are useful vehicles for exchanging information and analysis and for mobilizing acts of solidarity and support. Here, too, we should be clear about their limits. Strategic international coordination is dependent on the strength of national movements. What kind of internationalism can we expect among the United States, Mexico, and Canada if the American labour movement cannot yet organize its own South? If the Mexican labour movement does not yet have a common union across workplaces? If the Canadian labour movement has not yet been able to achieve major organizing breakthroughs in its own key private service sectors?

What is needed is the kind of internationalism that reinforces the space for, and contributes to, building the strategic and material resources for working-class struggles in each country to develop. Unions in the North need to throw their full weight behind campaigns that would commit each leading capitalist state to a policy of Global South debt cancellation, the most practicable immediate reform that can be won from the institutions of globalization today. But the political and economic debt owed to the South – long a bastion of past and ongoing Northern colonial expeditions – can only be fully repaid by achieving a transformation of working-class culture in each of the rich capitalist countries, so that unions can really do more than place workers as a class on the tail end of consumer society. Apart from ecological sanity, what is at stake here is the possibility of developing the kind of internationalism that alone will allow for the massive material redistribution – from the rich countries to the poor ones – that any progressive alternative global capitalism must entail.

If internationalism is conceived in a way that is an alternative to, or a substitute for, changes that are necessary at the national level, the results can only be negative, if not disastrous. There can be little tolerance for the kind of invocations of global working-class unity that, as was first made so tragically clear in 1914, has always produced more rhetorical heat than effective transnational solidarity and understanding. The most effective internationalism at this stage is for each labour movement to try to learn as much as possible from others about the limits and possibilities of class struggles that are still inevitably locally based. The world's working classes have changed, and the world's labour movements must change with them. There can be no doubt that it will be an enormous challenge to learn how to reinvent solidarity in this era of globalization. Winning international support for local struggles is more important than ever. But no less important is open discussion of each movement's weaknesses and ongoing problems.

Of course, in each country the landscape of political culture and organization is different. Still, common problems are present in every labour movement, North and South, including issues of sexism and racism, of intolerance and fragmentation, of undemocratic mobilization processes, of hierarchies built into labour aristocracies, and of organizational dialectics that reinforce member deference on the one hand and leader egoism on the other. What is needed now, above all, is common discussion of the experiences of each movement in trying to overcome problems, because advances made – and defeats suffered – by labour and its allies in any one province or state will have a greater exemplary effect than ever. In an era of accelerated globalization, successful new strategies for labour will have significant effects at the international level through converging and coordinated national pressures. A new labour internationalism that appreciates this common purpose is needed if working people are to develop the confidence and capacity to build a better tomorrow out of the great many popular struggles in evidence around the world today.

In developing a new strategy for Canadian labour, there will be much to gain from practising such an internationalism. Perhaps the main thing we can learn is that the first step in any new strategy must be to think ambitiously again and to orient other progressive social movements towards making new radical but concrete demands for the democratic control of capital. For instance, in adapting the seeds of the alternative vision to capitalist globalization much heard at the recent World Social Forums, we can build on their notions of localization by recognizing that they imply inward-oriented development strategies rather than export competitiveness. For this glimmer of an alternative to make sense to people, its meaning needs to be made much clearer and its strategic implications considerably developed. The key long-term condition for an alternative to globalization is democratic investment control within each state – the opposite goal to that of multilateral international negotiations. This shift must mean going beyond the type of quantitative controls on the inflow and outflow of capital allowed under the Bretton Woods system, let alone beyond the "Tobin Tax" on currency traders perennially advanced by many on the left today. A campaign for qualitative democratic capital controls is required that puts on the agenda what international investment is for and should be for – rather than governments themselves either taking a piece of the action (shades of tobacco and alcohol taxes) or just managing short-term capital flows in relation to currency stability, as they did under Bretton Woods.

Controls over foreign investment cannot be divorced from the need for democratic control over private domestic investment. This duality will not be adequately addressed by notions of pension fund socialism or labour investment funds that offer tax breaks to the workers that put their money in them.[27] Far from giving the labour movement control over jobs and the direction of the economy, such funds as now exist generally lack even the capacity to control any particular project, and many of them adopt no investment criteria other than profitability or require that the jobs created include unionization. Moreover, at the same time as shifting the risk of investment to workers' savings, these schemes envelop workers in the world of the stock markets and tax accountants: investors should be taxed and regulated, not subsidized, which is what accountants seek to achieve. Perhaps most importantly, approaching the issue of control over investment in this narrow way reinforces the conventional notion that the money in the banks is legitimately left to the capitalists to do with as they please.

But how does the notion of democratic investment control get on the agenda in a country like Canada, where even pension fund socialism sounds radical? Before finding its way onto the state's policy agenda, the struggle for democratic control must first entail a fundamentally different orientation of labour to the state. Rather than seeking a seat at the table, labour and other social movements must envision how to restructure the state so as to provide for meaningful democratic participation and control.[28] In many parts of Canada, our directly elected local school boards have the statutory responsibility to provide everyone under 18 years of age in their catchment area with a place in the school system and have been provided with the funds – or the means of taxation – to accomplish this. Why do we not have directly elected "economic planning councils" at the local level, vested with the statutory responsibility of providing everyone in their catchment area with gainful paid employment?

They would not have to provide the jobs directly but could vet and fund proposals for new projects to avoid displacing other workers. Further, staff employed by the economic planning councils could be assigned to work with labour and other social movements, doing various types of research in support of their efforts to develop job creation proposals. Like school boards, the planners would have to be given the funds, or the taxing powers, to accomplish these goals. The only really effective funding framework, given how costly it would be to do properly, would be to establish such control over the banks and other financial institutions as would allow for a considerable portion of our own money that passes through their hands as surplus to be designated for distribution to the elected local boards. This earmarking should be done centrally, and the money should be distributed by higher levels of government to each planning board to ensure regional parity.

This proposal is not for "socialism in one city"; it is a political as much as economic structural reform that would be implemented across the country. Even so, there would be no guarantee of success unless the labour movement, in conjunction with other progressive social movements, considerably enhanced its mobilizing capacity, so that real estate agents and property developers would not dominate among those elected to local boards. Moreover, such a municipal scheme for the democratic control of investment would have to be synchronized with sectoral councils that would bring together workers and other community groups in all industrial and service sectors, in contrast to the notion of industrial democracy at the level of single companies, which would leave workers balkanized and maintain competition between them. In the public sector, these councils would include public-sector employees and their clients, thereby involving democratizing the services that meet social needs but are now bureaucratically decided and provided.

Of course, such a strategy for labour is unmistakably socialist. This term is appropriate at a time when the label "anti-capitalist" is commonly attached by the media establishment and is openly embraced by participants themselves. There is a growing sense of the need to think in terms of class once again, but also to think about the question of socialist political organization again. The working-class mobilizations and struggles that launched the Keynesian welfare state era grew out of earlier capitalist crises and confrontation with reactionary forces, and these struggles were to a significant degree inspired and sustained by a broad socialist sensibility within the working class. Arguably, socialist ideas, at least in vague form, can on occasion emerge spontaneously from working-class experiences. In the main, the socialist project is "a creative act of collective will," and its development presupposes socialist political organizations to link and inspire concrete struggles.[29] Through the pivotal role these parties played in the struggles of that time, workers learned the importance of having their own political organizations: to give voice to their interests and aspirations; to give some overall political coherence to their diverse demands; and above all to build and sustain the struggles needed to make real gains.

There is no way ahead without taking up this daunting task once again. That collective bargaining can no longer achieve the gains it once did is an old story. As the foregoing chapters have shown, it is unhesitatingly apparent that the election of NDP governments cannot secure the needs, let alone the aspirations, of working people. The basic parameters of Canadian politics need to be changed, and this change still depends to a great extent upon a shift in the consciousness of working people. In the boom days of the postwar era and rising welfare state, when the focus of the struggle was on negotiating wage increases, it mattered less what the ideological dispositions of workers were. Now it matters a great deal: changing the political agenda has to begin and be sustained by a strong popular commitment to challenging the limits of actually existing capitalism and the actually existing state. Once the issue facing the labour movement is posed in this way, debating whether to leave the NDP is clearly not the real question. The desire of those who feel betrayed politically and want to punish the NDP by breaking with it is understandable, but in the absence of any alternative politics, this move does not itself constitute an advance.

Neither does it make much sense for union activists to throw themselves into trying to change the party from the inside. Such an intra-party battle, in which most working people would be uninvolved as spectators, could also have the effect of leaving a dangerous political vacuum. Moreover, a fundamental change in the party could only be achieved, if ever, after much bitter time and effort. In the short run, the internal party divisions would have severe electoral costs, and even in the unlikely case that the forces for change were successful, a great many on the centre and right of the party would split away rather than accede to the radical change in the nature of the NDP. The question of political organization is heard among political activists in labour and other social movements, most of whom have worked together for years in coalition campaigns. But there are strong voices among the new generation of young activists who have emerged in the anti-corporate and sweatshop campaigns and in the burgeoning protests against the institutions of globalization, police brutality, systemic racism, and the urgent need for environmental action.

The alienation from party politics remains, but there is an often-heard lament that something more than coalitions and campaigns is needed, some sort of organization within which to discuss and develop what a serious socialist strategy would amount to. Its immediate emphasis, sensitive to the historical moment of uncertainty on the left, would be transitional: to create the spaces and processes for collectively working out how to combine daily activism with the need for a broader alternative politics, as well as to increase the likelihood, through organizing the impressive commitments to radical change that already exist, that such energies will be organizationally cumulative rather than dissipated. Such a structured movement would neither take people away from the broad-based coalitions and organizations that concentrate on campaigns against the institutions of globalization, nor seek to undermine social democracy's electoral project. It would have a different project, a much longer term one oriented to developing a genuinely alternative vision and program to neoliberal globalization – and a genuinely alternative practice, especially in terms of the kind of leadership qualities and democratic and capacity-building processes discussed here.

Some tentative moves have been made in this direction in various Canadian cities, but they have not as of yet borne much fruit. A crucial challenge to any structured movement will eventually be how many trade union activists are prepared to join it. There was a time when local and even national labour leaders were prepared to risk trying to bring those whose confidence they had earned in the industrial arena with them into socialist political organizations. A significant change in labour movement culture among both leaders and members would have to take place in Canada before this would be likely to happen again on any scale. However, while trade union activists are among the most sensitive to the need for political organization, the current structures of political parties as well as governmental administration and policymaking are entirely unsuited to developing the popular creativity and consciousness necessary for a new type of politics to emerge. Existing union structures, and those of many social movements, are also not very well suited to the daunting task of trying to change the parameters of Canadian politics in a fundamental fashion.

This brings us to the most pressing issue, which a new strategy for labour must address as a condition of its own emergence and success, and that is the need for transforming labour itself. Not only new radical demands like democratic controls over investment bring this dimension to the fore. Even reforms that are currently on the agenda, such as a reduction of working time, a "right to disconnect," or "living wages," face limits that are internal to the labour movement. At the heart of a new strategy for labour must be a strategy for reorganizing and democratizing the labour movement towards developing the new capacities that workers and their unions require to start to change the structure of power. The objective would be to move unions beyond their current preoccupation with workers' interests as sellers of labour power (just workers) to become more inclusive of workers' full-life experiences – as producers, as family members and as citizens – taking up the human need to be productive and creative in and out of work. Union activists and leaders would need to engage directly – not just as surrogates who issue statements to support the vital issues taken up today by social movements – in the many spheres of working people's lives, from education and housing to racism and sexism, alongside the nature of the work that they do. It is not enough to win more leisure for workers via reduced working time; unions need to be concerned with working people when they are not at work, and that includes part-timers and those who are non-unionized and unemployed. Unions would also need to open themselves to the broader community to become centres of working-class life and ultimately vehicles through which working people develop the capacity and confidence to lead society.

This leadership and openness would necessitate significant changes to unions' collective bargaining priorities, how they deploy their resources, and how they relate to workers who are not unionized. Demands that integrate other interests, such as reduced work time or environmental issues, and facilitate capacity building (union-controlled education funds or more release time) ought to be centred. New and creative ways of relating to workers who are not members are also necessary. Servicing support ought to also be provided to non-members, and new types of membership could be created so that workers outside of organized bargaining units can establish at least some collectivity and become part of the labour movement. Educational and cultural activities would need to be greatly expanded and opportunities for non-members to participate in them created. And efforts would need to be devoted to building linkages among social movements at the local or community level.

Most crucially, a "movement-centred" unionism rests upon a fundamental democratization of the way unions function. Too often, solidarity within union structures – conceived primarily as loyalty to the leadership – has been purchased at the cost of internal democracy. The goal must be the creation of the most openly democratic procedures, affording members the opportunity and resources to make effective decisions at all levels of the union.

Unions in Canada, as elsewhere, have seldom come close to this model, nor has their postwar envelopment in a highly legalized collective bargaining framework been a salutary influence. It has exacerbated hierarchical developments within unions, whereby appointed officials, with technical skills and enormous power over the direction of the union, all too often have had little incentive or means for dialogue with the membership.

This structure is not just related to centralization in union organizations. The basic approach to union recognition – a certification process whereby labour boards normally set bargaining units at a workplace level – tends to fragment unions and weaken the basis for member participation and control over elected and appointed officials. The Rand formula, arguably the most important state sanction in favour of union solidarity, paradoxically loosened the link, so crucial to securing union recognition, between union finances and membership commitment. The legal framework by which a particular union wins exclusive bargaining rights has also sustained a proprietary notion of membership on the part of union leaders. This framework has imposed on labour federations, particularly the CLC, the unending and unsavory task of mediating jurisdictional disputes among their affiliates. It has been almost impossible for union members to secure help for the democratization of their unions by appealing to central labour movement structures or to retain federation affiliation if they move to form new, more democratic unions.

So much of what lay behind Canadian sections leaving American unions and creating or merging with Canadian unions related to the issue of union democracy. As a result, the CLC faced pressures to extend its concerns to the democracy of individual union structures, a problem not isolated to **international union** structures. Ongoing state intervention into union affairs coincides with growing demand by union members for internal democracy; the danger is that the latter will be used to justify the former. Unless labour centrals take up the question of internal union democracy, the state may step in further, as they have done with renewed vigour – with potentially great costs to unions' legitimacy and the significant possibility of further incursions on freedom of association. For their part, activists aware of the importance of democratic procedures and sensitive to their abuse all too often fail to pursue this issue, frequently confusing solidarity with democracy. Even in the case of the most blatant authoritarianism and/or corruption, little support is given to those trying to democratize their unions. There is a deep union culture involved here – a dialectic between rank-and-file deference and pride in the leader who can talk tough with an employer, and the paternalism of even a radical reform leadership that may genuinely have the members' interests at heart but believe the ranks are best served if the leaders maintain control.

Which precise constitutional mechanisms, democratic forums, and internal structures – not least as they pertain to the selection and payment of full-time staff – are technically best in terms of maximizing accountability and democratic decision-making is not the issue here. The point is rather to measure these mechanisms in terms of the contribution they make to developing democratic capacities whereby members overcome deference, leaders pass on expertise rather than hoarding it like their personal capital, and more frequent changes of leadership are made possible. Above all, debate needs to be encouraged rather than avoided, even over the most potentially divisive issues. The problem of avoiding debate – whether due to impatience, intolerance, or avoidance of tough questions – once again emerges out of a dialectic in which members' attitudes, as much as leaders' inclinations, are entwined. Only through open discussion and debate can members be brought to see that issues like race and gender, which are often treated by workers as divisive from the point of view of the narrow economics of bargaining, are constitutive of solidarity because of the diversity of the working class itself.

This relationship between democracy and class consciousness is, in other words, especially important in terms of those changes in the working class that are turning labour into a more inclusive social agent. Similarly, the most effective way to extend union organization to the unorganized is to identify as the main goal democratic capacity building among old as well as new members. What matters for this inclusiveness is the development of leadership just as much as the development of membership. Enhanced democratic structures can contribute to a more committed and involved membership, opening the way for unions to become, as far as possible, centres of working-class life and culture. In the final analysis, this development alone can root the labour movement in society. Democratization is directly related to possibilities for the kind of politicization that the movement requires today. Leaders must once again take the risk of talking radical politics with their members who, often enough, do not see the connection between their immediate reasons for joining or supporting unions and the struggle against capitalism as a system.

This risk can no longer be avoided. To accomplish this goal will mean educating those leaders who cannot see beyond defensiveness and economism and still hope falsely for an easy return to full union rights and the expansive Keynesian welfare state. It will also mean educating a membership that has only been exposed to the most caricatured or impoverished notions of social-ism, rather than the new possibilities for workers' creativity and self-deter-mination it could open. If the lessons drawn from the continuing assault on union freedoms can combine with the effusive tensions within unions today in such a way as to imbue the labour movement with a new radical purpose and practices, the result may yet lay the basis for the advance of the Canadian working class and that of other social movement actors.

Finally, one thing must be stressed above all: freedom of association for workers is an essential condition of democracy. Achieved through long, ardu-ous, even bloody, struggle, it was only accepted by the state at real cost to the further mobilizing capacities of unions. Moreover, it was always, in a capitalist society, open to challenge. Reforms, even reforms basic to liberal democracy, are always subject to limits and never guaranteed forever. They must be de-fended, extended, and transformed to further strengthen workers' capacity to conduct class struggle – or else they are always in danger of atrophying, or worse, being reneged on. In other words, the struggle to defend workers' free-dom of association is a struggle over the substantive meaning of democracy in Canadian society.

CONCLUSION: FIGHTING FOR THE FUTURE, TODAY

Permanent exceptionalism, the core subject of this book, is now wholly normed into the fabric of the Canadian state. The state has been successful for the most part, but with occasional retreat, because of the tremendous imbal-ance in class power that has only accelerated and broadened since the 1980s. The working class was transformed through the experiences of the 1930s where the CIO organizing campaigns, perhaps the largest social movement in the history of capitalism, advanced a new model of trade unionism, where the struggle was marked by sit-down strikes and mass political mobilizations for relief and work that were met by the repression of both the state and capital. These were formative events in the making of a working-class identity. And the radical left provided the organizational and ideological leadership in their work as organizers and educators.

The Canadian working class has again been transformed. The past 40 years have dissolved most of what was created in those struggles as well as those that followed through World War II and into the postwar period of welfare state building. It is time to start all over again, and part of this process is to move on from the black hole of social democracy. In the Canadian context, the NDP is a political space sucking everything in and from which there is no escape. It is both nothing, in terms of class political ambition, and everything, as it occupies such a huge and visible presence. And trade union sectionalism and conservatism contributes nothing to building class identity. There is no easy formula out of the abiding impasse of working-class politics, but there are, as noted above, two key considerations. Specifically, a new politics carried forward in a new type of party and a reconceptualization of the work of unions as the mechanism for building a class identity that extends beyond the workplace. The new type of party necessarily intersects with the new type of union. This political renewal is the only means to organizationally, ideologically, and culturally rearm the working class.

Failing the formation of a political vision "that encompasses the entire working class, and absent the goal of developing workers' capacity to democratize the economy and society," unions will simply remain, as Sam Gindin has noted, caught in what they are: "instrumental organizations" characterized by a "pragmatic exchange between active leaders and passive members."[30] In this regard, the question of a socialist party cannot be avoided. If trade unions and working-class communities are to not only resist but reverse the austerity and authoritarianism of the last four decades, rebuilding the capacities of organized labour to fight back against concessionary demands will be key, as will transcending what are often insulated labour and activist subcultures. If unions are to reappear as a movement and not simply hang on as a relic of the past, they will need to move beyond the limited defence of their own members' interests and fight for the interests of the working class as a whole. Doing so requires having feet both inside and outside the trade union movement – that is to say, rooted in an organizational form explicitly intent on building a broader working-class movement across the many cleavages among workers. As shown by the examples of the Democratic Socialists of America – which has grown from 5,000 to 100,000 members between 2015 and 2021 – as well as Corbyn's rise (and fall) within the British Labour Party and the growth in support for the Belgian Workers' Party and the Norwegian Red Party, among other such cases, we are clearly living through a period of the "revival of socialist ideas."[31] In Canada, despite rapidly growing inequality that has shone an intense light on the reality of capitalism, there is largely quietude rather than mobilization. This is due, at least in part, to the absence of the political infrastructure necessary to building a class-based alternative vision, culture, and capacity.

In light of historical and contemporary attacks against free collective bargaining and other democratic rights, it is increasingly clear that unions and oppressed persons generally can no longer, if they ever could, put their faith in the courts, laws, or governments to enforce the postwar class compromise. This postwar "consensus" has been thoroughly eroded in the face of trade union and social justice activists' inability to substantively counteract cumulative decades of concerted attacks. Organizing solely around specific issues, workplaces, and particular constituencies cannot add up to the kind of strength, organization, and structure that is needed to bring about wide-ranging change. As relevant today as when André Gorz argued four decades ago, the fact remains that the trade union movement is the best organized force within a broader array of social movements and this "confers on it a particular responsibility; on it will largely depend the success or failure of all the other elements in this social movement."[32] While trade unions must be a central part of any radical political renewal, their rebirth is equally dependent upon a broader revitalization of the left outside of organized labour and working-class politics as a whole – what Marx identified as a social and political formation united in difference.

The course of neoliberalism has thoroughly eroded what vestiges remain of trade union militancy, while social movements generally remain isolated in small-scale and resource-poor coalitions. Given the ongoing onslaught against all workers and working-class standards of living, the existing ways of doing things are not working. Recognizing this, in our view, is the only realistic starting point from which to move forward. The inability of both organized labour and community activists to confront this impasse belies the need for a new kind of radical, socialist political project suited to the current historical and social conjuncture, one that interrogates both its own historical failures as well as the transformations in the political, economic and cultural arenas under which we are struggling today. In the absence of this, organized labour will increasingly risk becoming an impediment to, rather than an instrument of, a renewed working-class politics. In other words, labour and social justice activists must lead left if austerity and authoritarianism are to be challenged. The failure to do so may regrettably amount to an historic class defeat. Revitalizing the political promise of a radical working-class politics remains a crucial step in resisting state and employer coercion and potentially realizing a better world that gets to the root of the problem – capitalism. Time will tell if a major resistance is in the cards.

Notes

1. From the Era of Consent to the Era of Coercion

1 Mark Thompson and Allen Ponak, *Canadian Public Sector Industrial Relations: Policy and Practice* (Pacific Rim Comparative Labour Policy Conference, Vancouver, 1987), 31, 41; P. Kumar, "Recent Labour-Management Approaches in Canada: Will They Endure?," in *Queen's Papers in Industrial Relations* (Kingston: Industrial Relations Centre, Queen's University, 1987), 4.

2 Donald D. Carter, "The Changing Face of Canadian Labour Relations Law," Working Paper No. 54 (Kingston: Industrial Relations Centre, Queen's University, 1985), 13.

3 Jamie Peck, *Constructions of Neoliberal Reason* (Oxford: Oxford University Press, 2010).

4 Gregory Albo, Sam Gindin, and Leo Panitch, *In and Out of Crisis: The Global Financial Meltdown and Left Alternatives* (New York: PM Press, 2010); Leo Panitch, Gregory Albo, and Vivek Chibber, *The Crisis This Time: Socialist Register 2011* (London: Merlin Press/Monthly Review Press/Fernwood Publishing, 2010).

5 David Harvey, "We Need a Collective Response to the Collective Dilemma of Coronavirus," *Jacobin*, 24 December 2021, https://jacobinmag.com/2020/04/david-harvey-coronavirus-pandemic-capital-economy.

6 Sam Gindin, "The Coronavirus and the Crisis This Time – The Bullet," *Socialist Project*, 10 April 2020, https://socialistproject.ca/2020/04/coronavirus-and-the-crisis-this-time/.

7 Editorial Board, "Virus Lays Bare the Frailty of the Social Contract," *Financial Times*, 3 April 2020, https://www.ft.com/content/7eff769a-74dd-11ea-95fe-fcd274e920ca.

8 Joel Dryden, "What Cargill Workers Want," *CBC News*, 1 December 2021, https://newsinteractives.cbc.ca/longform/what-cargill-workers-want.

9 Eric Tucker and Leah Vosko, "Designing Paid and Protected Employment Leaves for Short-Term Sickness and Caregiving," IRPP Insight 38 (Montreal: Institute for Research on Public Policy, 2021).

10 Vanmala Subramaniam, "The Pandemic Kickstarted Benefit Programs Like Paid Sick Days, So Why Are Essential Workers Falling through the Cracks?," *Globe and Mail*, 31 January 2022, https://www.theglobeandmail.com/business/article-paid-sick-days-covid-leave-essential-workers/. See also for Ontario: J. Freeman, "Ontario Extends Three Paid COVID-19 Sick Days through the End of 2021." *CTV News*, 31 August 2021, https://toronto.ctvnews.ca/ontario-extends-three-paid-covid-19-sick-days-through-the-end-of-2021-1.5568514; and Allison Jones, "Ontario Government Introduces Omnibus Labour Legislation, Including Right to Disconnect," *Global News*, 25 October 2021, https://globalnews.ca/news/8322699/ontario-covid-labour-right-to-disconnect-law/.

11 Canadian Press. "COVID-19: Quebec Teachers in Shock after Government Suspends Collective Agreements," *CTV News*, 19 March 2020, https://montreal.ctvnews.ca/covid-19-quebec-teachers-in-shock-after-government-suspends-collective-agreements-1.4859384; Michelle Bellefontaine, "Alberta Bill Removes Mandatory Vaccinations, Repeals Bill 10 Powers – CBC News," *CBC*, 12 April 2021, https://www.cbc.ca/news/canada/edmonton/alberta-bill-removes-mandatory-vaccinations-repeals-bill-10-powers-1.5984531.

12 Oxfam International, "Mega-Rich Recoup COVID-Losses in Record-Time yet Billions Will Live in Poverty for at Least a Decade," 25 January 2021, https://www.oxfam.org/en/press-releases/mega-rich-recoup-covid-losses-record-time-yet-billions-will-live-poverty-least.

13 Dave Macdonald, "Profit Squeeze: Excess Corporate Profits are Making Inflation Tougher for Canadians," *The Monitor*, 4 April 2022, https://monitormag.ca/articles/profit-squeeze-the-case-for-an-excess-profit-tax-in-canada-on-corporate-inflation-drivers; Will Daniel, "US Companies Post Their Biggest Profit Growth in Decades by Jacking Up Prices during the Pandemic," *Fortune*, 31 March 2022, https://fortune.com/2022/03/31/us-companies-record-profits-2021-price-hikes-inflation/.

14 H. Mackenzie and R. Shillington, *Canada's Quiet Bargain: The Benefits of Public Spending* (Ottawa: CCPA, 2009).

15 Statistics Canada, Household Actual Final Consumption (Ottawa: Government of Canada, 2019), https://www150.statcan.gc.ca/n1/daily-quotidien/190320/dq190320b-eng.htm.

2. The Postwar Era of Free Collective Bargaining

1 Claude D'Aoust and François Delorme, "The Origins of the Freedom of Association and of the Right of Strike in Canada: An Historical Perspective," *Rélations industrielles* 36, no. 4 (1981): 894–919.

2 James Armstrong and A.T. Freed, Report of the Royal Commission on the Relations of Labor and Capital in Canada, CP32-146/1889E-PDF; Z1-1886E-PDF
   (Ottawa: Government of Canada Publications, 2022), https://publications.gc.ca
   /site/eng/472984/publication.html.

3 Bryan D. Palmer, *Working-Class Experience: The Rise and Reconstitution of
   Canadian Labour, 1800–1980*, 1st ed. (Toronto: Butterworth, 1983).

4 James Rinehart, *The Tyranny of Work: Alienation and the Labour Process*
   (Toronto: Thomson Nelson, 2006).

5 Gregory Kealey, *Workers and Canadian History* (Kingston: McGill-Queen's
   University Press, 1996), 430.

6 Paul Craven, *"An Impartial Umpire": Industrial Relations and the Canadian State
   1900–1911* (Toronto: University of Toronto Press, 1980), 306. Craven notes
   (pp. 301–2) that H.D. Woods, despite arguing that the primary purpose of the
   IDIA was "the establishment of a bargaining relationship, and not, as commonly
   supposed, the delaying of strikes or lockouts," concludes that in practice it "was
   little more than a public-interest emergency-dispute policy." For the most nu-
   anced study of the interaction between "coercive and accommodative elements"
   in changes to the regime of industrial legality in Canada in the first half of the
   century, see Judy Fudge and Eric Tucker, *Labour Before the Law: The Regulation
   of Workers' Collective Action in Canada, 1900–1948* (Toronto: Oxford University
   Press, 2001).

7 Rinehart, *The Tyranny of Work*.

8 Dennis Lewycky, *Magnificent Fight* (Halifax: Fernwood, 1995); Norman Penner,
   ed., *Winnipeg 1919*, 3rd ed. (Toronto: Lorimer, 2019).

9 Kealey, *Workers and Canadian History*.

10 Herb Colling, *The Ford Strike in Windsor: 99 Days* (Toronto: NC Press, 1995);
   Irving M. Abella, *Nationalism, Communism and Canadian Labour: The CIO, the
   Communist Party, and the Canadian Congress of Labour, 1935–1956* (Toronto:
   University of Toronto Press, 1973).

11 Wilfred Eggleston, "King Reproves Labour's Attitude as Likely to Foment
   Strike," *Saturday Night*, 13 April 1946.

12 H.A. Logan, *State Intervention and Assistance in Collective Bargaining* (Toronto:
   University of Toronto Press, 1956), 75.

13 L. Sefton-MacDowell, "The Formation of the Canadian Industrial Relations
   System during World War Two," *Labour/Le Travail* 3 (1978): 175–96.

14 Hal Draper, *Karl Marx's Theory of Revolution, Vol. II: The Politics of Social
   Classes* (New York: Monthly Review Press, 1973), 234.

15 Mary E. Baruth-Walsh and Mark Walsh, *Strike!* (Newcastle: Penumbra Press, 1995).

16 The tenor of this new policy was graphically captured in Justice Rand's famous
   1946 ruling on union security: "Any modification of relations between the parties
   here concerned must be made within the framework of a society whose economic
   life has private enterprise as its dynamic. And it is the accommodation of that
   principle of action with evolving notions of social justice in the area of industrial
   mass production, that becomes the problem for decision. Certain declarations
   of policy of both Dominion and Provincial legislatures furnish me with the

premises from which I must proceed. In most of the Provinces, and by Dominion war legislation, the social desirability of the organization of workers and of collective bargaining where employees seek them has been written into laws…. The corollary from it is that the labour unions should become strong in order to carry on the functions for which they are intended. This is machinery devised to adjust, toward an increasing harmony, the interests of capital, labour and public in the production of goods and services which our philosophy accepts as part of the good life; it is to secure industrial civilization within a framework of labour-employer constitutional law based on a rational economic and social doctrine…. In industry, capital must in the long run be looked upon as occupying a dominant position. It is in some respects at greater risk than labour; but as industry becomes established, these risks change inversely. Certainly the predominance of capital against individual labour is unquestionable; and in mass relations, hunger is more imperious than passed dividends. Against the consequence of that, as the history of the past century has demonstrated, the power of organized labour, the necessary co-partner of capital, must be available to redress the balance of what is called social justice; the just protection of all interests in an activity which the social order approves and encourages." Justice I.C. Rand, "Rand Formula," *Canadian Law Reports* 2150 (1958): 1251–3. See also Colling, *The Ford Strike in Windsor*; Abella, *Nationalism, Communism and Canadian Labour*.

17 For an introduction to this, see Karl Marx, *Capital: A Critique of Political Economy* (New York: Penguin Random House, 1977); David Harvey, *A Companion to Marx's Capital* (New York: Verso, 2018).

18 William K. Carroll, *The Making of a Transnational Capitalist Class*, 1st ed. (New York: Bloomsbury Publishing, 2013); Jamie Brownlee, *Ruling Canada* (Halifax: Fernwood, 2006); Susanne Soderberg, *Corporate Power and Ownership in Contemporary Capitalism: The Politics of Resistance and Domination* (New York: Taylor & Francis, 2009).

19 Ellen Meiksins Wood, *The Origin of Capitalism* (New York: Verso Books, 2017); see also Carlo Fanelli and Jeff Noonan, "Capital and Organized Labour," in *Reading Capital Today: Marx After 150 Years*, ed. Ingo Schmidt and Carlo Fanelli (London: Pluto Press, 2017).

20 Harold J. Laski, *Trade Unions in the New Society* (London: George Allen and Unwin, 1950), 66–7, 10, 224, 232.

21 Laski, *Trade Unions*, 224, 232.

22 Paul Weiler, *Reconcilable Differences: New Directions in Canadian Labour Law* (Toronto: Carswell, 1980).

23 Logan, *State Intervention*, 26, 27. The "formal" equality of the ban on strikes and lockouts during collective agreements is, needless to say, illusory since the lockout is but one of several of capital's economic weapons.

24 Rand, "Rand Formula," 1252.

25 Hannes Lacher, "Embedded Liberalism, Disembedded Markets: Reconceptualising the Pax Americana," *New Political Economy* 4, no. 3 (1999): 343–60; Carlo Fanelli, "The Radical Keynes: An Appraisal," *Workplace* 25 (2015): 69–81.

26 Reg Whitaker and Gary Marcuse, *Cold War Canada* (Toronto: University of Toronto Press, 1995); Desmond Morton, *Working People*, 5th ed. (Montreal: McGill-Queen's University Press, 1999); Gad Horowitz, *Canadian Labour in Politics* (Toronto: University of Toronto Press, 1968); James Naylor, *The Fate of Labour Socialism* (Toronto: University of Toronto Press, 2016).

27 It is well recognized that the working conditions (including pay and managerial practices) of public employees were inferior to those of private-sector workers employed by major corporations in the immediate aftermath of World War II. It should be noted here that in 1944 the CCF government in Saskatchewan granted bargaining rights to provincial employees. See Stuart Jamieson, *Industrial Relations in Canada* (Toronto: Macmillan, 1973), 130 ff. The unionized proportion of the workforce did jump from 30 to 33 percent between 1952 and 1953, and then slowly declined to just below 30 percent in the mid-1960s. The 1952–1953 increase was due primarily to a contraction of 100,000 in the labour force. In British Columbia, new restrictions were imposed on the right to strike generally, while in Alberta, what were deemed "public interest disputes" were subject to more sweeping restrictions.

28 This position was common on the left as well as in mainstream thinking. For example, see Herbert Marcuse, *One Dimensional Man* (Boston: Beacon Press, 1964) and James O'Connor, *The Fiscal Crisis of the State* (New York: St. Martin's Press, 1973).

29 Ralph Miliband, *The State in Capitalist Society* (New York: Basic Books, 1969), 217.

30 Jamieson, *Industrial Relations in Canada*, 94–9.

31 H. Woods, *Canadian Industrial Relations* (Ottawa: Queen's Printer, 1969).

32 For a good overview, see Kenneth McRoberts and Dale Postgate, *Quebec: Social Change and Political Crisis*, rev. ed. (Toronto: McClelland and Stewart, 1980).

33 H. Arthurs, *Collective Bargaining by Public Employees in Canada: The Five Models* (Ann Arbor: Institute of Labour and Industrial Relations, 1971).

34 A. Heeney, *Report of the Preparatory Committee on Collective Bargaining in the Public Service* (Ottawa: Government of Canada, 1965).

35 There has been some suggestion that Jean Marchand, former president of the Confederation of National Trade Unions (CSN) and the most sought after of the "three wise men," made granting the right to strike a condition for remaining in the government (personal communication from E. Swimmer).

36 David Lewis, *The Good Fight: Political Memoirs 1909–1958* (Toronto: Macmillan, 1981), 393, 25, 151.

37 Lewis, *The Good Fight*, 151.

38 Logan, *State Intervention*, 76.

3. Permanent Exceptionalism: The Turn to Coercion

1 This boom was, in fact, the product of the historically specific set of conditions at the end of World War II: the unchallenged dominance of the United States

vis-à-vis the major capitalist countries that allowed it to order the international financial system; the extensive task of postwar reconstruction in Europe; discoveries of huge deposits of cheap resources; the colonial or neo-colonial dependency of most of the Third World; and the moderation of the labour movement in the West, not least due to the Cold War. While these conditions showed dim signs of passing by the mid-sixties, the formal announcement came in 1971, when United States president Richard Nixon renounced the Bretton Woods Agreement on which the postwar international financial order was based. See, for example, Ian Gough, "State Expenditure in Advanced Capitalism," *New Left Review* 92 (July/August 1975): 53–92.

2 See, for example, David Wolfe, "The State and Economic Policy in Canada 1968–1975," in *The Canadian State: Political Economy and Political Power*, ed. Leo Panitch (Toronto: University of Toronto Press, 1977), 228–51, and W.I. Gillespie, "On the Redistribution of Income in Canada," *Canadian Tax Journal* 24 (July/August 1976): 419–50.

3 See Leo Panitch, "The Development of Corporatism in Liberal Democracies," *Comparative Political Studies* 10 (April 1977): 61–90.

4 A discussion of these attempts in Canada and the reasons for their failure is found in Leo Panitch, "Corporatism in Canada?," *Studies in Political Economy: A Socialist Review* 1 (Spring 1979): 43–92.

5 Quoted in A. Price, "Back to Work Legislation: An Analysis of the Federal and Ontario Governments' Increased Propensity to End Strikes by Ad Hoc Laws, 1950–1978" (MA thesis, Queen's University, 1980), 98. Price concludes that seldom, if ever, was there such a threat. Rather, government intervention was designed to prevent serious disruption of immediate concern to a relatively small segment of society, or to prevent broad public inconvenience (p. 90).

6 Price, "Back to Work Legislation," 99.

7 Harry J. Glasbeek and Michael Mandel, "The Crime and Punishment of Jean-Claude Parrot," *Canadian Forum* (August 1979): 10–14.

8 Quoted in Leo Panitch, *Workers, Wages and Controls: The Anti-Inflation Programme and Its Implications for Canadian Workers* (Toronto: New Hogtown Press, 1976), esp. 1 and 18.

9 Quoted in the *Globe and Mail*, October 21, 1982.

10 For a cogent alternative view of the "6 and 5" legislation that mainly sees it as an attempt to renege on the collective bargaining rights granted to federal government employees, see E. Swimmer, "Six and Five," in *How Ottawa Spends 1984*, ed. A. Maslove (Ottawa: Carleton University Press, 1985), 240–81. While not disputing the specifics of his argument, the ensuing course of events seems to us to confirm the significance of the broader ideological factors we identify as being involved.

11 See "The Turning Point in Industrial Relations" and "Government Moves to Restrain Construction Wages," *Construction* 19, no. 3 (September/October 1983): 3–4, 17–19.

12 *The Canadian Air Traffic Control Association v. The Queen in Right of Canada* (Treasury Board) [1982] 1 S.C.R. 696.

13 In what the *Globe and Mail* termed a "radical decision," compensation commis
sioner Ed Peck confirmed on 14 March 1984 the government's "ability to pay"
and not a "fair wage" as the paramount consideration in overturning a binding
arbitration award of 5 percent to school support staff workers. Once the government set funding levels, collective bargaining had to take place within those
parameters. See Ian Mulgrew, "Province's Ability to Pay Wages Ruled Key to
Settlements in BC," *Globe and Mail*, 15 March 1984.

14 The following account is based on Bryan Palmer, "A Funny Thing Happened on
the Way to Kelowna," in *Canadian Dimension* 18, no. 1 (March 1984): 6; and
Larry Kuehn, "BC Teachers Strengthen the Labour Movement," in *Canadian
Dimension* 18, no. 1 (March 1984): 9–12.

15 Sid Tafler, "BC Job Cuts Partly Fake, Workers Say," *Globe and Mail*, 19 March
1984.

16 Perry Anderson, "Renewals," *New Left Review* 1 (January-February 2000):
5–24, 17.

4. Freeing Trade, Coercing Labour

1 Stephen McBride, *Paradigm Shift: Globalization and the Canadian State*
(Halifax: Fernwood, 2005).

2 Quoted in J. Deverell, "Ottawa Pushing 100,000 Workers into Strike Action,
Union Leaders Say," *Toronto Star*, 4 April 1987.

3 See J. Deverell, "End Strike and Back Post Office Business Group Urges," *Toronto Star*, 6 October 1987.

4 Quoted in J. Deverell, "Ottawa May Use Closure to End Strike by Posties,"
Toronto Star, 14 October 1987.

5 Interview by Michael Enright with Harvie Andre on CBC's *As It Happens*,
8 October 1987. The inclusion of this sanction in the legislation, ending the
lockout of longshoremen in Vancouver, very much caught the attention of Liberal MP Sheila Copps. *Hansard*, 18 November 1987, 1258. However, outside of
her intervention in the House of Commons, it generated little comment.

6 G. Sulzner, "Canadian Federal Labour-Management Relations: The Mulroney
Difference," *Journal of Collective Negotiations* 15, no. 4 (1986): 298. See also Wil-
fred List, "Crew's Dilemma Raises the Issue of the Right to Strike," *Globe and
Mail*, 7 July 1986.

7 Lorne Slotnick, "Federal Unions Angry at Plans to Amend," *Globe and Mail*,
14 January 1987.

8 G. Swimmer, "The Impact of the Dispute Settlement Process on Canadian
Federal Public Service Wage Settlements," *Journal of Collective Negotiations*
16, no. 1 (1987): 53–61.

9 M. Lim, "An Overview of Recent Compensation Settlements in the Canadian
Public Sector," *Proceedings*, Canadian Compensation Association Conference,
1985, 35–9. This conclusion was further underscored by the government's
decision to suspend the 50-year-old practice of posting a minimum wage

234 Notes to pages 62–7

schedule for any federal construction project for three years, beginning 1 April 1987. Since the schedule corresponded closely to construction union collective agreements, this practice essentially secured unionized federal construction projects. Suspending this practice – leaving the market to set a fair wage, as Labour Minister Pierre Cadieux blithely put it – opened federal construction to cut-rate non-union contractors. For the leaders of construction unions, who opted to leave the CLC rather than risk compromising their commitment to autocracy and unbridled class collaboration, the government's announcement was a humiliating if well-deserved slap in the face. See V. Bercovici, "Loss of Wage Schedule Helps Non-union Firms, Say Unions," *Ottawa Citizen*, 30 July 1987.

10 Quoted in G. Swimmer with Kjerstine Kinaschuk, "Staff Relations under the Conservative Government: The Singers Change but the Song Remains the Same," in *How Ottawa Spends 1992–93: The Politics of Competitiveness*, ed. Frances Abele (Ottawa: Carleton University Press, 1992), 277.

11 Swimmer and Kinaschuk, "Staff Relations," tables 9.1 and 9.2, 300–2.

12 See Gregory Albo, "Democratic Citizenship and the Future of Public Management," in *A Different Kind of State? Popular Power and Democratic Administration*, ed. Gregory Albo, David Langille, and Leo Panitch (Toronto: Oxford University Press, 1993), 17–33. Cf. Hugh Winsor, "Civil-Service Bill Merits Closer Look," *Globe and Mail*, 23 May 1992; and Marvin Gandall, "Public Service Perils: Meriting a Second Look," *Ottawa Citizen*, 19 March 1992.

13 See Graham Fraser and Virginia Galt, "PSAC's Strike Called Off: Negotiations to Resume," and Hugh Winsor, "Union Finds It Difficult to Go against the Grain," *Globe and Mail*, 18 September 1991.

14 B. Livingstone, "Alberta Labour under Attack," *Canadian Dimension* 18, no. 2 (May 1984): 21–2. See also the *Globe and Mail*, 3 July 1984, for a report updating this issue in view of subsequent board rulings.

15 L. Slotnick, "Proposed Bill Seeks to Curb Power of BC's Labour Unions," *Globe and Mail*, 11 May 1987.

16 Business Council of British Columbia, *BC Collective Bargaining Review and Outlook*, 1985, 24.

17 Business Council of British Columbia, *BC Collective Bargaining Review*. A good example of this trend was the "very tough deal" agreed to by workers in the forest industry. See R. Lester, "Causes and Effects of De-Accreditation on Collective Bargaining in the British Columbia Pulp and Paper Industry," *Proceedings*, 23rd Annual Meeting of the Industrial Relations Association University of Manitoba, 29–31 May 1986, 380.

18 D. Forkin, "IWA Defeats Contracting-Out," *Our Times* (February 1987): 12–13.

19 "Open Letter to the Premier," *Vancouver Province*, 1 May 1987. On the centralization effected by Vander Zalm, see J. Cruickshank, "Vander Zalm Runs a One-Man Show to Speed Reforms," *Globe and Mail*, 15 July 1987.

20 The implications of Bill 19, particularly regarding women workers, are incisively and wittily analyzed by Sharon Yandle in "The Women at Windermere," *New Directions* 2, no. 5 (June 1987): 3–6.

21 See Chapter 4, note 6; and D. Fudge, "ILO Condemns Restrictive Labour Laws in Canada," *Canadian Labour* January (1986): 15.

22 The government's revisions to the province's Labour Code went through two stages: Bill 60, introduced in June 1987, was scrapped due to business opposition to the minor changes the Bill proposed to the Employment Standards Act. See A. Noel, "The Americanization of Alberta Labour Law," *NeWest Review* (May 1988): 2. This opposition was quite remarkable, given how extensively Bill 60 expanded government powers to intervene in collective bargaining on behalf of business. These powers were reincorporated in Bill 22, which was finally enacted in 1988. Between the introduction of Bill 60 and the enactment of Bill 22, Bill 53 provided a temporary collective bargaining framework for the construction industry. Both Bills 60 and 53 were discussed extensively in the first edition of this book, pages 81–2.

23 J. Clark, "Labour Scene," *Journal of Commerce*, 15 June 1987. See also J. Bagnall, "Construction Workers Lead Labour's Retreat," *Financial Post*, 1 March 1986.

24 R. Sass, "Department of Labour: What's in a Name," *The Labour Reporter*, Saskatchewan Federation of Labour, February 1987.

25 See John Loxley, "Democratizing Economic Policy Formulation: The Manitoba Experience," in *A Different Kind of State? Popular Power and Democratic Administration*, ed. Gregory Albo, David Langille, and Leo Panitch (Toronto: Oxford University Press, 1993), esp. 192–4. For a perceptive earlier article on ideological shifts in the Manitoba labour movement, see Bob Ages, "Fresh Winds Blowing in the Manitoba Federation of Labour," *Canadian Dimension* (January/February, 1990): 45–7.

26 See L. Bissonnette, "Bourassa Triumphs over Unions," *Globe and Mail*, 3 January 1987; and CUPE, *The Public Employee* (Summer 1986): 13–14.

27 Carla Lipsig-Mummé, "Future Conditional: Wars of Position in the Quebec Labour Movement," in *Studies in Political Economy* 36 (1991): 73–107.

28 See E. Oziewicz, "Wages Frozen for 450,000 Quebeckers," *Globe and Mail*, 20 March 1991.

29 See M. King, "Three-Month Wage Freeze Backed by Heads of 6 Public-Sector Unions," *Montreal Gazette*, 24 April 1991; and the editorial, "Peace Is Worth the Price," *Montreal Gazette*, 17 April 1991.

30 C. Wallace, "Thousand Protest against Wage Curbs," *Montreal Gazette*, 13 April 1992. See also P. Wells, "Unions Reject Johnson Bid for Salary Concessions," *Montreal Gazette*, 20 February 1992.

31 M. Venne, "Québec court au désastre, avertissent les syndicats," *Le Devoir*, 14 May 1993. Cf. further protests during the summer, "Unions Told Freeze Might Come Sooner," *Montreal Gazette*, 17 June 1993. In May, the government proceeded with a piece of legislation (Bill 198), first introduced over two years earlier, which was designed to impose a mandatory hiring freeze in the broader public sector.

32 For incisive analyses of this, see Jean-Marc Piotte, "'Collabos' et Heureux de l'être," *Le Devoir*, 30 June 1992; and C. Lipsig-Mumme, "Wars of Position:

Fragmentation and Realignment in the Quebec Labour Movement," *Queen's Papers in Industrial Relations* 11(1990): esp. 21ff.

33 K. Stickney, "Nova Scotia's CLMB Confident It Can Extend Control," *Daily Commercial News*, 3 April 1987.

34 P. Gard, "Newfoundland Begins Labour Practices Overhaul," *Financial Times*, 3 May 1986.

35 Quoted in Michael Harris, "Under Siege Newfoundland Premier Assailed by Former Fans," *Globe and Mail*, 27 December 1984.

36 See W. List, "Exit of Labour Official Part of a Liberal Trend," *Globe and Mail*, 12 August 1986. The following draws largely on J. Deverell, "New Labour Minister Bill Wrye a Threat to NDP's Union Support," *Toronto Star*, 9 July 1986. See also J. Deverell, "Labour Ministry Officials Sabotaging Laws to Protect Workers, Brief Says," *Toronto Star*, 28 September 1986.

37 See "UAW Leader Urges Changes in First-Contract Legislation," *Globe and Mail*, 2 April 1986. As the title of this article suggests, the unions thought that improvements in the Act were possible, but the text shows that their reservations were few in number and marginal in nature.

38 Eric Tucker, "Worker Participation in Health and Safety Regulation: Some Lessons from Sweden," *Studies in Political Economy* 37 (Spring 1992): 119.

5. Consolidating Neoliberalism

1 This policy was foreshadowed by the Royal Commission on the Economic Union (McDonald Commission), which had emphasized Canada's failure to effectively integrate with global economic forces. See Canada, *Royal Commission on the Economic Union and Development Prospects for Canada* (Ottawa: Ministry of Supply and Services, 1985) 2: 290–301.

2 A. Jackson et al., *Falling Behind: The State of Working in Canada, 2000* (Ottawa: Canadian Centre for Policy Alternatives), 21–41.

3 Jim Stanford, "The Rise and Fall of Deficit-Mania: Public Sector Finances and the Attack on Social Canada," in *Power and Resistance: Critical Thinking about Canadian Social Issues*, ed. L. Samuelson and W. Antony (Halifax: Fernwood, 1998), 47–8.

4 Ann Duffy, Daniel Glenday, and Norene Pupo, ed., *Good Jobs, Bad Jobs, No Jobs: The Transformation of Work in the 21st Century* (Toronto: Harcourt Brace & Company, 1997).

5 Sam Gindin and Leo Panitch, *The Making of Global Capitalism: The Political Economy of American Empire* (New York: Verso Books, 2012).

6 Susan D. Philips, "The Liberals' Mid-Life Crises: Aspirations versus Achievements," in *How Ottawa Spends 1995–96: Mid-Life Crises*, ed. Susan D. Philips (Ottawa: Carleton University Press, 1995), 11.

7 As Murray Dobbin notes: "A study by CIBC-Wood Gundy concluded that Martin's cuts reduced economic growth in Canada by a huge 3.5 percentage points through 1994–1996. The resulting loss in tax revenue almost eliminated

the savings gained by making the spending cuts. The cuts combined with the zero-inflation policy of the Bank of Canada to create a recession lasting much of the 1990s." Murray Dobbin, "Paul Martin: He Has a Record," *Rabble*, 10 October 2008, https://rabble.ca/general/paul-martin-he-has-record/.

8   Toba Bryant and Dennis Raphael, *The Politics of Health in the Canadian Welfare State* (Toronto: Canadian Scholars, 2020).

9   Gene Swimmer and Sandra Bach, "Restructuring Federal Public-Sector Human Resources," in *Public-Sector Labour Relations in an Era of Restraint and Restructuring*, ed. Gene Swimmer (Oxford: Oxford University Press, 2000). The 3,500 workers at the Port of Vancouver were legislated back to work in January 1994.

10 Bill C-76 did not prevent prison guards from striking, but it empowered the federal government to order workers back to work at any time and to impose a settlement. Interestingly, the guards were only in a legal strike position due to a clerical error that left certain members of the union off of the designation list. The first-ever strike by federal prison guards lasted four days before the government ordered them back to their jobs, imposing a wage settlement of 6.5 percent over three years. See "Striking Prison Guards Ordered Back to Work: Union Leaders Condemn Government's Quick Move on Legislation," *Moncton Times and Transcript*, 31 March 1997.

11 Although the auditor general would clear Martin of any wrongdoing, the report outlined the misspending of $100 million in federal funds, some of which had been diverted through government agencies and advertising companies to Liberal supporters in Quebec.

12 See the articles by K. McCuaig, W. Roberts, and D. Langille on Ontario's NDP Government in Gregory Albo, David Langille, and Leo Panitch, eds., *A Different Kind of State? Popular Power and Democratic Administration* (Toronto: Oxford University Press, 1993), 220. For a good overall analysis of the Rae government, see Thomas Walkom, *Rae Days: The Rise and Fall of the NDP* (Toronto: Key Porter, 1994).

13 George Martell, *A New Education Politics: Bob Rae's Legacy and the Response of the Ontario Secondary School Teachers' Federation* (Toronto: Lorimer, 1995); Walkom, *Rae Days*.

14 The act repealed the ban on scabs, put limits on when unions could call strike votes (no sooner than 30 days prior to the termination of a contract), and set up a system of union certification that required a vote in all cases and made decertification votes easier to call. It also removed successor rights for public-sector unions.

15 Sid Noel, "Ontario's Tory Revolution," *Revolution at Queen's Park*, ed. Sid Noel (Toronto: Lorimer, 1997), 1–2.

16 Earlier that month, the OPP had shot Anthony Dudley George, an Indigenous activist, at a land claims protest at Ipperwash Provincial Park. There is currently a wrongful-death lawsuit pending against Harris, among others, for allegedly directing the police to use force, if necessary, to remove the protesters. Bill Dare, "Harris's First Year: Attacks and Resistance," in *Open for Business, Closed to*

People: Mike Harris's Ontario, ed. Diana Ralph, André Regimbald, and Nerée St-Amand (Halifax: Fernwood, 1997), 21.

17 The Days of Action, as they were known, captured widespread national and international attention. Beginning in London on 11 December 1995, the protests continued in Hamilton on 23 and 24 February 1996 (where more than 100,000 marched), in Waterloo on 19 April, and in Peterborough on 24 June. The strategy reached its apex on 24 and 25 October 1996, when some 200,000 people took over the streets of Toronto, shutting down Bay Street, the Stock Exchange, public transit, and a great many businesses and government offices. James L. Turk, "Days of Action: Challenging the Harris Corporate Agenda," in *Open for Business, Closed to People: Mike Harris's Ontario*, ed. Diana Ralph, André Regimbald, and Nerée St-Amand (Halifax: Fernwood, 1997), 165–76.

18 Sam Gindin, "Toronto: Days of Action, Days of Hope," *Canadian Dimension* (January–February 1997): 11.

19 Most of the private-sector unions, and especially the steelworkers, wanted to link the strategy to electoral politics by providing the NDP with a platform at the demonstration. The networks of social justice organizations that involved as many as 300 groups in Toronto and were supported by the CAW and most of the public-sector unions, wanted to clearly stress the extra-parliamentary aspect of the movement. Some elements on this side even looked forward to building towards a general strike. The debilitating division over both means and ends led to a five-month delay before the next Day of Action in Sudbury on 21–22 March 1997, which the local labour council failed to endorse, although many unions did contribute funds and organizers. Several smaller protests were organized over the following months, but all of the energy and enthusiasm created through the earlier successes in Hamilton and Toronto had by then withered away.

20 Leah Vosko, John Grundy, and Mark Thomas, "Beyond New Governance: Improving Employment Standards Enforcement in Liberal Market Economies," in *Regulating for Equitable and Job-Rich Growth*, ed. Colin Fenwick and Valerie Van Goethem (Geneva and Cheltenham: International Labour Organization and Edward Elgar, 2017), 63–87.

21 1996 Lancaster's Collective Agreement Reporter quoted in Joseph B. Rose, "From Softball to Hardball," in *Public-Sector Labour Relations in an Era of Restraint and Restructuring*, ed. Gene Swimmer (Don Mills: Oxford University Press, 2001), 66–95, 80.

22 R.D. Gidney, *From Hope to Harris: The Reshaping of Ontario's Schools* (Toronto: University of Toronto Press, 1999), 246–8, 256.

23 Duncan McLellan, "Neoliberalism and Ontario Teachers' Unions: A 'Not-So' Common Sense Revolution." *Socialist Studies/Études Socialistes* (2009), https://socialiststudies.com/index.php/sss/article/download/23746/17630.

24 Carlo Fanelli, *Megacity Malaise: Neoliberalism, Labour and Public Services in Toronto* (Halifax: Fernwood Publishing, 2016).

25 When the wage freeze provisions of Bill 52 expired in 1997, the Liberals attempted to transform them into a permanent 3 percent pay cut. After an

independent arbitrator working for the Ministry of Labour ruled against the government on this, Nova Scotia Supreme Court Justice Goodfellow reversed the arbitrator's decision. But when the NSGEU brought the case to the Nova Scotia Court of Appeal, it sustained the union's position, and the government eventually conceded that the wages of public-sector workers ought to be readjusted to pre-rollback levels. This decision lifted the spirits of what had been a very demoralized civil service and disgruntled trade union movement.

26 Sean Gordon and Jeff Heinrich, "Nurses Defy Order to Return," *Montreal Gazette*, 3 July 1999.

27 Yonatan Reshef, "The Logic of Union Quiescence: The Alberta Case," in *Public-Sector Labour Relations in an Era of Restraint and Restructuring*, ed. Gene Swimmer (Oxford: Oxford University Press, 2000), 132.

28 These acts included the Industrial Wages Security Act (1993), the Employment Standards Code Amendment Act (1994), the Labour Board Amalgamation Act (1994), and the Managerial Exclusion Act (1995).

29 Andrea Samoil, "Class Struggle and Solidarity in Neo-Liberal Times: The 1986 Gainers Strike" (Master's thesis, Trent University, 2014). https://digital collections.trentu.ca/islandora/object/etd%3A298/datastream/PDF/view; Alvin Finkel, *Working People in Alberta: A History* (Athabasca: Athabasca University Press, 2012).

30 Designed to prohibit unionized construction companies from spinning off non-union companies as permitted by the Devine government's Bill 24 of 1983, the NDP's Bill 93 (Construction Industry Labour Relations Act) disappointed the labour movement since it did not restore the bargaining structure that existed in the industry prior to 1983, thereby effectively leaving 80 percent of the industry non-union.

31 See Jocelyne Praud and Sarah McQuarrie, "The Saskatchewan CCF-NDP from the Regina Manifesto to the Romanow Years," in *Saskatchewan Politics into the Twenty-First Century*, ed. Howard A. Leeson (Regina: Canadian Plains Research Centre, 2001), 156–7.

32 Alex Netherton, "Paradigm Shift: A Sketch of Manitoba Politics," in *The Provincial State in Canada: Politics in the Provinces and Territories*, ed. Keith Brownsey and Michael Howlett (Peterborough: Broadview, 2001), 227.

33 Paul Phillips and Carolina Stecher, "Fiscal Restraint, Legislated Concessions, and Labour Relations in the Manitoba Civil Service, 1988–1997," in *Public-Sector Labour Relations in an Era of Restraint and Restructuring*, ed. Gene Swimmer (Oxford: Oxford University Press, 2000), 102–3.

34 The government also made changes in 1995 to the regulations governing public-sector employment under the Health Authorities Act, introducing a form of closed shop for five government-approved bargaining units in the health sector. Its commitment to strengthen collective bargaining in the health care industry again became questionable; however, the government legislated an end to a health sector dispute two days before the provincial election in April 1996.

6. Austerity and Authoritarianism

1 Brooke Jeffrey, *Dismantling Canada: Stephen Harper's New Conservative Agenda* (Montreal: McGill-Queen's University Press, 2015).
2 Chris Kutalik, "Power Threats, Legal Struggle Derail Conductors Strike at Canada's Largest Railroad," *Labour Notes*, 24 March 2007; Derrick O'Keefe, "Rail Strike's Strange Route," *The Tyee*, 22 February 2007.
3 Public Service Alliance of Canada, "PSAC Secures Reversal of Harper-Era Legal Changes Affecting Collective Bargaining, Sick Leave," PSAC, 3 December 2018, https://psacunion.ca/psac-secures-reversal-harper-era-legal-changes.
4 Michael Valpy, "GG Made Harper Work for Prorogue," *Globe and Mail*, 2009.
5 Steven Barrett, *Bill C-4's Impact on Federal Public Sector Unions*, Sack Goldblatt Mitchell, https://www.ourcommons.ca/Content/Committee/412/FINA/WebDoc/WD6320541/412_FINA_C-4_Briefs/BarrettSteven-e.pdf.
6 J. Gilmore and S. Larochelle-Côté, *Canada's Employment Downturn: October 2008 to October 2009* (Ottawa: Government of Canada), https://www150.statcan.gc.ca/n1/en/pub/11-010-x/2009011/article/11023-eng.pdf?st=6XXq5bIo. André Bernard, *Trends in Manufacturing Employment* (Ottawa: Government of Canada, 2009), https://www150.statcan.gc.ca/n1/en/pub/75-001-x/2009102/pdf/10788-eng.pdf?st=-b_av5Od.
7 Paul Bliss, "CAW Rejects Wage Cut Talk," *CTV News*, 18 May 2021, https://toronto.ctvnews.ca/caw-s-lewenza-rejects-wage-cut-talk-1.346797; "GM Canada Says Unprecedented Cuts Will Save $2b" *CBC*, 24 March 2009, https://www.cbc.ca/news/business/gm-canada-says-unprecedented-cuts-will-save-2b-1.841822.
8 John McCrank, "RPT – Chrysler Canada Cannot Afford GM – CAW Deal Source," *Reuters*, 16 March 2009, https://www.reuters.com/article/privateEquity/idUSN1650804820090316; Greg Keenan and Karen Howlett, "Find More Cuts, Premier Tells GM and CAW. Ontario's McGuinty Says Union and Car Maker Need to Show Taxpayers' Money Is Justified," *Globe and Mail*, 31 March 2009, https://web.archive.org/web/20090403150353/http://business.theglobeandmail.com/servlet/story/RTGAM.20090331.wgm0331/BNStory/Business/home.
9 "CAW Union Ratifies GM Concessions," *Reuters*, 26 May 2009, https://www.reuters.com/article/retire-us-gm-caw/caw-union-ratifies-gm-concessions-idUSTRE54O4NE20090526.
10 Herman Rosenfeld, "The North American Auto Industry in Crisis," *Monthly Review*, 1 July 2009, https://monthlyreview.org/2009/06/01/the-north-american-auto-industry-in-crisis/.
11 David McGrane, *The New NDP: Moderation, Modernization, and Political Marketing* (Vancouver: UBC Press, 2019).
12 David Camfield, "Fast Facts: Lessons of the Canada Post Lockout," *Canadian Centre for Policy Alternatives*, 30 June 2011, https://policyalternatives.ca/publications/commentary/fast-facts-lessons-canada-post-lockout.

13 CUPW challenged the appointment of the first arbitrator, retired judge Coulter Osbourne, on the grounds that he was unilingual and had no previous labour experience. A federal court agreed with CUPW's objections, removing Judge Osbourne as arbitrator. Next, Minister of Labour Lisa Raitt appointed former Conservative MP candidate Guy Dufort. Fearful that the arbitrator would be more inclined to legislate government policy rather than serve as an arbiter, CUPW challenged the appointment of Dufort in court. Dufort refused to remove himself despite his past partisan activities. Once again, a federal court sided with CUPW, removing Dufort as arbitrator. See Katherine Steinhoff and Geoff Bickerton (CUPW), *The Economic Impact of the Canadian Postal Strike and Lockout: Permanent Economic Damage or Temporary Inconvenience?* Twentieth Conference on Postal and Delivery Economics, 2012, Brighton, UK, https://www.cupw.ca/sites/default/files/CUPW_Rutgers_2012_en.pdf.

14 Scott Deveau, "Air Canada Attendants Opt for Hybrid Pension," *Financial Post*, 22 September 2011, https://financialpost.com/transportation/air-canada-attendants-opt-for-hybrid-pension; Canadian Press, "Air Canada Request to Review Deal Violates Agreement: CAW," *CTV News*, 24 October 2011, https://www.ctvnews.ca/air-canada-request-to-review-deal-violates-agreement-caw-1.715598?cache=jhiggtiw%3FclipId%3D89531.

15 Andrew Stevens and Doug Nesbitt, "An Era of Wildcats and Sick-outs in Canada? The Continued Decline of Industrial Pluralism and the Case of Air Canada," *Labor Studies Journal* 39, no. 2 (2014): 118–39; Andrew Stevens and Andrew Templeton, "Collective Action and Labour Militancy Interrupted: Back-to-Work Legislation and the State of Permanent Exceptionalism at Air Canada," *Economic and Industrial Democracy* 41, no. 1. The International Labour Organization issued a ruling that the law breached ILO conventions on freedom of association, the right to organize, and collective bargaining. The ILO has condemned Canadian federal and provincial labour legislation 73 times since 1982.

16 Scott Deveau, "CP Rail Talks Break Off as Back-to-Work Bill Looms," *Financial Post*, 27 May 2012. See also Thomas Walkom, "Walkom: The CP Rail Strike and Harper's Pre-emptive War on Labour," *Toronto Star*, 29 May 2012, https://www.thestar.com/news/canada/2012/05/29/walkom_the_cp_rail_strike_and_harpers_preemptive_war_on_labour.html.

17 Teresa Healy and Stuart Trew, *The Harper Record 2008–2015* (Ottawa: Canadian Centre for Policy Alternatives, 2015), https://policyalternatives.ca/sites/default/files/uploads/publications/National%20Office/2015/10/The_Harper_Record_2008-2015.pdf.

18 Toby Sanger, "A Dozen Reasons Why Bill-377 Is the Worst," Progressive Economics Forum, 21 June 2013, https://www.progressive-economics.ca/2013/06/a-dozen-reasons-why-bill-c-377-is-the-worst-bill/; Deirdre Wade, James Merrigan, and Lyne Duhaime, "Letter to Bob Runciman Re: Bill C-377 – Income Tax Act Amendments," Canadian Bar Association, 4 December 2014, https://www.cba.org/CMSPages/GetFile.aspx?guid=41dca1fd-6477-478f-991e-3cc32c3e2201.

19 Healy and Trew, *The Harper Record 2008–2015*.

20 Iglika Ivanova and Seth Klein, *Progressive Tax Options for BC: Reform Ideas for Raising New Revenues and Enhancing Fairness* (Vancouver: Canadian Centre for Policy Alternatives, 2013), https://policyalternatives.ca/sites/default/files /uploads/publications/BC%20Office/2013/01/CCPA-BC-Tax-Options_0.pdf.

21 Jim Beatty and Petti Fong, "Campbell Ends Strikes, Forces Deal on Nurses, Health Workers," *Vancouver Sun*, 8 August 2001.

22 Jim Beatty and Craig McInnes, "Hospitals Will Close Admits: Legislature Debates Controversial Labour Bills," *Vancouver Sun*, 28 January 2002.

23 Heather Whiteside, "BC's Recurrent Austerity: Victory Unfettered from Success," in *The Public Sector in an Age of Austerity: Perspectives from Canada's Provinces and Territories*, ed. Bryan M. Evans and Carlo Fanelli (Montreal: McGill-Queens University Press, 2018), 23–47.

24 David Camfield, "Neoliberalism and Working-Class Resistance in British Columbia: The Hospital Employees' Union Struggle, 2002–2004," *Labour/Le Travail* 57 (2006): 9–41.

25 Benjamin Isitt and Melissa Moroz. "The Hospital Employees' Union Strike and the Privatization of Medicare in British Columbia, Canada," *International Labor and Working-Class History* 71 (2007): 91–111.

26 Wendy Poole, "Neo-liberalism in British Columbia Education and Teachers' Union Resistance," https://files.eric.ed.gov/fulltext/EJ987320.pdf; Sara Slinn, "Conflict Without Compromise: The Case of Public Sector Teacher Bargaining in British Columbia," in *Dynamic Negotiations: Teacher Labour Relations in Canadian Elementary and Secondary Education*, ed. Sara Slinn and Arthur Sweetman (Montreal: McGill-Queen's University Press, 2011).

27 BC News, "BC's Striking Paramedics Ordered Back to Work," 7 November 2009, https://www.cbc.ca/news/canada/british-columbia/b-c-s-striking-paramedics -ordered-back-to-work-1.845542.

28 JoAnn Jaffe, Patricia W. Elliott, and Cora Sellers, *Divided: Populism, Polarization and Power in the New Saskatchewan* (Winnipeg: Fernwood Publishing, 2021).

29 Charles Smith, "Active Incrementalism and the Politics of Austerity in the 'New Saskatchewan,'" in *The Public Sector in an Age of Austerity: Perspectives from Canada's Provinces and Territories*, ed. Bryan M. Evans and Carlo Fanelli (Montreal: McGill-Queens University Press, 2018), 71–100.

30 Jaffe et al., *Divided*.

31 Charles Smith and Andrew Stevens, "The Erosion of Workers' Rights in Saskatchewan: The Sask Party, Labour Law Reform and Organized Labour, 2007–2020," in *Divided: Populism, Polarization and Power in the New Saskatchewan*, ed. JoAnn Jaffe, Patricia W. Elliott, and Cora Sellers (Winnipeg: Fernwood Publishing, 2021).

32 Jim Warren, "Joining the Race to the Bottom: An Assessment of Bill 6, Amendments to the Trade Union Act," Canadian Centre for Policy Alternatives, 2008.

33 Steven Tufts and Mark Thomas, "The Christian Labour Association of Canada: Between Company and Populist Unionism," *Labour/Le Travail* 80 (Fall 2017): 55–79.

34 Andrew Stevens, "Saskatchewan: A Beachhead of Labour Law Reform," *The Bullet*, 29 April 2013, https://socialistproject.ca/2013/04/b812/.

35 Duane Bratt, Keith Brownsey, Richard Sutherland, and David Taras, *Orange Chinook: Politics in the New Alberta* (Calgary: University of Calgary Press, 2019); Clark Banack, *God's Province: Evangelical Christianity, Political Thought, and Conservatism in Alberta* (Montreal: McGill-Queen's University Press, 2016).

36 Keith Brownsey, "Alberta and the Great Recession: Neoliberalism, Conservative Government, and Public Finance," in *The Public Sector in an Age of Austerity: Perspectives from Canada's Provinces and Territories*, ed. Bryan M. Evans and Carlo Fanelli (Montreal: McGill-Queens University Press, 2018), 48–70.

37 Meenal Shrivastava and Lorna Stefanick, *Alberta Oil and the Decline of Democracy in Canada* (Edmonton: Athabasca University Press, 2015).

38 Richard Gilbert, "Labour Law Changes Thrill Merit Alberta, but Leave Unions Crying Foul," Daily Commercial News/*ConstructConnect*, 16 June 2008; Ian Harvey, "Merit Contractors Takes Aim at Union Stabilization Funds," Daily Commercial News/*ConstructConnect*, 25 May 2009.

39 Lucas Edmond, "Neoliberalism Is Killing Manitobans," *Canadian Dimension*, December 1, 2020; Fiona MacDonald and Karine Levasseur, "Accountability Insights from the Devolution of Indigenous Child Welfare in Manitoba," *Canadian Public Administration* 57, no. 1 (2014): 97–117.

40 Errol Black and Jim Silver, "Manitoba's NDP: Time to Return to Its Social Democratic Roots," *Canadian Centre for Policy Alternatives*, 15 August 2012, https://policyalternatives.ca/publications/commentary/manitobas-ndp-time-return-its-social-democratic-roots.

41 David Camfield, "Manitoba: Fiscal Policy and the Public Sector under 'Today's NDP,'" in *The Public Sector in an Age of Austerity: Perspectives from Canada's Provinces and Territories*, ed. Bryan M. Evans and Carlo Fanelli (Montreal: McGill-Queen's University Press, 2018), 101–27.

42 "Manitoba Eliminates General Corporation Capital Tax Effective Jan 1," *Manitoba.ca*, 31 December 2010, https://news.gov.mb.ca/news/?item=10520.

43 Angela Day, "Work and Change in Atlantic Canada," in *Canada Since 1960: A People's History*, ed. Cy Gonick (Toronto: Lorimer, 2016), 412–17.

44 Thom Workman, *Social Torment: Globalization in Atlantic Canada*. Halifax: Fernwood Publishing, 2003, 29.

45 Workman, *Social Torment*, 52.

46 Workman, *Social Torment*, 55.

47 Workman, *Social Torment*, 107.

48 Workman, *Social Torment*, 60–4.

49 Workman, *Social Torment*, 65.

50 Jamie Gillies, "Between 'the Rock' and a Hard Place: Fiscal Policy in New Brunswick since 2007," in *The Public Sector in an Age of Austerity: Perspectives from Canada's Provinces and Territories*, ed. Bryan Evans and Carlo Fanelli (Montreal and Kingston: McGill-Queen's University Press, 2018), 189.

51 Geoffrey McCormack and Thom Workman, *The Servant State* (Halifax: Fernwood Publishing, 2015), 35.

52 Broadcast News, Budget Highlites, 11 April 2000, https://advance-lexis-com .libaccess.lib.mcmaster.ca/api/document?collection=news&id=urn:contentItem: 46YJ-1KT0-01G6-B1VS-00000-00&context=1516831.

53 Canadian Centre for Policy Alternatives, *Alternative Budget Moves Nova Scotia Forward, Not Back*, 22 March 2012, https://www.policyalternatives.ca /newsroom/news-releases/alternative-budget-moves-nova-scotia-forward -not-back.

54 Don Desserud, "The Political Economy of New Brunswick: Selling New Brunswick Power," in *Transforming Provincial Politics*, ed. Bryan Evans and Charles Smith (Toronto: University of Toronto Press, 2015).

55 Gillies, "Between 'The Rock' and a Hard Place," 195.

56 Sean Cadigan, "Newfoundland and Labrador, 1979–2011: Contradiction and Continuity in a Neoliberal Era," in *Transforming Provincial Politics*, ed. Bryan Evans and Charles Smith (Toronto: University of Toronto Press, 2015), 28–39.

57 Cadigan, "Newfoundland and Labrador, 1979–2011," 39.

58 Newfoundland and Labrador House of Assembly, Bill 38: An Act to Amend the Public Service Collective Bargaining Act No. 2 (2012), https://www.assembly .nl.ca/business/bills/Bill1238.htm.

59 The PC government had previously reinstated card-check certification in 2012 after a review of labour laws. The card check had been in place from 1945 to 1994.

60 Patricia Conrad, "Austerity in the Garden Province of Prince Edward Island," in *The Public Sector in an Age of Austerity: Perspectives from Canada's Provinces and Territories*, ed. Bryan Evans and Carlo Fanelli (Montreal and Kingston: McGill-Queen's University Press, 2018), 252.

61 Conrad, "Austerity in the Garden Province of Prince Edward Island," 51.

62 Legislative Assembly of Prince Edward Island, Bill 35, An Act to Amend the Labour Act, https://www.assembly.pe.ca/legislative-business/house-records/bills# /service/LegislativeAssemblyBillProgress/LegislativeAssemblyBillView;e= LegislativeAssemblyBillView;id=c35ef7a5-1eeb-46bc-899b-4bd77c696abd; chapter=21;bill_number=35;general_assembly=63;session=4.

63 Andrew Steele, "Lessons from Nova Scotia," *Globe and Mail*, 10 June 2009, www.globeandmail.com/blogs/andrew-steele/lessons-from-nova-scotia /article176683/.

64 *Chronicle Herald*, "NDP Platform: Cautious Change," 16 May 2009, http:// thechronicleherald.ca/print_article.html?story=1122234.

65 Deloitte, *Province of Nova Scotia Financial Review: Interim Report*, 2009.

66 Andrew Steele, "The Tax-and-Cut NDP," *Globe and Mail*, 21 April 2010, http:// www.theglobeandmail.com/news/politics/andrew-steele/the-tax-and-cut-ndp /article1526543/?cmpid=rss1&utm_source=feedburner&utm_medium= feed&utm_campaign=Feed%3A+TheGlobeAndMail-Front+(The+Globe +and+Mail+-+Latest+News).

67 David Bush and Doug Nesbitt, "Nova Scotia's NDP Revokes Paramedics' Right-To-Strike," *Rankandfile.ca*, 13 July 2013, https://www.rankandfile.ca/nova-scotias-ndp-revokes-paramedics-right-to-strike/.

68 Ontario Liberal Party, *Achieving Our Potential: The Ontario Liberal Plan for Economic Growth, Book #3* (Toronto: Ontario Liberal Party, 2003), 3.

69 Bryan Evans and Carlo Fanelli, "Ontario in an Age of Austerity: Common Sense Reloaded," in *The Public Sector in an Age of Austerity: Perspectives from Canada's Provinces and Territories*, ed. Bryan Evans and Carlo Fanelli (Montreal: McGill-Queen's University Press, 2018), 144.

70 Bryan Evans and Charles Smith, "The Transformation of Ontario Politics: The Long Ascent of Neoliberalism," in *Transforming Provincial Politics*, ed. Bryan Evans and Charles Smith (Toronto: University of Toronto Press, 2015), 176.

71 Evans and Smith, "The Transformation of Ontario Politics," 176.

72 Carlo Fanelli and Mark P. Thomas, "Austerity, Competitiveness and Neoliberalism Redux: Ontario Responds to the Great Recession," *Socialist Studies* 7, no. 1/2 (2010): 140–71.

73 Bryan Evans, "The Politics of Public Sector Wages: Ontario's Social Dialogue for Austerity," *Socialist Studies*, 23 July 2011, https://socialiststudies.com/index.php/sss/article/view/23615.

74 Carlo Fanelli and Mark P. Thomas, "Austerity, Competitiveness and Neoliberalism Redux: Ontario Responds to the Great Recession," *Socialist Studies*, 23 July 2011.

75 Peter Graefe and X.H. Rioux Ouimet, "From Bailiffs at Our Doors to the Greek Peril: Twenty Years of Fiscal 'Urgency' and Quebec Politics," in *The Public Sector in an Age of Austerity: Perspectives from Canada's Provinces and Territories*, ed. Bryan Evans and Carlo Fanelli (Montreal and Kingston: McGill-Queen's University Press, 2018), 163.

76 Peter Graefe, "Quebec Nationalism and Quebec Politics, from Left to Right," in *Transforming Provincial Politics*, ed. Bryan Evans and Charles Smith (Toronto: University of Toronto Press, 2015), 147.

77 Graefe, "Quebec Nationalism and Quebec Politics," 150–1.

78 Martin Robert and Martin Petitclerc, *Grève et paix: Une histoire des lois spéciales au Québec* (Montreal: Lux Éditeur, 2018), 175–85.

79 Robert and Petitclerc, *Grève et paix*, 186–8.

80 François Bolduc, "La décentralisation des négociations dans le secteur de la santé et des services sociaux québécois: qu'en disent les gestionnaires locaux?," *Relations industrielles* 70, no. 1 (2015): 110–30.

81 Lia Lévesque, "Fusion des syndicats dans la santé: la Cour d'appel donne raison au gouvernement," *La Presse*, July 7, 2011, https://www.lapresse.ca/actualites/sante/201107/07/01-4415883-fusion-des-syndicats-dans-la-sante-la-cour-dappel-donne-raison-au-gouvernement.php.

82 Henri Massé, "La sous-traitance : l'impact de la loi 31 sur le Code du travail du Québec," *Gestion* 29, no. 2 (2004): 88–9.

83 Robert and Petitclerc, *Grève et paix*, 189–200.

84 Robert and Petitclerc, *Grève et paix*, 192.

85 Robert and Petitclerc, *Grève et paix*, 195.

7. From Great Recession to COVID-19 Crisis

1 Bill C-234, *An Act to Amend the Canadian Labour Code (Replacement Workers)*, 1st session, 42nd Parliament, September 2019, https://openparliament.ca/bills /42-1/C-234/.

2 Bryden, Joan, "Senate Passes Legislation to End Canada Post Strike," *CTV News*, 2 November 2018, https://www.cupw.ca/en/two-year-contract-extension -membership-will-decide.

3 Martin Lukacs, "Justin Trudeau, Liberal Let-Down," *Canadian Dimension*, 8 October 2019, https://canadiandimension.com/articles/view/justin-trudeau -liberal-let-down.

4 Aaron Wherry, "For the Liberals, Taxing the Rich Might Be Politically Unpopular – and Risky," *CBC*, 8 October 2020, https://www.cbc.ca/news/politics /liberals-ndp-budget-pandemic-wealth-tax-gst-1.5754461.

5 On the issue of tax reform, Canadians for Tax Fairness have provided invaluable research, demonstrating that the federal government could generate over $90 billion annually through closing tax loopholes, increasing progressivity in personal and corporate taxes, tackling tax havens, and making polluters pay. See Toby Sanger, "Platform for Tax Fairness 2021," *Canadians for Tax Fairness*, 16 August 2021, https://www.taxfairness.ca/en/resources/reports/platform-tax-fairness-2021.

6 Harrison Samphir, "Private Investors Are the Big Winners in P3 Deals, Researcher Says," *CBC*, 27 March 2016, https://www.cbc.ca/news/canada/manitoba /federal-liberals-p3-privatization-1.3870100; Linda McQuaig, "Trudeau's New Bank Delivers for Investors, Not the Public," *Toronto Star*, 10 March 2021, https://www.thestar.com/opinion/contributors/2021/03/10/trudeaus-new -bank-delivers-for-investors-not-the-public.html.

7 John Loxley, *Ideology over Economics: P3s in an Age of Austerity* (Halifax: Fernwood Publishing, 2020).

8 Frédéric Tomesco, "Business Groups, Quebec Urge Feds to Intervene in Port of Montreal Labour Dispute," *Montreal Gazette*, 26 April 2021, https://montrealgazette .com/business/local-business/business-groups-quebec-urge-feds-to-intervene-in -port-of-montreal-labour-dispute.

9 Henry Lazenby, "Govt Inaction on Montreal Port Strike 'Incomprehensible,' says MAC," *Mining Journal*, 17 August 2020, https://www.mining-journal.com /politics/news/1393135/govt-inaction-on-montreal-port-strike-incomprehensible -says-mac; "Ottawa Ignores Calls from Provinces to Get Involved in Port of Montreal Strike," *CBC*, 17 August 2020, https://www.cbc.ca/news/canada /montreal/port-strike-quebec-ontario-call-on-federal-government-1.5689285.

10 Lia Lévesque and Frédéric Tomesco, "Port of Montreal Employers, Dockworkers Union Agree on 7-Month Truce to End Strike," *Montreal Gazette*, 21 August 2020, https://montrealgazette.com/business/local-business /striking-port-of-montreal-checkers-reach-tentative-deal-to-end-strike.

11 Canadian Press, "Longshore Workers Demand Negotiations after Special Law Forces Them Back to Work," *CTV News Montreal*, 1 May 2022, https://montreal

.ctvnews.ca/longshore-workers-demand-negotiations-after-special-law-forces
-them-back-to-work-1.5883937.

12 Canadian Press, "Nearly Half of Canadians Are within $200 of Financial Insol-
vency: Poll," *Globe and Mail*, 21 January 2019, https://www.theglobeandmail
.com/investing/personal-finance/article-nearly-half-of-canadians-are-within
-200-of-financial-insolvency-poll/.

13 Martin Lukacs, *The Trudeau Formula: Seduction and Betrayal in an Age of Discontent* (Montreal: Black Rose Publishing, 2019).

14 "Policy Responses to COVID-19," *International Monetary Fund*, 2 July 2021,
https://www.imf.org/en/Topics/imf-and-covid19/Policy-Responses-to
-COVID-19.

15 Government of Canada, "Canada Emergency Response Benefit Statistics," 15
July 2020, https://open.canada.ca/data/en/dataset/94906755-1cb9-4c2d-aaa6
-bf365f3d4de8.

16 Government of Canada, "Canadian Emergency Responses"; Government of
Canada, "Canada's COVID 19 Economic Response Plan," 16 February
2021, https://www.canada.ca/en/department-finance/economic-response
-plan.html.

17 Jolson Lim. "Federal Wage Subsidy Has to Cost Taxpayers Nearly $100 Bil-
lion, Says Budget Watchdog," *Ipolitics*, 16 December 2020, https://ipolitics
.ca/2020/12/16/federal-wage-subsidy-has-cost-taxpayers-nearly-100-billion
-says-budget-watchdog/.

18 David Milstead, "Most of Canada's Top CEO's Saw Pay Climb as COVID-19 Hit
Economy," *Globe and Mail*, 21 July 2021, https://www.theglobeandmail.com
/business/article-in-a-year-of-covid-19-ceos-pocket-more-pay/?s=09.

19 David Milstead, "Air Canada Granted Special Stock Awards and $10-Million in
Bonuses while Negotiating Government Bailout," *Globe and Mail,* 31 May 2021,
https://www.theglobeandmail.com/business/article-air-canada-granted-special
-stock-awards-and-20-million-in-executive/; Jacob Lorinc, "The Top CEOs Pledge
to Take Pandemic Pay Cuts but a Star Analysis Found Some Ended Up Getting
Millions More," *Toronto Star*, 10 May 2021, https://www.thestar.com/business
/2021/05/08/many-of-canadas-top-ceos-promised-to-take-pandemic-pay-cuts
-but-star-analysis-finds-that-some-actually-earned-millions-more.html.

20 D.T. Cochrane, "Report: Pandemic Profits and the Public Purse," *Canadians for
Tax Fairness*, 14 May 2021, https://www.taxfairness.ca/en/news/c4tf-report
-pandemic-profits-and-public-purse; "Wage Subsidies Were Meant to Preserve
Jobs. In Many Cases, the 110.6 billion Response Padded the Bottom Line" *Globe
and Mail*, 11 May 2021, https://www.theglobeandmail.com/business/article
-canada-emergency-wage-subsidy-data-analysis/.

21 Danny Dorling, *Inequality and the 1%* (New York: Verso, 2015), 53.

22 Heather Whiteside, "BC's Recurrent Austerity: Victory Unfettered from Suc-
cess," in *The Public Sector in an Age of Austerity: Perspectives from Canada's
Provinces and Territories*, ed. Bryan M. Evans and Carlo Fanelli (Montreal:
McGill-Queens University Press, 2018), 23–47.

23 Iglika Ivanova and Marc Lee, "CCPA Submission to BC Budget Consultations 2016," *Canadian Centre for Policy Alternatives*, 15 October 2015, https://policyalternatives.ca/sites/default/files/uploads/publications/BC%20Office/2015/10/CCPA-BC_BudgetSubmission2015_Nov12.pdf.

24 David Beers et al., "117 BC Liberals Falsehood, Boondoggles and Scandals: The Complete List," *TheTyee.ca*, 10 April 2017, https://thetyee.ca/Opinion/2017/04/10/BC-Liberal-Falsehoods-Scandals-Whole-List/.

25 Alex Cosh, "It Shouldn't Have Taken This Long for the BC NDP to Legislate Paid Sick Leave," *Canadian Dimension*, 30 April 2021, https://canadiandimension.com/articles/view/it-shouldnt-have-taken-this-long-for-the-bc-ndp-to-legislate-paid-sick-leave; Leslie Young, "Why Has BC Handled the Pandemic Better Than Other Provinces?" *Global News*, 21 June 2020, https://globalnews.ca/news/7085828/bc-coronavirus-strategy/.

26 Rob Shaw, "John Horgan," *The Canadian Encyclopedia*, 16 November 2020, https://www.thecanadianencyclopedia.ca/en/article/john-horgan.

27 Shaw, "John Horgan."

28 Andrew MacLeod, "So Long to 'Outdated' BC Labour Laws: NDP," *TheTyee.ca*, 1 May 2019, https://thetyee.ca/News/2019/05/01/So-Long-Outdated-BC-Labour-Laws/; Rob Shaw, "BC NDP Government Updates Labour Rules, Scrapping Liberal Measures," *Vancouver Sun,* 30 April 2019, https://vancouversun.com/news/politics/b-c-ndp-government-updates-labour-rules-scrapping-liberal-measures.

29 Robert A. Hackett, "Why It's Hard for BC's NDP to Be Greener," *TheTyee.ca*, 19 October 2020, https://thetyee.ca/Analysis/2021/10/19/Why-Its-Hard-BC-NDP-Be-Greener/; Justin McElroy, "10 Reasons Why the BC's NDP Had Its Most Successful Election Ever," *CBC*, 25 October 2020, https://www.cbc.ca/news/canada/british-columbia/ndp-wins-bc-2020-analysis-horgan-1.5776167; Iglika Ivanova and Kendra Strauss, "Paid Sick Leave Finally on the Agenda: Here's Why It Matters," *policynote.ca*, 27 May 2020, https://www.policynote.ca/paid-sick-leave/.

30 David P. Ball, "Where They Stand: The Parties on Making Life Better for Workers," *TheTyee.ca*, 10 October 2020, https://thetyee.ca/News/2020/10/19/Where-They-Stand-Life-Better-For-Workers/.

31 Lori Theresa Waller, "Saskatchewan Prepares to Gut Labour Laws with Bill 85," *rabble.ca,* 13 April 2013, https://rabble.ca/labour/saskatchewan-prepares-to-gut-labour-laws-bill-85/; David Doorey, "Saskatchewan's Bill 85: When Ideology Trumps Good Sense?" *Law of Work*, 2 May 2013, https://lawofwork.ca/saskatchewans-bill-85-when-ideology-trumps-good-sense/; Sunny Freeman, "Bill 85, Saskatchewan Employment Act, Erodes Union Power, Sets New Tone for Labour Relation in Canada," *Huffington Post*, 13 April 2013, https://www.huffpost.com/archive/ca/entry/bill-85-saskatchewan-employment-act_n_3039850.

32 "Saskatchewan's Infrastructure Funding 'Value for Money' Test Is Biased towards Privatization, New Study Finds," *progresspress.ca*, 4 October 2021, https://pressprogress.ca/saskatchewans-infrastructure-funding-value-for-money-test-is-biased-towards-privatization-new-study-finds/; Simon Enoch, "A Partnership in Name Only: How the Public Sector Subsidizes the P3 Model," *policyalternatives.ca*, 28 June 2020, https://www.policyalternatives.ca/sites

/default/files/uploads/publications/Saskatchewan%20Office/2020/06
/A%20Partnership%20in%20Name%20Only%20%28June%202020%29.pdf.

33 Simon Enoch, "The Futility of Austerity: Lessons for Saskatchewan," *Canadian Centre for Policy Alternatives*, 20 December 2020, https://www.policyalternatives
.ca/sites/default/files/uploads/publications/Saskatchewan%20Office/2016/12
/SASKNOTES_Futility_Austerity_Dec2016.pdf.

34 "Selling Saskatchewan: A Decade of Privatization 2007–2017," *Canadian Centre for Policy Alternatives*, 7 March 2018, https://www.policyalternatives.ca
/publications/reports/selling-saskatchewan.

35 David Macdonald, "Picking Up the Tab: A Complete Accounting of Federal and Provincial COVID-19 Measures in 2020," *Canadian Centre for Policy Alternatives*, January 2021, 4–49, https://www.policyalternatives.ca/sites/default/files
/uploads/publications/National%20Office/2021/01/Picking%20up%20the%20
tab.pdf.

36 Geoff Salomons and Daniel Béland, "The Presence of an Absence: The Politics of Provincial Sales Tax in Alberta," *American Review of Canadian Studies* 50 no. 4 (2000): 418–35.

37 "Bill 2 to Increase Corporate Tax Rates, Introduce Progressive Income Tax," *CBC*, 18 June 2015, https://www.cbc.ca/news/canada/edmonton/bill-2-to-increase
-corporate-tax-rates-introduce-progressive-income-tax-1.3119330.

38 Duane Bratt, Keith Brownsey, Richard Sutherland, and David Taras, *Orange Chinook: Politics in the New Alberta* (Calgary: University of Calgary Press, 2019).

39 David M. Price and Meaghan Albrecht, "Bill 17: Alberta's Family Friendly Employment Reforms and Curious Labour Changes," *stikeman.com*, 26 May 2017, https://
www.stikeman.com/en-ca/kh/canadian-employment-labour-pension-law
/Bill-17-Albertas-Family-Friendly-Employment-Reforms; Michelle Bellefontaine, "Labour Employment Code Overhaul Brings Alberta Law into 'Mainstream,'" *CBC*, 24 May 2017, https://www.cbc.ca/news/canada/edmonton/labour-employment
-code-overhaul-brings-alberta-law-into-mainstream-1.4130059; John Cotter, "NDP Announces Labour Law Changes to Bring 'Alberta's Workplaces into the 21st Century,'" *Global News*, 25 May 2017, https://globalnews.ca/news/3476075
/ndp-announces-labour-law-changes-to-bring-albertas-workplaces-into-the
-21st-century/.

40 Bob Barnetson, "Alberta Workers under the NDP, Part Two," *rankandfile*.ca, 10 January 2017, https://www.rankandfile.ca/alberta-workers-under-the-ndp-part-
two/; Anna MacMillan, "Failure to Address Old Equipment a 'Black Eye' in Alberta Farm Rules, Professor Says," *CBC*, 28 June 2018, https://www.cbc.ca/news
/canada/edmonton/bill-6-alberta-farm-rules-old-equipment-1.4725738.

41 Trevor Harrison, "Bill 1 and Alberta's Ongoing Descent into Authoritarianism," *Canadian Dimension,* 12 March 2020, https://canadiandimension.com/articles
/view/bill-1-and-albertas-ongoing-descent-into-authoritarianism.

42 Chris Alders, "Down the Authoritarian Rabbit Hole with Alberta's United Conservative Party," *Canadian Dimension*, 6 October 2020, https://
canadiandimension.com/articles/view/down-the-authoritarian-rabbit-hole
-with-albertas-united-conservative-party; see also Mitchell Anderson,

"Is Jason Kenney Ready to Bet Albertan Pensions on the Failing Fossils Firms?" *TheTyee.ca*, 15 July 2020, https://thetyee.ca/Analysis/2020/07/15 /Jason-Kenney-Bet-Failing-Fossil-Fuel/.

43 Jason Foster and Bob Barnetson, "Bill 47 Pt. 2 – Less Compensation for the Work-Related Injuries," Parkland Institute, 12 November 2020, https://www .parklandinstitute.ca/bill_47_reduces_compensation_work_injuries; Bob Barnetson, "Bill 2 Grinds Wages, Complicates Payroll, and Impedes Union Drives," Parkland Institute, 28 May 2019, https://www.parklandinstitute.ca/bill_2 _grinds_wages_complicates_payroll_and_impedes_union_drives.

44 *CBC News*, "Union's Bid to Appeal Alberta's Wage Arbitration Bill Rejected by Supreme Court," 12 March 2020, https://www.cbc.ca/news/canada/edmonton /aupe-bill-9-wage-arbitration-talks-alberta-appeal-supreme-court-1.5495058; Emma Graney, "MacKinnon Report: All 26 Alberta Government Panel Recommendations," *Edmonton Journal*, 3 September 2019, https://edmontonjournal.com/news /politics/mackinnon-report-all-26-alberta-government-panel-recommendations.

45 David Doorey, "Alberta Tests Right-Wing Republican Inspired Labour Laws," *Canadian Law of Work Forum*, 8 July 2020, https://lawofwork.ca/bill32 -alberta/; Jason Foster, "Tipping the Balance: Bill 32, the Charter and the Americanization of Alberta's Labour Relations System," Parkland Institute, 2020, https://www.parklandinstitute.ca/bill_32; Jason Foster, "Alberta's Bill 32 Is a Seismic Break in Labour and Employment Law," *Canadian Law of Work Forum*, July 10, 2020, https://lawofwork.ca/albertas-bill-32-is-a-seismic-break-in -labour-and-employment-law/; Case Littlewood, "A Return to Balance or Empowering the Powerful? Alberta's Bill 32," Centre for Constitutional Studies, 13 August 2020, https://www.constitutionalstudies.ca/2020/08/a-return-to -balance-or-empowering-the-powerful-albertas-bill-32/.

46 "Politics Blog: Jason Kenney's Bill 32 Is an Assault on Workers' Rights," *ufcw.ca*, 30 September 2020, http://ufcw.ca/index.php?option=com_content&view= article&id=32731:politics-blog-jason-kenney-s-bill-32-is-an-assault-on-workers -rights&catid=10189&Itemid=6&lang=en; Jeremy Appel, "In Canada Jason Kenney Is Launching an Assault on Alberta's Working Class," *jacobinmag.com*, 17 October 2020, https://jacobinmag.com/2020/10/canada-jason-kenney -alberta-working-class; Jeremy Appel, "Jason Kenney Is Trying to Kill Alberta's Labour Movement," *readpassage.com*, 23 July 2020, https://readpassage.com /jason-kenney-is-trying-to-kill-albertas-labour-movement/; Gil McGowan, "Celebrate Labour Day by Demanding Jason Kenney Resign," *TheTyee.ca*, 3 September 2021, https://thetyee.ca/Opinion/2021/09/03/Celebrate -Labour-Day-Demand-Jason-Kenney-Resign/.

47 "Alberta Ends Master Agreement with Doctors, New Rules to Be in Place April 1," *CBC*, 20 February 2020, https://www.cbc.ca/news/canada/calgary /alberta-government-doctors-pay-ama-agreement-1.5470352; "Opinion: UCP Government's War against Doctors Is All about Control," *Calgary Herald*, 25 August 2020, https://calgaryherald.com/opinion/columnists/opinion-ucp -governments-war-against-doctors-is-all-about-control.

48 Ashley Joannu and Anna Junker, "AHS Workers' Wildcat Strike Declared Illegal by Alberta Labour Relations Board," *Edmonton Journal*, 27 October 2020, https://edmontonjournal.com/news/local-news/alberta-health-care-workers-walk-off-the-job-aupe; Allison Bench, "Hundreds of Workers Disciplined by AHS after 2020 Wildcat Strike: Union," *Global News*, 23 February 2021, https://globalnews.ca/news/7657420/aupe-discipline-ahs-strike/.

49 Camfield, "Manitoba."

50 Mary Agnes Welch, "MGEU Workers Nix Austerity Deal," *Winnipeg Free Press*, 23 January 2011, https://www.winnipegfreepress.com/local/mgeu-workers-nix-austerity-deal-114443124.html; "MGEU Civil Service Members Vote Revised Final Offer," *npuge.ca*, 12 March 2011, https://nupge.ca/content/mgeu-civil-service-members-vote-revised-final-offer.

51 Baragar Fletcher, "Report on the Manitoba Economy 2011," *Canadian Centre for Policy Alternatives*, September 2011, https://www.policyalternatives.ca/sites/default/files/uploads/publications/Manitoba%20Office/2011/09/2011Report MbEconBaragar-smaller%20file%20size.pdf.

52 Simon Enoch, "Balanced Budget Painted Saskatchewan into a Corner," *Canadian Centre for Policy Alternatives*, 12 March 2021, https://www.policyalternatives.ca/publications/commentary/fast-facts-rickety-altar-balanced-budgets.

53 Amber McGuckin, "University of Manitoba Strike Ends after Faculty Association Approves New Deal," *Global News*, 22 November 2016, https://globalnews.ca/news/3081135/university-of-manitoba-strike-ends-after-faculty-association-approves-new-deal/; Nic Martin, "Labour Board Hearing UMFA Allegations of Unfair Labour Practice," *Winnipeg Free Press*, 27 May 2017, https://www.winnipegfreepress.com/local/labour-board-hearing-umfa-allegations-of-unfair-labour-practice-421083253.html.

54 Ian Froese, "Court Strikes Down Manitoba's 'Draconian' Wage Freeze Bill," *CBC News*, 11 June 2020, https://www.cbc.ca/news/canada/manitoba/manitoba-government-public-sector-wage-freeze-1.5608713.

55 "Brian Pallister's Government Demanded University of Manitoba Freeze Wages and Make Cuts Letter Shows," *pressprogress.ca*, 6 November 2020, https://pressprogress.ca/brian-pallisters-government-demanded-university-of-manitoba-freeze-wages-and-make-cuts-letter-shows/.

56 James Wilt, "The Devastation of Manitoba: An Autopsy of Pallister's Austerity Regime," *Canadian Dimension*, 28 August 2019, https://canadiandimension.com/articles/view/the-devastation-of-manitoba.

57 Molly McCracken, "Education Property Tax Cuts Worsen Income Inequality in Manitoba," *Canadian Centre for Policy Alternatives*, 18 May 2021, https://www.policyalternatives.ca/publications/reports/education-property-tax-cuts-worsen-income-inequality-manitoba.

58 Micheal Barkman and Molly McCracken, "Failing Grade: Manitoba Poverty Reduction Strategy and Budget 2019," *Canadian Centre for Policy Alternatives*, 16 April 2019, https://www.policyalternatives.ca/publications/reports/failing-grade-manitoba-poverty-reduction-strategy-and-budget-2019; Ian Hudson

and Benita Cohen, "Manitoba Inequality Update: Low Income Families Left Be-hind" *Canadian Centre for Policy Alternatives,* 6 June 2018, https://www .policyalternatives.ca/publications/reports/manitoba-inequality-update; Edmund Lucas, "Disaster Capitalism at Work in Manitoba," *Canadian Dimen-sion*, 30 April 2020, https://canadiandimension.com/articles/view/disaster -capitalism-at-work-in-manitoba.

59 "PST Reduction and Flat Carbon Tax Manitoba Going in the Wrong Direc-tion," *Canadian Centre for Policy Alternatives*, 30 March 2020, https://policyfix .ca/2020/03/05/pst-reduction-and-flat-carbon-tax-manitoba-going-in-the -wrong-direction/; Lynne Fernandez, "Change Starts Here: Manitoba Alternative Provincial Budget 2020," *Canadian Centre for Policy Alternatives* 3 March 2020, https://www.policyalternatives.ca/mbapb2020?mc_cid=c72fd822b9&mc _eid=[4b3c3d2ebe; Jesse Hajer, "Unspun 2019: Taxes and Deficit in Manitoba," *Canadian Centre for Policy Alternatives,* 9 September 2019, https://www .policyalternatives.ca/publications/commentary/unspun-2019-taxes-and-deficit -manitoba.

60 Lynne Fernandez and Shauna Mackinnon, "The Pallister Government Shifts into Gear," *Canadian Centre for Policy Alternatives,* 1 July 2019, https://www .policyalternatives.ca/publications/monitor/pallister-government-shifts -high-gear.

61 Edmond Lucas, "Brian Pallister's Long War on Workers Must Mark a New Era for Labour in Manitoba," *Canadian Dimension*, 13 January 2021, https:// canadiandimension.com/articles/view/brian-pallisters-long-war-on-workers -must-mark-a-new-era-for-labour-in-manitoba.

62 Macdonald, *Picking Up the Tab*; Lucas, "Neoliberalism Is Killing Manitobans."

63 Government of Nova Scotia, *Budget 2015–2016 Highlights* (Halifax: Department of Finance, 2016), http://www.novascotia.ca/finance/site-finance/media/finance /budget2015/Budget_Highlights.pdf.

64 TD Economics, "2020 Nova Scotia Budget," 25 February 2020, https:// economics.td.com/domains/economics.td.com/documents/reports/budgets /ns/NS_Budget_2020.pdf; TD Economics, "2019 Nova Scotia Budget," 26 March 2019, https://economics.td.com/domains/economics.td.com/documents/reports /budgets/ns/NS2019.pdf; TD Economics, "2018 Nova Scotia Budget," 20 March 2018, https://economics.td.com/domains/economics.td.com/documents/reports /budgets/ns/NS2018.pdf; RBC Economics Research, "Nova Scotia Budget 2017," 27 September 2017, http://www.rbc.com/economics/economic-reports/pdf /canadian-fiscal/nsbud2017_sep.pdf.

65 Peter Clancy, "Provincial Fiscal Strategies and Public-Sector Management in Nova Scotia," in *The Public Sector in an Age of Austerity: Perspectives from Can-ada's Provinces and Territories*, ed. Bryan Evans and Carlo Fanelli (Kingston: McGill-Queen's University Press, 2018), 233.

66 Clancy, "Provincial Fiscal Strategies," 233.

67 J. Jessome, Bill 30 – Essential Home-Support Services Act Update. Nova Scotia General Employees Union, 11 March 2014, https://nsgeu.ca/home_page /bill-30-essential-home-support-services-act-update/6242/.

68 Cecilia Benoit and Helga Hallgrimsdottir, eds., *Valuing Care Work: Comparative Perspectives* (Toronto: University of Toronto Press, 2011); Pat Armstrong, Hugh Armstrong, and Krista Scott-Dixon, *Critical to Care: The Invisible Women in Health Services* (Toronto: University of Toronto Press, 2008).

69 David Bush, "A Major Blow to the Right to Strike in Nova Scotia," *Rankandfile.ca*, 15 April 2014, https://www.rankandfile.ca/a-major-blow-to-the-right-to-strike-in -nova-scotia-2/.

70 Holly Fraughton, "The Liberals: Legislating Away Your Rights," *The Stand*, Fall 2014, 4–7, https://nsgeu.ca/wp-content/uploads/2021/06/webfall2014.pdf; Rachel Cardozo, "Nova Scotia Government Backs Away from Showdown with Health Care Unions, Avoids Charter Collision," CanLII Connects, 24 March 2015, https://canliiconnects.org/fr/r%C3%A9sum%C3%A9/36636.

71 Nova Scotia Legislative Assembly, *Bill 100 – Universities Accountability and Sustainability Act*, https://nslegislature.ca/legislative-business/bills-statutes/bills /assembly-62-session-2/bill-100.

72 Catrina Brown, "The Constraints of Neo-Liberal New Managerialism in Social Work Education." *Canadian Social Work Review/Revue canadienne de service social* 33, no.1 (2016): 115–23.

73 Jean Laroche, "Nova Scotia Universities Face Increased Financial Scrutiny with New Bill," *CBC News*, 22 April 2015, https://www.cbc.ca/news/canada/nova -scotia/nova-scotia-universities-face-increased-financial-scrutiny-with-new -bill-1.3044608.

74 Nova Scotia Legislative Assembly, *Bill 75 – Teachers' Professional Agreement and Classroom Improvements (2017) Act*, https://nslegislature.ca/legislative-business /bills-statutes/bills/assembly-62-session-3/bill-75.

75 Nova Scotia Teachers Union, "Memorandum: Update on Bill 75 Charter Challenge," 7 June 2019, https://nstu.blob.core.windows.net/nstuwebsite/data/June 7, 2019 Memo re. Bill 75 (Motions).pdf?fbclid=IwAR32UCxEW4EmDgx6 -hc9pGyx84acyPiSOHC0Hlj47jzvvX8uQSm8djNYV3g.

76 Nova Scotia Government and General Employees Union, "Bill 148 Update," NSGEU Homepage, 15 September 2021, https://nsgeu.ca/home_page/bill-148 -update/24765/; Nova Scotia Government and General Employees Union, "Update on Bill 148 Legal Challenge," NSGEU Homepage, 7 May 2021, https:// nsgeu.ca/home_page/update-on-bill-148-legal-challenge/23780/.

77 Nova Scotia Government and General Employees Union, "Update on Bill 148 Legal Challenges," NSGEU Homepage, 14 October 2020, https://nsgeu.ca/home _page/update-on-bill-148-legal-challenges/22183/.

78 "Update on Bill 148 Legal Challenges," NSGEU, 14 October 2020.

79 Robert Sweeny, "Newfoundland's Boom: A Study in the Political Culture of Neoliberalism," in *The Public Sector in an Age of Austerity: Perspectives from Canada's Provinces and Territories*, ed. Bryan Evans and Carlo Fanelli (Kingston: McGill-Queen's University Press, 2018), 281–4.

80 Canadian Union of Public Employees, "Dwight Ball's Crossroads – A Game of Budgets and Cuts for Newfoundland and Labrador," CUPE Homepage, 2017, https://cupe .ca/dwight-balls-crossroads-game-budgets-and-cuts-newfoundland-and-labrador.

81 Gillies, "Between 'The Rock' and a Hard Place," 211–12.

82 Don Drummond, *Public Services for Ontarians: A Path to Sustainability and Excellence*, Commission on the Reform of Ontario's Public Services (Toronto: Queen's Printer, 2012), https://www.opsba.org/wp-content/uploads/2021/02/drummondReportFeb1512.pdf, 10.

83 Gregory Albo and Carlo Fanelli, "Austerity against Democracy: An Authoritarian Phase of Neoliberalism?," *Teoria politica* 4 (2014): 65–88; Jason Hackworth, "The Neoliberal City: Governance, Ideology, and Development in American Urbanism," *Economic Geography* 84, no. 1 (2008): 121–2.

84 Laurie Monsebraaten, "Ontario Dead Last in Terms of Inequality, Poverty and Funding for Public Services," *Toronto Star*, 29 August 2012, https://www.thestar.com/news/canada/2012/08/29/ontario_dead_last_in_terms_of_inequality_poverty_and_funding_for_public_services.html.

85 Bryan M. Evans and Carlo Fanelli, "Introduction," in *The Public Sector in an Age of Austerity: Perspectives from Canada's Provinces and Territories*, ed. Bryan M. Evans and Carlo Fanelli (Montreal: McGill-Queen's University Press, 2018), 1–23.

86 Caitlin Hewitt-White, "The OSSTF Anti-Bill 115 Campaign: An Assessment from a Social Movement Unionism Perspective," *Alternate Routes: A Journal of Critical Social Research* 26, no. 1, https://www.alternateroutes.ca/index.php/ar/article/view/22317; Paul Bocking, *Public Education, Neoliberalism, and Teachers: New York, Mexico City, Toronto* (Toronto: University of Toronto Press, 2020).

87 "5 scandals Likely to Haunt the Liberals during Ontario Election," *Global News*, 2 May 2014, https://globalnews.ca/news/1307743/5-scandals-likely-to-haunt-the-liberals-during-ontario-election/.

88 Matti Siemiatycki and Naeem Farooqi, "Value for Money and Risk in Public–Private Partnerships: Evaluating the Evidence," *Journal of the American Planning Association* 78, no. 3 (2012): 286–99.

89 Bonnie Lysyk, Annual Report 2015, Office of the Auditor General of Ontario, https://www.auditor.on.ca/en/content/annualreports/arreports/en15/2015AR_en_final.pdf.

90 Canadian Press, "Bill Passed to End Five-Week Long Ontario College Strike," *Global News*, 19 November 2017, https://globalnews.ca/news/3869041/back-to-work-legislation-ontario-college-strike/.

91 Lisa Stam, "Everything You Ever Wanted to Know about Bill 148 but Were Too Afraid to Ask," *Employment & Human Rights Law in Canada*, 30 May 2018, https://www.canadaemploymenthumanrightslaw.com/2018/05/everything-ever-wanted-know-bill-148-afraid-ask/.

92 Aaron Saltzman, "Tim Hortons Lashes Out at 'Rogue' Franchisees as Employees Lose Even More Perks," *CBC News*, 5 January 2018, https://www.cbc.ca/news/business/tims-timhortons-minimumwage-wynne-liberals-ontario-1.4474836.

93 Bryan Evans, Carlo Fanelli, and Thomas McDowell, *Rising Up: The Fight for Living Wages* (Vancouver: UBC Press, 2021).

94 Devin Clancy, "Strike and Reclamation: Building Power in the Fight Against the Corporate University," *Upping the Anti* 21 (2019), https://uppingtheanti.org /journal/uta/number-twentyone.

95 Jordan Kirkness and Susan MacMillan, "Ontario Government Introduces Bill 47 to Reverse Most of Bill 148," *Canadian Labour and Employment Law*, 24 October 2018, https://www.labourandemploymentlaw.com/2018/10/ontario -government-introduces-bill-47-to-reverse-most-of-bill-148/.

96 Daniel Sheppard, "Bill 47-Making Ontario Open for Business or Just Sticking It to Workers," Goldblatt Partners LLP, https://goldblattpartners.com/experience /publications/post/bill-47-making-ontario-open-for-business-or-just-sticking -it-to-workers/.

97 Canadian Federation of Independent Businesses, "Small Business Applauds Ontario Government for Announcing Reversal of Punitive Labour Bill," CFIB, 23 October 2018, https://www.cfib-fcei.ca/en/media/small-business-applauds -ontario-government-announcing-reversal-punitive-labour-bill.

98 Ontario Federation of Labour, "Doug Ford Fails Ontario Workers with the Passage of Bill 47," OFL, 2018, https://ofl.ca/doug-ford-fails-ontario-workers-with -the-passage-of-bill-47-say-leaders-in-the-fight-for-15-and-fairness-movement -ontario-federation-of-labour-and-workers-action-centre/.

99 Paola Loriggio, "Province Introduces Bill to Prevent Strike at Ontario Power Generation," *CTV News*, 17 December 2018, https://toronto.ctvnews.ca /province-introduces-bill-to-prevent-strike-at-ontario-power-generation -1.4220710.

100 Lisa Xing, "1% Increase under Public-Sector Wage Cap a 'Slap in the Face,' Ontario Registered Nurses Say," *CBC News*, 11 June 2020, https://www.cbc.ca/news /canada/toronto/ontario-nurses-pay-increase-ona-covid-doug-ford-1.5607068.

101 Aidan Macnab, "Public-Sector Unions File Evidence in Charter Challenge of Law Capping Compensation Increases," *Canadian Lawyer Magazine*, 14 February 2021, https://www.lawtimesnews.com/practice-areas/labour-and -employment/public-sector-unions-file-evidence-in-charter-challenge-of -law-capping-compensation-increases/337805.

102 Ontario Federation of Labour, "Coalition of Ontario Unions to Launch Charter Challenge," OFL, 2019, https://ofl.ca/coalition-of-ontario-unions-to-launch -charter-challenge-vowing-to-defend-the-rights-of-all-ontarians-with -aggressive-campaign-to-repeal-bill-124/.

103 Steven Barrett, "Public-Sector Unions File Evidence in Bill 124 Charter Challenge," Goldblatt Partners, 2021, https://goldblattpartners.com/news-events /news/post/public-sector-unions-file-evidence-in-bill-124-charter -challenge/.

104 Shawn Katz, *Generation Rising: The Time of the Quebec Student Spring* (Fernwood Publishing, 2015).

105 Peter Graefe, "Quebec Nationalism and Quebec Politics, from Left to Right," in *Transforming Provincial Politics*, ed. Bryan Evans and Charles Smith (Toronto: University of Toronto Press, 2015), 157–8.

106   Union des producteurs agricoles (UPA), "Nouvelle Loi no. 8 – En relations de travail: les particularités du secteur agricole prises en compte," *L'UPA vous informe* 4, no. 1 (November 2014): 1.

107   Sid Ahmed Soussi, "Le travail migrant temporaire et les effets sociaux pervers de son encadrement institutionnel," *Lien social et Politiques* 83 (2019): 311, https://doi.org/10.7202/1066095ar.; Aziz Choudry and Mondli Hlatshwayo, *Just Work? Migrant Workers' Struggles Today* (London: Pluto Press, 2016).

108   *Rio Tinto: A Shameful History of Human and Labour Rights Abuses and Environmental Degradation around the Globe*, London Mining Network, 20 April 2010, https://londonminingnetwork.org/2010/04/rio-tinto-a-shameful-history -of-human-and-labour-rights-abuses-and-environmental-degradation -around-the-globe/.

109   Sandrine Rastello and Matt Townsend, "Alcoa's Quebec Workers Defy Union and Accept Offer, 'Exhausted' from 18-Month Dispute," *Financial Post*, 3 July 2019, https://financialpost.com/commodities/mining/alcoas-quebec-workers -defy-union-and-accept-offer-exhausted-from-18-month-dispute; Laurent Lafrance, "Quebec Premier Backs ABI in Extorting Massive Concessions from Locked-Out Workers.," *World Socialist*, 12 April 2019, https://www.wsws.org /en/articles/2019/04/12/abiq-a12.html; Laurent Lafrance, "Quebec ABI Workers' Struggle Betrayed by United Steelworkers Union," *World Socialist*, 11 July 2019, https://www.wsws.org/en/articles/2019/07/11/queb-j11.html.

110   International Labour Organization, Definitive Report – Report No. 392, October 2020, https://www.ilo.org/dyn/normlex/en/f?p=NORMLEXPUB:50002: 0::NO::P50002_COMPLAINT_TEXT_ID:4059244.

111   Heather Whiteside, Stephen McBride, and Bryan Evans, *Varieties of Austerity* (Bristol: Bristol University Press, 2021), 168.

112   Jamie Peck, "The Right to Work, and the Right at Work," *Economic Geography* 92, no. 1: 4–30.

8. The Right to Strike: Freedom of Association and the Charter

1   International Labour Organization, "Ratifications for Canada," 2022, https:// www.ilo.org/dyn/normlex/en/f?p=NORMLEXPUB:11200:0::NO::P11200 _COUNTRY_ID:102582; International Labour Organization, "Up-to-Date Conventions and Protocols Not Ratified by Canada," 2022, https://www.ilo.org /dyn/normlex/en/f?p=1000:11210:0::NO:11210:P11210_COUNTRY_ID:102582.

2   Re Service Employees International Union, Local 204 and Broadway Manor Nursing Home (1983), 4 D.L.R. (4th) 231 (ON Div. Ct.), affirmed on other grounds (1984), 13 D.L.R. (4th) 220 (ON C.A.).

3   "Just as the individual is incapable of resisting political domination without the support of persons with similar values, so too is he or she, in isolation incapable of resisting domination, over the long term, in many other aspects of life.... Freedom of association is most essential in those circumstances where the individual is liable to be prejudiced by the actions of some larger and more powerful entity, like

the government or an employer ... it has enabled those who would otherwise be vulnerable and ineffective to meet on more equal terms the power and strength of those with whom their interests interact and, perhaps, conflict.... There will ... be occasions when no analogy involving individuals can be found for associational activity, or when a comparison between groups and individuals fails to capture the essence of a possible violation of associational rights. This is precisely the situation in this case. There is no individual equivalent to the right to strike. The refusal to work by one individual does not parallel a collective refusal to work.... The legislative purpose which will render legislation invalid is the attempt to preclude associational conduct because of its concerted or associational nature."

4 A strong dissenting judgment was written by Justice Corry and concurred with by Bertha Wilson and Charles Gonthier, all of whom wrote: "Whenever people labour to earn their daily bread, the right to associate will be of tremendous significance. Wages and working conditions will always be of vital importance to an employee. It follows that for an employee the right to choose the group or association that will negotiate on his or her behalf with regard to those wages and working conditions is of fundamental importance. The association will play a significant role in almost every aspect of the employee's life at work, acting as advisor, as spokesperson in negotiations, and as a shield against wrongful acts of the employer. If collective bargaining is to function properly, employees must have confidence in their representative. That confidence will be lost if the individual employee is unable to choose the association.... A union can only exist if it is allowed to collectively bargain. That is the raison d'etre of a union. In order to carry out its function of bargaining it must be recognized pursuant to the provisions of the relevant labour legislation. However, such an association does not 'exist' under the Northwest Territories Act until it is incorporated as an 'employees' association.' The act thus effectively prevents 'unincorporated' associations from coming into existence and, by frustrating the employees' choice, thereby infringes the individual employees' right to association. To say that the union exists as long as the individuals can meet and discuss their grievances is, with respect, to cast a spell of unreality over the situation. The voiced grievances would have no more effect than casual complaints about the weather.... Arbitrary or totally discretionary restrictions placed upon the employees' right to choose their association must prima facie violate the freedom of association."

5 David Doorey, "Some Implications of a Canadian 'Right to Work' Law." *Law of Work*, 16 October 2018, https://lawofwork.ca/on-the-implications-of-a -canadian-right-to-work-law/.

6 Craig D. Bavis, "The Freedom of Association: The Emerging Right to Strike Consensus in International and Domestic Labour Law," LLM diss., York University, 2015, 1–19. https://islssl.org/wp-content/uploads/2015/10/Canada -CraigBavis.pdf.

7 Alison Braley, "'I Will Not Give You a Penny More Than You Deserve': Ontario v. Fraser and the Uncertain Right to Collectively Bargain in Canada," *McGill Law Journal* 57, no. 2 (2011): 353.

8 *Mounted Police Association of Ontario v. Canada (Attorney General)*, 2015, SCC 1, https://scc-csc.lexum.com/scc-csc/scc-csc/en/item/14577/index.do.

9 Brad Walchuk, "A Decade Later: The Legacy of the Supreme Court of Canada's Health Services Decision on Workers' Rights," *Global Labour Journal* 10, no. 1: (2019): 52–64.

10 In writing for the majority, Justice Abella noted: "It seems to me to be the time to give this conclusion constitutional benediction." *Saskatchewan Federation of Labour v. Saskatchewan*, 2015 SCC 4, https://scc-csc.lexum.com/scc-csc/scc-csc/en/item/14610/index.do.

11 Walchuk, "A Decade Later," 59; Charles Smith and Andrew Stevens, "The Architecture of Modern Anti-Unionism in Canada: Class Struggle and the Erosion of Workers' Collective Freedoms," *Capital and Class* 43, no. 4 (2018): 459–81.

12 Michael S. Dunn, "Many Questions and a Few Answers: Freedom of Association after Saskatchewan Federation of Labour, Mounted Police Association of Ontario and Meredith," *The Supreme Court Law Review* 17, no. 15 (2015): 387–411.

13 Claire Mumme, "The State Giveth and Taketh Away: Public Sector Labour Law, the Legitimacy of Legislative Override of Power and Constitutional Freedom of Association in Canada," *International Journal of Comparative Labour Law and Industrial Relation* 36 no. 34 (2020): 495–522, https://scholar.uwindsor.ca/cgi/viewcontent.cgi?article=1114&context=lawpub.

14 Leila Geggie Hurst, "A New Hope or a Charter Menace? The New Labour Trilogy's Implications for Labour Law in Canada," *Labour Rights*, 29 March 2017, https://labourrights.ca/sites/default/files/documents/brave_new_world_paper_final1.pdf.

15 Canadian Foundation for Labour Rights, *New Labour Trilogy*, NUPGE, 2015, https://nupge.ca/sites/default/files/documents/CFLR%20new%20labour%20trilogy%20forum.pdf.

16 Paul J.J. Cavalluzzo, "Postal Workers Win Court Challenge to Back-to-Work Law: Superior Court Declares Harper's Law Unconstitutional," *Cavalluzzo Law*, 27 November 2018, https://www.cavalluzzo.com/resources/news/news-item/postal-workers-win-court-challenge-to-back-to-work-law-superior-court-declares-harper's-law-unconstitutional.

17 Mark Zigler, *Legislative Developments and the Top 20 Cases of 2018–2019: 52nd Annual Canadian Employee Benefits Conference*, Koskie Minsky LLP, https://kmlaw.ca/wp-content/uploads/2020/09/2018-2019-Top-20-IF-Paper.pdf.

9. Labour's Last Gasp or Revival? Rebuilding Working-Class Resistance

1 Gosta Esping-Andersen, *Politics against Markets: The Social Democratic Road to Power* (Princeton: Legacy Library, 2017).

2 International Labour Organization, *Global Wage Report 2020–21: Wages and Minimum Wages in the Time of COVID-19*, December 2020, https://www.ilo.org/infostories/Campaigns/Wages/globalwagereport#introduction.

3 Statistics Canada. "Table 282-0223 Labour Force Survey Estimates, Employees by Union Status, North American Industry Classification System (NAICS), Canada, Annual."

4 Mark Thomas, "Global Unions, Global Framework Agreements and the Transnational Regulation of Labour Standards," in *Neoliberal Capitalism and Precarious Work: Ethnographies of Accommodation and Resistance*, ed. Robert Lambert and Andrew Herod (Cheltenham: Edward Elgar, 2016), 277–302; Don Wells, "Too Weak for the Job," *Global Social Policy*, 7, no. 1 (2007): 51–74.

5 Sam Gindin and Michael Hurley, "Working Class Politics after the NDP," *The Bullet*, September 1, 2014, https://socialistproject.ca/2014/09/b1030/.

6 David Bailey, *The Political Economy of European Social Democracy* (Abingdon: Routledge, 2009), 30.

7 Anthony Crosland, *The Future of Socialism* (London: Jonathan Cape, 1956), 378.

8 Frances Fox Piven, *Labor Parties in Postindustrial Societies* (New York: Oxford University Press, 1992), 18.

9 Stefan Collignon, "The Dawn of a New Era: Social Democracy after the Financial Crisis," *Social Europe*, 4, no. 1 (Autumn 2008): 9–13, 8.

10 Colin Crouch, *The Strange Non-Death of Neoliberalism* (Cambridge: Policy Press, 2011).

11 Maria Sosa Troya, "Socialist Youth Leader's 'Five-Star' Speech Goes Viral, then Vitriol Is Turned on Her," *El Pais* (English edition, 2013), http://elpais.com /elpais/2013/02/19/inenglish/1361300076_865976.html.

12 Larry Elliott, "Wanted: The Keynes for Our Times," *The Guardian*, 22 December 2008, https://www.theguardian.com/business/2008/dec/22/keynes-left -economics-economy.

13 Robert Taylor, "Does European Social Democracy Have a Future," *Dissent* (Summer 2008).

14 R. Lexier, *Party of Conscience: The CCF, the NDP, and Social Democracy in Canada* (Toronto: Between the Lines, 2018).

15 Sam Gindin, "Beyond the Economic Crisis: The Crisis in Trade Unionism," *Canadian Dimension*, 16 September 2013, http://canadiandimension.com /articles/5534/.

16 Michael Cross, *The Decline and Fall of a Good Idea: CCF-NDP Manifestoes, 1932–1969* (Toronto: New Hogtown, 1974).

17 Gregory Albo, "The Crisis of Neoliberalism and the Impasse of the Union Movement," *Development Dialogue* (January 2009), 119–31.

18 David Laycock and Lynda Erikson, "Modernizing the Party," in *Reviving Social Democracy: The Near Death and Surprising Rise of the Federal NDP*, ed. David Laycock and Lynda Erickson (Vancouver: UBC Press, 2014).

19 Sam Gindin and Michael Hurley, "Working Class Politics after the NDP," *The Bullet*, 1 September 2014, https://socialistproject.ca/2014/09/b1030/.

20 Gindin and Hurley, "Working Class Politics."

21 Sam Gindin, "Beyond the Impasse of Canadian Labour: Union Renewal, Political Renewal," *Canadian Dimension*, 21 May 2014, https://canadiandimension .com/articles/view/beyond-the-impasse-of-canadian-labour-union-renewal -political-renewal.

22 Carlo Fanelli and Jeff Noonan. "Capital and Labour," in *Reading Capital Today: Marx After 150 Years*, ed. Ingo Schmidt and Carlo Fanelli (London: Pluto Press, 2017).

23 Karl Marx, "The Different Questions – 1866," Marxists.org, http://www.marxists .org/archive/marx/iwma/documents/1866/instructions.htm#06.

24 Adolph Reed, "Antiracism: A Neoliberal Alternative to a Left," *Dialectical Anthropology* 42 (2018), 105–15; Vivek Chibber, *The Class Matrix: Social Theory after the Cultural Turn* (Cambridge: Harvard University Press, 2022); Barbara J. Fields and Karen E. Fields, *Racecraft: The Soul of Inequality in American Life* (New York: Verso Books, 2014); Martha E. Gimenez, "Women, Class, and Identity Politics," *Monthly Review*, 1 September 2019, https://monthlyreview.org /2019/09/01/women-class-and-identity-politics/.

25 Hugo Radice, "Responses to Globalization: A Critique of Progressive Nationalism," *New Political Economy* 5, no. 1 (March 2000): 14–15.

26 Sam Gindin, "The Auto Industry Concretizing Working Class Solidarity: Internationalism beyond Slogans," *Socialist Project*, 2004, https://www .socialisthistory.ca/PDF/SP/Auto%20Industry.pdf; Andrew Herod, "Labour Internationalism and the Contradictions of Globalization: Or, Why the Local Is Sometimes Still Important in a Global Economy," Middlebury, 2013, https:// sites.middlebury.edu/soan260/files/2013/08/Herod-Contradictions-of-Labor -Internationalism.pdf.

27 Kevin Skerrett et al., *The Contradiction of Pension Funds Capitalism* (New York: Cornell University Press, 2018).

28 Greg Albo, Stephen Maher, and Alan Zuege, *State Transformations: Classes, Strategy Socialism* (Leiden: Brill, 2021).

29 Sam Gindin, "Socialism with Sober Senses: Developing Worker's Capacities," *Socialist Register* 34 (1998), https://socialistregister.com/index.php/srv/article /download/5701/2597/7595.

30 Sam Gindin, "Unmaking Global Capitalism," *Jacobin*, 1 June 2014, https:// jacobinmag.com/2014/06/unmaking-global-capitalism.

31 Sam Gindin, "A 'Fatiguing Climb': Capitalist Competition and Working Class Formation," *The Bullet*, 13 July 2021, https://socialistproject.ca/2021/07 /fatiguing-climb-working-class-formation/.

32 André Gorz, *Critique of Economic Reason* (London: Verso, 1989), 231–3.

Glossary

ad hoc   Refers to things (like laws) that are put together for a special purpose.

Antonio Gramsci   Italian Communist leader, journalist, and philosopher who died in a prison cell under Mussolini's fascism. Gramsci is known for his insistence that the working class could not capture political power without creating an alternate and dominant (or "hegemonic") ideological and cultural practice that established broad consent to its leading role in society.

a priori   Refers to opinions or judgments established before considering the facts of a situation or case.

austerity   A strategy to constrain and disable the capacity of the state to intervene in economic and social affairs. This is achieved by constraining the fiscal capacity of the state (i.e., through cuts to taxation; requiring balanced budgets; prohibiting the acquisition of public debt); public-sector restructuring through privatization of state assets and requiring state enterprises to behave like for-profit businesses (marketization); and adopting policies that weaken trade union rights to bargain and erode legal protections for workers, such as minimum wage regulations.

authoritarianism   State-directed coercion that is insulated from democratic control. The power to make such strategic decisions is highly centralized within the state executive, and the state executive is prepared to bypass standard parliamentary and legal norms of accountability.

back-to-work legislation   Special "ad hoc" laws used to force trade unions (under pain of heavy fines and/or imprisonment of leaders) to end specific strikes, even though these strikes were undertaken with the support of the union's members.

Bretton Woods   The short-hand term for the postwar liberal international economic order set up at a US-led conference held at Bretton Woods, New Hampshire, in 1944. In addition to setting up the International Monetary Fund and the World Bank, Bretton Woods provided for fixed exchange rates based on the US dollar, backed by a US guarantee to exchange the dollar for gold at a fixed rate. US president Nixon withdrew this guarantee in 1971, and after a few years, floating exchange rates became generalized as part and parcel of the neoliberal free-market response to the breakdown of the postwar arrangements in the crisis of the 1970s.

coercion   The use of state power to constrain people or groups to obey, such as by ending legal strikes through back-to-work laws that establish special penalties for union leaders and members to force their compliance.

Consumer Price Index (CPI)   A measurement of the annual rise in prices of a range of basic goods and services purchased by consumers, used as an index of the rate of inflation.

corporatist   The incorporation of trade unions within the state or industry in a manner that diminishes or negates union independence; in liberal democracies, corporatism often involves consultative forums promoting collaboration among union and business leaders and government personnel, so that "**tripartism**" is often used as a synonym for corporatism.

democratic capitalism   The period following World War II corresponding approximately to the years 1945 to 1975. An era where trade union rights and freedoms were embedded through a legal framework; where a range of protections, again embedded in law, provided workers with rights to such benefits as paid vacations, minimum wages, health and safety, overtime pay, and more; and where the welfare state was expanded significantly to take a range of goods and services out of the market or at least do so to some significant degree (decommodification), such as with education, health care, social services, and even housing to some degree.

deregulation   Removing controls on the activities of private-sector companies, such as curbs on monopolies, environmental standards, and health and safety protection.

designation   Declaring specific occupations or sectors (generally in the public service) to be "essential services," with the effect that workers within are denied the right to strike. The actual number of workers so affected may be determined by the government unilaterally or through negotiations with the union(s) representing these workers.

economism   A type of practice or consciousness common in the labour movement that concentrates on immediate and narrow economic interests and identities of workers, paying little or no attention to broader political and cultural issues, practices, and identities (in contrast to a "hegemonic" practice of consciousness).

electoralism   An ideological and political orientation assuming that the most important (and sometimes the only) form of political action for the labour movement is that of supporting social democratic parties like the NDP in elections.

essential services   Any services (usually in the public sector) that a particular government has declared to be of such importance that they must not be interrupted by a strike. Such a declaration results in some or all workers delivering the service being "designated," thereby losing the right to strike that they would otherwise have had.

final offer selection (FOS)   A form of binding arbitration under which an arbitrator chooses between the final offers presented by both management and the union. FOS circumvents the system of free collective bargaining by allowing for the imposition of a settlement by a third party to end a labour dispute.

fiscal orthodoxy   The economic policy viewpoint that emphasizes balancing government budgets and eliminating deficits by cutting public expenditures and services.

Fordist   A term referring to a stage of capitalism based on the mass production of industrial goods through regimented control of workers and extensive division of labour; this is seen as the basis for conditions of mass consumption, stable employment, collective bargaining, high wages, and social benefits.

free collective bargaining   The regulation of relations between workers and employers through the recognition of trade unions and the negotiation of collective agreements governing wages, benefits, and working conditions; the state sets the legal framework, policing adherence to its provisions, governing collective bargaining without intervening in the content of negotiations. The state thus presents itself as an umpire between capital and labour.

freedom of association   The democratic right of people to join and act together to establish and advance their collective interests; particularly important for working people in terms of securing their independent organization and their capacity for collective action in relation to capital and the state.

globalization   The extension of capitalist production, trade finance, and communication on a world scale and the integration or subjection of local or national institutions in the process.

gradualism   An ideological orientation (characteristic of reformist in contrast to revolutionary political practice) assuming that society will make steady, step-by-step progress to overcome exploitation and inequality through the regular passage of social reform measures that are irreversible and cumulative.

Great Recession   The period following the 2007 financial crisis. This crisis began as a mortgage markets crisis primarily in the US but also Ireland and the UK; it soon spread globally and became a general economic crisis, the deepest since the Great Depression of the 1930s.

hegemony   A form of class rule over society exercised not only through economic and political power but expressed at the level of popular culture and consciousness. A hegemonic practice is one involving a type of class domination that incorporates some of the ideas, interests, and needs of other social forces, thereby securing an element of consent to the ruling of the dominant class.

ideology   An interrelated set of political viewpoints, ideas, goals, and strategies; any particular ideology may be more or less coherent, more or less illusory, more or less doctrinaire, and more or less closely tied to or reflective of the material interests of a given class, party, or group.

International Labour Organization (ILO)   An organization of the United Nations with business, labour, and government representatives that monitors trade union activities and rights around the world.

international unions   American-controlled or American-dominated unions with branches operating in Canada.

Keynesianism   The ideology and practice of economic policy whereby public expenditure and taxation are adapted by governments so as to combat the cyclical downturns of capitalist market economies. The term derives from the ideas developed by British economist John Maynard Keynes during the Great Depression of the 1930s; it came to be commonly employed to characterize the general economic policy orientation of western capitalist governments from 1945 to about 1975 and to define the reformism of social democratic parties as they dropped their commitment to socialist change.

liberal democracy   The form of capitalist political system defined by constitutional guarantees of basic civil liberties (including freedom of association) and regular multi-party elections to representative assemblies and governmental office whereby almost all citizens have formal voting rights.

monetarism   The ideological practice in economic policy whereby controlling inflation is stressed as the main goal for a healthy capitalist economy (in contrast to Keynesianism's commitment to full employment). The restriction of governments' deficits through public expenditure reductions, tight control of the money supply, and high interest rates are characteristic of the monetarist sets of policies that displaced Keynesian policies after the mid-1970s.

neoliberalism   An ideology and practice that surfaced in reaction to the economic and social crisis that began in the 1970s; it stresses the priority of individualism, competitiveness, and entrepreneurship over collective interests and needs, including trade union rights and universal welfare programs.

parliamentarism   An ideological and political orientation, characteristic of social democracy, which focuses strategy and popular attention almost exclusively on winning representation to, and on debates within, parliamentary assemblies. It also involves acceptance of the symbols and customs of the British parliamentary tradition, including the notions that parliamentarians serve a "national interest" overriding class interests, and that the elected representative is primarily accountable to the party leader or prime minister rather than to the party or constituency outside Parliament.

progressive competitiveness   The prime social democratic economic strategy that emerged in response to "free trade" and the dominant neoliberal free-market approach to globalization. This strategy stresses cooperation between labour and capital alongside extensive vocational training programs in support of a high value-added, high-skilled export production strategy. This was expected to enhance a country's competitiveness without having to cut back too far on wages and the welfare state.

public-sector workers   All employees in the broadly defined public sector, not only the federal and provincial civil service, but the municipal sector, the public education and health sectors, state-owned corporations, and so on.

Rand formula   An important provision in Canadian trade union laws that gives certified or recognized unions the right to compulsory dues check-off from all employees, in return for an agreement by the union that there will be no strike action or work disruption during the term of the union contract.

reformist ideology   A general term for the ideas, goals, and strategies that orient the labour movement towards defining its politics in terms of "gradualism" and "parliamentarism"; it denies the possibility or desirability of radical political upheaval as an aspect of fundamental social change.

right to strike   The right of workers to engage in collective work stoppages without interference, intimidation, or repression by the state or capital. This right makes "freedom of association" an effective means for workers to exercise collective power, whether as a form of pressure to achieve union recognition and to win specific demands from employers, or as a form of political mobilization and protest. The right to strike is not constitutionally established in Canada, and labour legislation only sanctions as legal strikes that comply with considerable regulations and restrictions.

"right to work"   A right-wing political notion promoted by private corporations and conservative politicians that stresses the rights of individual workers to refuse to participate in union activities and to continue working during strikes.

secondary strike action   Any form of strike action directed at targets other than the particular plant or government department whose workers have gone on strike. Examples include picketing of other enterprises owned by the employer or boycotts of other products produced by firms owned by the capitalist firm facing strike action.

social contract   A common term for a "social peace" agreement between governments and the representatives of unions and employers whereby trade unions agree to restrain or forego their full collective bargaining agendas and rights usually in the context of some broader plan that promises to advance economic growth, restrain inflation, cut public deficits, or redistribute income and wealth.

Social Credit   The "Socreds" are a conservative, populist, pro-business, and anti-labour political movement active since the 1930s. Their strength has been mainly in western Canada and they have controlled the governments of British Columbia and Alberta at different points as well as electing delegates to federal Parliament. The Reform Party of Preston Manning is in many ways the direct continuation of the Social Credit movement.

social democracy   A political ideology and political parties first emerging in the late nineteenth century that expressed working-class demands for political and economic democracy in addition to social and economic equality. Parties initially drew on the ideas of Karl Marx and Friedrich

Engels, but by the 1950s most such parties had replaced their formal adherence to Marxism with Keynesianism as their official policy orientation. Capitalism was accepted as the prevailing economic model but one where social democrats would use the state to redistribute resources to finance public goods and services and provide the working class, its core electoral constituency until the Great Recession of the 2000s, with various policy entitlements. Post-Great Recession, such parties typically turned to austerity and privatization and thus alienated large parts of their working-class support.

statutory incomes policies   The restriction of collective bargaining through legislation that directly regulates the scale of wage and salary increases for a given period and establishes specific penalties and sanctions to force compliance (in contrast to voluntary income policies, where unions agree to self-restraint, usually as part of a social contract). Such policies are sometimes accompanied by limited regulation of price increases, profits, and dividends.

tripartism   A term (often used as a synonym for corporatism) referring to a reformist ideology and practice that promotes institutional structures of formal collaboration among representatives of unions, business, and government.

vis-à-vis   In relation to.

wage controls   The use of coercion by the state to fix wages and salaries for a given period through suspending or imposing restrictions on the outcome of free collective bargaining and the right to strike; often used as a synonym for statutory income policies.

welfare state   The kind of government that assumes responsibility for protecting the living conditions of working people with public programs such as Unemployment Insurance, workers' compensation, medicare, old age pensions, and income supplements or benefits for people in poverty.

Index

*Page numbers in **bold** refer to glossary entries.*